THE LAW AS ARCHITECTURE: BUILDING LEGAL DOCUMENTS

Professor Jill J. Ramsfield
Georgetown University Law Center

Cover design: Carol A. Castro, Out of My Mind Design

To G, with love;

and

To All Legal Writers Who Want to Do Better

TABLE OF CONTENTS

ACKNOWLEDGEMENTS

My gratitude goes to those students and lawyers with whom I have worked over the last seventeen years. Your questions, solutions, criticisms, and creative energy percolate throughout this book. I also owe much to the teachers in my legal writing past: Mary Ray, Chris Rideout, and Jill and Chris Wren. To Scott Pernitz goes the thanks for mentoring and managing me, a rare occurrence in law firms these days. To my Georgetown legal writing colleagues, many thanks for the supple acceptance of my metaphors and the willingness to test many of the ideas contained in this book. To Melissa Bradley, thanks for the initial research and the patience in getting the book started, the photographic research, and the brilliant maneuvering through its early stages. To Ed Vermeer, thanks for cheerfully producing some examples and other details. To Paul Fakler, thanks for being audience and rhetorical critic in the early stages. To Joe Wylie, thanks for being the perfect reviewer—critical, prodigious, and willing, not to say brilliant. To Ross Wagner, thanks for being believer, productive analyst, and creative engineer in the middle stages.

To my family and friends, many thanks for the interest, cheers, and tolerance during this book's production. Thanks to Rob Lorey, Dave Harris, Kristin and Grant Miekle, and Beau Kaplan for photographs. Thanks to Howard Sharlach, who contributed exotic and beautiful pictures. To the best sister in the world, Judy Mahr, thank you for the interior design drawings, the artistic advice, the photos, and the loving, constant support. And thanks to my parents, Henrietta Ramsfield and Norm Pederson, for always believing in me.

To the Book Team: all glorious thanks. You have been creative, receptive, flexible, brilliant and willing. To Lisa Ritter, thanks for the innovative designs, diagrams and thoughts; the brilliant selection and exposition of examples, and the amazing technical facility for implementing any ideas. To Katlin McKelvie, thanks for the sharp critical eye, patient rework, careful selection and layout of photographs, and steady hand. To Kirstin Miller, thanks for finding beautiful photographs and generous permissions from artists, photographers, and architects. To Alex

Kymn, thanks for the patient work on layout and technical precision. To Kristen Murray, thanks for the versatility moving among tasks and chapters, offering excellent edits, and all with an amazing sense of humor. To Michelle Bell, thanks for the clear, constant, generous devotion to each detail. To Lisa Fine, thanks for the pinch-hitting on so many occasions. To Lisa Sharlach, thanks for the diverse and capricious photos and joyful execution of tasks at the end of the project. To Karin Scherner-Kim, thanks for the eagle eye on citations and proofreading. To Nicole Anzuoni, thanks for your generous help in the final stages.

Special thanks to the book's cover and interior designer, Carol Castro, whose technical expertise and positive attitude made beauty out of our home-made efforts. And thanks to the brave souls at The West Education Group who took the leap into color and images: Doug Powell, Pam Siege, Stephanie Syata, and John Och.

Thanks, too, to my colleagues who offered advice along the way, especially Richard Chused, Mike Seidman and Girardeau Spann. And to Noelle Adgerson, all thanks not only for taking the dictation that began this book, but also for taking my dictation day in and day out; you are the trustworthy wisdom and energy that bolsters all of my professional work. Then there is Gene, always Gene.

APOLOGY

To all architects, my sincerest apologies. This text cannot begin to approximate the complexity and sophistication of your work. I use architecture as a friendly metaphor because lawyers have responded so well and so creatively to it over the last few years. It helps us. Thank you.

This text uses mostly photographs of Western architecture because the thought patterns represented here are mostly western. While there are some photographs of buildings from other cultures, they are here for contrast, for we have not yet integrated into our legal documents the thought patterns of other cultures. That is another book.

PREFACE

It has always seemed a bit tragic to me that lawyers suffer so much as writers. While the act of writing has always been surrounded with a certain kind of romance, legal writing has always been surrounded with a lot of agony and very little ecstasy, either for the writers or the readers. Some of this agony has to do with the subject matter itself: ugly disputes, complicated desires, nasty transactions, crime, divorce, greed. But much of legal writing is creative dispute prevention, perhaps the most noble of our tasks. What draws many people to study and practice law is the challenging intellectual puzzle-solving of complex, intricate problems. To design a document that solves a problem creatively, that demonstrates dimensions of the problem others cannot see, that moves legal thinking in a new direction—now, *that* is creative, challenging, even inspiring work.

Why is it so hard? As I've observed thousands of law students and lawyers at their desks, in front of their computers, in individual conferences, I have seen intelligent people operating without a schema of problem-solving. Relying mostly on instinct and wit, two very helpful but sometimes unreliable sources, most lawyers fashion documents that they hope will serve their purposes. But these documents also often perpetuate the complaints about legal writing: turgid, impenetrable, inelegant, annoying. The fact is, many lawyers are actually unconscious of what they are doing as they write. This is a bit like engineers being unconscious about how they design a bridge. Yes, much literature explains why lawyers want to annoy their readers or keep them from understanding their prose, but, frankly, many lawyers are just as annoyed at their own prose and unable to do much about it.

It is so hard to produce clear, effective legal writing because we do not consciously study the means and the methods for doing so. Instead, we absorb information, both in law school and on the job, by reading, highlighting, and mimicking the bad prose we read. We do not break the chain of turgid legal writing by outsmarting it, by cutting through the confusion to create clear, coherent, concise prose. We give our readers no hope of understanding us because we ourselves do not design schematic structures that match our messages. We often work at cross purposes by using syntax that fights substantive messages, structure that fights meaning. Having read such writing, we simply reproduce it. Instead, we need prose that matches our modern purposes. Most often, we lawyers are advising, suggesting, recommending, informing, persuading, cajoling, or protecting. These are not purposes that need turgid prose.

This book suggests that we can produce good legal writing by studying it as an art. We can study what the good writers do. We can learn from the variety and richness of their methods, their design techniques, their style choices. We can also study legal writing itself. At once the law and what we use to talk about it, legal writing requires a level of scrutiny general style manuals cannot address. We must dissect its deep rhetorical aspects, such as the relationships between law and structure, between syntax and substance. For us, word choice is not just a question of personal taste, though our choice includes that; it is a question of substantive meaning and legal usage. For us, organization is not a simple deductive approach, but a complex synthesis of law, message, and purpose; of audience, scope, and the ultimate use our readers will make of the document.

We can design as architects do: by interviewing clients, understanding the products they have in mind, and designing structures accordingly. By knowing our materials, we can select from them carefully and design documents to fit budgets and tastes. By coordinating form and function, structure and style, we can create harmonious, unified documents that are accurate and elegant. We can create these consciously, deliberately, and even enjoyably because we can know much more about what we are doing and why. We can build a repertoire of techniques, designs, and strategies that will make document production smooth and even sweet.

By writing this book, I hope to make the legal writer's agony gradually disappear. The students and lawyers with whom I have worked over the years have been capable, intelligent, ready, willing. But many have been confused, frustrated, even angry with the experience of legal writing. I hope that this book will make explicit to them what has been implicit or merely formalistic. Implied writing rules or formalistic formulae are frustrating to the creative lawyer. They are limited and limiting. I hope this book explains some of the choices available to the legal writer, who is designer, architect, and artist. We can create useful, simple, affordable documents like the original Frank Lloyd Wright prairie homes, and we can also create ornate documents that embody grace as the National Cathedral does, or an Imperial Hotel that can withstand an earthquake. We need only apprentice ourselves to two areas of study: the legal writing *product*, whose architecture is based in classical rhetoric as peculiarly manifested in the United States legal community; and the legal writing *process*, whose techniques are created by lawyers to maneuver gracefully through document production.

This book's notions of modern legal rhetoric and good legal writing techniques are largely my own, derived from work with thousands of lawyers and students. Many ideas are borrowed from linguists and composition theorists, who have forged theories in other discourses. I have imported what I think can work in our discourse. What I suggest here must be modified according to personal preference and according to the local conditions of law practice and study. What I describe I have seen, but not empirically studied; what I suggest I have invented or observed, but not always personally tested. I leave the tests to you, the legal writer. Take or leave these ideas and implement them now or later. Use your doubts to cre-

ate new paths, not just to reinforce old habits.

INTRODUCTION

As a lawyer, you are a professional writer. You write for a living. You have to do so under very specific circumstances: the client has a sudden change of heart, the supervising attorney has been out of town and now returns to review a document three hours before filing time, the person working on the case has left the office and moved on to another job. Each law office has specific practices and traditions, and each lawyer brings to the job her own ideas about writing. These ideas and traditions can harmonize or clash, and you can get caught in the middle, watching the clock and becoming increasingly anxious about producing *something*.

This book suggests an approach to legal writing that allows you to write better and, eventually, faster. Even in the worst of legal writing circumstances, you can master the situation by being keenly aware of what to do when and why. To address making your writing better, this books describes the legal document metaphorically—as a building. It ushers you through the creative process by showing how your legal writing product is worthy of the same level of research, brainstorming, design, and expertise as any architectural achievement. For context, it describes our legal community: its features, its practices, and its expectations. It demystifies aspects of the community that often plague legal writers: how to translate traditional legal writing into readable prose, how to write simultaneously to non-experts and experts, how to shorten documents without damaging their precision. For design precision, this book sounds four rhetorical themes: *purpose, audience, scope,* and *stance*. For technical precision, this book suggests six "architectural" elements: *theme, materials, form, proportion, interior design,* and *finish*. And for efficiency, it weaves techniques on the *legal writing process* throughout the book.

This book suggests that, by designing documents with the same kind of care and expertise that good architects use, you can create accessible, accurate, and enduring documents. To frame design expertise, the book borrows from rhetorical theories and practical applications. From classical rhetoric come the elements of invention, arrangement, style, memory and delivery; from modern rhetoric, the element of audience. These elements manifest themselves differently in the modern legal writing community.

While they are rooted in persuasion, these elements may inform your legal writing decisions as you produce contracts, client letters, prospectuses, or international white papers. The book seeks to awaken in you a sensitivity to context, historical setting, and practical constraints, and to allow you to discover techniques for balancing your client's needs with the law's demands. It does, for example, try to show how the theme, or message, of legal documents can focus both process and product; how the purpose of a document can tailor its form, or arrangement; and how its audience can precipitate specific language that intricately connects legal substance with syntax.

To address making your writing faster, this book offers a variety of techniques for designing an effective legal writing process and eventually speeding it up. It suggests that your legal writing process includes certain steps that, broken out and analyzed, can become more efficient. One way to consider those steps in the legal writing process is to see them as a series of decisions to questions you ask yourself: *Do I start here or there? Do I use this resource or that? Do I need ten cases or will three do? Do I organize like this or like that? Do I use this word or that word?* These decisions fall on a time continuum that begins when the project is assigned and ends when you never have to see it again. This book ushers you through your own legal writing process, your own series of decisions, and suggests you continually ask yourself one central question: *What informs my decisions?*

As you read, review your decision-making process. Your answers to that repeated question, *What informs my decisions?* will help you design your best legal writing process. This book offers some ideas about how to create a process, but you will have to supply the rest from your personal experience and current situation. Whatever process you invent will involve writing techniques, such as using computer folders to organize your notes, using checklists to read a paper with fresh eyes, reading backward to proofread cites, and so on. This book offers techniques to make that review informative, to speed up your process, to make your product more effective. Adopt or adapt these techniques to create your own comfortable, creative, practical fit.

This book does not, however, suggest that all of these techniques are useful for all legal writers. Writing is ultimately personal; it is the way that each writer thinks, problem-solves, works. This book honors that personal aspect of legal writing by offering several techniques for making your legal writing product better and your process faster. Some of these techniques will seem ridiculous to you; if so, move on, forget them. Some of these techniques will make sense or will spark invention of other techniques that will be helpful to you. Stop. Note what they are. Start implementing them. Make your own list of techniques that assist you. This book's purpose is to leave you with that list, your personal list, of techniques that will help you to design creatively, to adapt to client and supervisor demands, to write better and faster. Tomorrow. And a year from tomorrow. And ten years from tomorrow.

CHAPTER 1
KNOWING THE ELEMENTS OF DESIGN

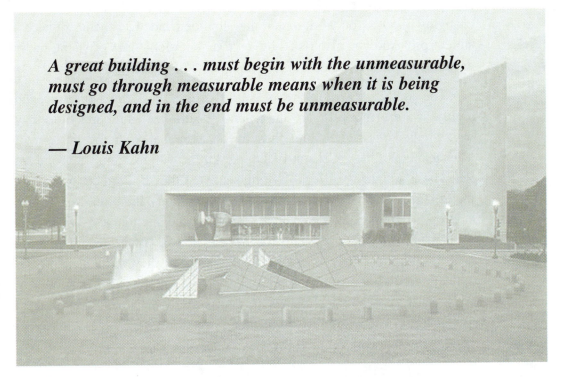

A great building . . . must begin with the unmeasurable, must go through measurable means when it is being designed, and in the end must be unmeasurable.

— Louis Kahn

Architecture is an art. The architect fuses the functional with the aesthetic, the practical with the perfect. He measures client with theme, form with function, interior with exterior. And he sees space as taking shape in habitable, usable ways. He frames the world we live and work in; he outlines our daily lives. At his best, he calls us to far-off places to see his work for its aesthetic beauty and endurance, for its majesty or its folly. Architecture is not just the grand, but the grubby; not just the monumental, but the mundane. It is what we use to define our similarities and differences, to measure our status and our stamina, to inspire our work and our relaxation. As an art, architecture calls upon the architect to be designer, engineer, artist, carpenter, critic, and genius. It requires years of training, including courses in drawing, computer science, engineering, history, and math, among other things. And it is a demanding art, expecting of its author nothing less than perfection. One wrong decision can ruin the plumbing, lose the client, or collapse the building.

The law as architecture calls similarly upon you. You are also artist, engineer, and measurer of materials. You are the reader of clients' needs, the matcher of materials with function, the designer of functional forms that serve specific purposes. You design documents both monumental and mundane. You must work with all kinds of landscapes, materials, deadlines, and changing minds. You work to add the often-demanded aesthetics of accessible prose. And you also risk—by a wrong decision—loss of client, badly decided law, or the collapse of a business deal or marriage.

The good legal writers are, of course, artists. Fastidious, creative, and highly aware of both the art and science of the law as architecture, they have studied their art. And they have pursued it with the passion of Michaelangelo, the precision of Leonardo, the whimsey and joy of I.M. Pei. These architects of legal writing see what they do as a serious, complicated undertaking, one that requires years of study and practice, one that calls upon the finest intellect and the most flexible intelligence. While they are capable of dashing off plans for the tract housing of a standard contract in a few minutes, they also know how carefully they must design each industrial building of a complicated transaction. Their repertoire of designs and techniques is enormous, their imaginations alert. And they, like architects, have developed the flexibility to work on their projects as moving targets.

Architecture: the art of creating a space.

- Yoshinobu Ashihara

Legal writing is its own art. It is a highly contextualized, practical, artistic act. It is performed under constantly changing circumstances, where clients change their minds, decision-makers shift policy, and the law itself changes. As a legal writer, your thinking evolves, and your reader's expectations rise. Time is of the essence, and technology inserts a series of learning curves into the recursive circle of writing. Researching methods shift: the explosion of new statutes, regulations, and decisions requires complex techniques for sifting and quick learning. All of this often occurs in a competitive setting where smart clients shop for good lawyers. Those shoppers want perfection in product and process: effective and efficient answers.

Designing useful, accessible, elegant legal documents thus challenges any aspiring legal writer. No less complicated than researching and designing a building, creating good legal writing requires a thorough understanding of the elements of document design. It also requires awareness of your own thinking, designing, and writing processes.

The materials themselves are overwhelming: statutes and regulations, constitutional provisions, cases, administrative decisions, executive orders, congressional hearings, and historical documents. The facts offer their own problems: the circumstances created by clients, or the circumstances clients wish to prevent; the facts as reported, the facts as they really happened, or the facts as they might happen. All of this is your moving target of ideas, concerns, problems, opinions, laws, public opinion, morals, and wants. Somehow you, as a lawyer, are supposed to create documents that withstand such movement, documents that survive the earthquakes created by human interaction. Sometimes your documents are meant to be temporary tents that serve a limited purpose; other times, you must build monuments on fault lines.

To perform successfully as a lawyer, you can be a versatile, willing, and quick artist. To operate with the expertise appropriate to any problem, you can use the elements of legal document design. What do you need to build such a wide range of structures? What materials? What information about foundations, proportion, and size? What knowledge of structural relationships? What information about rhythm, texture, visual effects? What knowledge of historical styles, contemporary tastes, practical solutions?

Knowing the elements of design in legal documents allows you to work intelligently, make informed choices, satisfy different clients' needs, work efficiently, and design creatively. Knowing these elements of design also allows you to move gracefully among the many demands placed on you as a modern lawyer. And knowing your own propensities, habits, and strengths allows you to build efficient techniques for on-the-job flexibility and speed.

This chapter introduces some basic elements of legal writing architecture. Those elements unfold and interact in the context of document production in the following chapters. Sprinkled among these discussions are two features that give dimension and context to the legal architect's work: technique sections that offer practical suggestions for document design, and "A Word on..." sections that offer more background for the book's main discussions. As a legal architect, you can use these sections in any way useful to you; you may want to read them consecutively for context, separately for emphasis on the practical or theoretical, or at random for what suits your immediate needs.

> Architecture is the flowering of geometry.
>
> -Ralph Waldo Emerson

The elements themselves need some context. Hardly springing from a vacuum, these elements emerge from well-developed features of a long-standing community. As architects or musicians or engineers or doctors define their profession, so do we. The more explicit we are, the more quickly we can acculturate, define, and eventually redefine our profession. The fact is, we define our legal profession largely by our writing.

Designing Documents In Specific Contexts

As you consider your approach to designing documents, reflect on your training and put your own writing in that context. Remember that, in the United States, novice lawyers traditionally apprenticed themselves to experienced ones. Those apprenticeships sometimes lasted for years while the young lawyer followed his mentor through all stages of document design, again and again. As a case developed or a business agreement was forged, the mentor explained each stage while the apprentice asked questions, drafted long-hand the document in question, and often copied the document long-hand for the clients, the files, and the courts. That training system remained intact until the 1970's, when the legal profession changed in size and mission. Today, you may be trained by a single mentor, but more likely you are working for many lawyers, none of whom actually teaches you the step-by-step process of document design. Law schools have been slow to pick up the training abandoned by practitioners, and until both groups forge a new kind of training, you may be on your own.

Focus on your own design training, then, wherever you are in your career. First, consider your situation, which includes all the constraints of law practice, including your law office's norms, past practices or traditions, and your own writing abilities. Second, consider your rhetorical situation, which includes audience, that is, all users of the document; the document's function; its size, setting, and perspective. Third, study the architectural elements of legal writing, including the materials lawyers use to build documents, the forms or structures that lawyers use to convey meaning, and the interior features of legal paragraphs and phraseology. Fourth, become aware of your own legal writing process, the sequence of tasks you perform to build a legal document. Fifth, be aware of the practical considerations, such as cost, durability, and deadline, that inform your design decisions. Finally, remember the larger legal culture itself, its history, norms, rules, expectations, goals, and limits as well as your local law office's practices and traditions. By being acutely aware of the many dimensions of legal writing, you can operate as a successful architect.

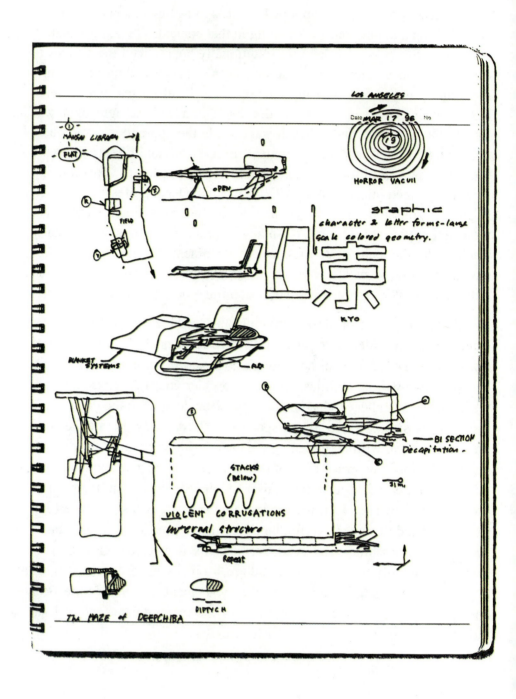

SOME SITUATIONAL ELEMENTS

TRADITIONS
TRANSITIONS
TRAJECTORIES

TRADITIONS

The legal culture places you in specific surroundings and under certain expectations. These circumstances spring from traditions whose origins may be obscure but whose followers are devout. You are expected to honor these traditions, such as using particular forms or formal openings, and to incorporate them into your writing. It helps to know, for example, how a specific kind of writing, such as a brief, compares to another, such as an agenda item or an opinion letter; it also helps to know how to adjust your approach, analysis, and style to make each work well. In legal writing, this is a complicated matter. A judge may need little legal foundation because she is experienced in that subject matter, while another who is inexperienced needs a more detailed orientation. A client may be general counsel to a business and therefore sophisticated in understanding the law, so he may expect your opinion letter to include citations and a fully technical analysis of his company's position. Another client may be dealing with a legal matter for the first time and may need an uncluttered explanation of his situation. You are expected to compose a letter both concise and yet comprehensive enough to protect yourself should your client act on the letter's advice. To do so, you combine the context, history, conventions, and norms of your situation.

In each writing situation, you may be expected to exercise certain analytical choices derived from forms or patterns developed within the legal community. Generally, the legal culture uses analytical methods that explore every aspect of a problem. You learn these methods in law school, but your repertoire continues to increase afterward. You may be aware of quasi-inductive approaches to problem-solving that require you to "discover" the law by assembling various holdings into one foundational rule;

you may be similarly aware of quasi-deductive approaches that move an analysis from a statutory basis to a conclusion about your client's situation. But you may not be prepared for the peculiar ingredient of policy formulation that invades your analysis in government service, or the negotiation of business elements that becomes crucial to building an effective series of transactional documents. Your analytical choices continue to become more complex as your practice grows. To become truly accomplished, versatile—good—you need to be able to speak the local legal language. You must translate your analytical choices into language that is accessible to all audiences who use it, lawyers and non-lawyers alike. You must be an interpreter. You must understand the patterns, language, and syntax of traditional, turgid legal prose. And you must be able to interpret that language accurately so that when you write, your readers understand you. You must become fluent not only in traditional Legal English, but also in modern Legal English, and even local legal dialects.

You must then situate yourself within these traditions and linguistic challenges. How comfortable are you with writing? How well do you know the fundamental rules of writing? How well do your organize your thoughts? What kind of writing have you done in the past? Is that writing situation the same or different from this one? Consider your professional situation, as well. Have you just started in this office? Have you switched areas of expertise? Do you feel experienced but in a kind of rut? Do things take too long, require too many revisions? Because legal writing is an art that is performed in specific situations, you need to define those situations to make the most of your training. You respond differently when you are learning for the first time (it may take much longer than you think and need to be broken into more steps) than when you are an expert adjusting to different audiences (you may work quickly, using similar document structures but shifting the tone). Your situation affects your document design process; your client's situation defines your document or product. Like the architect, you will do well with both when you can specifically define each.

> It is not an individual art, architecture. You have to consider your client. Only out of that can you produce great architecture. You can't work in the abstract.
>
> —I.M. Pei

Your design training reveals the nature of legal writing itself. When you consider the many different kinds of writing—novels, essays, op-ed pieces, graduate papers, letters, poems, knitting instructions, business summaries, investment prospectuses, short stories—you realize you are composing something very different from these. Your situation is different, as are your product and process. Compare, for example, writing an essay or poem with drafting a contract. When you think of writing an essay, what comes to mind? What kinds of planning events, feelings, visions of the final product do you experience? You might think of such writing matters as finding an original topic, presenting a strong point of view, using the standard pre-defined sections, introduction, and using elegant variation in vocabulary. Then consider a poem: what do you think of as a writer? Rhyme scheme, imagery, metaphor, economy of words, emotion, flow. Does the poem come from a different part of you than an essay? Do your reactions to poetry emanate from the same part of your mind as your thoughts about an essay? Do you feel the same behavior and activity being generated with an essay as with a poem? Then compare that with drafting a contract. There you consider the client's objectives, the appropriateness of the form, the legal accuracy of each section, and the precision of each legal term. Legal writing calls upon different bases for your decisions, many of them in the law itself. Like the architect, you must consider client and cost, not just word choice and phrasing. And, like the architect, you turn outward as you construct documents for others to use, not for yourself.

To do this well, you must be aware of your sequencing of writing tasks, your process. It is a complex decision-making process that is guided by the context within which it is produced. For lawyers, producing a document within a specific context includes such activities as collecting facts, analyzing facts, formulating preliminary issue statements, researching similar documents, researching the law, selecting sources, comparing and contrasting related laws, sifting through facts as redefined by the laws, organizing information, designing a document to meet several purposes, understanding several audiences' needs, drafting, rewriting, revising, polishing, incorporating comments, updating, and unifying the document when several people have commented upon it. All of these activities may occur in different sequences, depending upon the document and the circumstances of its production. And each of us chooses from among many techniques at each stage in the process.

Rather like designing a building, designing a useful legal document requires understanding many levels at once: selecting an overall theme, gathering the appropriate materials, seeing the overall form, fitting the materials into the form in the proper proportion, making the inside of the document harmonize with the theme and form, and polishing to perfection. You can train yourself to adapt to your situation, to increase your design repertoire (product), and to build versatility and variety into your techniques (process). Like the architect, you will do well with both when you can specifically define each and flow comfortably through whatever transitions you experience in a legal writing situation.

Transitions

You may find that you experience a kind of "before and after" whenever you design a document in a new situation: when entering law school, switching jobs, or working for a new client. These constant initiations can be complex and challenging. Just as a talented artist or engineer may find the study of architecture oddly familiar and strange, so you may find legal writing as you move into a new setting. Hardly just a matter of using English as you previously did, legal writing requires that your respond to specific conventions created by U.S. scholars and lawyers, to new language, and to expected behaviors. This phenomenon explains the difficulty many novices encounter when they first enter the community or experienced lawyers find when they switch jobs within it: poor organization, broken grammar, and incomplete analysis. The conventions are rarely defined explicitly and the methodology is usually trial and error. As a novice, you may have entered the community assuming you could "write," but that writing occurred in a different community whose conventions varied from the legal discourse community's. A transfer is necessary. For some, the transfer is swift and smooth, even intuitive. For others, the transition is difficult, especially if you try to import conventions from other communities into the legal discourse community. Legal discourse is neither journalism nor literature, engineering nor political science. And writing in one law office is not the same as writing in another. The discourse to which you have switched may bear similarities, but it has created its own conventions for specific purposes.

In a way, each time you switch, you become a novice. According to one observer of legal writers, Professor Joseph M. Williams, legal writers mature not in a step-by-step way, but rather by entering into the circle of the discourse community. Before entering law school, he says, legal writers are *pre-socialized*, that is, they write in other discourses and have varying degrees of familiarity with concepts used in the legal discourse community. They then enter the community, with varying degrees of comfort, in a kind of up-and-down initiation that allows them to feel comfortable one day, very unsure the next. This goes on for a while as they break into the circle.

architecture:
1. The art or science of building structures, esp. habitable structures, in accordance with principles determined by aesthetic and practical considerations.

-Webster's Third New International Dictionary

Once in the circle, they become *socialized* writers. That is, they learn to imitate what lawyers write, to echo patterns used traditionally within the community, to manipulate the lexis, to, in short, write like lawyers. For many, this means reproducing the famous turgid prose. For many, this is the end of progress in writing. They may indeed become experts, comfortable within the field, comfortable talking to other lawyers, comfortable writing. In fact, most lawyers remain in this acculturated condition of being a part of the fraternity-sorority of legal writers. Their writing remains technical, traditional, and mostly inaccessible to non-lawyers.

The final step, according to Williams, is to become *post-socialized*. These writers begin to recognize that non-lawyer clients and even busy lawyers prefer plainer, more accessible prose. These writers begin to think more about audience, more about translation. These experts produce documents that return to tenets of "good" expository writing in the more universal sense: stating a clear message, using an immediately recognizable organizational scheme, using plainer language.

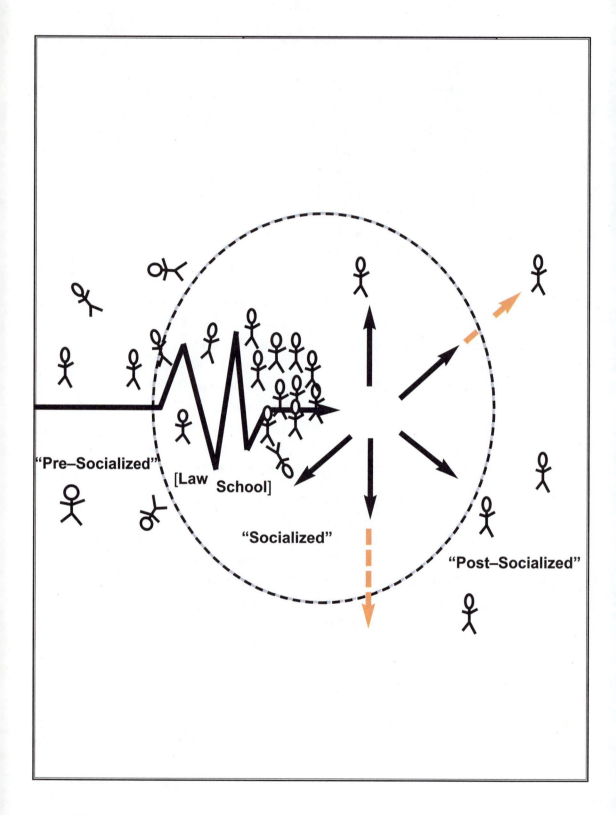

Adapted from Joseph M. Williams, *On the Maturing of Legal Writers: Two Models of Growth and Development*, 1 LEGAL WRITING 1, 17 (1991).

TRAJECTORIES

These expert legal writers, like expert architects, strive for creating beautiful works that, although possibly complex in their construction and design, appear simple and beautiful in their result. These experts design documents that draw readers in by their seeming simplicity, which is often a match between theme and form, between substance and syntax. They do the work for the reader, retaining accuracy, respecting the innate rhetorical soundness of doctrine and tradition (all buildings must have foundations and physics cannot be ignored), yet refreshing the reader with the sheer understandability of the result. These experts do not get trapped inside Williams' socialized circle, but rather build complex documents that look perfectly simple. Such accomplishment takes energy and will.

To know traditional legal writing well enough to break away from it requires moving on a trajectory out of the community. In fact, it may be that you experience not the up-and-down motion of entering the community, but rather a loop that carries you through pre–socialized and socialized writing, whatever your situation. Your design training requires you to engage in a dialectical process of discursive socialization, that is, you are drawn into the community through language and discussion. You cover a wide variety of terms and topics until you conform, sometimes without knowing why. It is that which keeps you socialized; imitation is a start, but is not original or creative. Without knowing the *why* underlying the field, legal document design, you cannot do more than imitate. Add to that the

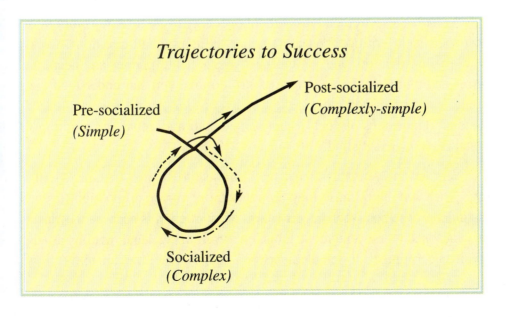

Trajectories to Success

Pre-socialized
(Simple)

Post-socialized
(Complexly-simple)

Socialized
(Complex)

constraints of your situation, and you can feel trapped. You may find yourself doing what you are told, then being criticized for it. You may unconsciously trade the clarity of your pre-socialized writing for the complexity of socialized writing, then becoming a mere conformist. You become one of the many socialized gate-keepers of our widely criticized turgid prose.

It often takes a tremendous amount of energy to create a trajectory into post-socialized writing. You must honor the norms and traditions, work within your situation, and yet catapult yourself into plainer architectural forms and more accessible language. To do this, you can understand the deeper meaning of both your project and your profession. You can understand all dimensions of your design so that both traditional and non-traditional readers are satisfied.

Very few lawyers, then, move on this trajectory to post-socialized writing. That may be because they are unaware of rhetorical possibilities or unguided by the post-socialized writers. Most often, it is because they lack the vocabulary and analytical tools for scrutinizing legal writing as an architect scrutinizes design elements or a doctor scrutinizes anatomy.

Much criticism falls on the legal community for its resistance to change, its turgid prose, its impenetrable language. This book suggests that those criticisms are valid; while you need to know the legal discourse community's conventions, you can still adjust the discourse to serve your many audiences' needs. You need to be versatile, to create more complicated structures, more difficult variations in design, and more specialized styles and features. As a legal writer, you are both interpreter and translator. You need to know the conventions within which to communicate, and then recreate, the discourse. You can move from Williams' socialized writing to post-socialized writing. By studying these elements, you can create a personal repertoire of design methods and techniques. You can, over time, become the post-socialized artist, the lawyer as architect.

KNOWING SOME ELEMENTS OF DESIGN

Underlying a fine legal product are fundamental rhetorical and architectural features. Like the architect, a well-trained lawyer examines all aspects of his case, including such rhetorical matters as the document's many audiences and their needs, the client's short-term and long-term objectives, the level of detail to be used, and the point of view to take. He also decides about the product itself, such as what the central theme is, in what order to present ideas, how to connect ideas, and so on. Because of law's complexity, these rhetorical and design elements offer many choices, many possible directions to take, from researching to deciding on the form of the product itself. While many lawyers make these choices intuitively, their audiences may not always make sense of those intuitions. These intuitions may also take too long to manufacture. The discussion that follows offers some terminology for identifying, analyzing, and characterizing the choices we make as document designers. By identifying and isolating these elements, you may be able to make quicker, more sound decisions as you design your document.

A Word On The United States "Legal Discourse Community"

Linguists and composition theorists have observed the phenomenon of interpreting and translating English within specific professional cultures. Some call those cultures discourse communities. When describing to non-native speakers of English the language that scientists, architects, doctors, and lawyers, for example, use to communicate among themselves, theorists call it English for a Specific Purpose, or ESP. The pun is too hard to pass over: it is the other ESP that seems necessary when first hearing the language spoken in first-year courses. Even native English speakers balk at the brand of English used by most lawyers, what is now known as English for Legal Purposes.

A discourse community, then, is a community within a larger culture that has created its own language, forms, and traditions for communicating with each other. Specifically, discourse communities are sociorhetorical networks that form in order to work toward sets of common goals. Those goals might include a socialization that maintains and recreates the sub-culture's social structure and world view. According to those adopting this perspective on discourse, known as the social view, discourse operates within conventions defined by the communities themselves, such as academic disciplines or social groups. So music historians will use terms to categorize their views of music history, such as romantic and baroque; philosophers will use language conventions appropriate to their goals, such as postmodernism; psychologists will create a discourse that incorporate's a particular world view, such as Freudian interpretation, and so on. Language itself creates meaning.

According to those adopting this social view, a discourse community is defined not only by the way community members use language but also by the way they behave. Discourse itself is a form of social behavior. The way that members of the community use language serves as a means of maintaining and extending the group's knowledge and is, in fact, epistemic or constitutive of the group's knowledge. In other words, members of discourse communities define themselves and their roles through the discourse itself. This is an important matter for newcomers to the community because experts use discourse as the means to initiate—or exclude—novices. Your first-year legal writing course initiates you into the community by introducing language, research sources, and analytical patterns. Your professors initiate you by using speech patterns that set up problem-solving sequences. Your supervising attorneys initiate you into the office by showing you approaches that members of that office use for designing and expressing ideas in documents. Your colleagues initiate you by giving you tips on the styles preferred by your supervising attorneys.

Writing in a discourse community, then, is not just an individual event. It is not just an inner-directed learning process. It is instead a complex, acquired response to the discourse conventions. Those conventions arise from preferred ways of creating and communicating knowledge within a particular community. Writing is a socially situated act.

You can work smoothly and quickly in any legal setting by identifying its overall characteristics. These characteristics, those that the community shares, may fall into the following categories, according to linguist John Swales. *See* JOHN SWALES, GENRE ANALYSIS (1990).

1.   A broadly agreed upon set of common goals;
2.   Mechanisms of intercommunication among its members;
3.   Use of its mechanisms to provide information and feedback;
4.   A register that uses particular genres to further its aims and a specific lexis, syntax, and phraseology; and
5.   A threshold level of members with appropriate expertise.

You encounter these characteristics in any new professional community. Consciously or otherwise, you adjust. The more consciously aware you are, the faster that adjustment, the more smooth the transition. Of course, you must also be willing to adjust; holding on to goals, habits, techniques, or even language that you used in other settings may impede your progress in your current circumstances. The following examples illustrate possible characteristics about the United States legal community at large and suggest situations that occur in practice. Consider more specifically the characteristics of your current setting.

First, the U.S. legal discourse community has a broadly agreed upon set of goals. These goals include serving clients, interpreting laws, and drafting legislation. They include resolving disputes, preventing disputes, and protecting those who cannot protect themselves. We also set goals for professional conduct and enforce those. Within the academic segment of the legal discourse community, those goals include creating scholarship through individual, original analysis and research; synthesizing complex concepts and creating legal theories that justify or explain behavior in and out of the legal discourse community. The U.S. legal discourse community has also agreed on encouraging service to the community at large, monitoring its members for proper behavior within the community, and establishing uniform guidelines for using and citing the law. These agreed upon goals, probably quite obvious and even unconsciously implemented to the expert, are unknown to the novice. Similarly, law offices may have a shared philosophy of practice, marketing goals, or training goals. You may want to research this aspect of the practice to make sure your choices are accurately informed by the local experts' goals and expectations.

Second, the U.S. legal discourse community also uses specific mechanisms of intercommunication among its members. Those mechanisms include classes, texts, exams, handouts, and e-mails in the classroom; meetings, memos, correspondence, newsletters, bar association publications, e–mail, and Internet for practitioners. The mechanisms serve to expedite communication among members. By these mechanisms, we inform each other of developments within the community, of changes in norms, of possibilities for developing areas of expertise, or of new decisions. We also assess performance, giving feedback to each other on analyses, development, and ability for prognosis. Within law offices, we invent other mechanisms: informal meetings, impromptu oral assignments, e–mail communications, or phone conferences, for example.

Third, members of the discourse community then use these mechanisms for information and feedback. Lawyers use newsletters and bar journals to get information about substantive changes in the law, amendments to rules of ethics, and lists of disbarred lawyers. We use correspondence to get feedback from clients, law journals for analytical approaches that develop new theories, and the *U.S. Law Weekly* to get information about U.S. Supreme Court decisions. The secondary purpose of these mechanisms and the members' use of them is that the profession improves, keeps up to date, moves more steadily toward the common goals. Law offices have formal evaluation processes, informal feedback meetings, and e-mail feedback on written work.

Fourth, the U.S. legal discourse community furthers its aims by refining its mechanisms to a specific register. Register refers to a discourse community's use of the language and instruments of communication themselves. The legal register is the unique combination of genres, terms, phraseology, patterns of discourse, and the syntactical conventions developed by the profession. Register includes the invention of specific genres, lexis, syntax and phraseology. Each genre, or type of document, fits a particular purpose and draws on particular forms and analytical patterns.

These patterns match the function of documents. So an appellate brief's overall form follows the local rules of appellate procedure; a contract uses a form derived from common law holdings, legal practices, forms, and local office traditions. The document's architecture is based on tradition and innovation: an opinion letter may use a deductive analytical pattern that moves from operative regulations to results; a contract may use an analytical pattern that places most controversial items at the beginning to avoid any confusion about final negotiations.

Through these genres, the community develops expectations about the discourse. Those expectations involve the form, function, and positioning of legal design elements, or a document's architecture; the roles the texts play in the community; and the appropriateness of subject matter, for example. Memos, letters, briefs, interrogatories, scholarly papers, and books, and other genres are used to further such goals as informing supervising attorneys of alternatives, advising clients, resolving disputes, developing legal theories, refining law for practical use, and informing clients of how law affects their activities. The genres themselves function in specifically defined settings; most require throughly expressed analysis that exposes each step in the reasoning, for example. These settings vary from trial courts to negotiation sessions to classes to professional publications, each of which has its own audience and purpose.

As another part of register, the U.S. legal discourse community has developed a specific lexis. This lexis is comprised of the technical terminology, or terms of art, that emerge from statutes, cases, and legal concepts. Those terms become a shorthand for members of the community, each term embodying principles, elements, and applications that are known to those who have studied the law. For U.S. lawyers, such terms as *demurrer*, *proffer*, *nuisance*, *unconscionability*, and *tortfeasor* have specific meanings, some embodying an action, some a doctrine. Similarly, abbreviations such as *F.R.C.P.*, *jnov*, *M/S/J*, and *UCC* stand for commonly used statutes and motions. The U.S. legal register encompasses both traditional and modern legal language. The traditional aspect of the register is the one most frequently caricatured; it is marked by doublets, repetition, Latinisms, and nominalizations. The Modern American Legal Register uses concrete subjects, verbs, and objects, rather than abstract ones; prefers active voice to passive voice; keeps subjects and verbs close together and uses footnotes rarely, if at all. (*See* Chapter 6.) For example, note the difference between the traditional sentence, *The doctrine of <u>res ipsa loquitur</u> requires that the defendant indicate the reasons for any accident by offering a reasonable explanation* *for all of the causes thereof* and the modern *Under the <u>res</u> <u>ipsa</u> <u>loquitur</u> doctrine, the defendant must reasonably explain the accident's causes.*

Moving throughout each genre are the other two parts of register: syntax and phraseology. While lawyers seem to use standard English syntax, they have developed some particular uses of syntax and some phraseology that identifies the discourse. Syntax, or the arrangement of words to form phrases and sentences, becomes particularly important in law because the arrangement of words may result in different meanings. For example, in the sentence, *The defendant refused to service the car belonging to the man who insulted him with good reason*, the placement of the phrase *with good reason* probably changes the intended meaning of the sentence. And in the sentence, *Ms. Ray suggested only filing a suit for adverse possession*, the placement of the word *only* in the last phrase is grammatically correct but legally ambiguous. Legal readers expect intentional decisions from the writer so that words are chosen and placed for a reason. Unintentional choices can lead to unnecessary ambiguity.

Finally, the U.S. legal discourse community establishes its threshold level of members with a suitable degree of relevant content and discoursal expertise using several methods. It uses exams, papers, class participation, and behavior to establish a threshold level of members of the academic legal community. The legal community at large uses the bar exam, rules of conduct, publication, and public performances. Law offices use assignments, deadlines, workload, and standards for promotion to establish "membership" within the office. Together, these methods regulate the profession, keeping within the community those members who have a threshold level of expertise.

These features of the legal discourse community incorporate traditions that require deference to certain members of the profession; that retain formal language in some settings, informal in others; that assume a knowledge of the U.S. legal culture, both national and local. More specifically, these broad characteristics then give way to more specific rhetorical elements, the elements of legal design. Once you have analyzed your current setting, you are ready to consider the approaches used locally to build useful legal documents. Embedded within the broader characteristics of your legal community are preferred systems for treating the more specific elements of legal design.

As you read the following discussions, remember that, like architecture, legal writing may be better experienced than explained. No system, list, or suggested plan can truly escape the terrors of formalism. Given a list, almost any novice is tempted to use it as both beginning and end; it is just easier that way. Even experienced attorneys devolve into following formal directions under pressure. Yet the intuitive trial and error method can be too dangerous and take too long, like physicians discovering what tools to use during surgery. The following discussions try to take a middle path of presenting some elements of legal design. To be useful, these discussions serve only to introduce design elements explored in later chapters. As elements, they may help you to identify forms, features, and functions of what you read and write. This identification alone may enhance your writing. The point, however, is for you to move beyond these elements to inventing your own; to move beyond any formalism to create, consciously and intentionally, documents that serve a variety of audiences. Read about these elements, then, in a spirit of criticism and creativity.

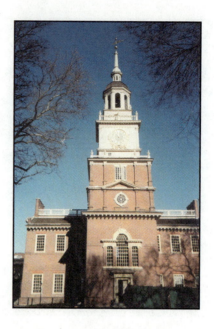

SOME RHETORICAL ELEMENTS

PURPOSE
AUDIENCE
SCOPE
STANCE

PURPOSE

An architect's first question is about function: to what use will the building be put? Is it a garage, church, home, office building? What is its purpose? Similarly, much legal writing is instrumental, that is, designed to serve a practical purpose: constructing transactions, setting up estates, or creating tax shelters. Some legal writing may be primarily expository—explaining the law, defining terms, or suggesting possible outcomes—but is usually embedded in a document that serves a larger purpose of informing, persuading, or advising. Very rare is legal writing an essay or verse. Legal writing may have purposes beyond informing, such

as to persuade, clarify, recommend, advise, summarize, annoy, obfuscate, deny, or console, for example. And, like many buildings, any one piece of legal writing probably serves several purposes. A brief may inform and persuade; a bad-news letter may inform, persuade, apologize, and prevent malpractice; a contract may capture an agreement, prevent future disagreement, and capitulate on some business points.

As you write, ask, *How should this document function?* What is it trying to accomplish? Is it persuading a decision-maker to decide in my client's favor? Is it created to account for all contingencies in a transaction? To anticipate all problems in a negotiation? To inform someone of the current law and its impact for the client? To motivate someone to take action? To dramatize? To memorialize? To protect? To create something not existing before? To correct a wrong? As you begin your design decisions, remember that the document may serve several purposes: Is the

same document informing, anticipating, and sealing a deal? Persuading, preventing, and informing? A dunning letter motivates someone to pay; a brief persuades; a letter may memorialize; a judicial opinion may create new law.

As a legal writer, you must decide not only on a document's purposes, but also on which purpose predominates. Doing so will generate decisions on theme, organization, tone, and style that conform to that hierarchy of purposes. Which purpose is most important? Try to decide what purpose predominates and design accordingly.

Remember, too, that what may seem primary as you begin designing may become secondary as you see the larger context. A judicial opinion may be creating new law in reaction to the legislature, which has struck down a previous ruling. A letter memorializing a conversation with a client may be subtly persuading the client to stop calling so often. Or a contract may be anticipating litigation over the deal. You can choose to state your purposes explicitly or to make them clear through the fusion of your theme, form, and interior design. Like the architect, you can design the document to fit multiple purposes.

AUDIENCE

Architects may enjoy designing a one-room addition to a single-family dwelling rather than an office building to be used by hundreds. Fewer decisions. Or not? Sometimes the fussy single client who keeps changing his mind will drive a designer crazy. Corporate clients may have more generic goals for the use of their offices. Similarly, legal audiences have specific requirements and tastes. They are not easy clients. Remember two characteristics about U.S. legal audiences, characteristics that may continually inform your design decisions: they read in bad faith, and there is usually more than one.

Legal readers have been trained to read very critically so as to ensure the content is complete, the analysis accurate, and the point of view consistent, among other things. They are looking for mistakes. Your clients will want to know exactly why they cannot do what they want to do. The opposing side in a negotiation will look for any wholes in your contract draft. No one will give you the benefit of the doubt because the stakes are too high, the results too concrete. This is law. (Even as you read this doc-

ument, you are probably looking more sharply for mistakes because this is a text about writing. The typo a few sentences ago probably stopped your critical eye.) You therefore must know your audience well and write to perfection. It takes longer and it takes excellent concentration sustained over long periods of time.

Further, you must write for several audiences at once. Most legal writing is viewed by several people, each of whom has a different point of view. For example, a brief might be read by a supervising attorney, a client, opposing parties, a judge, and that judge's clerk. To satisfy all of

these audiences and move beyond your sense of satisfaction to your read-ers' collective satisfaction, you must choose approaches, analytical pat-terns, and language that are widely acceptable but narrowly specific to the paper's content. This balance requires research into the specific readers' expectations, the norms used in the specific area of law, and the "local" conditions, traditions, and legal dialect.

Ask, *Who will be using this document?* Will it be just one client? Or will it be general counsel for a client and a number of executives who are non-lawyers? Will it be a defendant and his family? Will it be a defendant, opposing counsel, judge's clerk, and judge? The number of people using a legal document is a major factor in analyzing its architecture. For example, a judge's clerk may refer to a brief as a point of reference for research. The judge may refer to that same brief to study arguments that she knows have been developing over several years. Opposing counsel will use the brief to create the architecture for his own, and the client will use the brief to know that she is getting her money's worth from her lawyer. Again, decipher, if you can, your primary audience: who trumps whom? Is it the judge or the judge's clerk? Who will see it first? Is it the non-expert client? Or his gen-eral counsel, who is a lawyer? Expert writers, like expert architects, use audience to find a high common denominator, a design that pleases all users.

SCOPE

As you see a building, you are struck by its size. As you read legal writing, you might be struck by the same feature. Scope in legal writing refers directly to what the paper contains, indirectly to what has been omit-ted. Decide scope according to purpose, audience, law, and traditions. For example, a senior partner might want a short memo that answers a discrete question by using only the primary law in one jurisdiction. The client, another audience for the same document, may be willing to pay for only that short summary. Or several clients, parties to a class action, may want a comprehensive summary of all pertinent law on the same discrete issue, but analyzed in several jurisdictions and using mandatory and persuasive law. A judge may need more explanation because she is new to this sub-ject matter, while an expert requires less. You can decide the scope by con-sidering the hierarchies of purpose and audience established above; from those, you can balance thoroughness against over-inclusiveness and con-ciseness against relevance. You may find this tension unusual if you are used to writing within a specific community, such as the scientific or history communities. You may find that the variety in audience is so great that you have to learn different approaches for subordinating information to cover all that is required without boring the expert or losing the neophyte.

Ask, *How much will accomplish the purpose and accommodate these audiences?* How little can be included and still accomplish the purpose? Most legal readers extol conciseness; only the expert writers reach the perfect balance between accuracy and brevity. Striking the balance is often the lawyer's most difficult challenge. Does the document achieve this balance? Is it not repetitive, yet complete? Detailed, yet memorable? Are no sections, paragraphs, words wasted? Is there enough information that you can follow the document's meaning, message? Ask general questions about the document, too. What length is appropriate or required by the rules? How much information should be included; do the readers already know it? How many parties are there to the transaction? How many jurisdictions are covered? How much detail is used to explain or explicate the document? As you read legal writing, try to analyze what the writer included; try to infer what was omitted and why. As you write, match your document's scope to its hierarchies of purposes and audiences.

STANCE

Perspective brings a feeling to architecture. Michaelangelo chose monumental size and perfect alignment of the columns for St. Peter's to send a message of awesome grandeur and heavenly perfection. He designed David

to be seen from below in a niche. I.M. Pei designed such a sharp marble edge on the National Gallery's East Wing that one can stand at the bottom and see the edge's arrow shoot into the sky. Each designed with the user's perspective in mind, and with that perspective tied to both purpose and audience.

You create perspective in legal writing by similarly considering your audience, then taking a stance, or point of view. You tie that stance to purpose and audience. If you are informing, you may choose a quiet, objective stance, marked by an objective introduction and a careful balancing of elements. If you are persuading, you may choose an aggressive stance, or an offended one, or an indignant one. If you are trying to collect a bill, you may be firm, blunt, or pleading. Your selection of stance is informed by the document's purposes and audiences; in turn, it informs your decisions about structure, tone, and voice.

Ask, *What is my point of view?* What will best accomplish my purpose? What is my position in explaining or arguing or negotiating within this document? Should I be aggressive? cautious? firm? apologetic? impatient? kind? calm? surprised? conciliatory? candid? To keep the document

unified, present one overall stance. But, as with other rhetorical matters, stance may be complex. You may choose one overriding stance, such as firm, but you may incorporate others, such as kind or cautious. Shifts in stance confuse readers; consistency allows the reader to stay focused. Make sure your stance carries the design's purpose to its audiences.

SOME ARCHITECTURAL ELEMENTS

THEME
MATERIALS
FORM
PROPORTION
INTERIOR DESIGN
FINISH

THEME

For a Frank Lloyd Wright prarie home, it is blend with nature; for Chartres, it is *look up to see light illuminating spirituality*; for the Louvre, it is *let two powerful traditions unite*. These architectural statements, or themes, carry to our memories the peculiar offering of each of those remarkable buildings. For a tool shed, it might be *functional*, for a palace, *regal*, for a cabin, *cozy*. The themes of architecture help us to translate their import, to follow their logic, and to understand their functions. Audiences need just as much help in legal writing.

Your document should have a theme, that is, a message, thesis, or theory, a clear idea that can be stated in one sentence. If you were stopped in the hall of your law office and asked what is your document's theme, you should be able to say it immediately. Your theme can be simple: *We don't have to give up the documents because of attorney–client privilege* or *They have the money and we want it* or *The deal is that they give us widgets and we give them whatsits and three million dollars* or *The agency should change its mind because their latest decision is inconsistent with both the regs and their previous decisions.* Modern documents challenge you to make the complex simple. You may be tempted to let several points remain just that—disjointed and unassembled—a landfill instead of a building. Resist. Unify your message by creating a perspective that helps your audiences to assimilate the information. Negotiate this theme with anyone involved in the project, whether it is supervising attorneys, clients, or novices. Your theme unifies your document and helps you to build the connections among sections. State your theme directly in your document and include a verb, which transforms your idea from a topic to a theme.

Ask, *What is the theme*? Does it follow from purpose and audience? Does it unify all parts of the document? Can anyone understand it? Then decide where, if anywhere to put it. Is it an explicitly stated question? Is it a message given in the first few paragraphs? An explicit statement at the beginning of the contract? Then, more interestingly, determine what to emphasize. Because a legal writing document serves so many functions and is used by so many readers, your chosen theme may have to emphasize one aspect of your document over another. The issue stated in a case may address the immediate facts but the holding may incorporate a shift in philosophy or anticipation of legislative action. The message in a letter to a client may be that it is technically legal to go ahead with a proposed action; implicitly, the letter may suggest that, if the client does so, he will end the business relationship. Once you establish your primary theme, decide where in your document you will repeat or reinforce it. Use the theme to generate your form; use its terminology to frame its subparts.

MATERIALS

A grass hut, a log cabin, a concrete tower, a stone house, a glass office building: the architect's materials make a statement in themselves. They

are not just the substance out of which the building is formed; they are the media from which the message is forged. These materials give you an immediate sense of delicacy or durability, of sharpness or warmth, of celebration or ominous silence. You know that part of the architect's creativity is her ability to fuse materials that seemed incompatible, to use familiar materials in unfamiliar ways, to stretch, shrink, or modify.

And so your selection of your materials reflects your expertise. Selecting the appropriate materials is

a function of your research expertise. Whether you are gathering facts, forms, or law, you are carefully selecting the materials out of which you will build your document. Plan your research accordingly. Do the most you can for the maximum results under the circumstances. You may not need to stray past one jurisdiction's laws; you may be able to include only seven relevant facts on which the case turns; or you may need to anticipate every possible situation in a complicated transaction. Consider how long the document must remain functional, how many people will use it, how

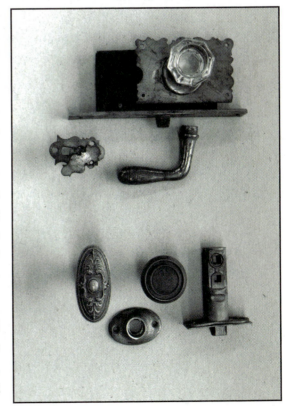

much time you have to build it, and how pretty it has to be. Also consider such practical matters as availability of the materials, their cost, how long it will take to get them, how long they will be good for, and how they work aesthetically. While you may like to think that every document you create is a thorough, perfect work that leaves nothing out, the truth is that you must often create pragmatic, inexpensive documents. You must be baroque or minimalist, depending on the situation. And you must usually be economical; very few clients will pay for materials that are not used in the construction.

Done well, your research should yield not only your materials, but also their place and proportion in your document. That is, when you leave the library, your document can be essentially written. You can know what materials you will probably use and their relative importance. You may have found one source that is essential because its facts, law, reasoning is so similar to your case. That source will figure prominently, while others may be combined in a single paragraph or not even merit one sentence. If you read critically, you can design your document as you evaluate the materials. The materials speak to you about design possibilities as they outline analytical patterns. They let you know how close or far from your client's situation they sit. If researched properly, even a form book will notify you of what is pertinent in your client's situation. Just as an architect understands the client's budget and requests and chooses her materials accordingly, so you can choose materials to fit the situation. You can discover the essential building blocks and be able to decide how much else will help achieve the document's goals. In researching consciously and creatively, you should gather very little extraneous materials, and your client will be pleased not to pay for more than is necessary.

Ask, *what materials answer the questions?* What do I absolutely need? What is most appropriate? How can I combine the materials to suit the purposes? What will my audiences find most pleasing? If necessary, what are the "cheapest" materials, those that will build the structure without any frills? What will I add for the next most expensive? And what is the fullest, finest version? Research, keeping in mind balance: most legal reader clients want enough to answer the question, nothing more and nothing less.

FORM

Sydney's Opera House broke all architectural traditions. Scoffed at on the drawing board, it is now Sydney's most recognizable draw. A great sea shell of white opening up into Sydney's harbor, it draws audiences not just for opera but for the sheer beauty of seeing its unusual form. Gaudi's unfinished cathedral in Barcelona spellbinds viewers with its unusual form. Even unfinished, its looming shape sears into the visual memories of visitors. And the swirling shape of the Guggenheim Museum draws viewers more interested in it than what it holds. Form, in the architectural sense, is the "frozen music" that makes its artistic mark on the people who inhabit it. It is architecture's dominating element, the structure that sends the message and performs the function.

> Architecture is frozen music.
> -Goethe

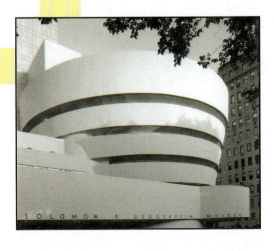

Your document's form, in the architectural sense, accomplishes the same objective. It carries the theme, performs the function, and offers your reader a schema for taking in the content and processing it. In reading a legal document, most legal readers comprehend first its large-scale form, the overall shape of the document. That form must account for the rhetorical elements listed above. It must also account for the materials you research, the organizational dictates of particular areas of law, any subset of traditional "logic" or patterns of thinking that go by that name, and tradition. This most essential architectural element is at once the most creative and critical aspect of your document. A well constructed form carries its content and purpose; a poorly constructed one collapses like a grass shack at the first critical gust of wind.

Your audiences appreciate knowing what kind of a structure they are entering and how they will proceed. Your design can be familiar, immediately recognizable. For example, your form may take cues from the law itself. You may choose to follow the parts of a statute in the order in which they appear, you may place jurisdictional issues first, or you may be presenting a balancing test that gives first one side, then the other, then the balance. Your form may draw on classical forms of western logic: deduction or induction. In U.S. law, traditional deductive organization presents the relevant general law (major premise), followed by specific definitions or examples (minor premise) as applied to the client's situation (minor premise), followed by a conclusion (conclusion). This deductive form is popular in genres such as memos, opinion letters, and briefs. Or you may be using the peculiar analogical paradigms developed in the U.S. legal community. Many judicial opinions follow an analogical organization by gathering examples and holdings from previous cases, contrasting them to the facts of the specific case, and then reaching a conclusion. Or your "logic" may be chrono- "logical" or topical.

If your purpose is to persuade, you may choose a form that moves from most important to least important. For example, a client wants to know his question and its answer in the first paragraph of a letter. A judge wants to know the issues immediately and perhaps the proposed remedies and a summary of the reasons.

Transactional work draws heavily on tradition: a structure that outlines the item to be purchased and its price, followed by terms, warranties and representations, and so on. Materials themselves dictate form: statutes with only scant legislative history and no cases may yield a lean analysis;

statutes with much legislative history and numerous cases offer several different and complex arrangements. And certain audiences simply prefer certain forms. A lawyer may primarily use one organizational scheme for certain types of transactions, his colleague another scheme, so that the novice attorney must learn to ghost write both. One judge may generally write deductively; another will often use the straw man approach of setting up arguments and knocking them down, so each clerk will have to adjust to those overall forms.

There are departures from these traditional architectural forms of legal documents. Complaints have been filed as poems, briefs have been written as plays, and charts sometimes replace writing altogether. Modern legal scholarship has also suggested departures from traditional organizational schemes by incorporating economics models, other interdisciplinary models, or personal experience. The document's form makes a powerful impression on the reader, who then looks for portions and proportions within that larger form.

These substantive architectural form choices are to be distinguished from technical legal forms and formats. Forms, such as for complaints or contracts, and formats, such as for appellate briefs or memos, are one–dimensional suggestions about blueprints. Like zoning requirements, they must be researched and incorporated, but they are not the basis for the

document's substantive dimensions. They do not account for law, logic, or purpose; they cannot reveal audience preferences, scope decisions, or local traditions. Like spell check, they are a point of departure, not a final plan. Like a sample blueprint book in an architectural firm, they reveal ideas and possible contours, but not the keys to final substantive decisions about space and structure.

Ask, *What are the design possibilities?* What possible ways can I assemble this document to meet the rhetorical needs described above? Should I use deduction to draw my reader to my inevitable conclusion in a brief? Should I proceed from most controversial to least controversial section of a document? Should I build the memo around the elements of the statute, but rearrange the elements in the order most favorable to my client? What works best in these circumstances? How does one part intersect with another? Can two parts be combined for more impact? Should one part be repeated for emphasis? Does the form follow the document's function? Convey the theme? Make the finest use of materials? These questions, and many more, may be the most central to your document's success. Your ability to create the appropriate form can make all the other elements click into place.

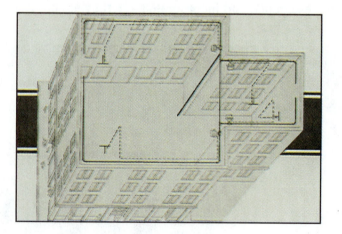

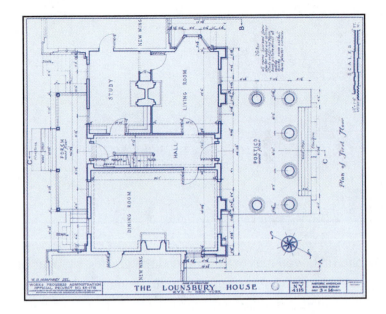

PROPORTION

You have probably, at one time or another, been in a building that made you queasy or uneasy. It might have been a claustrophobic doctor's office or a crowded department store. You may have felt uncomfortable in a too large living room or a tiny apartment. You may have been astounded at a master bathroom in a model home, that was equal to the size of the master bedroom. You have probably felt very comfortable in restaurant with the right-sized rooms, a kitchen with just enough space. You may have even chosen your current dwelling because of the proportion of the rooms to each other.

In legal writing, the proportion of the parts to each other and to the whole give similar messages to your audiences. Whatever overall form you choose, you can arrange proportionately the smaller pieces of the document, from sections to paragraphs. Your decisions on proportion send strong messages to your reader about your theme and purpose. If you choose to create a large section on a subtopic, the reader naturally assumes that subtopic is more important than one that takes up less space.

For example, if you are writing an appellate brief, within the required format (zoning regulations), you are creating an analytical, architectural form for your argument. If your choose an inductive form, each point heading will be an example of your overall point, perhaps creating a cumulative impact that is felt most powerfully at the end of the brief. You will then have to choose the order for each of those points. If you wish to present the

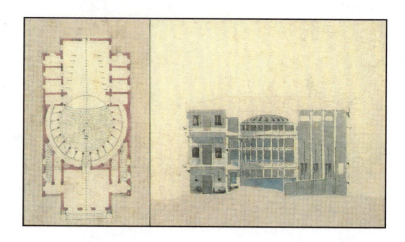

strongest one first, you may want to spend the greatest number of pages or use other devices to give that section weight. You may choose to bury your weakest point in the middle and make it short, then end with a longer next–strongest point. Or you may decide to move from strongest to weakest. With either choice, the proportion of space you spend on each point should match its relative importance. You may choose to bury the weakest argument to give symmetry to your brief; or you may choose the strongest-to-weakest version to create a flow of largest to smallest. Your decisions on proportion directly affect the reader, whose comprehension and sense of expectation are intensified by your design decisions.

Within sections of documents, proportion of paragraphs and sentences also affect the reader. If you use headings, you are creating doorways for your reader, signals of what is to come. Longer headings may indicate more importance, or you may choose to invert length and importance to draw attention to a crisp heading. If you design the headings as sentences that relate to each other and to the overall theme, you are indicating the proportions of parts to the whole. Such intentional designation reinforces your design decisions and keeps your reader comfortable by matching proportion to meaning. Legal

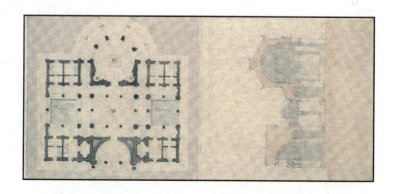

audiences appreciate such signals. The more complicated the document, the more assistance they need.

Ask, *What is the relative value of each part to the other?* What parts are more authoritative, carry more weight, and should therefore either fall in positions of emphasis or take up more space? What parts should be mentioned in passing? What parts should be eliminated altogether? What do I want to emphasize, de–emphasize? How does each part relate to the theme? Is each part proportioned so that audiences feel comfortable in that room and understand its place in the larger building or form? Does the proportion match the meaning? Such questions keep you focused at the mid–level design, the sections that audiences experience as one legal subset of the greater idea. Remember, too, that many audiences will go directly to one-room to use it, the way people find your kitchen, so each room must have its own integrity, its own coherent interior.

Interior Design

Flowered curtains, pillows, and couches are perfect for some people, anathema to others. The idea of having a designer "do" your home is often revolting, for the very reason that it often accomplishes only two things: telling you how bad your taste is and making your house ugly. So many designers simply have one way of designing and they carry it to every interior. Not the talented ones. They make your home look like a better version of your preferences. They position your favorite possessions as though you had put them there, but yet you would not have thought about that. It is not the flowered pillows they bring, nor the brass and glass, but the eye. They arrange with color, light, rhythm, texture, and shape in mind. They make what you have look good, rather than replace your tastes with theirs.

Paragraphs and sentences are the interior design of a document, the furniture and accoutrements that complement the document's architecture. As in interior design, so in law we have many interior designers whose one idea of writing paragraphs and sentences is to use flowered pillows or brass and glass–namely, their singular, inflexible "style." If Ralph Lauren is what the client wants, he can hire that kind of writer. But most audiences want something that makes sense, an interior that matches the document's purpose, form, and proportion. When paragraphs and sentences harmonize with a well-designed structure, they extend and intensify theme, form, and proportion. Here, more metaphors may help. The texture of sections and sentences may be thick, thin, rough, smooth, slippery, dry, and so on. Their rhythm can be slow, fast, or moderate; they can speed up, slow down, or stay the same. Your choices as a writer are like those of an interior designer. Words are your colors, sentences and sections your furniture.

For example, if your theme delivers an ultimatum and your architecture is direct and square, you may choose to use dry, short, staccato sentences: *You have not yet paid. You need to pay. You have five days.* If your

theme apologizes, you may wish to use smoother, more moderate sentences: *You have been patiently awaiting our reply on the difficult matter of splitting the litigation costs. After holding three meetings about the subject with our client, we have agreed to split the costs as you suggested. We apologize for the delay and hope that this news will expedite the closing of this case.* If you are matching your sections and sentences to a message that a government agency should reverse its policy, you may wish to speed up, using longer, more fluid paragraphs at the beginning, gradually converting to shorter, more staccato paragraphs at the end. The sentences within those sections may do the same.

The overall guidelines for proportion operate inside paragraphs and sentences, too. Just as important information appears in prominent places or is

relatively long, so important ideas can be in the main clause of a sentence. Conversely, a subordinate idea can appear in a subordinate clause, weak points can appear in the middle of a paragraph, and opposing arguments can be stated brusquely. Using proportion at the small-scale level also assists legal readers in comprehending and remembering the writer's message.

Your command over section structure, length, speed, and sound; over paragraph structure; over sentence structure, order, variety, and length; over word choice, order, sound, and sight—makes you able to match interior design to overall analytical form. This match is the second half of clarity; after matching your structure to your theme, match your syntax to your substance. Such conscious matching renders your document comprehensible, accessible, and memorable. The more you write, the more aware you become of these interior design possibilities; the more you develop your repertoire of possibilities, the more you can summon whatever is appropriate for your message and your audiences.

Ask, *Does the interior match the overall theme and form?* What subthemes do I want to introduce? What words or phrases encompass those subthemes? Where should I place them to unite a series of paragraphs or sentences within a paragraph? What phrases define the overall theme? When do I remind the reader of the relationship of the subideas to the overall theme? How often? How much clutter is in the interior design—lots of intrusive phrases, passive voice, complex conditionals that give paragraphs a baroque feel? Minimalist sentences that match a minimalist theme? Bring to your interior design an eye that makes the paragraphs and sentences work for those audiences. You may need to save your flowered pillows for your own living room.

Finish

Your document can have a finish, a quality that in itself expresses the theme. It may be shiny, like brass and glass, cozy like wood or warm like stucco. You can check the overall finish by looking at the document's level of refinement—highly shone or comfortably rounded. Tabs, colored pages, strong font and outlines give the product a formal finish; regular font, no headings, and no footnotes give a less formal finish. You can create an overall effect.

Whatever that effect, your reader expects perfection. The finest accomplishments fade with even the tiniest flaws. A color that doesn't match, a strident piece of furniture, a tile that is set the wrong way. Your architectural design must account for all parts, all aspects of the document. There should be no afterthoughts, no additions that do not match the overall form, no mistakes. Especially in the practice of law, details become crucial. One misplaced comma, one omission of the word "not," one phrase misstated, and the entire document can be misinterpreted. The standards are very high in the practice of law, as they should be. Your ability to develop a keen eye that can see the whole and all of its parts makes your work more solid and more satisfying.

In a sense, you finish where you began. One of your first considerations was the local conventions, the filing requirements, the contract forms used in your office, or the citation form used in your jurisdiction. You will make this a part of both your initial concept about the document, and you will finish by making sure the document conforms appropriately.

Ask, *Have I checked every detail?* Every heading, every section, every sentence, every cite? Is everything in its place, spaced properly in relation to the rest of the document? Is there any detail that I can add or subtract that will make the whole look better? Sometimes in design work, the best thing to do is to remove one piece of furniture, one painting from the wall to let the eye rest. Anything like that here?

Do you feel you have no time for this? Well, ask yourself: would you like a doctor who left in just one small sponge before closing at surgery? Left in just one staple when she did the follow-up? An engineer who omitted one cable on the bridge? An architect who forgot to put in the bathrooms? Perhaps the most frustrating and tiring part of your job, finishing is often what separates the finest architects from the mundane.

SOME PRACTICAL QUESTIONS

Cost
Time
Duration

As an architect of legal documents, you must account for the practical questions your clients will ask. From landscaping to water rights to property lines, you have to fix the aesthetics of your design into your client's situation. You may have the luxury of working for that client for whom money is no object, but often cost will limit your selection of materials or time for assembling the document. You may want to build the house of the future, but your client needs only a tent that lasts a week. Like the architect, you need to place your document in a practical context.

Cost

Ask, *What can my client afford?* Consider this from the beginning so that you temper your design accordingly. You may need to scale down both your research and the size of the final written product. If your client has a modest budget, you may choose to write a short letter explaining your findings or report in a phone call. You may limit your research by jurisdiction or by date, using the cluster of crucial cases without explaining tangential cases. If your client can afford exhaustive research, you may produce a large document with a Table of Contents and an executive summary or a series of documents on various aspects of the client's situation. Your design should match the client's budget, offering the best design within the budget.

Time

Ask, *How much time do we have from beginning to absolute end?* Your client may also have a specific time schedule in mind. Anyone who has worked with contractors knows how frustrating it is to be given a date of completion that is unrealistic or even dishonest. Measure the depth and breadth of the project carefully so that you can give honest projections of time invested. If your client has a short deadline, consider what you can do best in that amount of time, measured against your other clients' interests. One of the keys to your success will be your ability to find techniques that free you to work well under time pressure.

Duration

Ask, *How long must this document last?* The document may be something that is needed to confirm a short telephone exchange or a memo on a subject that will become moot shortly. Both are useful only for a short time,

so you may not invest the time and resources you would in a document that will last longer. Those documents may be legislation that you are drafting, intended to last for years and to withstand all interpretations; contracts that are intended to bind parties for several years; or opinions that become law. Your design decisions can account for that duration, for the document's use by several audiences over time, for the possible interpretations of the document as policies shift. Your planning may therefore require more discussion about possible materials, forms, proportions, features. Be aware of interpretive possibilities, uses that will be made of your document, additions or corrections that may be proposed in time. You may design the document so that

it allows for additions; conversely, you may wish to make it so internally consistent and tight that no additions would make sense. Many legal documents are like public buildings and must be able to withstand a lot of traffic over time; others are for the private use of a limited audience. Think about your materials, form, and features accordingly.

SOME CONTEXTUAL ELEMENTS

HISTORY
LEGAL CULTURE
RELATION TO CURRENT LAW
UNSTATED ASSUMPTIONS
CONVENTIONS

Restricted covenants ensure the uniformity of architecture: low, adobe buildings in Santa Fe and Spanish architecture in Santa Barbara. The planned community in Kohler, Wisconsin was designed, landscaped, and administered by Frank Lloyd Wright's disciples, using strict guidelines. Such restrictions prevent someone from building anything that is strident aesthetically; they also prevent any innovation. You explored your specific situation above and now you, like the architect, can align your design decisions with the traditions in your specific setting. You may not have started with the contextual elements described in this section, but you may need to incorporate them to refine your decisions.

In the legal community, writing serves both as communication and as the law itself. Much of what we initially read as law students is the latter; much of what we produce is the former. Both are highly dependent on context and both have highly stylized modes of interpretation. As communication, legal writing may function as shorthand messages among members of the community or as complicated translations to those outside the community who are nevertheless affected by legal writing.

Try, then, to figure out the document's *context*. Reading for and understanding context requires looking before and after the document's genesis. What was going on? Who wrote this? What precipitated the need for the document? What assumptions has the author made about your understanding of legal culture? Is the document context-independent, that is, it does not require you to go outside the text to understand the whole?

Or did you have to be there? What conventions has the author observed or broken, whether in format, form, citation, or local practice? Where do you place this document—traditional or modern?

As much as is possible, consider these questions and examine the document accordingly. You may be reading a contract that was drafted in the context of a specialized, technical, delicate, one–of–a–kind transaction. Or you may be reading a standard form contract. The first may use very technical, specific language, the latter more general language. The first may have a long section laying out the parties and their rights, the latter a shorter section, and so on. Imagine the players and the motives of the writer. You may be reading a judicial opinion that creates a new area of law in a jurisdiction or a standard case that reinforces old law. Again, the first may be more detailed, and give more background information; the second may use abbreviated explanations that refer to a line of previous cases. What is happening in the development of the doctrine? Where does this jurisdiction stand on it? What is likely to follow from this decision?

You can, then, divine the context within which a document is created. You can observe, then articulate, evoke, and even create your own forms within a context. Doing so enhances your reading and invigorates your understanding of legal architecture, so to speak. You are then better able to write well. As you observe the examples in this chapter, note the rhetorical, design, and contextual elements, and study how the writer uses the elements to create a specific effect. Read for deeper rhetorical matters, such as purpose and stance. Try to decipher the theme, the reason for including the materials, the form the author selects, the proportions of parts to each other within the whole, the document's interior design, and its finish.

History

Note the document's *history*. Much of law school class discussions are designed to create context, to build a schema for understanding what motivated legal trends and the development of legal doctrines. Much of your reading and research in the law is a mini–version of the same phenomenon, but for narrower questions in the law. Your job is to read for what preceded an opinion, what motivated an agency to pass a regulation, or what suggested a policy shift. Your ability to succeed with your clients requires you to set their circumstances in context: what has happened before and what is likely to happen in the future. You begin this process by reading for these circumstances.

Legal Culture

In observing legal texts, also consider *legal culture*. The culture is generally nervous and distrustful. Mistakes in legal writing lead clients and legal writers into court. So many of the motivations for the writer's decisions find their roots in excessive care. This care often results in longer documents, packed sentences, and servile honoring of what has been written before. At its extreme, such behavior results in fossilization: the unthinking preservation of forms and sections and even language used for decades. Is the document showing signs of slavishness? Does the form look old? Is there a clash between what seems standard and what seems new? Is there a clash between the writer and his text? Tension between the lines because the writer has not engaged the traditional format? Is the text disembodied, that is, it seems as if so many people have so over refined it that it has no immediacy or life? Or does the text seem watertight, so well conceived and thoroughly worked over that no reader could find any holes in the content? Study the traditions of the genre, the office that produced the document, the writer who drafted it, and the standards in that area of law. Critically read to distinguish the traditional from the modern.

Relation to Current Law

Consider, too, the document's *relation to current law*. In documents where authority appears explicitly, read for its placement and use. Does authority weave throughout the analysis, intertwining with the author's own statements? Is authority quoted or paraphrased? Which happens more often? Does the author do the work for you in using the authority as specifically relevant to this document? Or is the authority quoted and dumped, leaving you to figure out its relationship to the analysis? Is each authority helpful or is the author giving his own research report, including most authorities she found without sorting through them? Does the authority appear next to statements so that its direct relationship is immediately apparent or is it relegated to a footnote? Listed in a string cite? Do signals indicate how to use the authority in relation to propositions or do the signals seem random, imprecise?

Unstated Assumptions

Perhaps the hardest things to read for are *unstated assumptions*. If you cannot follow the writer's reasoning, it may be because too much is left unsaid. What is missing? Is there a general statement and then a conclusion? Are all parts of the transaction included in the document? Is anything context-dependent, that is, you had to be there or you would not understand it? Or does the document stand alone?

Conventions

Note how the writer's use of *conventions* affects your reading of the document. The question is credibility, a feeling of confidence that the writer has done the work, that the reader does not need to leave the document to do further research or to check the use of authority. The care with which the writer presents authority telegraphs her research strategy and understanding of how authority works. Weigh the writer's use of authority against the theme and the form. This is the mortar that holds the document together.   Note also how the document honors local conventions on format and citation.

These contextual elements set the document in a landscape, an analytical zone of specific circumstances that make it unique. Even if it closely resembles another document, it has peculiar features that set it apart, such as facts, conventions, or perspectives. By divining its context, you can better understand why the document is built as it is.

A Word on Context

Context in legal writing includes both a shared understanding within the community and a sense of what will be interpreted outside the community. As law, legal writing has the intended function of regulating behavior. Context here also includes a broader and yet more technical understanding of modes of interpreting and implementing law. Such a powerful use of analytical patterns and language distinguishes our discourse community from others, whose use of both may be more casual, symbolic, or oblique.

For example, consider the following text:

> *If the consumer disagrees with the information in the report, the agency must investigate again.*

To contextualize this sentence, the reader will try to relate this passage to something familiar, some overall pattern that will account for this event. Many patterns are possible, but perhaps the most common one will involve assumptions relating to past experiences. The reader may assume that a consumer received a report about a purchase and disagreed with the description of events. Now we see the related bits of information as forming part of this pattern: that there has been a purchase, that there was some trouble about the purchase, that the consumer filed a report with an agency, and that the agency has already investigated the matter once. The pattern has to include knowledge of federalism: knowing that an agency is governmental body that is an extension of the executive branch of government, that the consumer has certain rights, and that these rights are protected by laws and regulations invoked by the agency.

If we add new information that the consumer is a radio station and the agency is the FCC, the pattern adjusts because then he may assume that other, specific regulations are involved that have to do with radio stations and that the report may put the station in danger of closing or of paying a fine, for example. If we then add the following information:

> *...before it turns over the matter to a criminal court.*

he must adjust his pattern to include the possibility of fraud or white collar crime. The radio station owner may have been duped or may have been involved in an act that violated both a federal statute and state criminal laws. To interpret and assimilate this information, the reader needs to have in place content schemata that include an understanding of where agencies fit into the authority hierarchy, of how consumer law protects innocent listeners, and how federal administrative law and state criminal law intersect. These schemata, inherent in the "socialized" U.S. lawyer's understanding of analytical paradigms, are simply absent for novices and non-lawyers.

Similarly, legal writers use familiar schemata when writing, sometimes forgetting that some of the target readers will not share these assumptions. They may not have the same understanding of the assumptions underlying the law, much less the analytical conventions used within certain subject areas. They may not know all of the history that led to these patterns of thinking and writing.

As you write, you can consider these patterns in the invention of the genre, or type of document, itself. Within the wide array of forms or genres that we use to communicate within our community are genres whose sources reach back through legal history. Conventional language and forms develop from repeated use and from substantive origins in cases and sometimes statutes. Knowing that a legal writer must both honor convention and be accurate forces you to investigate the origins of some genres. To do so, you can ask questions about all the elements discussed above, but you may also have to penetrate the reasoning behind some genres.

Often you know exactly what the genre is. It might be a standard letter demanding payment, a contract similar to those drafted several times in your office, an agenda item, a regulation, or a brief to a specialized court. Quite often the genre itself has been so specially developed in law that conventions give you many signals about how you will shape your document. Those genres have evolved over time, within particular settings, for very good reasons. For example, certain offices may develop a format for interoffice memos that incorporates business practices; certain agencies will create specialized genres for addressing agency law. And certain law offices will use language in contracts that draws literally from previous cases decided in this field. That seemingly conventional language is "safe" because the legal issue behind it has been litigated. Penetrating the reasoning behind the creation of the genre helps you to see how it functions, to read it more critically, and to create your own versions more creatively.

To read critically and write well, you must know what you are looking for, what analytical form a text takes, as discussed above. And that analytical form depends on context, too, context that often relies on unstated assumptions. For example, all members of the U.S. legal discourse community assume certain matters. They assume that authority will be cited according to the relationships dictated by federalism. That is, they expect that the writer understands what authority is predominant, how the sources of authority are linked, and what weight is given to each in coming to a conclusion. The answers to those questions help the writer design a specific analytical form for each legal problem. Further, the members of the community assume certain matters about the content of the document: that all relevant authority will be included and that omitting any is a violation of the code of ethics; that all irrelevant authority will be excluded; that legal holdings will be stated explicitly when relevant to advancing the analysis; that legally significant facts will be explained in detail when they resemble the facts being analyzed; and that authority will be cited according to a uniform system accepted by the readers involved. All of these assumptions build our cultural "logic"; all might be assimilated more effectively if made explicit to readers.

Other assumptions become more complicated for the reader. While the U.S. legal community still uses Aristotelian principles of deductive and inductive reasoning as adapted to federalism, it has gradually embraced other notions of analysis, including deconstructionism and anecdotal rendering. The community itself is in controversy over the value of using these methods of analysis, or whether or not they can even be called forms, or analytical patterns, as this book uses those terms. As the community incorporates new theories, new forms, and new analytical tools, the reader's work increases. And, quite often, we assume that the reader has done the work of figuring out context or can infer patterns and assumptions from the discussions. Some readers can, but the acculturation process can be hastened if some of these analytical processes and paradigms are made more explicit in rhetorical terms.

THE LEGAL WRITING PROCESS

One way to think about what you do as a lawyer and professional writer is that you go through a process of making decisions. From beginning to end, you are making choices. You start the project by receiving information in one of several ways. A client may call; an e-mail may appear on your screen; your supervising attorney may call you in and explain the assignment orally; or a memo may appear on your desk that outlines the project's parameters. Whatever way the project begins, you start your series of decisions. *Should I start here or there? Should I use this resource or that resource? Should I research the facts or get some legal background? Do I organize this way or that way? Do I go back to the assigning attorney or not? Do I use this word or that word?* And so on. That series of decisions, taken together, constitutes your legal writing process.

What follows are some sample legal writing processes compiled by both professional and novice legal writers. Note how the processes differ. Some lawyers like to begin right away and to ask a lot of questions, as in example 1.1. Others focus on the deadline and the time allotted for completing the project. Others are more theoretical, preferring to begin with the large picture and narrow it down to the small picture and smaller tasks at the end. Note also the complicated, recursive nature of the legal writing process. Experienced writers often return to the person who gave the assignment. They find times to review their work and to reformulate the issues. They also allow enough time to make the document utterly accurate. None of the experienced writers bunches activity at the end, for example. Even the busiest writers try to create a rhythm to the project so that there is enough percolation time to think about it. In fact, most experienced legal writers have rejected the "last minute" syndrome, knowing that any mistakes made in the process of producing a legal document can be fatal to the client's goals or leave them professionally liable.

Such high stakes force legal writers to create sophisticated and careful approaches to each project. It is a long journey from the process used on the first legal writing project to the processes of experts. In example 1.2, three law students sketch their writing processes during the first two weeks of law school.

Example 1.1. Writing Processes of Experienced Lawyers.

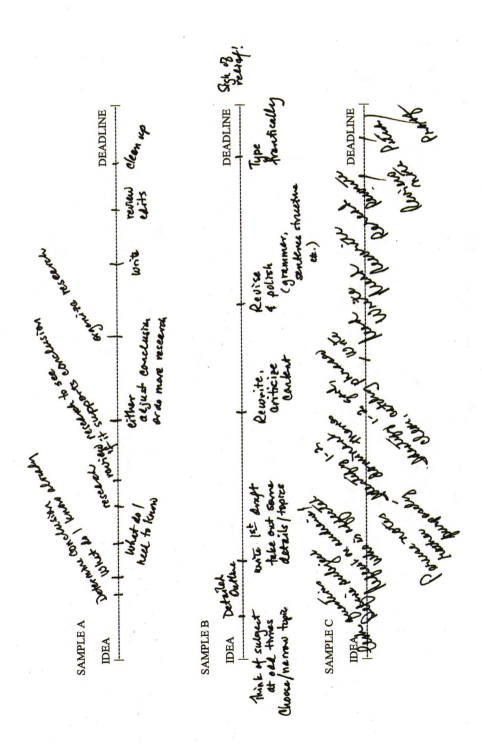

Example 1.2. Writing Processes of Entering Law Students.

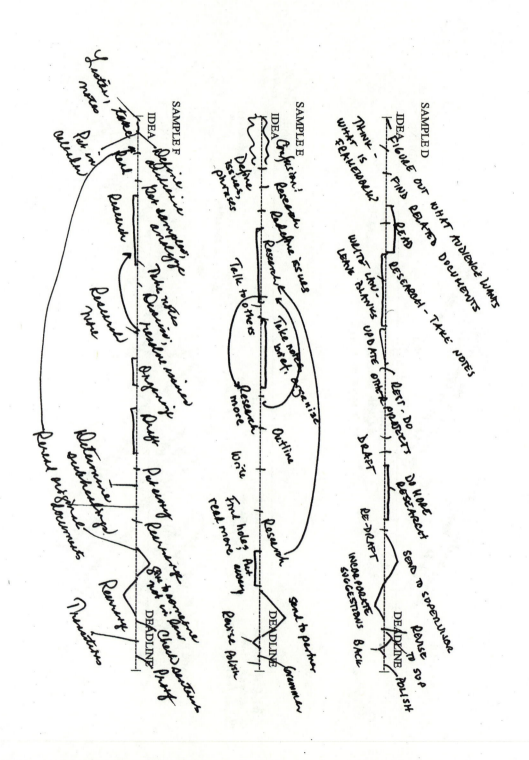

These novices tend to have fewer writing activities. This is quite natural because previous experiences did not include legal research or as many recursive swings to verify factual and legal sources. Some novices have not written for many years. The first example is from an engineering major whose writing experience was limited to reports, if anything. The second example is from a liberal arts major who had some experience writing papers in undergraduate school. The third example is from a second career student whose first career gave her many publishing opportunities. In any case, it is not at all uncommon for a novice's writing process to have worked quite well previously. That process may, however, break down when the novice switches situations, either from undergraduate school to law school or from law school to practice. When she enters law school, a novice discovers two complicated and time–consuming matters that federalism adds to her writing process: researching the law and designing complex analytical paradigms. When he switches jobs, an attorney discovers that his new office's priorities and conventions differ and he needs to factor in those and any approaches to new subject matters.

A Word on Writing Process

For many of us, writing classes focussed exclusively on the written product. It was either right or wrong. Our teachers "corrected" our papers, period. This school of teaching writing, known as the Controlled Composition school, was formalist in nature, offering us five–part essays, fourteen-line sonnets, and five-line Haiku forms to fill in. The trouble was, for many writers, such an approach taught nothing about transferability. If a six-part essay was required, or a twenty-page paper, we were lost. As schools of thought come and go, the pendulum swung in the 1970's to the Expressivist school, which taught us that forms did not matter at all, the writer did. Thus, out the window went grammar, sentence–diagraming, and five-part essays. In came free forms, the author's authenticity, and spontaneity and individualism in writing.

As individuals discovered what they wanted to say, they also discovered how they were producing it. Some researchers started asking good writers what they did to create good pieces of writing. That is, they focused not just on the product, but on the process. They discovered that good writers planned, translated, and rewrote. The more they investigated writing processes, the more they uncovered possibilities for helping all writers. Some techniques could be carved out, explained, attempted. This school of teaching writing, known as the Process school, opened up all writers to the many possible ways for writing successfully.

This study of writing processes did not seem to complete the writing picture, however. Individual preferences in either product or process did not matter so much in certain, specific settings. That is, where the writing was not in the form of novels, poetry, or essays, for example, writers operated under other constraints. Those constraints seemed to be indicated by the subject matter itself, or the discourse community. Doctors were required to use certain terms, forms, genres for communicating. So were engineers, music critics, and journalists. Thus, an individual's writing process was somewhat informed by the circumstances within which she was writing. Those who follow this view, the Social Constructivist school, believe that writers perform best when they factor in the social circumstances, the discourse community's features, and their own preferences.

In our community, we know that our decisions about writing are informed by the law, our research choices, conventions, and audience, among other factors. Does this mean that we have no individual choices?

Certainly not. Each of us develops a process by which we uncover and discover meaning in creating a document. Each of us discovers techniques that work well. We build our own processes through experience. We can streamline those processes by comparing our techniques to others and by becoming more aware of what we are doing, and when, how, and why we are doing it.

To further complicate our writing processes, we are also caught in an unusual form of teaching and learning. Until the late nineteenth century, legal writers referred to classical rhetoric for many of their writing cues. Tenets of argumentation and logic from the Enlightenment offered schemata for thinking and writing—a deductive, formalist approach to learning. But at the end of the century, academics, including those in law, rejected classicism and replaced it with the inductive, scientific approach. The case method theory removed from the law school any study of rhetoric as such.

The study of rhetoric was resurrected by the modern rhetoric movement. Those in the modern rhetoric movement are concerned chiefly with how audiences will react. This is not that different from what the classicists did, but it shifts the emphasis. According to modern rhetoricians, the life of the reader—because now rhetoric is defined mostly in written terms rather than oral—is what concerns the teachers of rhetoric. That internal reader-editor and the writer, both of them "me," talk to each other to produce a result that will affect its audience. ANTHONY C. WINKLER & JO RAY MCCUEN, RHETORIC MADE PLAIN 7 (5th ed. 1988). Such an approach means that the writer is not self-centered, carefully links sentences and paragraphs together, and tailors writing to the intended audience. *See Id.* at 8-9.

The new rhetoricians also emphasize that writing is a process. Composing is a recursive process, one where the writer goes back and forth in reaching conclusions about how to present something. The topic, they say, can make a difference by informing and defining the writing. In this process model, writing does not automatically improve with use. The responsibility is on the writer to develop and to become more conscious of who he is in relationship to his audience and in relationship to his own development. *See Id.* at 10-15. The new rhetoricians do also pick up on the first two elements of classical rhetoric, invention and arrangement. What they awaken is a kind of self-awareness on the part of the writer, so that the writer feels dedicated to and responsible for his work. Modern rhetoric shifts the focus from the product to the process and therefore away from the formalism to the discovery of meaning. The kind of invention varies, depending on the rhetorical situation in which the writer is situated. *See Id.* In the legal discourse community, then, we discover our meaning in varied rhetorical situations, from negotiations to the courtroom. Our writing processes are defined through the complex combinations of individual choices and rhetorical situations.

The causes of bad legal writing quite often lie in poor techniques or improper sequences in the legal writing process. Successful legal writers seem to be able to create a flexible process that allows for surprises, analytical twist and turns, and expanding issues. By knowing your legal writing process, you can adapt it to whatever situation occurs. If you have six weeks to complete a project, you can spread tasks over that amount of time. If you have only two hours, you may collapse or combine tasks to complete the project well. And if your process repertoire is large enough, you can vary approaches to conform to your workload, energy level, or familiarity with the topic. Such command over your process should increase your efficiency and improve your writing. What follows are some ideas about how to create a legal writing process that works for you not only now but also in the future.

Like the architect, you have a lot to consider. You have to concentrate on what the product is supposed to look like by studying the genre, the conventions, and the context; by knowing the audiences' expectations; by researching the materials thoroughly; by preparing, designing, and executing the document. You also have to think about exactly how you are going to do this. When do you consider each of the questions raised in this chapter? When do you design your form? When do you actually discover your theme? When do you use your legal research to formulate your argumentation? When do you reconcile conflicting clauses in form contracts you have been asked to read to prepare for the contract that you are drafting? When do you translate your complex ideas into a draft? When do you cut and paste? When do you repair sentences? When do you proofread? And what do you do when you are working collaboratively?

The process of constructing a legal document is personal, yet predictable. Only you can design and implement it. You know how your mind works, what sequences of events you prefer. You may approach most documents using the same sequence, such as writing small segments of the document as you go or outlining everything before you draft. Instinctively, you may shift your process, using some sequences for short projects, others for longer ones. Whatever your process, your work may fall into the following categories.

Certain terminology will help isolate and focus on certain aspects of the legal writing process. Please keep in mind that these are areas to consider in the legal writing process, but not necessarily in the sequence presented here. Some projects will take more or less of each of the things discussed and others will call for inventions of things that cannot be covered here. Consider the terminology and the reference points as exactly that: starting points and not ending points. Whether considering the legal writing process or the product, it is important to escape formalism.

SOME LEGAL WRITING PROCESS ELEMENTS

PREWRITING

WRITING

REWRITING

REVISING

POLISHING

PREWRITING

Prewriting includes anything you do before you actually start composing a draft. It includes collecting facts, analyzing facts, talking to others, researching, gathering forms to compare, holding conference calls to determine the dynamics of a deal, formulating preliminary questions, taking notes, making calls, or just plain looking at the ceiling—percolating. These activities include making decisions about purpose, audience, scope, and stance; gathering materials; considering possible forms; finding out about local conditions or traditions; interviewing assigning attorneys; or just figuring out the law. This stage also includes designing, whether by formal outlining or by a less formal way of organizing and prioritizing materials. Prewriting includes making most of the critical decisions about the document: theme, materials, form, proportion, and some matters of interior design. Done well, prewriting determines the document. Many experienced attorneys put most of their time into this part of the process, which creates fewer drafts and more architectural accuracy.

WRITING

The writing stage simply includes translation from idea into prose. For many writers, writing is done sequentially, after prewriting is finished. For others, writing occurs throughout prewriting, a kind of note–taking that translates into a draft. For yet others, writing moves by "rooms" of the document. That is, certain segments, such as the Conclusion, Recitations, or Statement of the Case, are written first, followed by others out of the sequence in which they will appear in the final document.

REWRITING

Rewriting a document means checking that it is correct, complete, and coherent. This is a stage when you can review your architectural choices. Is the theme working? Does it need to be refined or redefined? Are the materials appropriate, or should some be added or subtracted? Is everything stated correctly? Is the form appropriate for the clients' (readers') needs? Too many "rooms" or ideas? Too little harmony among the parts? Does everything fit? Does the structure need to be rethought, refined? Do the proportions work? It is during this stage that you can make substantial changes to streamline a document, to make it fit together perfectly. It is not at this stage that you look for details because, in legal writing, whole sections may move, disappear, or reappear at this stage. Why fix a sentence you are going to get rid of? During rewriting, others may also suggest substantial changes to the document. A client may change his mind about the results he seeks; a supervising attorney may remember a sticky policy question that must be addressed, or a new theory of the case may emerge. This stage is the lawyer's; the next is the writer's.

REVISING

Once the document's form and proportion are in place, its interior can be refined. Where does the theme appear? What words does it use? Where do those words reappear? How are the "rooms" of the document connected, with what cohesive devices? What are the document's subthemes? Where do they appear? Does repeated language create topic strings where appropriate to keep subthemes understandable? Does sentence structure match meaning, that is, are ideas expressed with syntactical devices that match their relative importance to each other? This is also the stage to check personal idiosyncracies, such as propensities for legal jargon, overly long sentences, or footnotes. It is during this stage that you test your ability as an interior designer—can you design for the setting or do you just have one flower–print style that you use for all of your clients?

POLISHING

Just when you think you are done, the perfectionism must kick in. For this stage, allow much more time than you think you will need because the legal reader expects perfection, often even in early drafts. Whether or not you are a "detail person," you need to become one in this field. During this stage, you must make sure the document has absolutely no mistakes—no inconsistencies, no citation errors, no mispellings, and no typos. (Didn't that mistake just jump off the page? And in a writing book!) Care during this stage often separates the good architect from the bad; oddly enough, there seems to be a strong correlation between a good finisher and a good architect. The best do it all and account for the time necessary to perfect.

Your activities during these stages, the order in which you decide questions, and the techniques you use are what create your personal legal writing process. That process is never the same twice for the sensitive legal writer. It is always influenced by such factors as the time frame dictated by the

client, the amount of money or time the client is willing to spend, the difficulty of the legal question, the legal writer's experience, the resources available to the legal writer, and so on. The art of writing well is creating a flexible process that uses techniques appropriate to all of these factors. This book will periodically suggest process techniques; for more information and checklists on these stages, see MARY B. RAY & JILL J. RAMSFIELD, LEGAL WRITING: GETTING IT RIGHT AND GETTING IT WRITTEN (3d ed. 2000).

Creating a flexible process puts you in command of constructing your writing. You must be able to select techniques and sequences that fit the circumstances. To do so, you can heighten your awareness of your writing process.

USING THE ELEMENTS

Product and process work together. You consider both as you create a legal document. The process is recursive, that is, you consider elements, research, reconsider, write, reconsider, rewrite, and so on. Your experience may be more accurately reflected in the following:

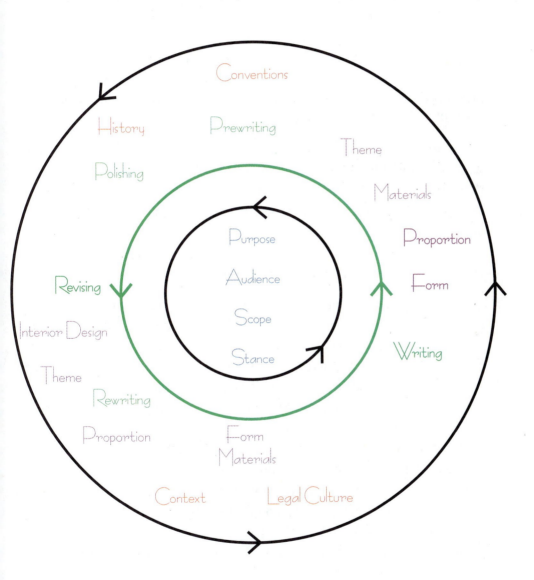

You—and your reader—learn by comparing what is new to what is old. You compare your schema of what writing is to those definitions and behaviors your observe in your surroundings. And, just as you become comfortable within certain surroundings, you graduate or switch jobs or get a new supervising attorney. Definitions and behaviors change. You compare the new to the old. And you adjust or you don't. As you develop your designs approaches throughout your career, be flexible. Observe and record them rather than become them. Any schema assists us in learning but puts us on the precipice of formalism. That formalism, a slavish attachment to a certain schema or a belief that the elements or habits are themselves the system of learning or teaching a problem, impedes progress. It prevents quick adjustments, the development of more complex schemata, the brilliant invention of a new approach.

Use this book similarly. As you consider the notions of classical and modern rhetoric discussed here, look beyond them immediately. See them as points of departure, as old ideas that lead to your new ones. As you read about a technique, take the useful features from it and create a technique of your own. As you see technology offering you new choices for producing documents, take them. Create your own complex schema for legal writing, one that allows for new information and techniques at all times.

As you travel through this book, you will see techniques set aside in green boxes. Consider them. Can some of them help transform a weakness into a strength? Can some of them speed up your process? Can some of them make your legal writing more enjoyable? Adapt these as you see fit, one at a time. Deciding whether or not to try a new technique is up to you. You hear an idea and you try it. If it does not work the first time, you try again. Some new techniques take a great deal of repeated behavior before they work, but your persistence may be rewarded with a breakthrough. Keep an open mind about what is and is not working in your process. As you do this, you will need to work smart. When you discover that a formerly successful technique is sometimes slowing you down, don't automatically drop the technique. Keep it in your repertoire of techniques and invoke it when it works. Conversely, when you discover that you are sticking doggedly to old habits when they are no longer working, drop them. For example, one of the hardest habits for many legal writers to break is the habit of trying to write an entire document in one sitting. This is a bit like trying to build a building in one day. In modern law practice, such marathons are almost entirely impossible unless you work on weekends and evenings. Such marathons may also ruin the product, which becomes as tired as you do. Blend process and product to work smart.

Writing is, after all, a provisional necessity. Many of us would rather talk. Many of us would rather use the power of our presence to make a point, not just words on a page. We may well return, or move on, to oral communications as our communication paradigms change. In the meantime, we will use the written page to try to say what we mean. In the ecosystem of legal writing and understanding, each choice we make affects something else. Each decision affects our readers; each selection affects meaning.

Your success in the discourse community depends on your thorough understanding of its changing features and of your position within the community. Watch carefully to continually define both, to make informed decisions in dynamic situations, and to enjoy the complexity of your situation. Observing critically is a vital complement to writing effectively. It also keeps you informed of the community's norms. Your process, then, must fit your circumstances. Despite any personal propensities for one sequence or another, any habits that dictate a particular approach, you must adjust to rhetorical, design, and practical elements so that you finish the job on time. This requires that you move quickly from novice to expert status. And being an expert in law, as in any field, requires versatility and consistency. Each project you undertake offers opportunities for practice and growth— in technique and understanding. Add to your repertoire a new technique each time, one that improves your performance. Strive for consistency over time. We each do one thing well, some time. The expert does all things well all of the time. That is the architect your clients want to hire.

CHAPTER 2

OBSERVING FORM AND FUNCTION

Form ever follows function.

–Louis Henry Sullivan

So Sullivan taught Frank Lloyd Wright, whose organic architecture fused form and function so completely that buildings were *of* the hill, not *on* it, *of* the forest, not *in* it. To study the landscape, to research a building's function on that landscape, to diagram every current in the stream, tree on the hill, rock in the cliff—is to allow form to emerge from function. While all architects no longer strictly subscribe to the concept, many still honor its manifestations. The same is true in law.

A document's form may be informed by its functions, which are varied and complex. A legal document may be home to an entrepreneur's dream business. It may construct a new doctrine, change policy, or grant new rights. It may construct a series of transactions that shape a business for years. It may house good news. Deciding how to construct any legal document requires sensitivity not only to design elements but also to sheer aesthetics, not only to precedent but also to purpose. Your decisions may best flow from observing the work of expert legal writers. Study their documents to see what design decisions they have made and why. Just as an architect studies the history of architecture, drawings of Italian cathedrals, photographs of great works, and actual buildings themselves, so you can study and observe the architecture of legal writing.

Law takes its analytical form through writing. In that sense, legal writing is analytical architecture. It is a multi-dimensional fusion of elements, set in a specific situation, sprung from established traditions. Unfortunately, much of what you read is poorly constructed, badly thought through, or decaying, as is some architecture. Buildings have crumbled, walls have cracked, and huts have fallen back into the earth. But the wall on which Leonardo painted "The Last Supper" in Santa Maria delle Grazie in Milan was the only church wall left standing when the city was bombed in 1943. The reasons for durability and timelessness may be structural or mystical; either way, your ability to observe the legal design elements will help you to construct legal documents more consciously and carefully.

You can observe legal architecture by reading each work critically. Reading critically is observing the author's treatment of these design elements. Analyze a legal text to see what it aims to do, what it actually does do, and what it fails to do. By observing the effect the text has on you, by breaking it down into its elements, and by noting how the elements combine in the whole document, you are studying legal architecture. You are apprenticing yourself to the discourse, traditional and modern. You are also playing the role of audience. From Aristotle to post-structuralists, observers of rhetoric and writing have suggested that audience is the cause of writing, that reader and writer are inextricably intertwined. The more you play the role of audience and observe writing's effect on you, the more sensitive you become to your audiences when you write. To closely observe legal writing for its manifestation of architectural elements, for better or worse, is to expand your own design repertoire.

OBSERVING CRITICALLY

As you observe legal documents, read for a number of reasons. You are accustomed to reading legal writing for the materials it yields, the parts you will use as a writer. As a law student, you read cases for individual holdings or policy statements and you read for connections among a series of cases that develop a doctrine. As a practitioner, you read for connections among authorities that invoke a doctrine and help you to draw legal parameters for your client's case. As a legislative drafter, you read previous statutes and definitions to make choices about what form and language you will use to achieve accuracy and consistency among the statutes. And, as a legal historian, you read law to see what happened between the lines, to understand, for example, context and social setting.

Read also as a writer, an architect studying the author's use of architectural elements. All elements of communication are interwoven, and you can observe the means by which the writer succeeds in communicating with you. You can observe the writer's design choices, the overall effect the document has on you, whether or not form follows function, how its proportions affect you. When you are not conscious of these elements as you read, you may get certain vague messages; you may be moved in certain directions. Or you may be manipulated. Being conscious of these elements increases comprehension and intensifies your awareness. Being conscious of them also makes your own writing more conscious, your decisions more informed. Ultimately, active observing makes you a better writer, even when you must observe badly written texts. By demystifying legal texts, you are less likely to be duped: you see how to use or not use the texts.

Most importantly, by observing critically, you are constructing your own schema of interpretation and architectural design. Each bit of your reading finds its place among previous readings and previous interpretations. Your world of legal understanding depends on how you observe. What are you looking for? What are you remembering? How are you assimilating what you observe? What are the connections among the parts?

The more you become aware of yourself as audience, the more sensitive you become to your own audiences. And the more you may become transformed, both as reader and writer. Because audience can be thought of as the cause of writing, the interrelationship of reader with text becomes a dynamic part of constructing a document. Few architects have built buildings that they intended should not be used. The users, then, inform the entire construction process. In that sense, audience sparks the strategic choices a writer makes to respond to how she construes the reader's prospective interpretation of the document. Any information a writer has about a reader's perspective and predilections informs the writer's choices during the writing process. The writer tailors her message in a way that allows the reader to internalize and understand it. She also maximizes the utility of her writing by considering the reader's practical needs. Such an interactive process allows the writer to achieve both a transformative aim— to change the attitudes and opinions of her readers—and a utilitarian aim— to win.

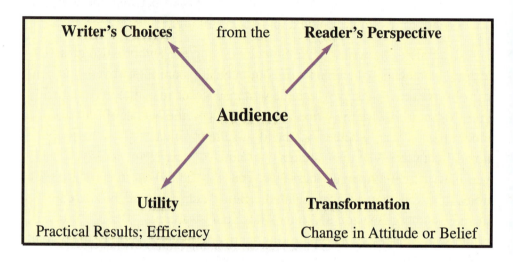

By using your audience as the cause of writing, you become more keenly aware of how to build the most effective document. Like the architect, you make your choices based not just on your expertise, but on your client's perspective. Such perspective informs decisions on themes, form, proportion, on scope and stance. Then you are more able to construct a document that not only fits the landscape—is utilitarian—but also transforms the audience's outlook—makes the audience *see* the landscape differently.

In this way, when you read, you inform the writer's decisions; you are the catalyst for the direction the writing takes; you generate meaning together. Reading critically is a process, a creative, rather than passive, interaction between you and the text. Rather than sitting outside the text and trying to discern its meaning, which is certainly one way to read (*I wonder why the architect built my house that way? Where is the entrance?*), you join the writer at the center of the creative process, and you may even replace the writer as creator of meaning (*That's a very interesting plan, but I need a living room that will hold my furniture*). As an intelligent legal reader, then, you can be a live and sympathetic reader, willing to participate in the quest for meaning that is writing. The more you do this, the better you will write.

This chapter asks you to experience legal writing as the audience of its art. Read to see how it succeeds in its purpose, how it guides you through each part, how it is decorated, how beautiful it is. You enter a document as you might enter a building, having identified its general architecture from the outside: a contract, a letter, a brief, a prospectus. Within that structure, the writer has made some design choices about the order of the information, the relationship among the parts of the document, the overall effect it should have on the reader. If the document's form follows its function and message, you will probably be affected positively, and you will not be lost. If it does not, you will find yourself wishing you could somehow get out, though you

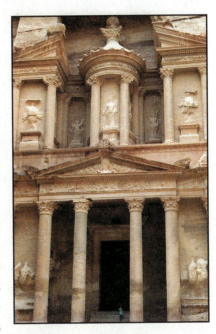

may not know how. Chapters 3–7 elaborate on law's repertoire of design elements; this chapter asks you to observe some examples and to participate creatively in the interpretation of meaning; it also suggests some methods for deciphering a document's rhetorical underpinnings, design elements, and context. As you observe legal architecture, you may want to begin by differentiating between traditional and modern legal documents and compare the manifestations of architectural elements in each.

A Word on Critical Reading

As audience, lawyers interpret meaning professionally. As managers, researchers, students, and professors, lawyers are in the business of constructing—and deconstructing—texts. Law school offers several theories for doing both, but not in the architectural sense. Within the legal discourse community, we "share interpretive strategies not for reading (in the conventional sense) but for writing texts, for constituting their properties and assigning their intentions. In other words, these strategies exist prior to the act of reading and therefore determine the shape of what is read rather than, as is usually assumed, the other way around." STANLEY FISH, IS THERE A TEXT IN THIS CLASS? 171 (1980) (*cited in* Edward M. White, *Post-Structural Literary Criticism and the Response to Student Writing*, 35 Coll. Composition & Comm. 186 (1984). What this means for legal readers is that there may be some stability of interpretation among different readers because they belong to the legal community, for example, that they understand the plain meaning canon of reading statutes. It also means that a single reader will regularly employ different strategies and thus make different texts because he belongs to different communities, such as the legal and business communities, or the legal community at large and the scholarly subset or the tax subset. *See id.*

As readers, we have to be careful. We can find ourselves in a "grim sameness" when we respond to legal writing, a "uniform code of commands, requests, and pleadings" that demonstrates that the reader "holds a license for vagueness while the [writer] is commanded to be specific." Nancy Sommers, *Responding to Student Writing*, 33 Coll. Comp. & Comm. 148, 152-3 (1982). Rather than interact with the writer as we are responding, we read in bad faith, asking the writer to divine our "ideal text," to write as we would have done it—in our final version (*Build my dream house perfectly, but don't ask me any questions until you're done*).

Instead, we can bring a kind of practical intelligence to our critical reading, a willingness to interact with the text. Whether that text is something presented as an associate's draft or a published statute, we can read with some understanding of the interaction between writer and reader. We can look for the architectural features of the *product*; we can try to decipher the manifestations of the writer's *process*; and we can read with some sense of the document's *context*. I suspect that this kind of practical intelligence will make texts progress, either mid-process (*the materials we have chosen will not work in this humid climate*) or at the end (*as it turns out, I spend more time in the kitchen than in the living room, so please enlarge the kitchen*). Part of our practical intelligence may be to understand how readers assimilate ideas, then how materials, writer, and reader interact.

We form, remember, and assimilate ideas not in isolation but by comparing new information to old information, according to schema theory. Old, familiar information is stored in patterns, or *schemata*, in our brains. If we are aware of the schemata, we can welcome new schemata and information more readily. See FREDERIC C. BARTLETT, REMEMBERING 199–200 (1932) (citing SIR HENRY HEAD, STUDIES IN NEUROLOGY 605–06 (1920)). "'Schema' refers to an active organisation [sic] of past reactions, or of past experiences, which must always be supposed to be operating in any well– adapted organic response." *Id.* at 201. In other words, text itself does not carry meaning; rather, "a text only provides directions for listeners or readers as to how they should retrieve or construct meaning from their own, previously acquired knowledge." Patricia L. Carrell & Joan C. Eisterhold, *Schema Theory and International Reading Pedagogy*, *in* METHODOLOGY IN TESOL: A BOOK OF READINGS 220 (Michael H. Long & Jack C. Richards eds., 1987). This background knowledge provides the basis for the reader's interpretation of a text and most certainly for that reader's recreation of a text in the target discourse. This interpretation "is guided by the principle that every input is mapped against some existing schema and that all aspects of that schema must be compatible with the input information." *Id.* at 220-21. Previous experience and prior texts allow us to recognize genres, see JOHN SWALES, GENRE ANALYSIS 83 (1990), but when there is neither, the difficulty of entering a new discourse community and comprehending its patterns increases.

Patterns, or *schemata*, are hierarchically organized from most general at the top to most specific at the bottom. Schema theory suggests that there are two basic modes of interpretation: *bottom-up processing* and *top-down processing*. Bottom-up processing is evoked by the incoming data, which drive the reader up toward the more general information. Thus bottom-up processing is often called data-driven. Top-down processing is conceptually driven because it "occurs as the system makes general predictions based on higher level, general schemata and then searches the input for information to fit into these partially satisfied, higher order schemata." CARREL & EISTERHOLD, supra, at 221. Both levels should be occurring simultaneously as a reader interprets. That is, the data that are needed to fill out the schemata become available through bottom-up processing while top-down processing "facilitates their assimilation *if they are anticipated by or consistent with the listener/reader's conceptual expectations.*" *Id.* (italics added). Bottom-up processing ensures that the reader will be sensitive to information that is novel or that does not fit her ongoing hypotheses about the content or structure of the text; top-down processing helps the reader resolve ambiguities or select between alternative possible interpretations of the incoming data. See *Id*.

In legal reading, we use bottom-up processing when we gather data from one case at a time; we use top-down processing when we hold general discussions about legal theory or hypothesize about a theory of the case. Reading several cases that interpret a UCC provision gives us data about specific conclusions on specific facts; discussions may reveal not only the general rule being interpreted but also the rules of interpretation used by courts who apply UCC law. Both are happening simultaneously. But this information, particularly the theory, may differ from our expectations or experience. If the difference is too great, we have difficulty assimilating the information.

As readers, not only must we process the schemata, but we must also understand the kind of schemata we are using. The schemata themselves break into two groups: *formal* and *content* schemata. Formal schemata assume background knowledge of different types of texts or genres, such as narratives, newspaper articles, memos, briefs, or opinion letters. Content schemata assume background knowledge about the content area of a text, such as the economy of Switzerland, Mardi Gras in New Orleans, the First Amendment, or a United Nations treaty. So "when content and form are familiar the texts will be relatively accessible, whereas when neither content nor form is familiar the text will be relatively inaccessible." SWALES, supra, at 87 (citing Patricia L. Carrell, *Content and Formal Schemata in International Reading*, 21 TESOL Q. 461 (1987)). In other words, comprehension or a faltering interpretation results when the writer has failed to provide sufficient clues to invoke either or both of these schemata or when the reader does not possess the appropriate schemata.

This becomes more complicated if the reader enters this culture from another one, switches law offices or practices, or possesses a background different from those invoked in the reading. "One of the most obvious reasons why a particular content schema may fail to exist for a reader is that the schema is culturally specific and is not part of a particular reader's cultural background." Carrell & Eisterhold, supra, at 223. The reader can't make the match. That is, "the implicit cultural content knowledge presupposed by a text interacts with the reader's own cultural background knowledge of content to make texts whose content is based on one's own culture easier to read and understand than syntactically and rhetorically equivalent texts based on a less familiar, more distant culture." *Id*. (citing Margaret S.

Steffenson et. al., *A Cross-Cultural Perspective on Reading Comprehension*, 15 READING RES. Q. 1:10 (1979); Patricia Johnson, *Effects on Reading Comprehension of Language Complexity and Cultural Background of a Text*, 15 TESOL Q. 2:169 (1981); and Patricia L. Carrell, *The Role of Schemata in L2 Comprehension*, paper presented at 15th Annual TESOL convention (1981)). Of course, content schemata in U.S. law are new to the law student; content schemata in a legal specialty are new to an inexperienced lawyer.

Schema theory also suggests that if a reader cannot follow a text's schema, she cannot reproduce it or create new problem-solving strategies using that schema. This is further exacerbated when she gets no help. In the U.S. legal discourse community, *content schemata* are often implicitly, not explicitly, defined. That is, the teaching uses *bottom–up processing*, not *top-down processing*. Deductive learners suffer. Further, *content schemata*, and the teaching methods themselves may assume certain cultural preferences innate to the legal discourse community but foreign to newcomers or readers.

As we read, then, we import the patterns from previous experiences with texts into the current reading. If we have neither prior experience nor experience with prior legal texts, we may import other patterns, such as those used in undergraduate school—sociology, business, or history. If we have been working in a law office that uses texts a certain way, we may naturally import those patterns to our new jobs.

One antidote to this is for an expert to intervene during a novices's process of writing. As managers or professors, we can participate in the process if we want a specific result (*yes, I do want a tool shed attached to the garage; no, I don't want an elaborate entrance because the house itself is too simple*). The more reasons we provide to the writers (architects), the more capable they are of inventing what suits our needs. Especially if we are in the position of using our reading to train legal writers, we are obligated to articulate—in a manner that is as organized, well-structured and as specific as what we are expecting from them—the reasons, theories, and methods for producing types of legal documents.

Another antidote is to bring our practical intelligence to decipher how materials, writer, and reader interact. By analyzing the design elements as demonstrated in this chapter, we can fuse the writing with its effect on us as readers. These effects in turn sensitize us as writers to our readers' needs.

DIFFERENTIATING BETWEEN TRADITIONAL AND MODERN LEGAL DOCUMENTS

In the United States, traditional legal writing betrays its link to oral traditions and the doctrine of *stare decisis*. There: even a Latin phrase to describe it. Common law decisions, traditionally delivered from the bench, were often rambling in form, luxurious in texture and rhythm, and utterly inaccessible to the uninitiated. Early opinions carried the weight of hundreds of years of formal discourse. These conventions spawned the famous "turgid" prose, still with us today. The features of this traditional legal writing, whether judicial opinions, contracts, letters to clients, or scholarship, include long, complex sentences; doublets; Latinisms; long paragraphs, and analytical patterns that, no matter how eloquent they seem, often show leaps in logic and poor organizational structure in general, which make it hard for the legal reader to maneuver, much less remember or use. It is rather like the sentence you just read, which included intrusive phrases, too many ideas, and a punctuation mistake. Hard going, wasn't it? Much of legal reading is. Consider this example of traditional legal writing:

Example 2.1. Traditional Legal Text.

It is alleged as the ground of recovery that on the 13th day of November, 1904, the defendant was the owner of a certain island in Lake Champlain, and of a certain dock attached thereto, which island and dock were then in charge of the defendant's servant; that the plaintiff was then possessed of and sailing upon said lake a certain loaded sloop, on which were the plaintiff and his wife and two minor children; that there then arose a sudden and violent tempest, whereby the sloop and the property and persons therein were placed in great danger of destruction; that to save these from destruction or injury the plaintiff was compelled to, and did, moor the sloop to the defendant's dock; that the defendant by his servant unmoored the sloop, whereupon it was driven upon the shore by the tempest, without the plaintiff's fault; and that the sloop and its contents were thereby destroyed, and the plaintiff and

his wife and children cast into the lake and upon the shore, receiving injuries.

Ploof v. Putnam, 81 Vt. 471, 71 A. 188 (1908).

Comment: One sentence. 170 words. This paragraph is the entire fact summary for the opinion. It uses subordinate phrases to recite the facts, jargon as adverbs, and a chronological schema that may help you remember the events but does not foreshadow the logic of the opinion. If your own lawyer wrote to you in such a manner, you would not likely retain him. Lawyers are gradually moving to more modern ways of presenting complicated information. This book advocates such a move. But traditional writing is legal history, so you must observe it carefully, interpret it, and hone your abilities to translate and compose in modern prose.

Contrast the previous example with the following presentation of facts from another case:

Example 2.2. Modern Legal Text.

Plaintiff was standing on a platform of defendant's railroad after buying a ticket to go to Rockaway Beach. A train stopped at the station, bound for another place. Two men ran forward to catch it. One of the men reached the platform of the car without mishap, though the train was already moving. The other man, carrying a package, jumped aboard the car, but seemed unsteady as if about to fall. A guard on the car, who had held the door open, reached forward to help him in, and another guard on the platform pushed him from behind. In this act, the package was dislodged, and fell upon the rails. It was a package of small size, about fifteen inches long, and was covered by a news-

paper. In fact it contained fireworks, but there was nothing in its appearance to give notice of its contents. The fireworks when they fell exploded. The shock of the explosion threw down some scales at the other end of the platform, many feet away. The scales struck the plaintiff, causing injuries for which she sues.

<u>Palsgraf v. Long Island R.R. Co.</u>, 248 N.Y. 339, 162 N.E. 99 (Ct. App. 1928) (Cardozo, C.J.).

Comment: Again, a chronological scheme, but this time directly related to the substantive analysis. Several sentences. Strong connections. Simple words. A complicated series of facts made immutably clear. These are the features of modern legal writing that, on the surface, look simple. An arch looks simple but is a complex feat of engineering. Fred Astaire said of his dancing: "I work so hard so that it looks simple." As an audience of legal writing, you often appreciate the same effort. How do the expert legal writers do it, translate the complex to the accessible? The key may simply be a way of seeing. If a writer's vision is broad enough to see a subject from many angles, she may find the most "simple" way of constructing a document.

Increasingly, legal audiences are impatient with traditional norms and forms. You, as audience, probably appreciate reading documents that are useful and accessible on the first read. You expect a legal writer to be both

> [All] systems of thought, all ideological constructs, are in need of constant, conscious criticism; and the process of revision can come about only on the assumption that there is a higher and more universal standard against which to measure the existing system. History provides both the ideas that are in need of criticism and the material out of which this criticism is forged. An architecture that is constantly aware of its own history, but constantly critical of the seductions of history, is what we should aim for today.
>
> —Alan Colquhoun, Three Kinds of Historicism in Joan Ockman, Modernity and The Classical Tradition, in PROGRESSIVE ARCHITECTURE 118 (1990).

interpreter and translator. Often without saying so, you expect that writer to read, interpret, and understand traditional legal writing, but not to write in the same way, even though her writing is naturally affected by her reading. Remember, it is a bit hard to write consistently well when you are reading bad prose. But there it is. In a way, a legal writer is being asked to read nineteenth century French—legal English is a bit like a foreign language— but to write modern French. That translation is most effectively accomplished when the writer is fluent in both.

Traditional legal writing still predominates; there are relatively few good examples of modern legal writing. This can be very frustrating to the legal writing modernist, who wishes to design, consciously and conscientiously, documents that break from tradition. Many legal writers prefer the traditional (Williams' "socialized") world of legal forms, phrases, and themes. Because law is by nature a conservative profession, looking to its past for guidance, reluctant to force change too quickly, reliant on case precedent for prediction, legal writers hesitate to innovate. They fear that any changes may cause inaccuracy or force forward an issue that had previously lain in peace, so they refrain from making anything but minimal changes to previously created documents. The result, over time, is that they build a library of choppy documents, cut and pasted by several authors and made inaccessible to non-experts. These documents may function well enough. They may satisfy clients who do not feel they need to understand the documents, but they offer tough navigating for other users, a labyrinth of hidden meanings and obscure details.

Observe in the examples that follow some of the ways in which both traditional and modern legal texts present meaning. A document's design elements all flow from the writer's intention, whether consciously or not. Your job is a tough one: as observer, you must be able to identify and interpret traditional elements; as a modern writer, you must decide whether you can break those traditional molds. Add to or subtract from the elements and ideas stated here your own critical reading criteria. Set your own standards for analyzing a document and observing its contours and content. See how all pieces relate, from choice of construction materials to form to finish. Put the document in context and use your information to develop your own theory of architecture, your own theory of legal writing. These pages merely suggest the possibilities.

Observing Rhetorical Elements

As you encounter a text, consider its rhetorical features. What kind of a document is it? For what purpose(s) was it created? Who will read it? Who "counts" the most? How large is the document? What is the writer's point of view, or stance? You may be able to answer these questions before you begin to read, just from the nature of the genre or your knowledge of the author. If the document works well, these rhetorical features will show consistency early in the document. As described in Chapter 1, you can observe the document's elements by asking specific questions as you move through the document, analyzing it for the answers the writer provides and for consistency and accessibility.

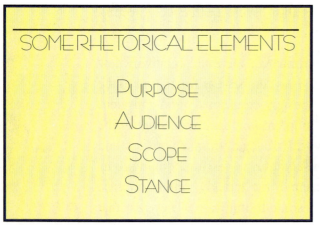

SOME RHETORICAL ELEMENTS

PURPOSE

AUDIENCE

SCOPE

STANCE

TECHNIQUES

- *Record the document's rhetorical features, as you observe them, perhaps as "rhetorical outlines."* Then number the possibilities; assess your perceived hierarchy of what the author intended.

Your reading notes might look something like what follows.

PURPOSE	1. sway to client's point of view 2. remind reader of regulations pertinent to this question 3. satisfy client we are representing him well
AUDIENCE	1. agency lawyer who has been assigned the response to this letter 2. head of agency, to whom it is addressed 3. client
SCOPE	4 pages, single-spaced statute subsection and accompanying regulations on drug approval 3 previous FDA opinions
STANCE	courteous careful and thorough firm

Example 2.3.　Notes on the Rhetorical Elements of a Letter to Federal Agency.

PURPOSE	1. obtain agreement 2. get in everything the client wants 3. get troubling parts of transaction changed/omitted 4. satisfy client we are representing him well
AUDIENCE	1. partner 2. other party to agreement 3. client 4. court (I hope not)
SCOPE	90 pages, double-spaced client's demands boilerplate their points, recast
STANCE	"neutral" tough

Example 2.4.   Notes   on   Rhetorical   Elements   of   a   Contract   for
International Business Partnership.

PURPOSE	1. convince client to bargain 2. inform of law, arguments 　　against him 3. close case 4. impress supervising attorney
AUDIENCE	1. over-eager client 2. supervising attorney, who 　will sign letter 3. ofile
SCOPE	7 pages, single-spaced
STANCE	concerned forceful

These rhetorical outlines sharpen your analysis of the writer's decisions and drive you more deeply into the text. Theoretically, you could
compare notes with the author and ask, "Was this what you were attempting to do?" There should be a match between what the author intended to
do and what you, the audience, understood. Should you have difficulty
understanding the document's rhetorical elements, or should they seem
inconsistent to you, or undecided upon, then you will probably see some
other problems in the text. You may see analytical pieces missing, inconsistent points of view, shifts in tone, or incoherence. Without a strong
sense of how the rhetorical elements work together, many authors have difficulty uniting the pieces of a document. If, however, they capture this specific relationship among the rhetorical elements, then the document more
likely unifies the architectural elements, as well.

OBSERVING ARCHITECTURAL ELEMENTS

Once you have considered the document's underlying rhetorical features, analyze what design decisions the writer has made. What is your
overall impression? Do you perceive a theme, a message? Do the materials work, that is, do they build a document that is appropriately durable?
Do you understand the analytical form? The proportion of one part to
another? Do the interior features, the paragraphs and sentences, match the
theme and the analytical form? And does treatment of the design elements
match that for the rhetorical ones?

Analyzing documents architecturally yields fascinating results. Quite often, the writer has a design in mind that works from one point of view, but that design may not be appropriate for the document's purpose, for its audiences of varied backgrounds, for its scope of limited pages, or for the stance chosen by a supervising attorney. Look for a match. When architectural elements match rhetorical decisions, you should feel consistency among such elements as purpose and theme, form, proportion; among audience and materials, message, and form; between stance and interior design.

Reading documents without doing so critically, without looking for the match between rhetoric and architecture, sometimes makes it impossible to tell what was going on. For example, the design may be a compromise design negotiated by a committee of writers who have lost sight of or disagreed upon the rhetorical aspects of the situation. Or the supervising attorney and original drafter may have simply negotiated a result that pulls rhetoric from design because they did not know how to voice their differences. Or a document may be cut and pasted from previous documents without the writer understanding why. Because design elements are more evident than rhetorical ones, you may find it easier to recognize design elements first, then infer how the writer may have incorporated rhetorical ideas. As you read critically, ask specific questions about each architectural element.

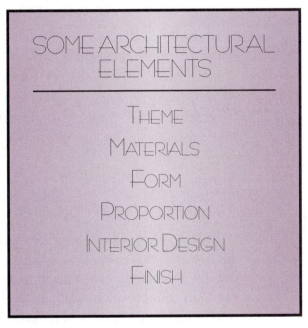

SOME ARCHITECTURAL ELEMENTS

THEME

MATERIALS

FORM

PROPORTION

INTERIOR DESIGN

FINISH

THEME OR MESSAGE

Try to state the document's theme or message in one sentence. What is the one message the document conveys? Is it ever explicitly stated? If not, could any legal reader infer the same message? Does a brief have a theory of the case, a contract a clear statement of purpose, a statute a theme of proscribed behavior? Try to spot the themes in the following example.

Example 2.5. Thematic Opening from a Memo.

You have asked me to examine whether or not Local Bank can successfully move to dismiss this case based upon the *forum non conveniens* doctrine or to transfer the claim under 28 U.S.C. § 1404(a). The bank could be expected to argue that most of the alleged discriminatory actions occurred in North Carolina, Texas, Mississippi, or Illinois, and that the bulk of their witnesses, documentation, and other proof needed to defend this claim reside outside this state, thereby making other venues more appropriate and convenient. As a result, they will assert that the complaint should be dismissed or transferred.

Comment: But can they?   We have a question raised but not yet answered. This message is, *You asked me to investigate this question and I did.*   Most lawyers do not find this helpful; it goes without saying. Instead, the message might have been, *Local Bank can successfully move that his case be dismissed or transferred.*   This is an example of how mechanically following previously written documents can perpetuate vague openings.

Example 2.6. Thematic Opening from a Letter.

This is in response to your April 29, 1993 inquiry whether affiliated insured state nonmember banks may provide certain services to one another's customers pursuant to a recently enacted Minnesota statute, without filing branch applications with the Federal Deposit Insurance Corporation ("FDIC") and receiving the FDIC's prior written consent. . . .

Generally, the banks involved enter into a contract whereby each bank agrees to act as agent for the other bank in providing specifically enumerated banking services. Examples include an agent bank accepting deposits, cashing checks and receiving loan payments for customers of the other bank. These arrangements commonly are referred to as "contract branching," "accommodation branching" or "facility banking."

Comment: same problem, even though the information offers more detailed context. The subject is introduced, but not the theme. Eventually, the document will answer the question of whether or not the banks can provide services to one another, but the reader will have to wait. Again, the theme is, *You asked a question.* Well, yes, the reader did, but he already knew that theme.

Example 2.7. Thematic Opening from another Letter.

This letter confirms our conversation of January 12, 1997, in which I explained to you both the Food and Drug Administration's (FDA) position regarding the above case and our desire to settle this case with a Consent Decree. As I informed you on the telephone, FDA maintains its stated position: "BUG–RID" Cat Cleanser, produced by your client Cuddle Laboratories, does not fall within the protection of the Grandfather Clause of the 1962 amendments to the Food Drug and Cosmetic Act ("the Act"), and BUG–RID is therefore not exempt from review as a new animal drug.

Comment: now here is a theme. The question and answer reside in the first paragraph of this letter. The reader knows that *BUG–RID is not exempt from FDA review as a new animal drug.* The theme promises that the document will discuss this explicit finding. We would know even more if a *because. . .* clause or sentence were added explaining precisely why does the product does not qualify under the grandfather clause.

Example 2.8. Thematic Opening from a Brief.

The court should dismiss the case on ripeness and standing grounds because the Compliance Policy Guides (Guides) serve only to guide FDA personnel; they do not declare all compounding by pharmacies illegal. The policy is familiar, the practices not new.

The Guides outline circumstances in which compounding by pharmacies may amount to manufacturing and thus may be subject to regulatory action by the Food and Drug Administration (FDA) under the adulteration, misbranding, and new drug provisions of the Federal Food, Drug, and Cosmetic Act (Act). See CPG 7132.16 at 6. They are not proscriptive about all compounding. The Guides are intended to be both internal guidance to FDA personnel, see CPG 7132.16 at 6, and notice to the industry of what the agency will consider in deciding

whether or not to initiate enforcement **action against pharmacies that engage in compounding. See id. at 4.** Such guidelines are in keeping with past practices and policies. . . .

The Guides do not interfere with the traditional practice of pharmacy. See CPG 7132.16. The Guides do not affect the compounding of drugs in reasonable quantities upon receipt of a prescription for an individually identified patient from a physician or other licensed practitioner. See CPG 7132.16 at 1. Nor do the Guides require that pharmacies submit a new drug application ("NDA") **for all medications they compound, as plaintiff asserts. See id. The issue, as plaintiff describes it, is not** grounded in the Guides, is therefore not ripe, and should be dismissed.

Comment: the court knows its mission from the first statement. The message is *Dismiss the case because nothing new has happened to depart from past accepted practice.* The theme resides at the first part of the argument and is developed in more detail in the next paragraphs. The audience also expects a matching symmetry in developing the discussion's form so that it shows conformity with past practices.

The theme welcomes the audience and drives the document. It shows the interrelationship between rhetorical and design elements. If the theme

is *BUG–RID is not exempt from FDA review as a new animal drug because you invented it too late*, then the purpose of convincing the reader not to try again may be best achieved by a form that emphasizes the chronology of dates when the regulation was passed and when the product was invented. If the theme is *Dismiss the case because nothing new has happened to depart from past accepted policy and practice*, then the purpose of persuading the judge may be best achieved by either a form that follows the symmetry of describing previous policy and then previous practice or a form that contrasts the consistency with the past versus wrongly stated (by the opposition) inconsistency.

MATERIALS

From what materials is the document constructed? What does it contain? What has the writer decided to include and omit? How do the legal materials relate to the message? In a letter, the writer may choose to restate legally significant facts so that he can double check their accuracy with the client. He may omit technical citations and detailed descriptions of regulations because the client may not need that information to understand the letter's message. In a contract, the writer may include boilerplate sections even when the circumstances do not look likely to invoke them because the traditions of the practice require that she do so. Or she may create new sections describing details of a complicated transaction, details that do not appear in previous contracts. In a memo, the writer may include materials from several jurisdictions or one, charts explaining their interrelationships, or statistics relevant to the case's outcome. Materials are the building matter of the document: law, facts, technical information, results of negotiations. Materials are directly related to the document's scope: more materials, larger scope. As you read critically, try separating what the author found in her research from what is a product of her own thinking. Note how materials carry forth the document's purposes, suit the audiences' needs, and match content and form.

Example 2.9. Materials from a Memo.

The power of an attorney general to bring suit in a representative capacity, including on behalf of state instrumentalities, charitable trusts, and as <u>parens patriae</u>, has generally been recognized as a question of state law. <u>See</u> <u>e.g.</u>, <u>Arizona ex rel. Lawrence v. Omega Corp.</u>, 666 F.3d 998, 999 (11th Cir.) (holding that an attorney general has authority under state law to file Sherman Act suit on behalf of state agencies and political subdivisions), <u>cert. denied</u>, 666 U.S. 111 (1999)); <u>Alabama v. Alpha Corp.</u>, 667 F.3d 1212, 1215 (5th Cir. 1999) (holding an attorney general has authority under state law to file federal antitrust suit on behalf of direct purchaser University of Alabama). Even after the passage of the Hart-Scott-Rodino Antitrust Improvements Act of 1976, which authorized state attorneys general to file <u>parens</u> <u>patriae</u> actions, courts turned to state law to determine whether various attorneys general could file such actions. <u>See</u> <u>Arkansas v. Southern Distribution Co.</u>, 668 F.3d 101, 103 (6th Cir. 1999) (holding that four attorneys general were authorized under state law to file a federal antitrust suit on behalf of consumers); <u>Tennessee v. John & John Co.</u>, 669 F.3d 777, 779 (6th Cir. 1999) (same).

Comment: this example uses four cases as material to demonstrate that courts look to state law to determine the power of attorneys general to file suits as representatives. The question is, do four cases satisfy the theme,

"generally. . . recognized"? Are four cases "general"? Are three of thirteen circuits "general"? And, if so, does the reader have enough of a feel for this rule? Has anyone said attorneys general do not have authority? In fact, the memo from which this is pulled states three pages and forty-one lines of footnotes later, in the middle of a paragraph, "In most states, however, basic issues in this area of law are unsettled." Ah. Perhaps that should have been stated at the beginning of the section. If the purpose of this paragraph is to demonstrate the relative strength or weakness of the opening statement, then the materials used might need to be more extensive if they are to match "generally." If the point is that there is not "general" recognition of this, then perhaps the materials are appropriate, but the sentence needs to use a phrase such as "in narrowly defined situations," or "in only four cases have. . . " This use of parentheticals also impairs understanding because the reader may skip over them, assuming they match the paragraph's message identically, which they do not. Combined with the footnotes, these string cites make the reader hunt down the materials and double check their validity, a bit like having a client double check the bricks and mortar out of which her house is being constructed. These materials should be more carefully selected and presented.

Example 2.10. Materials from another Memo.

The fact that Mr. Figetakis and Richard Delmore are sentimentally attached does not imply that the former alienated the affection of the latter towards his children. In Utah, alienation of affection actions have applied only to married couples, not to gay couples. In those cases, plaintiff must show the following elements to have a cause of action for alienation of affection: 1) the fact of marriage; 2) that the defendant willfully and intentionally alienated the wife's affections, resulting in the loss of the comfort, society and consortium of the wife; and, to justify punitive damages, 3) a charge of malice. See Wilson v. Oldroyd, 1 Utah 2d 362 (1954). The previous case refers to a husband and wife relationship, but it is equally applicable to father and children. In that sense, when one of the points previously stated is missing, the cause of action does not exist. It is clear and can be proven in a court of law that through the first year that Mr. Figetakis and Richard Delmore met, it was for business purposes. In that year and after that there has never been the will and intention of Mr. Figetakis to alienate the affection of Mr. Delmore towards his children, and for that reason the cause of action that is being brought against Mr. Figetakis will fail. The plaintiff will have to prove what's stated in the previous paragraph, which is extremely hard to do. So even if it was true, Mr. Figetakis has evidence to prove otherwise. Mr. Figetakis can prove that in fact all the meetings, telephone conversations and other

contacts he had with Richard Delmore were business related. The fact that the company doubled its sales once Figetakis and Delmore teamed up speaks for itself. This was the result of hard work on the behalf of the defendant and Richard Delmore, which sometimes had to be done at odd hours and places. A jury should be understanding of this, because in some degree most persons have experienced putting extra hours into their jobs and taking calls late and night. They should be even more understanding of Richard Delmore because he runs his own company.

Comment: this example, written by a lawyer from another country, assumes the audience knows much more than he does. The writer also assumes that the audience trusts the writer's judgment. Although there are many facts, there are very few citations, very few references to the law. This lack of legal materials raises doubts for the U.S. reader, who wonders, *Says who*? The materials are simply missing, which fails to fulfill the purpose of informing the reader about the relevant law and its impact on the facts.

Example 2.11. Materials from a Brief.

Plaintiffs' prayer for future damages is far too speculative to begin to meet the minimum legal standard. Damage awards based on unsubstantiated expert testimony, speculation, or mere guess work are not permitted. <u>See</u> <u>Smith v. Jones</u>, 666 So. 3d 1314 (Fla. 1999); <u>Brown v. Green</u>, 555 So. 3d 422 (Fla. 1999); <u>Jeremy v. Bradford</u>, 544 So. 3d 345 (Fla. 1998). When expert testimony on future damages is not supported by evidence in the record, it is speculative and should not be admitted. <u>O'Brien v. O'Sullivan</u>, 554 So. 3d 37 (Fla. 1998).

Comment: this example also uses materials, four cases, that directly support the statements in the second and third sentences. Here, audience and materials intersect. If these cases are familiar to the very experienced judges who will hear this case, this presentation is perfect: concise, tight, lucid. There is no need for elaboration through the specific holdings or facts of the cases, even though the Bluebook requires elaboration on string cites. If, however, this is a new judge, the writer may want to illustrate why these cases support the statements. Audience informs the writer's decisions on materials.

Form

Law, too can shelter a client's problems, it can contain a negotiation about to go awry, it can exalt, stimulate, cajole, direct, or even inspire the person reading it. The document's architectural form should give you the strongest impression of its message, purpose, content—how you will use and experience the document. When you pick up a document, what do you see first? What shape does it take? How many parts are there? In what order do the parts appear? Why?

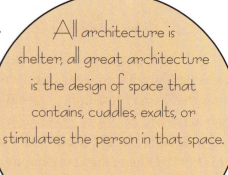

All architecture is shelter, all great architecture is the design of space that contains, cuddles, exalts, or stimulates the person in that space.

— Philip Johnson

Form emancipates analysis. The reader interprets meaning through the structure of the document, whether it be the chronology of the transaction, the relationship among statutory elements, or the delicate weighing of two sides of a balancing test. Observe how the writer has shaped the document. Coherence and comprehension go hand in hand.

Analytical Form

Like the architect, the lawyer designs space, analytical space. The document's analytical form reveals the intersection of materials and theme to achieve specific purposes for several audiences. In this sense, the document's form may be its most creative part. The form is the scheme or structure or pattern used to move the audience from one point to another, such as from premise to conclusion in argumentation. Traditional classical forms are still used for proof. In memos, briefs, and opinion letters, for example, U.S. lawyers often use some form of *deductive reasoning* to move the reader from general law to specific conclusion. Often some kind of *analogical reasoning* is embedded within the deductive structure to demonstrate how precedent requires a specific outline consistent with previous examples. A *chronological* form may analyze the sequence in which events occurred in determining the outcome of a statute of limitations motion; an *inductive* form may convince a court that several actions result cumulatively in violating a client's constitutional rights.

Neo-classical forms are also still popular. Some documents use an overall *deductive* form that moves from a general rule to a specific result. Embedded in that overall form is *analogy*, a subset of *induction*. The current case is compared to previous cases to establish a minor premise and reach a specific result.

In modern legal architecture, form follows another function such as the *policies* of legal realism, the *balancing tests* of law and economics, or the *narratives* of critical race theory. Modern legal writers also borrow other analytical forms from general expository writing and narrative. For example, they use *definition* in assessing the plain meaning of statutes and building an analysis around that principle of statutory construction; *illustration* to argue with examples from persuasive jurisdictions; and *enumeration* to clarify a statutory analysis by listing its elements. They may use *narrative* techniques to persuade audiences by the sheer force of the story. Within the legal culture, not only the forms themselves but also the traditions of their usage are subsumed in interpreting and using them. For example, traditional statutory interpretation strategies have evolved beyond the canons of construction, as have traditional principles of *stare decisis* reasoning.

You will read more critically if you can consciously describe the document's analytical form. If you can compare and contrast forms at all times, recognizing the parts and sequences of new patterns, you will see how legal writers design texts to achieve specific purposes. If you can similarly understand the assumptions underlying the text, you will be able to enlarge your understanding of how various forms function in text and context.

Try, then, to identify the document's analytical form. See if you can recognize the order of the ideas and the relationship of form to function and theme. As you enter the document, observe how it is analytically shaped. Is a contract organized as the transaction will proceed? By most important part of the transaction to the least important? Substantive points first, then boilerplate? In a memo or opinion, is the analysis' approach overtly deductive or inductive? Does the structure follow the elements of a doctrine or statute, such as a balancing test or a four-part statute? Is the document following some particular method of interpreting statutes? Is analogical reasoning being used? Or is the structure just a list of points, randomly organized? Is the writer simply rambling?

Does the form, the design of the space, seem intentional? The patterns may reveal that the writer is struggling with the meaning, is himself unable to see the relationship among ideas. They may also reveal a listing, rather than a synthesis, of sources, which may indicate that the writer does not understand the overall purpose of the document. Or they may reveal intentional building to a conclusion, structuring of an inductive argument, or sequencing of a transaction. Recognizing an analytical form is difficult in some legal writing. A judicial opinion may ramble because the judge has simply transcribed an oral opinion; a letter may seem to hide its message in the middle because the writer is concerned about delivering bad news; a contract may have been cut and pasted from previous contracts. Even the structure of the document may be context dependent, that is, hard for an uninvolved reader to decipher.

Once you determine the analytical form, try to identify possible reasons the author may have had for choosing that structure. Such an

approach will often expose problems in the document's content: a missed step in the reasoning, a provision omitted from a contract, a promise of content that is not delivered. Such an approach also alerts you to possible structures for your own writing; by studying how the analysis is presented, you study how you may imitate, borrow, or reject such an approach.

Example 2.12 Analytical Form of a Memo

Issue: Do the pre-existing deficits in earnings and profits carry over if the corporation's wholly owned subsidiaries are now revived when the subsidiaries took a worthless stock deduction, were left dormant for several years, but did not formally dissolve?

I.   Effect of the Worthless Stock Deduction

A.   The de facto dissolution doctrine has been generally accepted by the courts to determine whether or not a corporation's existence has ceased for purposes of federal taxation.

B.   The de facto dissolution doctrine has been applied by the courts to disallow carryback of excess profits tax credits.

C.   Thus far, the de facto dissolution doctrine has not been successfully applied to tax attributes other than excess profits tax credits.

D.   The de facto dissolution doctrine will most likely be applied to allow carry over of deficits because they do so with net operating losses, and no unique policy concern justifies different treatment of the two.

Comment: this analytical form shows how the various uses of a particular doctrine have developed to demonstrate why the doctrine may be used in this case. It uses an analogical schema, contrasting where the doctrine has been applied with where it has not been applied, and fits these circumstances between the two. In this form, it is difficult to see how the writer got from point C to point D, that is, where did net operating losses come in and what do they have to do with excess profits tax credits? The text itself might explain this, or an experienced tax attorney may have no difficulty with this, but the average reader might need some stronger connection in the text of the headings. Or does "other than excess profits tax credits" include deficits and net operating losses? Overall, the analogical schema seems to work, though, at least by demonstrating the parameters of the doctrine's use.

Example 2.13. Analytical Form from a Contract.

CONTRACT FOR SALE OF MICROCHIPS

PART I
1. **Duration of Contract**
2. **Parties**
3. **Purposes**
4. **Background**
5. **Duration of Contract**
6. **Consideration**
7. **Seller's Obligations**
8. **Buyer's Obligations**
9. **Sending the Computer Microchips and Inspection**
10. **Payment**

PART II
11. **Default or Breach**
12. **Notification and Change in Design**
13. **Termination and Right to Terminate**
14. **Notice for Breach or Termination**
15. **Force Majeure**
16. **Time is of the Essence**
17. **Limit on Resale by the Seller**
18. **Damages and Liquidated Damages**
19. **Mediation or Arbitration**
20. **Change in Parties**
21. **Extensions of Contract**
22. **Warranties**
23. **Headings and Table of Contents for Reference Only**
24. **Signatures**

Comment: this analytical form divides the transaction into two parts: positive completion of the contract and possible negative results. Part I outlines the transaction itself: there is some mutual consideration, the parties agree to do business, the business starts, chips are sent, payment is made. Part II outlines the problems: if default or change in design or breach or termination or *force majeure* or late delivery happens, then the seller resells or damages are determined through mediation or arbitration (and if parties change, they are subject to mediation or arbitration). If the contract is fulfilled, then it may be extended. The last two provisions relate to the contract itself. This order sets the transaction itself, then allows for contingencies.

Example 2.14. Analytical Form from a Brief.

TABLE OF CONTENTS

B.   **Wisconsin Statutes Sections 632.32 and 632.43** Do Not Prevent Insurers From Limiting Their Liability By Contractual Reducing Clauses.

   1.   The statute is clear and unambiguous because the plain meaning of the word "indemnify" does not encompass liability coverage.

   2.   If the court finds the statute ambiguous, then the statute's scope, history, context and purpose indicate that insureds are not allowed to stack indemnity and liability coverage.

II.   HORACE MANN IS NOT LIABLE UNDER THE UNINSURED MOTORIST'S PROVISION OF THE MULLEN POLICY BECAUSE THE WISCONSIN SUPREME COURT'S INTERPRETATION OF WISCONSIN AUTOMOBILE INSURANCE STATUTES ALLOW INSURERS TO CONTRACTUALLY LIMIT THEIR LIABILITY.

   A.   Neither The Wisconsin Supreme Court nor the Court of Appeals Has Expanded Wisc. Stats. Secs. 632.32 and 631.43 To Prevent Insurers From Contractually Limiting Their Liability in Some Circumstances.

   B.   The Reducing Clause in the Mullen Policy Is Permissible Because It Appropriately Prohibits Stacking of Indemnity Coverage With Liability Coverage.

   C.   To Require Stacking of Liability and Indemnity Coverage Would Be To Convert Liability Coverage to Indemnity Coverage in a Manner that was Unauthorized, Unanticipated, and Unregulated by the Legislature.

III.   PERMITTING STACKING OF LIABILITY COVERAGE AND INDEMNITY COVERAGE WOULD ENDANGER CONSUMERS' INTERESTS BECAUSE RATES WOULD INCREASE, SMALLER INSURANCE COMPANIES COULD GO BANKRUPT, AND CONSUMERS WOULD BE ENCOURAGED TO BECOME SELF–INSURED OR UNINSURED.

A. **Stacking of Liability Coverage and Indemnity Coverage Will Greatly Increase Overall Costs to Consumers.**

B. **Smaller Insurance Companies Will Not Be Able To Financially Bear the Risk of Stacking of Liability Coverage with Indemnity Coverage That Is Thus Far Not Regulated or Mandated by Statute.**

C. **Consumers Will Be Encouraged To Become Self–Insured or Uninsured Because of the Increased Costs and Risks Resulting From The Stacking of Liability Coverage with Indemnity Coverage.**

Comment: this analytical form relies on a strict plain meaning interpretation of the statute. The form takes its cue from a literal reading of the insurance statutes by ushering the reader first through the consistency of the language with the statutes, second through the consistency of this interpretation with the policy behind the statutes, and third through a discussion of how a different interpretation would result in bad practices. Each "room" in the document is devoted to a specific aspect of interpretation and each "room" is about the same size. As such, it is an inductive schema, using examples to show the general conclusion that the statute must be consistently interpreted.

As you read, distinguish form from format. The analytical form reveals the contours of the legal analysis or the structure of the transaction, for example. The "zoning requirements" of traditional formats do tell you what kind of document it is: contract, appellate brief, or federal regulation. As you read documents critically, observe both form and format and how they affect the document's success.

TRADITIONAL FORMATS

Check to see what overall format the author selected. Does it make sense? Is there a beginning, middle, and end? Or does it look thrown together, random pieces floating near each other? Might the author be scrambling the format to confuse the reader, as some lawyers do in inter-rogatories or negotiating letters? Can you recognize a connection between the format and the document's rhetorical elements?

Example 2.15. Traditional Format of a Contract.

EMPLOYMENT AGREEMENT

[1] _____ *[company]*, located at [2] _____ *[address]*, City of [3] _____, County of [4] _____, State of [5] _____, herein referred to as company, hereby employs [6] _____, of [7] _____ *[address]*, City of [8] _____, County of [9] _____, State of [10] _____, herein referred to as employee, as [11] _____ *[state capacity in which employee is to be engaged]*, to serve and to perform such duties at such times and places and in such manner as company may from time to time direct.

Employee agrees to faithfully perform the duties assigned to [12] _____ [him *or* her] to the best of [13] _____ [his or her] ability, to devote [14] _____ [his *or* her] full and undivided time to the transaction of company's business, to make to company prompt, complete, and accurate reports of employee's work and expenses, to promptly remit to company all monies of company collected by employee or coming into employee's possession, and not to engage or be engaged or be interested in any other business during the existence of this agreement.

In consideration of such service by employee, company agrees to pay employee compensation at the rate of [17] _____ Dollars ($____) per [16] _____ and employee's reasonable and necessary traveling expenses incurred in company's business while away from [17] _____ [*designate geographical area*].

Employee shall, when required by company, reimburse it for the expenses of a fidelity bond secured by company and not to exceed [18] _____ Dollars ($____).

This agreement shall be in effect from [19] _____ [*date*] until it is terminated by either party at any time on [20] _____ days' written notice to the other party.

At the termination of this agreement in any manner, the payment to employee of salary earned to the date of such termination shall be in full satisfaction of all claims against company under this agreement.

In witness whereof, each party to this agreement has caused it to be executed at [21] _____ [*place of execution*] on the date indicated below.

[*signatures and date(s) of signing*]
[*Title of person representing employer*]

Comment: this contract follows the schema generated within a law firm for these kinds of contracts. Tradition, litigation, and experience with clients often dictate

sticking to the format plan, though a client's situation might require rear-ranging or recasting certain sections. Audiences tend to glaze over when they see these forms (did you read all the details?), so consider whether or not that was one of the document's purposes. When you analyze a form, make sure you know why the parts are in the order they are; try to unravel the reason behind the format. Chronology? Easy information, then hard? Factual information, then transactional activity, then boilerplate legal requirements?

Example 2.16. Format of a Law Office Memo.

Introduction

(QP/BA/Context)

Discussion

Conclusion

Comment: this format plan allows the reader to get the most important information at the beginning of the document, the question and answer. This kind of "front-loading" allows busy readers to glance at a document to get its essence, then to see more detail in the later Discussion section. The Conclusion recommends a direction to take. This plan permits the reader to make optimum use of the analysis because the Question Presented and Brief Answer provide a distilled version of the entire Discussion. The reader can "enter" the document at any heading and understand its results.

Example 2.17. Format of an Appellate Brief.

COVER PAGE

TABLE OF CONTENTS

TABLE OF CASES

ASSIGNMENTS OF ERROR

STATEMENT OF THE CASE

ARGUMENT

CONCLUSION

APPENDIX

Comment: this format disciplines all writers to frame issues that match their discussions. The format requires several blueprints from which the readers can judge the document's validity. The Table of Contents gives the arguments in one coherent place so the readers can see the connection among the parts. The Table of Authorities outlines the materials, a starting place for clerks to check the research and the place where the reader can check the writer's thoroughness. The match between Issues and Assignments of Error requires that the writer show the reader the precise bases for the appeal. The correspondence between the issues and the point headings also requires the writer to balance the argument with the issues. Such a format ensures disciplined organization for the writers and conformity for the readers' tired eyes. In this case, the format anticipates the form by requiring the writer to match substantive concepts among Issues, Assignments of Error, and Point Headings.

The form, not the format, will give you clues about proportion, or how big each section should be. To read critically, revisit the rhetorical elements and start to see how an author apportions size to each of the document's segments.

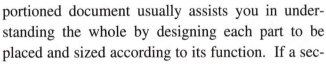

PROPORTION

As you read, observe the document's internal proportions. A well-proportioned document usually assists you in understanding the whole by designing each part to be placed and sized according to its function. If a section is central to the document's purpose, it appears in an important place, perhaps even in the center. If a section is unimportant, it may be annexed to another or added at the end, even in an appendix. If a section connects two points, it may be constructed as a hallway by making it a transitional paragraph or section.

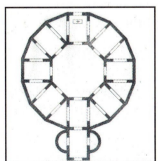

Try to identify the relative proportions of sections and paragraphs. Are important sections emphasized, either by their position, the use of graphics, or their length? Are less important sections treated in an opposite fashion? Where are the important ideas located and how much "space" is devoted to them? Are legal points emphasized or is each paragraph a "mini-brief," a kind of chronological summary of one case, where the important information is buried in the middle of the paragraph or in a subordinate clause? What relation do the sections have to the theme? Are the more important ones placed at positions of emphasis, that is, the beginning or ending? Or are they longer? Does the pivotal section lie at the middle of the document, balancing the analysis on either side? Do smaller "rooms" separate the larger ones? Are the central themes centralized? Then check the paragraphs within sections. Ask the same questions, testing whether or not the paragraphs carry the appropriate proportion for their respective values to the section's theme.

Unfortunately, at the section and paragraph levels, much traditional legal writing rambles. It is often difficult to determine a section or paragraph's importance to the theme, either by its placement or its length. Section breaks may seem more cosmetic than analytical, as though the writer were tired of that section and wanted to make a bit of white space on the page; then the next section shows no relationship to the old ones. Is there ever a short section? Are relationships among the sections explicit? Understandable? What about within the section: are the paragraphs in an understandable sequence? Do topic sentences connect ideas? The same questions on proportion can be asked at the paragraph level. Much legal writing collapses at the section and paragraph level, so studying its proportions may assist you in interpreting the document.

Example 2.18. Proportions from a Brief.

ARGUMENT

I. THE EXCLUSION OF BREAST CANCER FOR TREATMENT WITH HDC/ABMT IS NOT A DISABILITY-BASED DISCRIMINATION.

OPM previously argued, and continues to argue, that the exclusion of breast cancer for treatment with HDC/ABMT is not a disability-based distinction. The coverage was based on the suitability of the

treatment, not the disability. However, the EEOC rejected OPM's argument, finding that the exclusion is a disability-based distinction. The EEOC's rationale for concluding that OMP's exclusion of breast cancer for treatment with HDC/ABMT is a disability-based distinction pursuant to the EEOC Interim Guidance, June 1999 (Guidance), is that "the distinction in this case applies to a specific disability, breast cancer, and affects only persons who have this <u>disability</u>. As such it is <u>neither a broad distinction, nor one which affects both persons with and without disabilities</u>." <u>See</u> EEOC Decision, April 3, 2000 (Decision), pages 13-14 (emphasis added).

> This is the longest paragraph in the argument, and it is devoted to the other side! This is the strongest position of the document, and here is the other side's brief. They already had their chance when they filed! The message is that their argument is more important; the proportion and position indicate that it may be a *stronger* argument. despite its words.

The ADA defines disability as a physical or mental impairment that <u>substantially limits one or more of the major life activities of such individual</u>; a record of such an impairment; or being regarded as having such an impairment. <u>See</u> 42 U.S.C. § 2000 (2) (   ) (emphasis added). The regulation defines a physical impairment as any physiological disorder, or condition, cosmetic disfigurement, or anatomical loss affecting one or more of the following body systems: neurological, musculoskeletal, special sense organs, respiratory (including speech organs), cardiovascular, reproductive, digestive, genito-urinary, hemic and lymphatic, skin, and endocrine." 29 C.F.R. § 1 (   ).

The EEOC in this case erroneously assumed that all breast cancer is a disability. However, "the determination of whether an individual has a disability is not necessarily based on the name or diagnosis of the impairment the person has, but rather on the effect of that impairment on the life of the individual." 29 C.F.R. 2, App. (2000); <u>see</u> <u>also</u> <u>Adgerson v. ELR Corp.</u>, 1999 WL 99999 (E.D. Tex.).

In a recent decision, <u>Kinnear v. Diskette Rainbow, Inc.</u>, 99 F.3d 999 (5th Cir. 2000), the United States Court of Appeals for the Fifth Circuit held that an employee did not establish that her breast cancer was a "disability" within the meaning of the ADA. The court found that "a physical impairment, standing alone, is not necessarily a disability as contemplated by the ADA because the statute requires an impairment that substantially limits one or more of the major life

> This is the next longest paragraph. It is a mini-brief. The treatment of this case continues into the next paragraph. . . .

activities." Id. at 1001. The Court of Appeals referred to appellant's testimony in which she noted that she never missed a day of work during her treatment for breast cancer and that she was "back to normal in three to four months." Id. In affirming summary judgment for the employer, the court concluded that "the evidence did not create a material fact issue on whether her cancer and treatment 'substantially limited' her major life activity of working. Obviously, her ability to work was affected; but, as reflected in the above–quoted statute and regulations, far more is required to trigger coverage under § 2000." Id. at 1002.

> . . . .where, in the middle, we discover that this case is "erroneous." But its proportion suggests it is very important.

The EEOC in this case, in contrast to the Fifth Circuit, has defined breast cancer, per se, as a disability. As a result, it has concluded that the exclusion is a disability-based distinction. However, the EEOC's assumption is erroneous. The proper standard for determining whether breast cancer or any other illness is a disability, as defined by the ADA, is dependent on whether it has a substantial impact on one or more major life activities.

Other cases have also held that for the purposes of the ADA, a disability must substantially limit one or more major life activities. See e.g., Butcher v. Wilder Shipbuilders, 55 F.3d 100 (5th Cir. 2000) (ADA requires that in order to be a disability, an impairment must substantially limit one or more major life activities); Blocher v. State University, 2000 WL 99999 (E.D. La. March 17, 2000) (a material factual issue was raised as to whether plaintiff was substantially impaired from mastocytosis); McKinna v. Accidental Ins. Corp., 2000 WL 11111 (S.D. Tx. October 5, 2000) (a person claiming to be disabled must establish that he satisfies the requirement of the definition of a disability under the ADA and its accompanying regulations).

> The writer's arguments occur in these last two paragraphs, but only some of the sentences affirmatively state the writer's argument, and the strongest holdings are relegated to the short parentheticals in paragraph 6!

According to the Guidance at pg. 6, distinctions which "constrain individuals both with and without disabilities, are not distinctions based on disability." While breast cancer may constitute an impairment as defined by 29 C.F.R. § 1, as the Fifth Circuit correctly held, not all breast cancer is a disability as defined by the ADA. To the extent that the EEOC Guidance excludes from the definition of disability based distinctions "broad distinctions which affect both persons with and without disabilities," breast cancer should also be excluded because it affects persons with and without disabilities. The EEOC's decision, therefore, is erroneous because it assumes that all breast cancer is a disability. As a result, the EEOC's conclusion that the insurance carrier's policy which excluded coverage of ABMT for the treatment of breast cancer constitutes a disability-based distinction is erroneous.

Example 2.19. Proportions from a Contract.

EMPLOYMENT CONTRACT (for a psychologist)

I. **General Provisions**
<u>Introductory paragraph</u>: parties are identified, agreement is identified
<u>Term</u>: length of agreement, notice of renewal
<u>Freedom to Enter Contract</u>
<u>Contract Termination</u>

II. **Expectations of Employer**
<u>Duties</u>: duties of employee
<u>Holidays</u>: when office is open, when employee is expected to work
<u>Sick Leave</u>: amount of time allowed annually
<u>Noncompetition</u>: employee will not practice in same area if he leaves the company

III. **Benefits to Employee**
<u>Salary</u>: amount of compensation, when compensation will be made, increases in salary/bonuses
<u>Moving Expenses</u>: amount
<u>Benefits</u>: health insurance, disability, life insurance
<u>Vacation</u>: length
<u>Liability Insurance:</u> what kind the company will provide
<u>Office and Equipment</u>: location, dimensions, supplies, furniture
<u>Professional Development</u>: training, credentials

IV. Characteristics of the Agreement

Binding Agreement: agreement shall bind parties/heirs

Entire Agreement: this contract represent entire agreement

Applicable Law: law of Texas shall apply

Severability: if one provision of contract is invalid, the rest of contract remains

Paragraph Headings: are descriptive only and have no legal force

Comment: the overall message of this contract is *Please come work for us*. Notice how the section with the most provisions is entitled "Benefits to the Employee." At the same time, the expectations of the employer are clearly identified. The writer has tried to make some of the more contentious provisions, such as those provisions that come into play when there is a lawsuit—applicable law, severability, termination—fall under neutral headings like "Characteristics of the Agreement" or "General Provisions." The proportions give a welcoming message to the prospective employee.

Example 2.20. Proportions from a Judicial Opinion.

The affidavit on which the warrant was granted did not allege that on April 17, 1922, the liquor was still in the garage, though the return and this motion both show that this was the fact. The question is, then, whether it was enough, to justify a search two days later, that a truck had gone into the petitioner's garage loaded with liquor. Had the

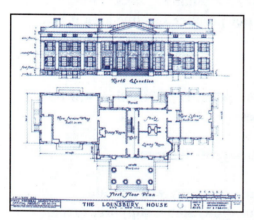

agent seen the liquor unloaded from the truck, that would be some evidence of illegal possession by the owner of the garage. Had he waited, and the truck come out empty, that, too, would have been some evidence, or, if the whisky cases had borne any evidence of ownership by Casino, it would have been quite different. The affidavit shows none of these things.

On the contrary, it only says that a truck loaded with whisky drove into the petitioner's garage, which for all that appears may have been doing business as a public garage. That, it seems to me, is not

enough to give a right forcibly to search the premises two days later. It is equally consistent with a stop by the truck at the garage for repairs, oil, gas, air, or water, or even to pay a visit. It will not, therefore, serve as prima facie evidence that the liquors were illegally retained upon the premises when the warrant issued.

<u>United States v. Casino</u>, 286 F. 976, 976 (1923) (Learned Hand, J.).

Comment: here, the proportions fulfill the dual purposes of outlining what a warrant should do and scolding the issuer of the warrant. The greatest proportion of these paragraphs is given to possible grounds for issuing a warrant, none of which appeared in the affidavit. The text suggests many possibilities, beginning with what the affidavit should have said and did not. The first paragraph ends by repeating the error, then re-emphasizes the point at the beginning of the next paragraph. Both give greater proportion to the error. Such repetition about the missing grounds for the warrant emphasize that the affidavit was insufficient to justify the warrant.

Interior Design

Once you have a sense of the document's form and the relative pro-portion of the parts to each other, you are prepared to look inside the rooms. Critically read to discover the document's interior design. What is

the sentence order within paragraphs, the word order within sentences? What is the sentence structure, the syntax? The word choice? Is there a repetition of syntactical structures, of certain phrases, of terms of art? Is there a topic string that establishes a theme within a section or paragraph?

To identify the document's interior design is to uncover the writer's most idiosyncratic choices: what word to use, what order to place the sentences in, whether or not to make connections explicit. In traditional legal writing, the interiors tend to be baroque, overstuffed, flowery. Sentences tend to be long, using complex conditionals, dependent clauses, intrusive phrases, and compound subjects and verbs. In modern legal writing, the interiors are cleaner, more minimalist, but functional. Sentences are shorter, subjects and verbs are simpler and closer together, and explicit cohesive devices connect sentences and paragraphs.

Observe the document's interior. Is it predominantly traditional or modern? It may be traditional if it uses technical language that cannot be understood by a non-lawyer or unusual discourse markers, such as *whether* to begin a question. It may be modern if it defines all terms within the document and uses them consistently, if it makes the document's message explicit and repeats it throughout. Note the writer's use of language. In traditional legal writing, these word choices often included Latinisms; doublets, such as *on or about, by and for*, and *by and between*; intensifiers, such as *said* and *such*; jargon, such as *instant case, aforementioned,* and *the case at hand*; and formal introductory phrases, such as *It might be argued that,* or *It is well-established that. . . .* In modern legal writing, most of these conventions are dropped: *On July 14, 1997. . .* , and *Party A and Party B agree that. . .* Reference to the writer's case is more likely *in this case* or *here*; and sentences begin with the argument, not a formal introduction: *Breast cancer is not a disability for the purposes of this Act.*

By identifying the patterns used by the writer, you are identifying some of the means intended to work on you, the reader. Is there inflammatory language? Subtle word choice that suggests meaning not made explicit? Slightly altered use of terms of art? Try to identify the writer's selection and use of language, keeping in mind that your very identification of the devices enriches your own repertoire of what to do and not do in your own legal writing.

Example 2.21. Interior Design of a Contract.

SECTION SIX

INCORPORATION; PERMIT TO ISSUE SHARES;

PAYMENT OF SUBSCRIPTION

The incorporators shall cause the corporation to be formed under the provisions of § 22.5, formed within twenty (20) days from the date of this agreement, and thereupon with all reasonable diligence shall cause the corporation to apply for and secure a permit authorizing issuance of stock as hereinabove subscribed and sale of stock to the public in accordance with an approved prospectus.

Upon incorporation, the subscribers shall pay the amounts of their respective subscriptions to America's Bank at 2020 Avenue of the Americas, New York, NY 10001, which is hereby agreed upon and designated as trustee for subscription issued, and then pay over the same to the corporation upon its proper organization, or return the same to the several subscribers on refusal of the state to issue such permit.

Comment: here is the overstuffed interior that makes some readers feel comfortable and plush, others suffocated. Each paragraph is one sentence long. Each is invaded by intrusive phrases (e.g., *with all reasonable diligence, as herinabove subscribed, which his hereby agreed upon and designated as trustee for subscription issued*) and jargon (e.g., *hereinabove, hereby, such*). Each separates subject from verb (e.g., *incorporators shall cause. . .and secure. . ., subscribers shall pay. .or return*). And each stuffs all legal concepts into a small space.

Example 2.22. Interior Design from a Letter.

The undersigned ocean carriers appreciate the opportunity to submit comments on the proposed Code 7 program. An open dialogue between the government and industry is critical to the effective and efficient operation of the defense transportation system. This is particularly true with respect to the proposed Code 7 program, the potential consequences of which extend far beyond the confines of the shipment of household goods. Indeed, the government may not fully appreciate the implications of the Code 7 program. The purpose of these comments is to articulate our concerns.

We believe that the Code 7 program is imprudent for several reasons and therefore should not be implemented. First, the projected savings are illusory because the government has not considered all of the economic implications of the Code 7 program. Second, the Code 7 program provides a lower quality service than the Code 8 program. Third, the program jeopardizes the maintenance of a healthy merchant marine under the United States flag, which is needed to serve military sealift requirements. We discuss each of these points below.

Comment: this interior design is businesslike, sharp, and a bit foreboding, like the law office interior that suggests clients' money is being well spent. The sentences are varied, but of average length—2-3 lines. They are neither traditionally formal not modernly minimalist. They simply present the information. Subjects and verbs are close together (*carriers appreciate, government may not appreciate, program provides, program jeopardizes*), word choice is no nonsense (*critical, true, illusory, lower, healthy, needed*), and the paragraph structure uses straightforward tabulation to outline what is coming (*first, second, third*). Direct, unadorned, and strong, this letter's interior matches its message that *You will save money, improve quality, and maintain a healthy merchant marine if you abandon the Code 7 program.*

Example 2.23. Interior Design from a Judicial Opinion.

Here, for example, the mere fact that Bostick did not feel free to leave the bus does not mean that the police seized him. Bostick was a passenger on a bus that was scheduled to depart. He would not have felt free to leave the bus even if the police had not been present. Bostick's movements were "confined" in a sense, but this was the natural result of his decision to take the bus; it says nothing about whether or not the police conduct at issue was coercive.

Florida v. Bostick, 501 U.S. 429, 435 (1991) (O'conner, J.).

Comment: this is the more open modern interior. It uses *Here,* not *In the instant case* to begin the paragraph. The second and third sentences are relatively short; combined with the semicolon sentences, they offer variety to engage the audiences' collective eye. The defendant and his movements occupy the subject of three of the five sentences, emphasizing him as the theme, not the police. This choice places the defendant in the spotlight, not the police. The repetition of his name suggests the volition of his actions.

Such interior design choices alert the reader that seizure is a function of the defendant's choices, not the police actions. Note, too, the symmetry of the first sentence: Bostick's feeling does not mean police seized him. The sentence structure itself states not just the theme but the relation of each part to the other.

Example 2.24. Interior Design from a Memo.

ISSUE

Has Congress recently enacted, or proposed, any lobbying reform legislation? If so, what impact will the measures have on the following lobbying activities:

1. **ENTERTAINING: Is it still permitted, for instance, to take a congressional aide to a professional baseball game or to a concert?**

2. **DINING: Is it still permitted to pay for a congressional aide's lunch at a local restaurant?**

3. **GIFT–GIVING: Is it still permitted to give a congressional aide a nominal gift, such as a holiday popcorn basket?**

BRIEF ANSWER

Although several lobbying reform measures have been introduced, both in the last and in the current congressional sessions, no bills (and only one rule change) have been enacted to amend the current federal lobbying laws. Thus, depending on the actual dollar value of the "gifts," the above-mentioned lobbying activities are still lawful under current Senate and House ethics rules.

Comment: this interior is homey, comfortable, to be used among friends. Its sentence structure follow familiar forms (question/answer, simple sub-ject–verb combinations). The word choice is concrete (*entertaining, base-ball, gift-giving*), and the sentences in the brief answer are three lines long. These may foreshadow the length of each section in the Discussion section. The transitional words in the brief answer (*Although, Thus*) show the ana-lytical relationships between the ideas.

Example 2.25 Interior Design from a Brief.

Other jurisdictions support this ruling. For example, an Illinois court of appeals affirmed a directed verdict for plaintiff when defen-dant train company offered no reasonable explanation for its train col-liding head-on with another train. See Smith v. Atchison, Topeka & Santa Fe Ry. Co., 288 Ill. App. 2d 340, 771 N.E.2d 393 (1999). A Minnesota Court of Appeals also sustained a directed verdict for the plaintiff when the defendant bus manufacturer offered no reasonable explanation for the carbon monoxide leakage into the passenger com-partment. See Deazy v. Reliable Bus Mfs., 290 Minn. Ct. App. 49, 456 N.W.2d 76 (1999).

Similarly, defendant can offer no reasonable explanation here, and thus the court should have directed the verdict for the plaintiff. No smell of gas indicated a gas line failure, so that was not the cause. No failure of the Bastion Blessing control occurred, so that was not the cause. No failure of the pressure or temperature valves occurred, so those were not the cause. And no testimony indicated any intervening cause.

The only causes of the accident, then, could be improperly func-tioning controls, non-functioning controls, improper combustion, or misuse of the compound Soot Destroyer. All of these were in the con-trol of the defendant, who negligently maintained and used the con-trols, the equipment, and the compound.

Defendant offered no reasonable explanation for his negligent maintenance of the gas heater and thus the trial court should have directed the verdict for the plaintiff.

Comment: this example of a modern interior uses three devices to drill home the theme: topic strings, parallel structure, and substitution. The topic string of *should have directed the verdict* appears in three different places. Parallel structure, used in the second and third paragraphs, offers lists that separate piles of evidence. And substitution occurs in the final-paragraph, where the general terms of art, established in the first paragraph, are substituted with the specific terms of this case: *Defendant offered no reasonable explanation here.* Substance matches syntax, as discussed in Chapter 6.

FINISH

The perfect sheen on a walnut table gives a particular vibration to a room. A stucco finish offers a familiar, solid, friendly feeling, while a glass skyscraper suggest sheer cleanliness. The finish of a document is not just its perfection, but its feel. Observe what sheen the document gives off or what overall impression it makes. Do you get a sense that the writer has let the document breath long enough to reveal its rough edges, and that the writer has then smoothed those edges, whether they be in creating clearer topic strings, finer transitional devices, or proper spacing following punctuation? Observe how finely finished the document is. Is every detail in place, every coma properly put, every citation properly polished? Are there any typographical errors, any spelling mistakes or cultural misspellings?

Flaws in the document's finish are the first things to hit the audiences' eyes, and any failure in finish damages credibility. Finish reveals the document's overall effect. It also serves as the "punch-up" list used in construction. Everything is almost done, but a wall needs the paint patched, a hinge needs to be replaced, a door hanging needs adjusting. You can live in the building, but some things just aren't right. Oddly, it is those things that will grow to bother you the most, taking your eye from the otherwise perfectly finished details. How did you react when you saw the typo in the previous paragraph? Especially in a book on writing? You, as audience, probably appreciate a fine finish.

Example 2.26. Finish from a Letter.

Gentlemen:

This will acknowledge receipt of your letter of May 12, 1999.

Please be advised that the attorney representing the injured, has not been able to give us a satisfactory explanation of his theory of liability, which are position is none.

We would appreciate it if you would drop us a line indicating your theory of liability, if you have any. We are not engaged in any settlement discussions with the attorney representing the injured.

Very truly yours,

Fred. B. Waters
CLAIM DEPARTMENT

Comment: this example may seem extreme, but it is authentic. It was actually sent. The letter's overall finish is rough, to say the least. Such "typographical" mistakes happen too often in the rush of legal practice. The finish here may be so off-putting as to render the letter unusable.

Example 2.27. Finish from a Lease as Quoted in a Brief.

Thomas Krauss went out of his way to make sure that the Thomases understood that the farmhouse was an older house and that it lacked a lot of the cosmetic appeal of a newer house. (TK dep. pg. 56.) Further, he indicated that there were no plans to fix up the farmhouse, as in further plastering or painting. (TK dep. pg. 56.) The lease itself reflected the entire agreement that Thomas Krauss entered into with the Thomases regarding the renting of the farmhouse. There were no other written documents modifying the lease, nor were there any other verbal agreements modifying the lease. (TK dep. pg. 56.)

At lines 79 through 83 the text of the lease provides as follows:

> **Lessor shall not be liable for any damage occasioned by failure to keep said premises in repair, and shall not be liable for any damage done or occasioned by or from plumbing, gas, water, steam or other pipes, or sewerage, or the bursting, leaking or running of any cistern, tank, wash stand, water closet, or waste pipe in, above, upon or about said building or premises, not for damage occasioned by water, snow or ice being upon or coming through the roof, skylight, trap door or otherwise, or for any damage arising from acts or neglect of co–tenants or other occupants of same building.**

(Exhibit A, pg. 1)

The terms of the above quoted clause cover the facts of this case. The plaintiff, Daniel Thomas, was injured in a gas explosion when he attempted to light the pilot light on a water heater. If the facts are as the plaintiff suggests, this explosion was caused by a faulty mechanism that allowed gas to escape from the water heater. The above quoted clause indicates that the lessor shall not be liable for any damage done by or from gas or water. The accident in this suit comes within the terms of the exculpatory clause contained in the lease.

Comment: here the mistake in finish is more egregious. A punctuation error, the comma after "steam," is now being litigated. Is it gas or gas pipes? The finish needs to be perfected!

TECHNIQUES

- *Record your reactions as you read.* Writing down the document's effect can uncover its use of architectural elements. Are you properly informed, convinced, or motivated, depending on the document's primary purpose?

- *Write a descriptive outline of the document that captures its analytical progression.* What goes first, second, third? Why? Does it work? Such "reverse" outlining can serve both to enhance textual analysis and to build a repertoire of possible analytical structures. (See example 2.29.)

- *Read for one thing at a time.* You may read only to see how the materials are used and if they can be transferred to your project. You may read only to see if the form is appropriate for that kind of building, such as element-by-element progression through a statutory analysis. Or you may read only for historical context, to see whether or not, or how, your subject has been treated previously.

- *Read separate sections out of order.* You may be interested only in the dining room, not in a whole tour of the house. See what may of use there, but keep in mind context and setting before transferring the architectural ideas wholesale to your design.

- *Read as mentor.* If you are reading a document in progress, use it to teach. Note what works and why. Try to decipher the writer's intentions and best design directions; then use your responses to draw out the best architect in that writer. Use the draft not only to finish that project, but also to teach about future projects. Build together.

- *Read for the document's most important needs.* If you are responding to a document or writing together, focus on the most important questions, rather than everything at once. A writer can only fix one thing at a time. In legal writing, nothing works without a strong sense of rhetorical purpose and audience.

- *Read actively, rather than passively.* Participate in the document's discussion. I once went to Chartres with a woman who declined to take Malcolm Miller's tour of the glass and sculpture. She was tired. She walked around once and sat outside. We, meanwhile, were breathless as he brought to life the famous "Chartres blue" and the detailed faces in the "infancy windows." We had each brought binoculars so we didn't miss a detail (he was impressed!). An hour passed like a minute. By trying, by looking, by listening, by bringing some energy to your reading, you will learn more and tire less.

- *Keep notes from project to project.* Be specific about design patterns, use of materials, techniques that work in what you read. You may not need them for this project, but you can use them later. Imitate the great writers. Innovate from what you record.

OBSERVING CONTEXT

Finally, observe documents in context. See how they work as an architectural whole. They are set in a landscape, built at a certain time, and meant to function in certain ways. By putting them in context, moving around and through them, you participate in their meaning. Annotate them for their use of architectural elements. Note if form follows function, and how all elements intersect. In this chapter, you have been observing examples of design elements in isolation. One of your most difficult jobs as a reader is to observe the whole, to decipher the document's overall effect, especially in context. When you analyze architecture, you begin from the outside and walk through each room, observing how themes emerge, materials unite, and the form and proportion fulfill the function. As you enter Chartres cathedral, you look up, up at the windows, up at the arches, up at the sculpture. For its builders, that whole effect was to take man out of himself. As you enter a ranch style home, you are looking across the rooms, all on one level, level with the land. The rooms are a continuation of the land.

As you enter and tour the following opinion letter, observe its effects similarly. See how form and function interact, how the materials are used, how the proportions relate to the theme. Consider the context of the document, where in the legal process it was generated, what the relationship is between reader and writer, and what effects the letter has. The comments are one observer's reactions. You may react differently. Experience the text as its user, Mr. Smith, and measure the overall effect of the legal architecture.

I am an eyewitness to the ways in which people relate to themselves and to each other, and my work is a way of scooping and ladling that experience.

- Richard Neutra

Ramsfield & Litsinger
600 New Jersey Avenue, NW
Washington, DC 20001

April 12, 1994

Mr. Neil Smith
Smith Architects & Associates
One Trafalgar Square
London, England

Dear Mr. Smith:

Example 2.28.
Comments on the Design
Elements of an Opinion Letter

Paragraph 1- Entrance: Introduces the history of the case and provides a brief answer.

Here is the theme, including the reason; good news!

Practical context: make a note that she has to see the works.

When we spoke last week, you asked me to advise you about a potential copyright action against George Ikopi. You expressed concern that a work of Ikopi's that was recently profiled in Architectural Digest was a copy of one of your designs. As this letter explains, you probably can make a claim against Ikopi because your relationship with ProTech was such that you should own the copyright to your work, and because Ikopi had access to your work before producing a similar work that he marketed as his own. I must caution, however, that I cannot be certain of this opinion until I have seen the two works myself.

Paragraph 2- Hallway: Transitions from the brief answer to the facts relied upon by the writer and cautions me to review the pertinent facts of the letter before relying on the legal conclusions drawn.

I will explain the reasoning underlying these conclusions in just a moment. Before doing that, however, I must ask you to review the facts as I have written them below. My conclusions are based on the facts as I understand them, and if there are any mistakes in those facts the conclusions will not be accurate. Please review the facts briefly and let me know right away if there are any mistakes or omissions.

Facts

Paragraph 3- Familiar room, proportion appropriate because these paragraphs summarize chronologically the relevant facts and the events leading to the presentation of the architectural plans at the meeting of the ProTech Board of Directors.

As I understand the situation, ProTech commissioned you in November 1990 to design a new building for the corporation's headquarters. You worked on this project in your London office for sixteen months, traveling to Miami a few times to finalize the details. You completed the design in March 1992.

Paragraph 4- Central part of the room taking shape: Summarizes the events of the Board of Directors meeting. I'm comfortable, familiar with this and pleased to see my own things cared for properly—this is an accurate summary.

A month after you finished the plans, you presented your design at a ProTech Board of Directors meeting. In addition to the board members, major shareholders were specially invited to attend. One of the shareholders who attended was James Knokof, a partner in the Miami architectural firm of Ikopi & Knokof. At this meeting you displayed architectural plans, design drawings, and a model of your proposed building, and you distributed brochures about your firm. The brochures included design drawings and pictures of the model that you had just proposed. After this meeting ProTech officials told you that a major investor had withdrawn and that the project was being placed on hold.

Paragraph 5- Central part of this room: Summarizes the facts that show the copying after he had seen the plans at the meeting of the ProTech Board of Directors.
Yes, this is the question.

This February, Architectural Digest magazine featured a project by Ikopi. The article included copies of a model, design drawings, and pictures of the completed external structure of a building. You were struck by the similarities between that project and your proposal to ProTech and contacted me to discuss the possibility of a copyright infringement action.

Paragraph 6- Anteroom to Main Rooms: Transitions from the facts to five questions of law presented, beginning with the general question of whether the design is copyrightable to the final specific question of whether Ikopi infringed on the copyright.
I'm ready.

If anything in this statement of facts is inaccurate, please let me know. Assuming that these facts are correct, the case turns on the answers to a series of questions. I have briefly answered each question here, but I would be happy to discuss any of them further if you wish to know more.

Is an Architectural Design Copyrightable?

Paragraph 7- Main section, first room: Presents the threshold question of statutory definition of copyrightable material as including "architectural works" and uses deduction to conclude that since the design is an architectural work, it is protected by the copyright laws. I follow.

The first question is whether or not the design you created is protected by the copyright laws of the United States. The answer to this question is clearly yes. The law was amended in 1990 to specifically include "architectural works." Architectural works are defined as "the design of a building as embodied in any tangible medium of expression, including a building, architectural plans, or drawings." The copyright protects "the overall form as well as the arrangement and composition of spaces and elements in the design." In addition, copyright law has long protected the physical plans and designs themselves from being copied. Therefore, this case would actually involve two copyrights, one in the conceptual design itself and another in the physical representations of that design.

Uncluttered, the materials are standard law, the interior is modern, uncluttered, almost minimalist (no citations, jargon).
Nice.

Who Owns the Copyright?

Paragraph 8- Main section, second room: Asks and answers questions and gives general reasons. Makes sense.

The second question is who owns the copyright to this work. The answer is that you own it. Although corporations sometimes own the copyright to works which they pay to have created, that should not be the case in this situation because you were an independent contractor rather than a salaried employee.

Paragraph 9- An attractive furniture arrangement: gives the factors supporting my classification as an independent contractor from among a list of factors developed by the courts, including where the design work was performed, who had control over the work schedule and assistants, if any, and whether the design services the service was part of the corporation's normal business

Courts have said that corporations own the copyrights to works created by salaried employees, but not to the copyrights to works created by independent contractors. Courts distinguish between the two types of relationships by looking at a list of factors which indicate how independent the creator was from the corporation. In your case, these factors show that you were quite independent. You worked in your own offices in London rather than a ProTech office, you set your own work schedule rather than reporting to work when told to do so, you worked with ProTech on only this one project, you had complete control over hiring any assistants, and you performed a service for ProTech that is not part of their normal business trade. All of these characteristics show that you were an independent contractor. Therefore you should own the copyright to your work. In researching this conclusion I am assuming that the proposal you presented to ProTech was your original work. If you have any question as to whether that is true, please let me know right away, as that could change the situation.

What Rights Does Copyright Ownership Give You?

Paragraph 10- Main section, third room: Elaborates on good news, what rights copyright gives, and returns to the theme—potential copyright infringement actions. Materials are consistently uncluttered and accessible.

The third question is what rights your ownership of the copyright gives you. The answer is that you have three rights: you may prevent others from (1) reproducing your work, (2) distributing copies of your work to the public, and (3) preparing derivative works based on your work. All three of these rights may have been infringed in this case. Reproducing a work means creating any reproduction of you work in any tangible medium, such as a design drawing. Distribution to the public means showing these reproductions to anything more than a very limited private audience. Publication in a magazine would be a distribution to the public. Preparing a derivative work means adapting the original work to fit another medium or format. Building a structure from your design-drawings would be considered creation of a derivative work. Therefore, Ikopi has infringed your rights if he has used our work in any of these ways.

Proportion is increasing as information about the main theme emerges.

I follow. I like this room—I do have rights.

Did Ikopi Infringe Your Rights?

Paragraph 11- Main section, fourth room: Turns attention to the central theme by giving full paragraph to a reminder of both theme and practical need to see works.

The fourth question is whether or not Ikopi did in fact copy your work. I cannot yet give you an answer to this question because I have not yet seen the two works. However, based on your description of the Architectural Digest article, I am hopeful that we can prove this element of the case.

Paragraph 12- Large furniture arrangement here: Analyzes whether Ikopi infringed on Neil Smith's copyright by focusing on the two criteria, access and substantial similarity, used by the courts to infer copyright infringement.

Since direct evidence of infringement is almost impossible to collect (we would have to find someone who would testify in court that he or she actually saw Ikopi copy your plans), courts will infer copying where the plaintiff shows two things: access and substantial similarity. Access is defined as an "opportunity to view" the work that was allegedly copied. We should not have trouble convincing a judge or jury that Ikopi had an opportunity to see your materials once we show that you gave copies of your work to his partner at the ProTech board meeting.

Paragraph 13 - Largest piece of furniture: substantial similarity. Analyzes most difficult element by devoting long paragraph to it. Proportion seems appropriate.

Substantial similarity is the aspect of this case about which I cannot yet give solid answers because I have not yet seen the works. I will tell you a bit about this step of the case generally for now, and then we will discuss it more specifically as soon as I have had a chance to look at the two works. The test for finding substantial similarity is a vague one. Basically, although the two works do not have to be identical for the court to find that one was copied from the other, the similarities must be more than slight or trivial. Therefore, if virtually every aspect of Ikopi's building is exactly the same as your design, you have a good chance of proving that he copied your work. But each difference between your design and his reduces the chance of winning the case. If you have no objection, I will arrange to have a messenger pick up copies of your designs and the Architectural Digest article from your office so that we may discuss this aspect of the case in detail when we talk.

<u>What Relief Can You Sue For?</u>

The fifth question is what relief you may ask for from the court. The answer is that you may ask for both actual damages and an injunction against future infringement by Ikopi. Actual damages would be a monetary award designed to compensate you for the amount of loss you suffered because of Ikopi's infringement. This award would be based on the injury Ikopi caused to the market value of your work. For instance, if ProTech no longer wanted to build from your designs, you could be awarded the amount that you would have profited had they used your design as originally planned. The second type of relief, an injunction, would prevent Ikopi from future use of any design aspect copied from you. Such an injunction, however, would probably not prevent completion of the building currently under construction. Judges are reluctant to order the destruction of useful buildings. Instead of extending the injunction to the current construction project, the court would probably add to your monetary award to compensate for this use of your work. Most likely, Ikopi would be forced to turn over his profit from this project to you.

As you may know, there are other forms of relief available in some copyright cases. Awards of attorney's fees and awards of special statutorily determined monetary damages are sometimes granted. Unfortunately, these are not available in this case. Because your copyright was not registered at the time it was infringed, American copyright law does not offer you these special types of damages. The law has this restriction because of a compromise between traditional American copyright law (which required all works to be registered) and an international agreement to which the U.S. became a party which requires the U.S. to give protection without registration). The resulting system offers you copyright protection without registering, but prevents you from receiving some desirable forms of relief in infringement actions. However, you should not be discouraged from pursuing your suit because of this limitation. Both actual damages and injunctions are significant forms of relief. I mention this limitation merely so that you would not be confused if you had read about other copyright infringement cases which involved awards of attorneys' fees or statutory damages.

Paragraph 14- Main section, fifth room: Moving toward the back part of the building, this analyzes the remedies available to me should copyright infringement be established.

Furniture arrangement of possible remedies. Proportion is large, which gives hope for some possible results.

Paragraph 15- Another furniture arrangement, to the side. Attractive, but not suitable. Needs a bit of explaining, so proportion is a bit too long for something not functional. Analyzes award of attorney's fees or special statutorily determined monetary damages and determines they are not available in this case. OK, I get it.

Is this Case Likely to Succeed?

Paragraph 16- Last room of the house: Summarizes the primary issues and assesses the likelihood of success on the case. Restates the theme.

As I said above, I cannot be certain in my advice until I see your designs and Ikopi's work. However, if the works have very few differences, you have a good chance to succeed because there is the strong evidence that you were an independent contractor and because it will not be hard to establish that Ikopi had access to your work before "creating" his.

Paragraph 17- Back Entrance: suggests practical directions. Closes discussion. I'm ready to leave.

At this point you must decide how you wish to proceed. Please note that we have many options; we may pursue remedies short of full scale litigation if you would prefer that option. I must advise you that this letter does not create any legal rights, but merely expresses my opinion. I will call you in a few days. In the meantime, I will send a messenger to pick up the materials which I need to see so that I may review them before we talk. I look forward to speaking to you soon.

Sincerely,

Karen Litsinger
Attorney-at-Law

MOVING FROM OBSERVING CRITICALLY TO DESIGNING CAREFULLY

The more you experience the architecture of legal writing, the more ideas you get as an architect. Observing form and function forces you to break legal writing down to all of its elements and to see it as the result of a complex process. You realize how important are the landscaping, zoning requirements, and traditions. You also know you must honor basic matters such as physics and the nature of the materials themselves. Wood burns. Steel is less flexible than aluminum.

The remainder of this book is devoted to your work as a legal architect, the designer. As a designer, you are always negotiating meaning. Such negotiations should spark your most creative energies. Building documents amidst shaky terrain, changing minds, and dynamic materials requires you to be innovative, practical, careful, and quick. As a legal architect, you are all of those and more.

The great thing about being an architect is you can walk into your dreams.

-Harold E. Wagoner

CHAPTER 3

INVENTING THE THEME

The job of buildings is to improve human relations:
architecture must ease them, not make them worse.

– Ralph Erskine

What welcomes you into a building is often its theme, its statement. The theme may be *Relax elegantly* as in this French
country home. It may be *This building brings together all
nations,* as in the United Nations, *This building is itself a work of art*, as in

the Guggenheim, or *Let's have fun*, as in Philip Johnson's capricious works. The theme is the building's message and, as such, draws you in: *Do business here*, *Eat here*, or *Relax here*. You may not care nearly so much about its aesthetics as its practical use (the gym). Or you may visit it precisely because its architecture has been so beautiful as to redefine what follows (the Parthenon, the first skyscraper). A building can improve human relations when its theme harmonizes design elements. It is no coincidence that the ancient Chinese art of Feng Shui suggests setting, designing, constructing, and decorating buildings to improve human relations. Centuries of observation taught the Chinese the power of a well-designed building in easing human relations. A well-designed legal document can do the same thing.

Your document's design begins with its theme. This theme is a message, that precise question, answer, and reason in your memo; advice and justification in your letter; or final resolution in a negotiation. The theme unifies the document. All design elements in turn generate the theme and respond to it. By analyzing the rhetorical possibilities (the client, her needs, the document's size, point of view), the zoning requirements (genre and format), and the landscape (the context), you can invent a theme that unifies all the necessary parts. In turn, you can select materials (research), design the space (arrange the ideas), assign proportions to the parts (decide how long each subpart is), and design the interior (choose paragraph and sentence structure, phraseology, connecting devices) to carry out that theme.

"The principle of the Gothic architecture is infinity made imaginable"

-Samuel Taylor Coleridge

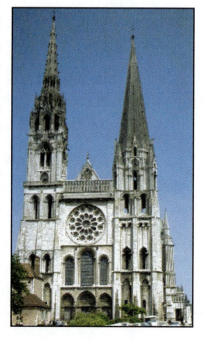

By inventing a unifying theme, you trigger the reader's memory and recognition and, by doing so, create the mechanism by which the reader processes your document. Because legal documents can be so complex, and because legal readers are often overloaded with information and work, your theme becomes a reader's essential tool. Readers can process one idea into which several other ideas fit more easily, and retain it longer, than processing several, separate ideas. Engage and keep your readers by inventing a theme that allows them to test and remember that theme throughout your document.

For example, this chapter's theme is *Invent a theme that unifies your document by incorporating all design elements*. That invention is a recursive process by which you discover both the parts and how to unify them; the theme is your starting point. When you begin a project with a theme in mind, you have an eye on coherence from the beginning. Then, as you discover the parts, you revise and hone that preliminary theme until it matches the structure. To assist you in inventing your theme, this chapter explores three sub-themes that help you discover your theme: 1) use the classical idea of *invention* to get started, 2) fuse classical with modern rhetorical elements to discover your theme, and 3) apply classical and modern elements to create specific writing techniques. You now have a general idea and a preview of the parts. As you read each part, you expect to see some justification for the part, some connection to the main theme. You remember more as you experience each part because you are relating it to a unified idea and to the other parts. You have probably already constructed three rooms and may wonder how they relate to each other. Your reader will similarly follow your theme's architectural directions.

Just so you know, the previous paragraph was revised a number of times before it matched the rest of the chapter. What I started out doing was different; the original theme was *Invent a theme that accounts for all parts of your document*. That seemed too mundane and did not pick up on either the ideas of the first chapters nor did it emphasize the critical importance of doing something smart right away, rather than exploring aimlessly until you settle on something. So I changed it to *Invent a theme that incorporates rhetorical elements and unifies design elements*. That picked up on the previous chapters but did not emphasize the timing point. I tried two more: *Your first task is to invent a theme, using a recursive process, that incorporates rhetorical elements and unifies design elements*. Too much, really. Then two other parts, because I just could not fit in the critical part about where arguments reside and that you have to start right away: *Inventing a theme is a recursive process by which you discover the fusion of rhetorical and design elements that unifies your document*. Its corollary theme is *To invent an effective theme, you need to start right away*. Too daunting, just like legal writing. I had to choose. Finally, I decided to emphasize the corollary in other ways, so both the theme and the parts united under it are fused.

USING
CLASSICAL INVENTION

As you develop your theme, you are *inventing*, in the classical sense, all of your arguments, positions, or ideas. You are discovering what result you seek, what facts are significant, what goals the client has in mind, what practical limitations exist. You are choosing ideas to advise your reader to negotiate a bargain or decide on a business deal. You are selecting ideas that connect to form your conclusions. Whether or not your document is overtly persuasive, you are also anticipating and refuting possible arguments. In other words, as you invent your theme, you are also discovering the reasoning, the thoughts themselves.

All buildings have foundations. Physics has not changed much since the Parthenon was built, but tastes and areas of emphasis have. The classical rhetoricians thought a great deal about how to research, organize, and communicate; how to transform the thinking of others; and how to prove a legal case. Some of the rhetorical physics of what they developed may still be useful to you as you approach a project.

Invention, in classical terms, was a system or method for finding arguments, not just an idea bestowed by a muse. In fact, the greatest proportion of classical rhetoric was devoted to explaining the various systems for finding the ideas that would make up the subject matter. This was not research in the traditional sense of simply finding some materials to work with; it was rather a way of thinking about the materials once they were found. In some cases, the speaker was simply *discovering* what was there, as in the case of witnesses, oaths, or testimonials. This was so-called *non-artistic appeal*: the materials were just there, waiting to be discovered. In other cases, the speaker was inventing arguments by appealing to reason, emotion, or ethics. This was the so-called *artistic appeal*: the speaker discovered these arguments, too, but by exploring specific topics or classes of arguments and by using his imagination. As a systematic way of generating ideas on a subject, *invention* suggested means by which a speaker could make sure he had covered all the possibilities for his argument. He had to start right away. He had to pick a topic and then use *invention* to prove or disprove it.

A Word on Classical Rhetoric

Systems for inventing themes emerge from rhetoric, which classically focused on persuasive speech and, some argue, writing. Many commentators suggest that all legal writing is persuasive. Whether or not it is, most genres within our community borrow some elements from rhetoric; probably all can glean techniques from studying it.

> rhetoric... 1: the art of speaking or writing effectively; *specif*: the study of principles and rules of composition formulated by critics of ancient times. 2a: skill in the effective use of speech.

MERRIAM-WEBSTER'S COLLEGIATE DICTIONARY 1004-5 (10th ed. 1993).

> *Rhetoric* is "the art of putting one's case in the strongest and best possible way... [It is a] combination of audience expectation and writers' desire to please that operates like a force of nature....This desire of writers to please—to communicate with their audiences—is the basic law of rhetoric."

ANTHONY C. WINKLER & JORAY MCCUEN, RHETORIC MADE PLAIN 4-5 (1988).

The rhetoric of law borrows elements from both classical and modern definitions. While the elements of classical rhetoric are not exhaustive or necessarily representative of the way lawyers view legal discourse, they are central to the manner in which lawyers construct it. And while they provide perhaps only reductionist and rudimentary means for solving human problems, these classical elements are nevertheless the forerunners of modern legal reasoning. Originally classified by Aristotle, they percolate through modern legal discourse. Knowing them well increases both your ability to interpret texts and to engage audiences by speaking and writing. Knowing them may help you discover your theme, the message you wish to send.

Invention was the speaker's topic, including his arguments; *arrangement* was the order he selected for presenting them, presumably for the greatest effect; the *style* was the particular choice and order of language and syntax, again to get the greatest effect; *memory* ensured that he owned the information so thoroughly that he could be commanding, yet spontaneous; and *delivery* included inflection, tone, physical gestures, posture, and eye contact, to gain and keep his listener's attention. Classical commentaries spent the most time on invention, which included the discovery of the topic and the arguments

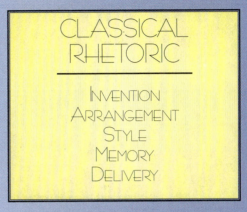

which could be used to explore it, ultimately to influence the audience. *See* EDWARD P.J. CORBETT, CLASSICAL RHETORIC FOR THE MODERN STUDENT 22–28 (1990).

Invention, according to the classical rhetoricians, required discovery by examining the topics, the places where arguments resided. This is how a theme emerged. *Definition* required that the meaning of key terms be explained; *comparison* set two or more things together for the purpose of studying their similarities and differences; *relationship* examined how one thing affected another, whether through cause and effect, antecedent and consequence, contraries, or contradictions; *circumstance* demonstrated that a proposed course of action was possible or impossible, that it had happened or would happen; and *testimony* argued through material gathered

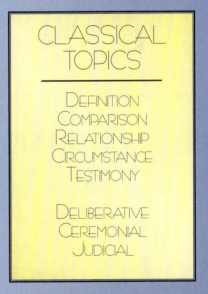

elsewhere, namely, *authority*, *testimonial*, *statistics*, *maxims*, *law*, and *precedent*.

Classical rhetoricians also identified three kinds of special topics. The first was *deliberative*, or political hortative: adversarial speech in which one deliberated about the future of public affairs or politics. It was concerned about the future; its special topics were the expedient and inexpedient, and its persuasive means were exhortation and dissuasion. Another was *ceremonial* oratory, also known as epideictic, demonstrative, or declamatory. This was the oratory of display and was the most literary. In this kind of oratory, the speaker was not so much concerned with persuading as with pleading with or inspiring the audience. It was concerned primarily with the present; its special topics were honor and dishonor, and its means were praise and blame. A third was *judicial* oratory, sometimes referred to as legal or forensic oratory. This was the oratory of the lawyers in the courtroom and it was the kind of discourse in which a person sought to defend or condemn some action. Forensic oratory was concerned with the past; its special topics were justice and injustice, its means accusation and defense. *See id.* at 28.

The classical rhetoricians, then, narrowly defined the rhetoric of law. Not only did legal rhetoric use *forensic* argument in the courtroom, but it also used the first of the two means of persuasion available to speaker, the *non-artistic*: laws, witnesses, contracts, tortures, and oaths. *See id.* at 22. So, for example, if politicians were suggesting that a tax be repealed, they quoted statistics, existing laws, historical documents, and the testimony of experts. They were not inventing those arguments; those arguments already existed and the speaker was simply presenting them. Thus the orator's research was that of searching, finding.

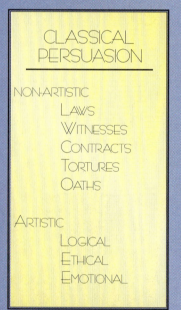

CLASSICAL
PERSUASION
────────────
NON-ARTISTIC
    LAWS
    WITNESSES
    CONTRACTS
    TORTURES
    OATHS

ARTISTIC
    LOGICAL
    ETHICAL
    EMOTIONAL

Classical lawyers also used the second kind of argument, the *artistic* proof, which appealed to the audience's sense of character (*ethos*), right and wrong (*pathos*), and reason (*logos*). Because legal rhetoric was usually classified as forensic oratory, then, theoretically, within accusation and defense, the lawyer might invoke *ethos*, *pathos*, and *logos*. All were part of invention.

Some of what we now consider legal writing was then considered "non-artistic," that is, not requiring the art of the orator. These documents stood by themselves; they did not need to be invented, only used. The orator did not have to create or invent supporting arguments, only find them in these documents or sworn-in entities. He needed only look them up. *See id.* at 22–23. Similarly, you may find standard, prescribed documents and use them as supporting evidence.

But if you are required to create these documents in the first place, you must be artistic in doing so. Even standard architectural forms, which guide you according to certain rules, facts, and laws, may require you to make artistic decisions. For example, your research, which includes finding these laws, facts, and witnesses, requires you to sort, cull, and synthesize those sources. Designing a standard contract may still require you to reorder the sections according to your ultimate purpose, and preparing witnesses requires you to ask questions in a carefully planned way.

Finding and deciding how to use these materials also requires you to see the context within which they will be used, the ultimate purpose of their use, and their cumulative effect on the audiences who will see them.   For example, you may be working on a document that has what appears to be a pre-ordained format, a contract for the sale of goods.   Your office may have created several of these kinds of documents and you may have selected one or two of the most recent versions on which to base your contract. Far from finished when you "discover"—in the classical sense—these two documents, you must begin the

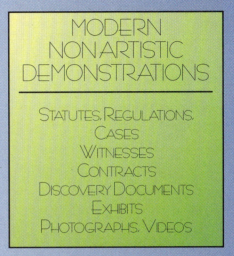

MODERN
NON ARTISTIC
DEMONSTRATIONS

STATUTES, REGULATIONS,
CASES
WITNESSES
CONTRACTS
DISCOVERY DOCUMENTS
EXHIBITS
PHOTOGRAPHS, VIDEOS

complicated task of researching the contract by reading it, researching and updating relevant law, researching why your colleagues drafted it this way. You may find, for example, that the substantive law requires special language, that a previous client added a provision not relevant for your current client, or that another party to the contract has been particularly sensitive to one provision in previous dealings. As a litigator, you will use the exhibits, photographs, or videos as they are, but you will investigate where and when they can be used most appropriately in your case, just as classical lawyers did.

Classical rhetoric, then, offers keys to comprehension that have been used in western thinking for centuries. In modern law practice, for example, if you think your theme may be that *Our client can sue the manufacturer under a products liability theory because the manufacturer did not exercise due care*, you can explore the topic, define your research, and structure your argument using these ancient topics. You can *define* the terms of art, "products liability" and "due care." You can *compare* this case with other cases where the circumstances were similar to measure the outcomes in those cases. You can show the *relationship* between the action and the injury, for example, that the first caused the second. You can give the reader context by explaining the *circumstance* in which the accident occurred, and you may use expert *testimony* to prove your case. You can invoke many aspects of classical rhetoric in your own invention.

It is this concept of invention that helps modern lawyers discover cogent themes. Through the discovery of a theme, the lawyer can explore materials, such as arguments, facts, laws, testimonies, and policies. This discovery process in turn redefines the theme. Classical rhetoric categorized the discovery process itself, seeing invention as an intellectual exploration of the theme. Thus invention was the major category in classical rhetoric. There resided all ideas, facts, laws, arguments, and circumstances that united to become a theme. Because the overall purpose of classical rhetoric was to persuade, more categories became helpful, categories that reveal some history of legal discourse. Such classical categories put legal writing in historical perspective: seeing where legal rhetoric fell in the classical scheme may awaken invention in a modern context.

You can do the same. By selecting a theme right away, you prepare yourself to read systematically, to *discover* the materials that prove or disprove your theme. You can then adjust accordingly. This recursive inventing process allows you to select a general theme, investigate its possibilities, revise it, investigate more, and so on until you settle on a theme that unifies the document. For example, you may have a desired theme after a client phones with a problem, such as, *My client does not have to pay the gift tax*. This theme works initially because it is the one the client wants to hear, and it is specific about what person, what tax, and what result. But the most important clause is missing, that following the sentence: *My client does not have to pay the gift tax because ....* To *discover* what to fill in, or to reverse the message because of your research findings, you could choose to follow the classical rhetoric system by *defining* the term of art, "gift tax," and thinking about how others might define it; *comparing* this situations with others; *relating* this situation to others, looking at such things as cause and effect, for example; examining what *circumstances* give rise to the payment or non-payment, to the gift or non-gift; and perhaps using other cases or law review

articles as *testimonials* to your thesis. This system gives you a template for exploring your theme, testing it, reviewing it, and refining it.

A theme may be general, such as *We agree to exchange goods for services because it is in our mutual interests*. It might be a theory of the case: *We cannot allow police activity to erode the Fourth Amendment because there is more at stake than drug wars* or *Drug trafficking requires us to make exceptions to the Fourth Amendment because it is unusually surreptitious activity*. Or it may be a specific message, such as *You are exempt from review by this agency because your activities occurred before 1998*. It might be the delivery of bad news:

You have to pay the tax because your activities fall within section 23(a) or *You have to pay a fine because you didn't file on time.* It might be a complicated conclusion: *Our client is exempt from the requirements because of an obscure regulation that has been adjudicated in only one case* or *Our client can win on a theory that borrows from and combines three doctrines previously uncombined.* It may not be a conclusion at all: *There's much more than what you thought here* or *We need to know if you want to continue with this negotiation.* Your theme may appear in the second sentence of a letter or in the conclusion of a brief. It might be a recommendation: *Our client should go into arbitration or he risks losing everything* or *Our client should carefully reconsider his case because no one has succeeded in pursuing his argument and our attempt will be costly in time and resources.*

Your theme may ultimately be implicit, as in a contract or statute: *We agree* or *That behavior is prohibited.* You can also make that message explicit: *We agree to restructure this debt* or *Peyote use is prohibited except in certain, specified religious rites.* You may indeed transform a general theme of *We agree* into a specific message of *You agree to pay us in timely, monthly installments or we will take back the goods.* Your

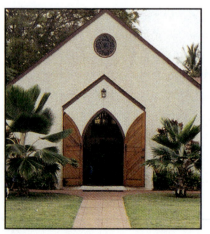

opening to a contract may also be a specific message, such as *Bank of Main Street agrees to restructure the debt and Allied Plumbing agrees to pay the debt in monthly installments.*

Wherever or however it appears, your theme is the document's entryway, the place your readers search for a message, a reason for reading the document, the idea that is new or unique about this communication. Your theme can also be an entryway for you, the writer, in this reader-oriented process. Sometimes your materials will yield an obvious theme an inevitable result that all researchers and readers would reach. This is rare. More often, as the expert, you invent the theme, to unify the document's disparate parts into one comprehensible message. If you leave the inventing to the reader, your document is harder to use. The document may contain the appropriate information, provisions, or arguments—all accurate and important pieces. But without a theme to give the parts coherence, the document is more like a landfill, not a building. The reader can see the information and even count the parts, but is unable to assemble them coherently.

To invent a theme, then, is to discover all of its parts and unify them. Your discovery includes searching for those aspects of your case that, if changed, would change the outcome. They may be factual, legal, or policy-oriented; they may be financial, negotiable, or interchangeable. As you research the document's possibilities (Chapter 4), you discover not only the materials you need, but some ideas about their configuration (Chapter 5). Together, these yield a theme that synthesizes the document's parts into a whole, accessible to all potential users.

This theme is so essential to a legal reader's understanding of the document that you may want to incorporate specific techniques for framing legal issues and, by doing so, discovering possible arguments or points for negotiation. You can use these techniques even when the final document does not explicitly state a theme. By using them, you can explore all questions raised in a certain situation and assure your client that you have thought of everything: past, present, and future. Some of these techniques are ancient, some modern, but all serve to get to the essence of your theme. Then, other elements of design follow. The more focused the theme, the more sharply purpose fuses with form, audience with interior design. Discovering the theme requires asking a series of questions that ensure appropriate exploring of facts, issues, and strategies. Inventing the theme requires patience and planning, a systematic approach to beginning a project.

INVENTING AS A MODERN LAWYER

As a modern lawyer who is often informing clients or preventing disputes, you can transform the vestiges of classical rhetoric and oratory into the design elements discussed in Chapters 1 and 2. Both the classical and new rhetoricians recognize that law is a specialized kind of rhetoric. You, the modern lawyer, are specifically situated within a community where you use certain developed means of presentation and argumentation, as Chapters 4 and 5 discuss in more detail. Thus you invent topics and analytical means or arguments peculiar to the legal discourse community in general and your local situation specifically. The law itself sometimes defines those arguments, whether they be rules of statutory interpretation, customs of analogous reasoning dictated by centuries of *stare decisis*, or local application of specialized rules of procedure. Your office may also prescribe methods for inventing your theme—*discovering* it, in the classical sense—including following decisions from policy-makers, traditions from the office practice, or preferences from individuals.

Architecture begins where engineering ends.

- Walter Gropius

More particularly, for a modern lawyer, inventing a theme means framing the issues accurately and answering them by giving the reasons. It means interviewing the client so that all aspects of a transaction are discovered. It also means exploring any argument that may arise when legal issues are raised. While the final document may select only some of these concepts to emphasize or explore, your inventing process carefully considers all of them. Inventing the theme, then, is a complicated path of discovering laws, arguments, policies, customs, and attitudes that surround a legal issue. This discovery can be unwieldy at best, out of control at worst. It requires recording, remembering, recalling, and re-forming these means of analysis into a theme comprehensible to any legal reader, lawyer or not. This is not easy. Such a process of discovering,

uncovering, rearranging, and generating information and ideas calls for a systematic approach. You can create your own approach, based on the elements of modern legal rhetoric.

Using Modern Rhetorical Elements to Invent the Theme

To determine a building's theme, the architect takes stock of the entire situation, particularly the foundation on which it will sit. You may similarly use the rhetorical elements to start building a legal document. Your answers to the rhetorical questions are the document's foundation.

Whether or not you know the theme ahead of time, you may want to check with your client or the assigning attorney to discover responses to these questions. Your initial "take" on a transaction may be perfectly valid, but may clash with your client's idea of the transaction's purpose. Your theory of the case may be brilliant but will not work with the trial judge hearing the case. Some architects make a similar mistake, designing their own idea of a house, ignoring the landscape and client's needs. If you wish to make your document useful to all audiences, whether they are non-lawyers, judges, or businesses, consider several points of view in discovering the answers to these rhetorical questions.

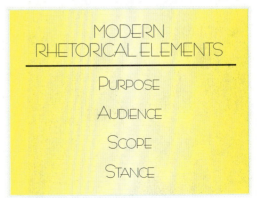

MODERN
RHETORICAL ELEMENTS
———————————
Purpose

Audience

Scope

Stance

If you are assigning a project, you may want to set it in the context of these rhetorical elements. Rather than just starting with the facts, you may want to put the project in context, discuss the rhetorical elements, and give a researcher an opportunity to ask about them. You can assign like this: *This is a very good client who is concerned about paying the tax. I think he's OK, but please confirm that. I want to keep his business. Write him a letter reassuring him, but don't make it too technical. Here is what happened. . . . I think the issue is probably. . . .* By giving a researcher that kind of information, you start the invention process.

If you are the researcher, you can ask questions that evoke this information—even before you hear the facts. Remember that reasonable minds may differ about the document's rhetorical elements, so you want to clarify them as soon as you can. You may think that the purpose of your letter is to deliver routine news to a client; your partner may see the letter's primary purpose as building business. You may think that the audience for your memo is a colleague in the law office; she may intend to send the memo to a client. Or you may think that your brief should exhaust all possible arguments; your partner may think it should use one direct argument and persuade by its brevity. You may think that you should take an aggressive stance toward a bothersome client; your colleague may suggest a conciliatory one, and so on.

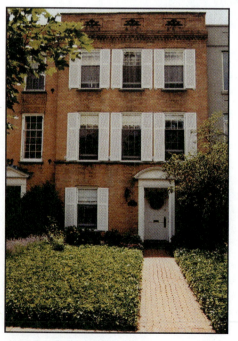

Your investigation of these rhetorical elements informs your theme. If your purpose is to inform a supervising attorney about law with which she is only vaguely familiar, your theme may be *It used to be true that Wisconsin prevented stacking of insurance policies, but now consumer interests have outweighed insurance company interests and consumers can buy as many insurance policies as they would like* or *What you thought was pretty settled law on insurance fraud just exploded.* If your purpose is to use a memo to set up a brief in the same cases, your memo theme may be *Our best theory is that this trend to allow consumers to buy whatever they want must stop because insurance companies can keep paying out at this rate* or *All bets are off; we can make new law on insurance*

fraud. Similarly, if your audience includes all parties to a transaction, your theme for a contract may be *We all agree that we will set up four franchises and share the profits and losses equally despite the risk that at least one of the franchises may not make a profit in the first two years*, but your letter to just your client might have the theme *You can have the franchise for two years, but you may experience heavy losses during all of that time.*

Scope questions frame research when they are accurately anticipated. If you are drafting a prospectus for a company, you must include all contingencies, and your research must include examining several prospectuses, interviewing your client extensively, and studying the business aspects thoroughly. Your theme may be *Invest in this because it is both socially conscious and will yield good results.* But if you are drafting a brief for a trial judge, you must limit your research to those matters the judge must consider, rarely more than that. There is simply no need to over-research the case and try to convince by a deluge of information. Your resulting theme may be *To decide in our favor is not to change the law at all.*

TECHNIQUES

• *Interview the assigning attorney.* Do this as vigorously as an architect interviews his client, and use a system for taking careful notes. By writing out the information as you take it in and transcribing it after it has been spoken, you may find inventing your theme becomes easier. For most modern lawyers, it is rarely sufficient just to make mental notes, for the mind slips and slides among too many projects, and brilliant thoughts dissipate. If you had only one project at a time to work on, you might be able to explore its questions without a system or without taking notes, but most lawyers—certainly many of the best writers—need to write out issues and explore them systematically. This part of your process is prewriting, more particularly getting started.

Working backwards from the readers' perspectives helps you measure your scope before you do more than you or your readers need.

Finally, thinking early on about your stance may also guide your invention. If your assigning attorney wants to discourage a client from taking a certain action, you may approach your research so that you can accurately justify that advice. If your letter to an agency seeks approval for a client's course of action, you may research under what circumstances they approve similar actions, what stance the agency itself takes in opinions on similar matters, and adjust your stance as you research.

You are the architect who thinks of the possibilities, but always with a mind on the function, client, size, and perspective on the building. And, as with many aspects of building, you cannot always know at this early stage all answers. Remember that the process is recursive; you are discovering your theme. The positions and arguments reside in the materials. You may have to adjust, just as the architect adjusts for an unexpectedly discovered water main or a shift in the client's needs. You may find adjusting easier if you have made some preliminary decisions on these rhetorical elements.

TECHNIQUES

• *Discover the rhetorical elements.* Whether you are asking directly or indirectly, find out as must as you can about purpose, audience, scope, and stance. You may infer this as you listen and then confirm it at the end of your interview: *So, as I understand it, we are writing a letter that delivers bad news to a valuable client whose business we want to keep.* You may have thought, as you listened, that this was going to be a long memo; make sure you confirm. So you would prefer that we put this in a long memo to the file... No? Ah, a short letter to the client. So we do not want to get technical, but want to include enough information that he understands both the bad news itself and our valiant efforts to have searched for good news—is that right? Include stance, which often goes unmentioned and creates a lot of editing later on. Is this a business transaction or more friendly? Is this client accustomed to informal exchanges or does he prefer a very formal letter? Like a good architect, you are already anticipating the materials you will gather, the size and setting of the building, and the nature of its users. Use the interview to glean everything you can about the rhetorical elements.

USING MODERN TOPICS TO INVENT THE THEME

Because legal work is so complex in combining information and law, custom and change, technical language and plain English, it helps to maneuver problem-solving intentionally and systematically. The rhetorical elements offer foundation for the project; the modern topics help you discover what parts go into the whole. To discover these parts, you may create your own system, or you may borrow from some systems here. Some more specific techniques are discussed in the last section of this chapter. The systems require you to be alert, deliberate, and concentrated during the first stages of inventing the theme, the crucial moment of first impression.

Many successful legal writers employ their systems immediately to take advantage of the fresh, first moment. Their systems resemble those suggested by the classical rhetoricians; these systems essentially use modern topics to discover facts, negotiating postures, arguments, and overall approaches. One system, for example, begins with a two-step process that examines first the facts, then reaches more specific legal questions of sub–issues, defenses, and relief (in litigation) or positions, business concerns, and results (in transactions). This system yields a starting point for your research and a legal framework for your discovery or construction of a transaction.

Exploring Modern Topic 1, the facts, allows you to separate and categorize your information, especially if you have a complicated document. You separate the facts into categories: *who, what, where, when, why,* and *how*. *See* CHRISTOPHER J. WREN & JILL R. WREN, THE LEGAL RESEARCH MANUAL: A GAME PLAN FOR LEGAL RESEARCH AND ANALYSIS 30 (2d ed. 1986). This system also helps you to discover what you have and what you do not have. By brainstorming through this list, you naturally raise questions that may not be obvious at the outset. As a lawyer, you need to have the fullest set of information possible, and this system permits you to collect it. By separating the purely factual from the legal, you prevent yourself from jumping to premature conclusions.

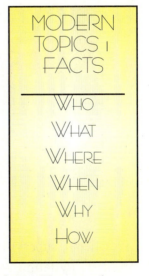

MODERN TOPICS 1
FACTS
___
WHO
WHAT
WHERE
WHEN
WHY
HOW

In a separate category, then, you can analyze the facts. You can choose from Modern Topics 2 and 3 (or more appropriate topics that you invent),

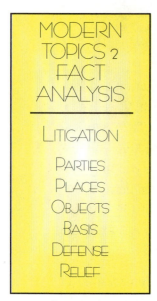

MODERN TOPICS 2 FACT ANALYSIS

LITIGATION

PARTIES
PLACES
OBJECTS
BASIS
DEFENSE
RELIEF

MODERN TOPICS 3 FACT ANALYSIS

TRANSACTIONS
PARTIES
POSITIONS
BUSINESS GOALS
AGREEMENTS
DISAGREEMENTS
TECHNICAL POINTS
RESULTS

depending on your practice. If you are doing litigation research, you can use a system that explores arguments according to the status of the parties, location of the incident, type of object involved, possible bases for causes of action, possible defense (these last two categories yield arguments) and relief.

If you are doing transactional research, you can use a system that explores parties, positions, business goals, agreements, disagreements, technical points, and desired results. You can also use a terms sheet, an interviewing document that serves as a checklist for all the questions you ask your client and for all the parts that should appear in the document. By initially analyzing according to a system, your invention process proceeds carefully and thoroughly. You discover your document's parts in relation to your theme and see their relationships to each other. You start connecting parts. Such an approach both focuses your discovery of the appropriate law or contract provisions and hastens your process. You search purposefully.

Heredity is a strong factor, even in architecture. Necessity first mothered invention. Now invention has little ones of her own, and they look just like Grandma.

—E.B. White

KNOWING THE THEME AHEAD OF TIME

Clients, supervising attorneys, and colleagues may make your invention easy by telling you the theme. They may have thought through the problem, may have decided about its outcome, or may know something more about the topic than you do. They therefore may present you with a

message and ask you to write it up. Sometimes this works. For example, this may be the fourth contract forming a limited liability company that has been done in the last week. They may ask you to find the last one, take out the old client's name, and put in the new client's name. Either way, the theme will be *The parties agree to form a limited liability company under the Maryland Limited Liability Company Act and its amendments.* Or you may be filing a motion for summary judgment and the pre-ordained theme may be *This court should find in our favor because the parties do not dispute the material facts and we are entitled to judgment as a matter of law.*

Beware. These are very general themes. They may work. Substituting new names for the old ones may work, but using such generic themes makes it hard on the reader. What distinguishes this document from any other agreement or motion? How can the reader remember the document? How can he organize the information so as to make it useful? Your *purpose* reappears here. Some lawyers will argue that their purpose is to make the information obscure or inaccessible. If so, a vague theme works. If your purpose is to clarify or persuade, you might need something more specific, such as *We are entitled to judgment as a matter of law under ERISA because we have not breached any fiduciary duties* or *Because Ms. Smith failed to file her claim within the statute of limitations time period, we are entitled to judgment as*

In architecture as in all other operative arts, the end must direct the operation. The end is to build well. Well building hath three conditions: commodity, firmness, and delight.

—Sir Henry Wotton

a matter of law. Your ability to frame the theme precisely requires you to know the case yourself, to know its nuances, and to synthesize all aspects of the document.

To do all of this well, create a system for validating the theme you have been directed to present. This "pre-ordained theme" situation recalls those papers where the teacher gave you the topic; few people got an "A" for literally following directions, for really telling what they did on their summer vacation. The "A"s often went to those who transformed one aspect into a short story or created a poem to capture the essence of summer. You, too, may have been given a theme and your assignment, for the purposes of time and efficiency, is not to change it. Fine. Just make sure you understand what you are perpetuating so that you can do the task well. Use your judgment to analyze whether or not you should be transforming the document into a more original piece.

For example, you may be asked to design a limited liability contract. You do so by pulling out the most recent form and substituting names. You read through it once, it looks good, you finish. What you do not notice, because you are eager to follow directions, is that the percentage interests are different than in the last contract. More subtly, you do not notice that the managing member has a limited term. In other words, you must know the transaction well enough to account for different details and to reconcile them with the whole. Similarly, you may be writing a complaint for a client who has filed similar complaints in five other jurisdictions. You take the most recent complaint, copy it, and are ready to file. What you did not *discover* is that the standard of review is different in this state, which requires a different strategy to win, a strategy that starts with the complaint.

In a sense, then, you must still invent or re-invent the theme, unless you are sure of its similarity to other documents. Distinguish between apprenticeship and creativity here. There are times when the advice you get comes from an expert whose specific directions will take you on the proper path. Ask enough questions to assure yourself of that, and then do the job. Other times, the assigning source, whether client or supervisor, is not sure, assumes that this case is similar to others, and gives you directions accordingly. Use the techniques suggested below to protect your client and yourself, to make sure that your invention comports with the situation. One test you may find useful is the context-independent test: can you answer, without anyone around, all the questions about this document? Can you recognize the theme even if you haven't seen the document in six months? Do you know why you are wrote what you wrote? Can you justify each sentence? If you are particularly new, use your own time to study documents in this way; that is, understand and justify each sentence until you see the design elements as discussed in Chapter 2. Then you will be more sure of what to do when someone gives you your answer ahead of time.

Not Knowing the Theme Ahead of Time

Some clients are more vague. An architects who is designing a building for the undecided client or in an unexcavated landscape proceeds differently. He negotiates meaning. As he surveys the landscape, researches the zoning requirements, and tries to understand the client's desires, he allows himself to watch the theme emerge. He may have thought he was building a one-story, three-bedroom house. He may end up building a two-story, five-bedroom house, one that accommodates a den and an exercise room. Similarly, if you are inventing the theme as you go, such as in developing a theory of liability or structuring a transaction or drafting a judicial opinion, use techniques that help you explore your topics systematically. In this "What should I do?" scenario painted by your client, you carry the burden of sorting out the facts, the legal issues, prospective problems, and unmentioned circumstances. Cut a path through the unknown by anticipating the possibilities.

Some lawyers are able to discover their documents' themes and accompanying designs in their heads. They think about them and produce brilliant documents. Mozart could not write fast enough to keep up with the music pouring out of his brain and Schubert grabbed place mats in bars to compose some of his finest songs. Frank Lloyd Wright designed Falling Water in one-and-one-half hours, though after months of anticipatory thinking. Indeed, some projects may seem to write themselves. It is the difficult projects that call for systematic paths to discover the theme.

In writing process terms, you are in the midst of prewriting when you begin a document. Everything that happens between the time you receive the information and the time you actually start drafting is prewriting. Systems for prewriting are as varied as the people who use them. The only constant is that most good writers have a system. What follows are some suggestions from successful legal writers, systems that allow you to discover your possibilities and invent an appropriate theme.

Beginning a legal writing project without knowing the theme requires both a sense of adventure and a sense of restraint. Usually, the situation calls for careful weighing of several factors, including time, cost, and experience level, not to say materials and form. Restraint is appropriate, but many lawyers are so restrained as to prepare nearly identical documents, without thinking. While this approach seems safe in the short term, it can be dangerous in the long term.

Restrained adventure may yield better results. By being aware of the role that theme plays in unifying all parts of the document, you may be able to honor both tradition and local terrain. You can incorporate what is known, but think about it. You can decide what to keep or omit, add or subtract, change or leave alone by investigating the contents through the theme. By using the theme, you make each document self-sufficient; you also train yourself to be a versatile architect. You may even manage to give voice, direction, and energy to your document. You will have time because you will see the document differently; you will see the whole as you gather the parts.

You may find the theme to be your most powerful way of discovering the document's materials, form, proportion, and even interior design. Begin each project as though it were brand new. Begin with the familiar and then reshape the materials to create a document that honors the old but is shaped for the situation. The key to both is beginning immediately and using techniques that get you off the mark quickly.

TECHNIQUES FOR PREWRITING

- Analyzing Rhetorical Elements
- Collecting the Facts
- Analyzing the Facts
- Formulating the preliminary issues
  - Getting the client to clarify the issues
  - Getting the assigning attorney to clarify the issues.
- Researching
- Talking to Others
- Taking Notes
- Organizing
- Outlining
- "Percolating"
- Addressing Practical Matters
  - Determining the due date
  - Determining the amount of time to be put into the project
  - Determining the amount of resources the client is willing to put the project
  - Measuring how the project fits in with other projects
  - Determining how much turn-around time must be factored into the time line
  - Determining own level of expertise on the topic

USING MODERN
TECHNIQUES TO INVENT
THE THEME

As a modern lawyer, you can create specific techniques for inventing your theme, techniques that incorporate the classical idea of invention as the major activity in developing discourse. By using modern topics that duplicate and extend the classical topics, you can structure and discipline your discovery process. By analyzing the type of discourse you are working within, you can frame your document's form from the start. These techniques, used consciously or unconsciously by some of the finest modern legal writers, use the early stages of document development to invent, discover, create, and analyze the best possible choices. Using the theme as the focal point, these techniques allow you to explore all aspects of the writing situation, from facts to business preferences, from arguments to negotiating stances. As a part of your prewriting, these techniques take advantage of your freshest moments and help you to own the information with confidence and creativity.

Like a good architect, you can use these techniques to precipitate appropriate ideas. You know that certain clients cannot afford an elaborate building, so you ask them the questions that will allow you to design the most effective building while making the least expenditure. You know that, before you start ordering building materials, you need to investigate the terrain, sketch the landscape, research the zoning laws, and check out the neighborhood. You also need to have a clear understanding of the building's function, its users, its size, and the direction its opening will face. You need to know how much the client can spend, when she wants it completed, and how she envisions it looking. As you listen, you are already sketching in your mind; you might be literally sketching the first drawings to compare them with her ideas. Knowing that you both want to minimize any phone tag or too much mind changing, you review together what you have, where you are going to start. Having experience with many clients who change their minds or give you unrealistic budgets or deadlines, you use particular techniques to get a reasonable agreement for both before you part. You also probably allow for expenses for changing your mind. Then you go to work.

When do you actually invent your theme? When do you decide what you are going to say? It may be early. You may have been given the theme by your client (*Get me out of this mess because I paid all my taxes on time*) or from a supervising attorney (*We move for summary judgment because*

we did not breach a fiduciary duty under ERISA). You may have to wait until you explore the problem more fully. You may have no idea what the theme is, just that your client wants to start a business or escape liability. It may come upon you early or late, especially with more abstract projects. You may, for example, have to invent a new theme, such as for an international client who wants to structure a business transaction between his company and a company in a newly-formed republic. Use techniques that leave you open to inventing the theme at the appropriate moment.

Classical lawyers did the same thing, using invention as a careful exploration of ideas. The topics offered a discipline of places to discover the theme. For modern purposes, those topics may be too limiting, although they survive as useful topics even to this day. The techniques in this section include those classical topics and offer others. The examples

TECHNIQUE

• *Collect the facts.* Take notes by separating the facts into the Modern Topic 1 Facts categories, Who, What, Where, When, Why, and How. As you interview or read or listen, you can fill in a chart or use the categories to take notes. As you take in the facts, use the modern topics to brainstorm what other facts you need. If the assigning attorney is not providing enough information about dates and sequences, use the When column to ask about those before you leave.

offered here are just that, examples of some of the many ways you can make the most of the very first part of your design process. See them as a point of departure, as is the spirit throughout this book. Only you can create the best techniques for yourself. These techniques come from experienced, successful lawyers, who, like experienced architects, see invention as perhaps the most critical stage in effective document design.

Your legal document usually starts with a phone call, e-mail, or a file plunked on your desk. You are seeing what situation your client is in, what kind of building you may need to build to protect, defend, or promote your client. How you take in the first bit of information can have a ripple effect on your entire process. This crucial moment of initial impact when the project hits your mind and your memory can have some order. You have several choices for exploring your theme; they all have in common the thorough examination of your ideas, from all sides, before you arrive at your final, precise theme.

Your moment of first impression is the cleanest, purest moment of your discovery process. When the information first hits your brain, you start to assemble it into your own schema. You start to make sense out of it. Your translation of the information then is re-translated as you think, question, analyze, invent. If you are systematic about taking the information in, your re-translation has a better chance of making sense to your reader. You have a better chance of inventing a cogent, coherent theme. You may find that your closest ally is writing, both at the moment of first impression and throughout your inventing process.

Unfortunately, a very popular method for intake in law offices is to listen as someone gives the information orally. While this method may be friendly, it is, in fact, the least efficient form of information transfer. You have played telephone. By the time the information gets reprocessed, it can become inaccurate. By the time it is turned into a draft, several other theories, directions, or tangents may have been explored. The assigning attorney wonders what the writer has been doing. Of course, the writer wonders what the assigning attorney was doing. The moment of first impression was fuzzy, especially if it was complicated by any hazing or power games, tests of whether or not a new attorney can "figure it out."

Instead, interview the attorney using the design elements, modern topics, or other categories suitable to the project. Find out what you can about rhetorical, practical, and architectural elements. You may want to create a checklist or charts you can fill in as you listen. The design elements give you a schema for asking appropriate questions and making the most use of your valuable time together.

Whether you are interviewing an attorney, reading an e-mail, or talking to a client, start categorizing the information so that you can own it well enough to work flexibly with it. Many successful legal writers begin by taking notes of some kind, whether they are notes on a legal pad as the assigning attorney is talking, notes on the computer as they are transferring information in from an e-mail, or notes on an interviewing document as the client is speaking.

Example 3.1. Using Written Instructions for a Memo.

You can use Modern Topics 1 with the following memo.

MEMO

To: Associate

From: Jill Ramsfield

Re: Laffon – copyright of derivative work, File No. 05–843

Date: June 18, 2000

Monsieur Edouard Laffon just telephoned me with a question about one of his newest works of art. He would like to copyright the piece in order to protect it from being copied, but he is not sure that he can do so under U.S. copyright law.

Laffon is a naturalized U.S. citizen, who brought his studio to the United States about five years ago. In France, he enjoyed a reputation as an avant-garde artist who mixed some Daliesque surrealist touches with Warhol-like streaks of sacrilege. That reputation was well-established in France, but he came to the U.S. to escape France's exorbitant tax rates and to find "fresh ideas." Once here, he grew accustomed to the lifestyle, traveled throughout the country, and made his home in New York in 1989. Since then, he has exhibited at a few galleries in New York, Santa Fe, and here, and has sold one or two major pieces to collectors.

Two days ago, Laffon finished his newest piece, a sculpture of Meryl Streep, his favorite actress. The sculpture is entitled, "Four Meryls," reminiscent of the Andy Warhol piece featuring Marilyn Monroe. The sculpture rests in a rectangular frame which is hung on a wall to resemble a painting, but the figures in the "painting" are three-dimensional. There are four quadrants that contain sculptures of Meryl Streep's face, each in a different-colored background, just as Warhol's "Four Marilyns" showed four Marilyn faces in different colors. Laffon intentionally created this piece to remind its admirers of the Warhol piece, but he has changed Warhol's piece in order to make a different statement. Laffon has sculpted different facial expressions on the face in each quadrant, to show the emotions that the actress expresses, while Warhol's "Marilyn" used four identical faces. Rather than the loud and vibrant colors used in Warhol's piece, Laffon has used realistic tones that vary from quadrant to quadrant, depending on the emotion expressed by that face.

M. Laffon would like to copyright his work; however, he is afraid that because it is derived from a piece by another artist, he will not be able to do so. That would leave Laffon without any legal recourse if anyone were to copy his sculpture. If he cannot copyright it, he will refuse to display the piece rather than risk exploitation.

Please provide me with a memo discussing whether or not M. Laffon may copyright "Four Meryls." I think the Warhol piece is in the public domain, so there is no question of copyright infringement. I would like to see the results of your research by September 6 so that I can keep track of the case. Please have a draft of the memo to me by September 13 so we can report to M. Laffon before October. Thank you.

Using the Modern Topics 1 to collect the facts you have and brainstorm the ones you do not, your notes on this case might look like the following chart:

WHO	WHAT	WHERE	WHEN	WHY	HOW
Edouard Laffon reputation avant-garde	derivative work	Seattle - created in US.	6/18/00 - created How long to create?	To remind admirers of the Warhol piece while making a different statement	Four quadrants with realistic tones
	Sculpture "Four Meryls" 3-D variation in faces, realistic tones, Dali-esque, "Warhol-like"	Naturalized U.S. citizen from France. Five years ago came to U.S.		fresh enough? Escape tax rates and find 'fresh ideas'	Sculpture Variations in faces
Andy Warhol's estate?	"Four Marilyns" painting loud colors vibrant colors identical faces	In public domain? (c)? In U.S? Is timing a factor?		Sculpture diff from painting? Part of statement?	Each face in a different colored background using loud and vibrant colors
Marilyn Monroe?					faces identical
Meryl Streep	How different?			3-D difference matter?	painting
Potential copiers					

Example 3.2 Chart for Collecting the facts

Using these techniques is a generative process. That is, you see not only what facts you have but also what facts you do not have. Rather than giving you just a literal summary, this technique allows you to think of what you do not have, to start your discovery process, to ask questions of the client while she is on the phone, or to prepare questions for the next meeting with the supervising attorney. This is significant. You have accomplished at least two steps in one. Also, many times, while you are working through a problem, you discover that the issues turn on information that was not initially known or considered important. This technique may allow you to anticipate that information. It also takes very little time. You can fill in this chart at the end of the day, while you are listening, or right after you take in the information. Allow your mind to expand and create before narrowing too much. The client or the assigning attorney may have been very specific and limited about the information, but often you need either a larger context to understand the issues, to spot other issues not yet recognized by them.

Then, once you have collected the information, you have to analyze it. This second step allows you to generate language that shapes your analysis throughout your process. You are not only inventing your topic and preparing to research, but you are also writing. By generating language here, you are preparing your text. Your selection and translation of terms begins when you fill in this chart. And, by writing out your terms, you are

TECHNIQUE

• *Analyze the facts.* You can create your own template to do this translation, preferably one that conforms to the practice area invoked by the facts. For example, if you do a lot of research in a certain publisher's system, you might want to use categories that conform with the publisher's system. If you are doing a transactional document, you might want to create a checklist for assembling the document. You can use the same technique: fill in the template. You can choose to use a system that matches the one your favorite publisher uses. The following is the system that most resembles West Publishing Company's system. If you prefer Lawyers' Coop, use Things, Acts, Persons, Places. *See* CHRISTOPHER J. WREN & JILL R. WREN, THE LEGAL RESEARCH MANUAL: A GAME PLAN FOR LEGAL RESEARCH AND ANALYSIS (2d ed. 1986).

Example 3.3. Chart for Analyzing the Facts

PARTIES	PLACES	OBJECTS	BASIS	DEFENSE	RELIEF
Edouard Laffon	New York state, U.S. federal	Sculpture, "Four Meryls"	U.S. copyright law? Case law?	Substantively changed Warhol's Four Meryls	Own copyright of Four Meryls
Andy Warhol's estate	France?	same as painting, "Four Marilyns"?	Derivative works	Prevent distribution of Four Meryls	Prevent distribution of Four Meryls
potential copiers		work fixed in a tangible medium	State copyright?	different medium?	
		Infringement?			
		colors neutral v. vibrant	Warhol?	public domain so OK	Prevent future copying
			artist's rights?		Preserve right to imitate but state different effect
			substantial similarity?	not substantially similar	

• *Compare the arguments.* You can also use a prewriting method that contrasts your client's situation with the opposing side's situation, or compares the strengths of your client's positions with those of another. Such contrast allows you to measure, as an architect does, the degree to which certain parts of the building need to be emphasized, the manner in which the materials need to be gathered. Your theme may begin to emerge in this contrasting process because, combined with the information about the rhetorical elements, these strengths and weaknesses start to suggest the result the client wants.

Example 3.4. Comparing the Arguments to Invent a Theme for a Memo.

Arguments for	Arguments against	Possible sources
Laffon's work makes a different statement than Warhol's; the work is original.	"Four Meryls" simply copies "Four Marilyns."	U.S.C.A.? Case law?
"Four Meryls" is original because it is a sculpture, not a painting like "Four Marilyns."	"Four Meryls" is not original; M. Laffon has simply copied "Four Marilyns" into a different medium, sculpture.	Case law interpreting U.S.C.A.? Definitions?
Not similar colors & neutral	Same idea, same quadrants	Nimmer on © Derivative works?
Same faces - different faces	Actress' face	Painting v. sculpture?
Idea v. expression	Color same faces diff; just reversed	2d cir? Color v. expression? 9th cir?

Preliminary Theme: M. Laffon can copyright "Four Meryls" because it is different enough to not be a derivative work.

triggering your memory. So, you receive four benefits from one task: invention, research, writing, and memory.

Setting the arguments in this fashion is a less formal method of exploring topics. A memo or brief lends itself to such a presentation of arguments. A contract, however, requires a different approach. In transactional work, your template must allow you to absorb and navigate a complex series of possibilities; you must also begin the project in such a way as to keep the document internally consistent.

TECHNIQUES FOR STARTING CONTRACTS

- *Use interviewing documents or checklists.* See if your law office already has one. Evaluate it for your needs by making sure it has covered all contingencies. Develop over time if you need to, thinking of all possible questions to ask the client.

- *Try to get client to identify issue.* Determine the limits of client's goals, e.g., borrow $50 million? Get a mortgage loan? Get a complete set of criteria from the client about parameters for making the deal.

- *Get partner to identify issue.* Make sure the assigning attorney has a good idea of the legal issues to be researched. Use any discussion to probe hidden legal issues that must be researched to build the document.

- *Balance business concerns against legal ones.* By focusing on the commitment letter, try to determine the business issues at stake and how they intersect with or challenge legal restrictions.

- *Evaluate the economics of the deal.* Try to determine how hard the client wants to negotiate to set up this transaction. Try to eliminate any irrelevant questions and get to the heart of the client's economic goals.

- *Research the forms.* Discover what forms exist for this type of transaction. You may want to get original drafts of forms before final matters were negotiated on those transactions. Make sure you gather at least three and study them for what they have in common, for what is specific to one transaction, and for what makes them internally consistent.

- *Then get the right "flavor" for the form.* Decide what pieces you must include, e.g., Parties; Price; Payment Schedule; Description of security, collateral; What the parties are agreeing to; Representations; Warranties; Time of performance; Conditions for execution; Remedies; Signatures; Date.

- *Create a library of master forms.* While you work on this project, keep in mind its category so you can create your own library.

- *Choose an organizational plan.* You have the same design choices with transactional work as with persuasive. Analyze the rhetorical value of organizing chronologically, typically, or by decreasing importance. You can create your own design for this type of document concentrating on the modern rhetorical elements.

Example 3.5. Interviewing Document for Transaction.

You may choose to be much more formal as you listen to the first information on about the document. A transactional document is often all-inclusive, and many questions are predictable but may be forgotten without the assistance of an interviewing document. Because such a document frees your mind from remembering what to ask, it may allow you to develop your theme as you listen. Before you are finished, you may have a good sense of exactly what the client wants the document to say.

[Borrower Name]

CONFIDENTIAL DRAFT

Term Sheet for Loan

<u>Important Notes</u>

(A)   THIS TERM SHEET DOES NOT CONSTITUTE AN OFFER OR A COMMITMENT AND IS INTENDED TO SERVE ONLY AS A BASIS FOR DISCUSSION OF THE MAJOR PROSPECTIVE TERMS THAT WOULD APPLY TO INVESTMENT IN THE PROJECT. THE DECISION TO INVEST IN THE PROJECT IS CONTINGENT ON THE APPROVAL OF MANAGEMENT AND THE EXECUTION OF FINAL DOCU-MENTATION IN FORM AND SUBSTANCE SATISFACTORY TO LENDER. THIS TERM SHEET IS NOT TO BE RELEASED TO ANY PARTY OTHER THAN TO THE BORROWER WITHOUT THE PRIOR WRITTEN CONSENT OF LENDER.

(13)   ALL FIGURES, TERMS AND CONDITIONS HEREOF ARE SUBJECT TO CHANGE.

1. Borrower
    [Borrower Name] (the "Company").

2. Project
    The construction and equipping of a [facility capacity] [facility name]' to be located in the [province] of [Country Name].

3. Sponsor(s)
    [Sponsor(s)' Name(s)] (the "Sponsor(s)").

4. Project Cost and Financial Plan
    The estimated total financing required for the Project is US$_____ million equivalent, including base cost, contingencies, provisions for escalation, working capital and financing charges during construction. The Financial Plan is made up of:

	US$ million (equivalent)	Percent
EQUITY		
[Sponsor Name]		
[Other Shareholder]		
Total Equity		
LOANS		
Loan		
Export Credits		
[Local Bank Loan]		

Total Loans
        [Cash Generation]
        Total Financing

5. Letter of Information

A letter of information, providing a detailed description of the Company, the Project and the Financial Plan and certain representations and warranties concerning the Company, shall be submitted to Lender by the Company before presentation of the Project to Lender's Management for approval.

6. Principal

   a. Loan Agreement between Lender and the Company Documentation providing, inter alia, for the Loan.
   b. Share Retention Agreement between the Company, X and Lender providing for the undertaking of X not to dispose of its shares in the Company until the Loan is fully repaid.
   c. Guarantee Agreement between Guarantor and Lender for the guarantee by Guarantor of the Loan.
   d. Security documents.

7. Loan Amount

Ten million Dollars (US$10,000,000).

8. Repayment Terms

20 approximately equal semi–annual installments payable on October 15 and April 1 in each year, commencing on April 15, 1999.

9. Prepayment

Prepayable in whole or in part, upon Loan not less than 45 days' notice; in case of partial prepayment, amounts prepaid will be applied to the outstanding repayment installments on pro rata basis. There will be no premium on prepayment.

10. Interest Rate

5% per annum, above 6 months LIBOR.

11. **Default Interest**

   2% per annum over normal interest rate or such higher rate charged by other lenders.

12. **Interest Payment Dates**

   Interest payable semi-annually on October 15 and April 15 in each year.

13. **Commitment Fee**

   $1/2$% per annum on so much of the Loan as shall not have been disbursed to the Company, commencing to accrue on the date of the Loan Agreement.

14. **Front-end Fee**

   1% of Loan amount.

15. **Estimated Date for Signature of Loan Agreement**

   March 1999.

16. **Security**

   The Loan will be secured by a mortgage on all Immovable assets of the Company (collectively, the "Security").

17. **Conditions for Disbursement**

   a. The front-end fee and all amounts immediately due under the Loan Agreement shall have been paid by the Company.
   b. No Event of Default or Potential Event of Default shall have occurred and be continuing.
   c. All governmental, corporate and other consents and approvals necessary for Lender's investment, the Project, the Financial Plan, and the Security shall have been obtained.
   d. The Security shall have been duly executed and perfected.
   e. Lender shall have received a legal opinion, in form and substance satisfactory to it.

18. **Covenants**

   a. <u>Affirmative Covenants</u>:
   (i) carry out the Project and conduct its business with due diligence;
   (ii) install an accounting, management information and cost control system satisfactory to Lender;
   (iii) appoint auditors satisfactory to Lender;
   (iv) provide information required by Lender;
   (v) maintain in force the Security and consents and approvals referred to above;
   (vi) provide financial statements quarterly and at the end of each fiscal year;
   (vii) proceeds of Loan disbursement to be applied only to Project.

19. **Events of Default**

   a. non–payment of principal interest or any other amounts due in respect of the Loan;
   b. failure to perform any obligation under Loan Agreement;

c. any representation or warranty found to be incorrect;

d. expropriation seizure or nationalization of property or other assets;

e. bankruptcy, insolvency or liquidation of Company or any of its property or assets;

f. non–payment of any other indebtedness under any other loan agreement;

g. security no longer in effect or loses its priority.

20. Jurisdiction
Non–Exclusive Jurisdiction of the courts of the Country.

TECHNIQUES

- *Ask for written directions.* To the extent that it is possible, request your client or your supervising attorney to write out the assignment. If you assign anything and want better results, then do the same: write it out. The minutes spent at this crucial moment of first impression are usually saved in mistakes or backtracking later. Use e-mail or dictate, but try to transcribe and organize the initial information.

- *Write out the facts and have them checked.* If you receive the information from a client or supervising attorney, transcribe and organize them so that you are sure of their completeness and validity. Use them for your own purposes in understanding the document; if you are unsure, have them checked.

- *Write out the theme, including any specific issues and answers, and have it checked.* To make sure you understand the theme, put it into your own written words. Keep amending it as you work, and if the amendments are significant, have it checked by the supervising attorney. This will ensure that you both have the same focus.

- *Brainstorm.* Use a systematic technique to separate facts, such as *who, what, when, where, why, how* or an interviewing document. Let your mind go as you fill in the categories. Think not only of what you have but of what you do not have. Just let the mind go; it will generate questions as well as categorize information. Then analyze the facts, using a system such as parties, places, objects, basis, defense, relief or things, acts, persons, places.   In these categories brainstorm terms of art, that is, translate factual information into search terms. It is best to separate these steps so that facts and legal language--and the relationship between the two--remain precise.

- Write down ideas as quickly as they come to you.
- Use short kernels of ideas, not long phrases--just enough to capture and recall the idea and move on.
- Avoid discussing ideas, in your own mind or with others. Just let them flow.
- Avoid judging the idea's value, singly or in relation to other ideas. Keep going.
- Set a specified period of time, such as fifteen minutes. Work with the clock.

- *Interview the audience himself.* If it is a partner, create an interviewing checklist, perhaps using some of the categories listed in the brainstorming technique.   If it is a client, create a list of possible questions, especially about the facts.   If it is a client in a transactional setting, use a term sheet to make sure all parts of the transaction are covered.   Also ask what forms, conventions, or procedures that person prefers.

- *Discuss the audience with the assigning attorney.* How experienced or expert is that audience? How much information do we have? Has there been response to any other writing by that same audience?

- *Interview people who have written for that audience before.* Experienced writers can often describe the features necessary to write for a particular audience. They might know the foibles of a client (Just the bottom line, no details) or of a supervising attorney (cover all the bases). Incorporate their experience into your invention.

- *Write down the page limit you would want for this document if you were the primary reader.* This limit should derive from audience and help you define the scope of your research. For example, if you are writing for a trial judge, put down the number of pages you think she would read on this topic.

- *Estimate the number of appropriate sources before you research.* Is it appropriate to include secondary authority, treaties, or esoteric documents? Is it appropriate to use anything beyond the jurisdiction in which the question arose? While your research will give you a definitive answer, it may help you to control your research if you think first about how this document might look even if you have no experience in it. Remember you know more than you think you know.

- *Select, prepare, and repair forms.* If you are using forms, think ahead of time about how you will research them. What should they contain, how many will you get, and how will you decide what to take from each? Think about the audience as you do this so that you remember consistency, wholeness, coherence, right from the outset.

- **Write out all preliminary question or legal issues. For the latter, include law, legal question, legally significant facts. These are the keys to your theme. What is being asked? How might the questions either break down or be united under one theme?**

- *Before you write, consider the level of detail that will be appropriate for the audience.* Do they want a law review article? Or do they want practical information with enough authority to justify the results? Carefully calculate how big this house should be.

CLASSICAL RHETORIC: MEMORY

In classical Greek oratory, an early mnemonic device was based on an architectural metaphor. As the person seeking to memorize worked through the information or argument, he walked through his house and assigned pieces of data to different objects in rooms. Because he knew his own house very well, this gave a concrete and easily remembered framework into which he could put his information. The trick was to assign objects to ideas or facts based on some similarity between the two, no matter how attenuated. The process of seeing the similarity would precipitate the memorization.

Whatever approach you develop, the idea remains the same: that you are systematic and thorough in examining, developing, and investigating the information you receive. With thorough understanding of the information you have received, you are starting to commit your project to that part of your memory that can analyze the information accurately. By the end of your intake process, you should have collected enough information to decide on the preliminary issues. Whatever method you use for gathering information, your goal is the same: to remember.

In classical rhetoric, memory referred to memorizing, something that became less important as the written word became more important. Orators trained through constant practice, but also used mnemonic devices to remember. These charts, lists, and the arguments and topics you discover serve similarly to make an imprint on your memory. While you do not have to memorize a speech, you do have to keep your various projects clearly framed in your mind. For most of us, our memories are simply not trained as well as those of classical orators. Relying on someone else's writing, by doing such things as highlighting and nothing else, can rob us of memory, especially when we are overloaded with several projects. By transcribing or rephrasing them ourselves, we activate memory. So, brainstorming language using any of the above techniques offers at least three advantages:

1)   generating search terms;
2)   categorizing information for future reference; and
3)   identifying terms that may be placed strategically in headings, sentences, and paragraphs to develop the theme, connect concepts, or emphasize points.

Be careful, of course, not to get "set" on a theme in these early stages. Even if the assigning attorney has been quite explicit about the information, you may discover facts later that change perspective. Even if you are sure you can construct a reliable transaction, the law may have changed since you last constructed a similar one. You still have to check. These techniques give you a firm grasp on the information so that you can remember it well and judge it accordingly as you proceed to develop the theme. Whatever approach you develop, the idea remains the same: that you are systematic and thorough in examining, developing, and investigating the information you receive. With thorough understanding of the information you have received, you are starting to commit your project to that part of your memory that can analyze the information accurately. By the end of your intake process, you are ready to take the next step in developing the theme: deciding on the preliminary issues.

Framing the Preliminary Issues

Framing your preliminary issues, whether they become explicit or implicit in your document, shapes your research, your thinking, and ultimately your design of the document. These questions, written out, talk to you. They demonstrate exactly in what direction you are heading analytically. If your invention is left as a noun, e.g., *derivative work*, *gift tax*, or *products liability*, it is probably too general and vague for effective note-taking, analysis, and composition. Even if you are doing a general policy paper or a contract, you can formulate the issues to help focus the aspects of your case.

You can frame your preliminary issues in three parts. These three parts are the general law, the legal question, and the legally significant facts. The general law is that law under which you are asking the question, such as section 2503(e) of the tax code, or New Jersey law on products liability. Sometimes this is one statutory provision; sometimes it is a series of cases that develop a doctrine. The legal question is that part without which an issue statement does not exist; it is the subject, verb, and object of the question, for example, *does our client have to pay the gift tax?* or *did the malfunctioning of the butane pipe cause an injury?* The legally significant facts are those facts which, if changed, would change the outcome of the case. These might be *when his mother paid $23,000 for his medical expenses last year* or *when the butane pipe caught fire while Mr. Gupta was lighting his cigarette.*

You can use these three parts even when you have no experience in this area, there is no developed legal doctrine, or you have no crisp facts with which to work. Your general "law" may be about policy, your legal question may be a negotiating question, and your legally significant facts may be projected circumstances. In fact, using these three parts of an issue reveals what you have and what you do not, which will in turn lead you to effective research strategies and questions to ask your client or partner. You can use the following to frame any preliminary issue statement.

Example 3.6.   Template for the Preliminary Issue.

LAW   *Under...*

LEGAL QUESTION   *did (or was, can, is, etc.). . .*

LEGALLY SIGNIFICANT FACTS   *when...*

For a concrete memo, such as in the Laffon case, you might draft preliminary issues as follows.

Example 3.7.   Preliminary Issues for a Memo With No Specific Law.

LAW   Under U.S. copyright law—stats? cases?

LEGAL QUESTION   can M. Laffon copyright his sculpture

LEGALLY SIGNIFICANT FACTS   when the work is based on an existing painting?

Example 3.8. Preliminary Issues for a Memo With Specific Law.

If you were given a statutory section, you might draft a few issues, one for each subquestion, to start.

17 U.S.C.A. § 101.

A 'derivative work' is a work based upon one or more preexisting works, such as a translation, musical arrangement, dramatization, fictionalization, motion picture version, sound recording, art reproduction, abridgment, condensation, or any other form in which a work may be recast, transformed, or adapted. A work consisting of editorial revisions, annotations, elaborations, or other modifications which, as a whole, represent an original work of authorship, is a 'derivative work.'

> Under U.S.C.A. § 101,
>
> > is M. Laffon's sculpture "based on a preexisting work"
> >
> > > when it is a sculpture, not a painting, and it shows different faces, not the same ones?

> Under U.S.C.A. § 101,
>
> > is M. Laffon's sculpture "based on a preexisting work"
> >
> > > when it is "reminiscent of the Andy Warhol piece featuring Marilyn Monroe"?

Example 3.9. Development of Preliminary Issues Using General Law.

If you are working on an area about which you do not yet know the specific source, you can still begin inventing the theme. Your issue simply starts the discovery process; your research helps you to become more specific. An issue that begins as,

> Under New Jersey products liability law,
>   is a retailer liable for damages
>   when a butane pipe malfunctioned, caught
>   fire while Mr. Gupta was lighting his cig-
>   arette, and caused second degree burns to
>   his hands?

can become,

> Under New Jersey Statutes sections 2A:58–C2,
>   did the malfunctioning of the butane pipe render
>   the retailer liable for damages
>   when that pipe caught fire while Mr.
>   Gupta was lighting his cigarette and
>   caused second degree burns to his hands?

Similarly, a tax question can begin as,

> Under the I.R.S. Code ???,
>   does our client have to pay tax
>   when his mother paid $23,000 towards his
>   medical bills last year?

and become,

> Under I.R.S. Code 1986, §2503(e),
>   does our client have to pay the gift tax
>   when his mother paid $23,000 towards his
>   medical bills last year?

If you are inventing a theory, your preliminary issue can say,

> Under federal and international law,
>   can our client set up an international partnership
>   when they are incorporated in Delaware
>   and ship goods to ten countries?

and your research can then refine your direction if the law restricts your client in one country.

By framing such a preliminary issue, you direct your invention. You also speed up your process because you can identify useful materials. You can ask how any materials either help answer or modify the question. In each issue, then, the first part of the question cues you about the research strategy you need to use to fill in any blanks, the second helps you to narrow the topic, and the third helps you to filter through the blurbs or paragraphs describing possible sources. As you read, you redefine, reshape, restate the issue, using your research to hone it for the purposes of your document.

Using the three-part issue statement or something like it offers several more advantages. First, you are discovering, in a more focused manner, what materials you have and what you do not have. Your general topics now give way to more specific ones, whether you are gathering law, testimonials, policy, precedent, or argument. Everything you gather helps you to answer or modify your theme. Second, you are using a temporary form of deductive organization (*see* Chapter 4) as you move from the general law to the specific, legally significant facts. You may be able to preserve this form throughout your invention because it is so predominant in modern legal design. If it is not working, you may use it to discover more sophisticated designs, as discussed in Chapters 4 and 5.

Third, you know where to begin your research. If you have the statute, you can begin with the statutes annotated; if you have a more general issue, you know you will have to determine what law applies by beginning with the index to the statutes annotated, a secondary source, or a digest, for example. In each situation, a research strategy starts to develop. In the tax problem, you know the statutory provision, which means you can begin researching in the code itself. Language in the code should help you to refine the legal question, which, in turn, will indicate exactly what facts are legally significant. In the products liability problem, you need to research that body of statutes and cases that are invoked by these facts. By filling that in, you can refine the other two parts. In the international law problem, you need to research international partnership law to discover what possible laws are invoked, what customs and practices are used, what countries are involved. And in the contract question, you need to research a specific question in contract law before deciding on the language you will use as you draft the document.

Fourth, you can filter through sources more effectively by comparing them to the blurbs. Rather than copy everything in sight, you can select

sources according to the facts you list in the third part of the issue statement, even if you are not sure that they are legally significant. Your recursive reading process allows you to check the facts against the blurbs, and
vice versa, as you go along. Your listing of potentially significant facts in
the third part of the preliminary issue statement allows you to filter your
research. You rarely need to copy every case you discover on your first
look through an initial source. This is often a form of procrastination that
puts off your analysis. Instead, look for the cases closest to that outlined
by your list of facts. You want the cases that most closely match yours. As
you read them, look at your issue statement and ask yourself, *How does
this source help answer or redefine that question?* If your question is more
general or is developing a field of law in which there are very few cases or
sources, the third part of your preliminary issue statement will project possible facts. You will glean these projections from your analogy to other,
similar sources, or from your analysis of the policy underlying these areas
of the law. As you read, then, you may hone your issue statement to read,
*Under international trade law, can our client form a partnership with each
of twenty companies when the resulting sales may violate some current
trade sanctions?*

Finally, you have begun an internal indexing system by placing the
name of the statute at the top of your issue statement. You can refer back
to this issue statement if the topic comes up again. You may want to file it
electronically by listing issues by statutory sections or topics.

Once you have decided what the possible issues are, you can put them
in an order to unify your theme. What informs your decisions? Depending
upon your level of expertise, you may have some initial idea of the order
in which you should research the issues. If so, you can number the issues
accordingly; if not, you may want to anticipate an order. You can choose
the order according to level of controversy, urgency to the client, or layout
in the document. Whatever order you choose, let it be dictated by the document's parameters, not your whim or taste. If you are presenting a white
paper or a memo or even a client letter, such an arrangement of your issue
may also help determine your architecture. This template of the issue statement moves from general to specific, addressing the most general statement of applicable sources, narrowing the question, and stating those particular facts that distinguish this case. Quite often, we use this overall template in explaining the law, so you may have already outlined your document. (*See* Chapter 4.) You have many other, more sophisticated or more

narrowly fashioned choices for your architecture, but this may give you an organizational plan that will help you to understand the issue better.

Your theme often evolves from a series of preliminary issue statements. Rarely does a document address just one narrow issue. Instead, you may have framed as many as ten issues like this, each raised by the situation your client is, or may be, in. Your research strategy (*see* Chapter 4) depends on your arranging these issues according to what you think is their importance to the document. You may be able to determine that arrangement early on, for example, to research jurisdictional questions before substantive ones. Other times, the questions are too general or equal to dictate an order. In either case, you can arrange your research deliberately so that, as you gather and filter, you will give each source a "home" in your note-taking scheme.

Just as an architect sketches ideas that then take more specific order and form, so you can use your issues to frame the analytical contours of your theme. Your transcribing of these issues probably precipitates a quicker intellectual response as you discover your theme, especially if you are not too wedded to your preliminary issues. You can use the issues to carve through sources, whether or not your final document uses an issue statement as such. This technique forces you to sharpen your thoughts by subdividing sections of your analysis. It forces you to discover your theme. You also may remember more when you are guiding your research with your written issues. With so many interruptions, so many new projects, and so much shifting of your daily tasks, you may need to write more, sub-divide more, and break your work into smaller steps.

This activity, of framing the preliminary issue and using your reading to hone it, is a writer-based activity for a reader-based result. Your docu-ment may not require any issue statement; even if it does, your preliminary one will probably not appear because you will have developed it in response to your reading. It may evolve into the second sentence of a letter answering a client's question or the introductory paragraph of a cover memo explaining a contract to a client, or a more specific question presented in a memo to a supervising attorney. You may instead simply use it to clarify the problem in your research-ing process. However you use it, it will focus your thinking in the crucial stages of research intake.

TECHNIQUES

- *Write out all the issues, using the three-part schema.* The three parts continue the role that topics started: giving you a systematic way of generating ideas. The questions beget answers and relationships among those answers. You also must decide on the relationship among the pieces of the issue statement, which should help you invent your overall theme.

- *Put the issues in a preliminary order.* Choose some order, such as what seems most important, what will probably end up being most important, what is most controversial, what is most difficult, or what will take the most resources.

- *Consider what will make some issues irrelevant.* Some may be eliminated because of jurisdiction, sequential relationship in the law, or possible power of other issues, for example.

- *Talk to others.* You can often hear what you cannot see. If you talk through your ideas and try to tell your listener the theme, you may discover you have been writing one thing and thinking another. Verbalizing may help you discover your theme.

- *As you research, fill in the charts.* Use them as templates for finding out information, theories, legal points, etc. The charts, or your equivalent, keep you steadily discovering, rather than randomly shopping for sources.

- *Take notes about both content and organization.* These techniques will be discussed more completely in Chapters 4 and 5. As you begin, commit yourself to recording your discovery process so that you can formulate your theme from what you have, not what you remember.

- *Percolate, rather than procrastinate.* Use the charts to capture information and ideas. Then allow yourself to percolate on them, to imagine and discover ways of unifying them into a theme, ways of seeing them originally.

- *Address practical matters.* Make a note, perhaps in your calendar of the due date. Consider turnaround time if you are working with others. Factor in your expertise and experience, which may determine how long it will take you. But be professionally skeptical; the invention process more often than not produces unanticipated questions. Determine—or ask—how much time and money should be put into the project. And measure how the project fits in with other projects so that you do not have clashing due dates.

A WORD ON THEORY OF THE CASE AS THEME

You have invented your theme when you develop a solid theory of your case or a theory for negotiating a transaction. Your recursive process begins to produce an idea that unifies your document. An architect may have a theory that *Buildings can get larger at the top and still stand* because she has researched the possibilities and knows the elements of engineering and design well enough to make a building do this. That theory unifies the building.

You similarly develop a theme when you establish your theory of the case. You begin with general theoretical notions. Those may be based on the standard of review in appellate practice (*Courts always use de novo review for constitutional matters so argue every fact*), dispute resolution in negotiations (*The other side always has a right to arbitrate, which we want to avoid*), or local conditions (*This judge never lets defendants go*). You may develop that notion more specifically into *Police should not be allowed to break rules just because of drug traffic*, a theme that unifies your arguments about each infraction the police have committed. You may build your document differently if you use that general perspective than if you use a more specific theme, such as *The evidence should be suppressed because police did not have a warrant to enter his home and were not operating under any of the exceptions to the Fourth Amendment*. Your general theme may be that *The law is the law*, but your may invent a more specific theme that *Defendant does not qualify under any of the exemptions to the Civil Rights Act of 1983 and is therefore liable*. Or your theory may be that *A deal is a deal* and your specific theme is *We are negotiating this for the last time*.

Inventing a theme ensures that you understand the whole, that you see a system and can therefore communicate it to your reader. If you do not see a system that explains your document, you could, again, be presenting your reader with several different points but preventing him from connecting or understanding them. Many briefs do just this. They present several points, period. If the reader looks at the beginning, he sees several sentences, but no theme that explains the document. When he looks at the end, he sees *For the foregoing reasons*, which sends him back into the list. He really does not know why he should rule in the writer's favor. The opening and closing of this brief reveal such an approach:

Example 3.10. Incomplete Theme in a Brief.

> **Acme's opposition to Deadwood's Motion for Judgment on the Pleadings rests in large measure on "conclusory verbiage," similar to that reflected in its Complaint, which is of a kind that this Court has previously held to be an inadequate substitute in antitrust actions for proper allegations of fact. [cite] Thus, Acme retreats to the position from which it began this litigation—that the asserted regulatory violations of which Acme complains can be bootstrapped into a federal case rather than an administrative action before the City's Cab Commission, where Acme is apparently reluctant to have its grievances aired....**

> **For the foregoing reasons, and those stated in Deadwood's Memorandum in Support of its Motion to Dismiss, Acme's complaint should be dismissed.**

The writer's theme seems to be that the court should dismiss, but we do not have the other half of the theme, which is the reason. What follows the sought-after *because? Because Deadwood did nothing illegal? Because Acme doesn't know what it is doing? Because this Court does not have jurisdiction to hear this Commission matter?* Nor do we have a more general, unifying theory. Is it that *Opponents cannot retreat and expect to win?* Or *Swindling the court into thinking this is not administrative law but a federal case means that the swindler loses?* Or *Courts should defer to appropriate regulatory bodies?* Here, at the two most important positions of emphasis, the beginning and the ending, the reader is searching for a system that unifies this document, for a theory and a message. The writer could write as follows.

Example 3.11. Full Theme in a Brief.

> **Acme's moves the court to dismiss Acme's complaint because this court does not have proper jurisdiction to hear this matter.**

Plaintiffs are required to exhaust administrative remedies before seeking action in a federal court. [cite] Deadwood's Motion for Judgment on the Pleadings is properly heard before the City Cab Commission because it involves matters occurring between a passenger an driver. Such matters must be heard before the Commission first [cite], which has not happened here.

Further, Deadwood's Motion should be granted because there is no dispute as to material facts. Acme's allegations are "conclusory verbiage," which is an inadequate substitute in antitrust actions for proper allegations of fact. [cite]. Acme itself seems to acknowledge this problem because it no longer makes this argument....

Because this case should be heard before the City Cab Commission and not this Court, the Court should dismiss Acme's complaint.

Here the more general theme is *Courts cannot hear cases over which they do not have jurisdiction*, and the specific theme is *The court should dismiss this action because it does not have jurisdiction to hear this case*. Similarly, your negotiating team should agree on a theory of completing the transaction. Your invention may reveal several issues that put your client in a weak negotiating position. Your more general theme may be *Compromise will get us better long-term results or Hard negotiating establishes the company more strongly in the long run*. Your theme may be *It's worth it to give these up to get the rest of the agreement* or *We can't give up even one of these and still get what we want*.

You can see where this is going. Differences of "opinion" in creating documents often are based in disagreements over theories of the case. Worse, these "opinions" have no articulated theory; they just "feel right." Such amorphous approaches to document design build documents on mud; they slip easily from the reader's—and writer's—mind.

TECHNIQUE

- *Try out several theories; write them out.* Look at them. Discuss them with your colleagues. Try to determine the best general theory for your document. Then hone your theme or message accordingly.

Honing Your Theme

As you continue to invent your theme, you observe its metamorphosis. Your research and note-taking (*see* Chapter 4) reveal details that help you to hone the preliminary issues, whether by breaking them into parts, uniting them, or changing their emphasis. What was preliminary becomes informed by your researching, your thinking, your own interpretations, your formulation of a theory. You may also experience the changed or evolving thinking of those around you: a client who changes his mind, a supervising attorney who thinks of another issue or angle, a negotiation that introduces more work. A theme is often a moving target. Your invention evolves as the situation does; your approach must be flexible and responsive.

Your theme helps you move. Your grasp of detail combined with your overall understanding may in fact anticipate or precipitate some of the very changes. Again, the essence of these changes is the message. Your research on a gift tax may uncover legislative intent or even specific purpose statements that show the statute was not intended to cover the situation your client is in. Your message may evolve from *Does my client have to pay the gift tax?* to *Whether Congress intended that I.R.S. Code 1986, §2503(e) require an indigent son suffering from AIDS to pay the gift tax when his mother paid for $23,000 of his medical bills last year.* What seemed like a simple decision whether or not to file a motion may become a new theory of the case. And what was a complicated negotiation may break into something simple when one issue is cleared up. Your notes allow you the mastery of the situation; by remembering the details, recording them in an organized fashion, and alerting yourself to the legal and linguistic connections among ideas, you are better able to anticipate changes and fashion favorable outcomes. You are researching the possibilities (*see* Chapter 4).

The language you finally settle on for your theme cues both your architectural design (*see* Chapter 5) and your placement of language in prominent places such as headings, first sentences, verb phrases (*see* Chapter 6). For example, if you choose to include a standard of review, *arbitrary and capricious*, when you are appealing an IRS decision, you can repeat that phrase when describing the treatment of that agency's decisions in previous appeals. If you choose to negotiate for *time is of the essence* in several provisions of the contract, then include that language in the purpose statement as well as in each appropriate provision. Your invention should become refined as the center of the document whether or not it actually appears as one sentence.

Your theme is your own invention. Attend to it throughout your project so that it is both accurate and comprehensive. Your reader is searching for it; you are, too, when you begin the project. Discovering it as you read; through materials, as you see the connections, as you incorporate various audiences' needs, as you investigate your ultimate purpose—permits you to create the unique message that makes your document useful, even memorable. Keeping your eye and your pen, so to speak, on your invention keeps you honest, focused, creative. Anticipating possible language, recording specific language, and matching your thoughts to what you find—permit you powerful possibilities. Avoid the blank discovery of seeing what's there before you decide anything; guide yourself to the message that ultimately will guide your reader. Your companion in this invention is, of course, your legal research strategy, your method of uncovering the document's possibilities.

CHAPTER 4

RESEARCHING THE POSSIBILITIES

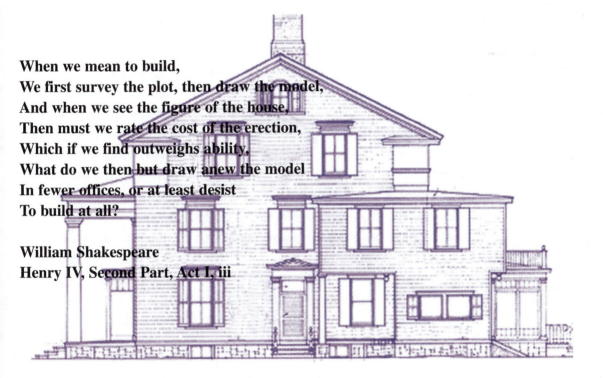

**When we mean to build,
We first survey the plot, then draw the model,
And when we see the figure of the house,
Then must we rate the cost of the erection,
Which if we find outweighs ability,
What do we then but draw anew the model
In fewer offices, or at least desist
To build at all?**

**William Shakespeare
Henry IV, Second Part, Act I, iii**

magine the architect's job. First she meets with the client to decide what kind of a building to construct, say, a house on a ravine that juts out over a creek. The client also mentions certain preferences of style, size, or basic design. Then, having established the theme—the large, contemporary house on the jutting ravine—the architect may explain preliminary research questions she needs to explore, such as what zoning laws permit and how the far the land juts out over the creek. The architect then researches by inspecting the land, consulting the zoning laws, and studying any environmental impact standards that may limit the kinds of materials that she can use, where she can place the building, and so on. The architect may consult again with the client to talk through adjustments that conform to the standards. Then she may sketch some possible designs, taking into account both her research results and the client's preferences. She discovers the project will be well over cost if it is done as the client specified. So she returns to the client to make suggested adjustments. In the meantime, the client has changed his mind about some aspects of the house. She must still design a house on this plot, but now must redesign in light of the new information. She is aware of the cost of the materials and of not going over budget and she sets about to discover a good compromise solution. The process is recursive and interactive—thoroughly informed by the architect's research and the client's preferences.

The same is often true about legal writing process and product. You have both creative possibilities and constraints. And what appears to be a constraint may liberate your most creative idea. Researching the possibilities for your document's materials and design requires you to work smart, tailoring your research strategies to the circumstances, which include your experience level; available time, money, and sources; and the document's ultimate design. Once you have considered the landscape into which the document must fit—the answers to the underlying rhetorical questions— and developed an initial theme, you are ready to research the possibilities for your document. Those possibilities should yield the document's appropriate materials, possible forms, proportions, and some aspects of its interior design.

This chapter's theme is *Research is analysis*. It is not a shopping spree. As a legal architect, you can use your theme, the answers to rhetorical questions, and your client's situation to assess the validity and value of the sources you touch. As a designer, you can use your knowledge of basic logic to assess a source's strengths and weaknesses. As a critical reader, you can recognize forms and proportions of sources. As you decide what you may need, as you develop a strategy, and as you read and digest the materials, you are analyzing.

Researching can be creative and fascinating, a way of seeing sources and possibilities. Sometimes you have many constraints, from budgets to tastes. Other times your drafting board is clean; you can create what your imagination suggests. You may work from particular legal sources and ideas to create a document. Or you may create something from nothing, inventing ideas and theories not yet used. You may build a document identical to previously successful documents or you may be comparing plans—or legal formats—themselves, figuring out what is required in a jurisdiction for motions briefs or what is required for a specific kind of contract. Your research ranges from the concrete to the abstract. Overall, an architect researches the possibilities for a range of buildings—from row houses to skyscrapers, shopping malls to mosques—by combining research and imagination, by seeing several ways to solve the client's problem. As a legal architect, your ability to see several possibilities for building a legal document should similarly help you solve your client's problem.

You need flexibility and a sharp eye to read critically and keep your research focused. Your sources and your imagination are your tools. Your ability to maneuver nimbly among them dictates the success of both your product and process. Old forms were not written for this client. Old successful briefs worked in that setting; they need to be updated, fit to this client's legal landscape, or put aside if not appropriate. You may see sleeker solutions than did your predecessors, but only if you know tradition well enough to choose between honoring it or breaking from it. Your imagination can build on the past's traditions, and your design can fit today's setting. You can build a research strategy that reveals the best choices.

As a process matter, researching is still part of *prewriting*: you are culling and sorting. You may begin to draft notes or parts of the document while you are researching. As a rhetorical matter, researching continues your *inventing of the theme*, as discussed in Chapter 3. If you have formulated some of the possibilities in your theme, you have something with which to compare your research findings. If you continue to reformulate your theme as you read and gather, you are making informed decisions about why you select a source, a quote, a fact, or a policy statement. Liking a source is not enough. If the materials do not help further your theme, theory, or message, they are extraneous. Very few legal readers tolerate clutter, so use your research strategies to cull critical material earlier rather than later. That is, work smart. Stay focused. Analyze.

To do so, know your sources and keep design elements in mind as you read to see both the large picture and the small pieces as you solve your analytical puzzle. You are deciding what will work or not work and even where you might use an item. Your discrimination and close reading before, during, and after you gather the sources should reveal possibilities for designing your document: a consistent method of analyzing an often-used statute, a policy that permeates all opinions on a regulation, a sequence of items in a form.

As you research, develop a keen eye for analyzing analyses, for forming forms, for researching the research. Your ability to use your researching time simultaneously as analysis not only shortens the time you spend on a project, but also sharpens your document.

This chapter, then, suggests strategies for seeing your document develop as you research. Essentially, you will be using legal architecture to read. Introduced here is classical legal architecture, whose forms can reveal some of your sources' strengths and weaknesses. As classicism, however, it is only the beginning of architectural modeling. Chapter 5 explores more advanced forms that can also be used in assessing the relative relationships of your sources or forms to your theme.

As you begin using architecture to read, consider what techniques you will use to find and record the sources essential to building your document. Like a trusty drafting board, your computer or legal pad should both liberate and discipline your thinking. Create a system for following your thinking as it develops, keeping in mind your client, your budget, and your setting. Remember that your system will vary for the project and that your system is what will cast your research into your memory. It will also be recursive, which can be confusing and tedious. Ironically, though, the "owning" of the materials through using such a recursive system is what liberates your creativity. As you see the architectural models others have constructed and understand them well, you begin to create the appropriate model for your project.

The techniques suggested in the following pages liberate such models. Used by successful legal architects, they allow creative and productive designing in the context of a busy practice. Rather than adding time, they save it, because these techniques allow you to see enough possibilities that you are likely to choose the best form for your project. There is usually much less rewriting and revising. As always, choose what works well and

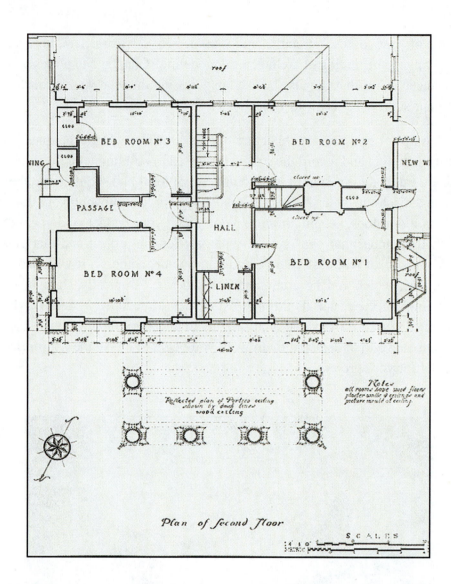

Plan of second floor

add it to your repertoire. Avoid getting pigeon-holed as a thorough but slow researcher or an electronic whiz who misses some cases.   Imagine yourself as the architect of your client's project. Develop a diversified repertoire of strategies for researching and designing strategically.

RESEARCHING THE MATERIALS' POSSIBILITIES

RESEARCHING STRATEGICALLY

The better you know your research sources, the more adept your research strategy and document design will be. Each source offers information uniquely. Each source attempts to organize complicated information. Each source tries to make that information accessible. Like a great meeting of sages, mentors, and some imposters, the law library speaks. Success is usually a matter of asking the right questions in the right order and listening carefully.

This takes some loving attention to each source. You can understand its features, including a bit about its history. You can know how it has performed for researchers in the past, and you can discover if it is something that will work for you. One temptation is to go to the friendliest, not always the best, source. Another temptation is to use sources in the same order each time. Know all your sources well enough to use them comfortably and to tailor your search strategy to your situation. Know their rela-

tionship to other sources. Granted, law sources do not make researching the research easy. As sages, sources are a cranky sort, seemingly unapproachable at times. The newer ones may move too quickly and the older ones not at all.

While such volume and variety are valuable, you must constantly balance time with results. To do so, you can conduct your research at three levels: *researching the law*, *researching the research*, and *researching possible analytical frameworks*. As you research the law, you are using a specialist's eye to search for how a source answers or redefines your question. As you research regulations, contract provisions, or cases relevant to this topic, you can also keep a generalist's eye watching for new sources and new ways of finding old sources. For example, if you are researching an agency's opinions on an esoteric topic, you can use the agency's electronic database rather than sending for hard copies of opinions as you had before. You are at once gathering the appropriate materials and expanding your understanding of how sources are connected.

As you examine a source, you can also research that research. Note how much weight it has subsequently, how favorable or unfavorable it has become, how it compares to the other sources you have uncovered. Research, too, any new sources and topics for future use. Keep your strategies and your list of possible sources as updated as you keep the research itself.

Finally, as you are reading the research, note the analytical frameworks, or forms, used to reach results. If there is a pattern, note it, or note the departures from traditional patterns, such as classical deductive or modern element-by-element approach. Derive from your reading possible forms for your own document's design. Note the possibilities for a source's relative proportion to other sources in your document.

By researching strategically on all three levels, you use the research process itself to design and build your document. You see the materials yield certain forms, you see the relative proportions of the sources to each other, and you see certain terminology and phrases that will define your interior design. As you gather, you know you may eventually reject some ideas and emphasize others, but you are starting to see the ideas emerge. Simultaneously, you are creating an increasingly rich and helpful personal library of sources and strategies tailored to your practice. From this library, your specific design can be drawn. It all starts with a good research strategy.

A Word on Researching Practically

The combined legacies of federalism (multiple sources), capitalism (multiple publishers), and individualism (multiple pronouncements on the same subject) make legal researching messy. No matter how well you may have researched in another field or another office, no matter how comfortable you may be in a certain sub-part of the law, you often face a daunting search when you start a new topic. Even when the topic is not new, you may be faced with a very complex transaction, a very long brief, or a white paper that covers multiple subjects. Such researching requires not only familiarity with the sources, but efficiency in sorting through them.

As you research in the law library, you may find yourself still importing research techniques from previous research experiences. Such techniques may fail or slow you down in the law library. In other disciplines, sources are sometimes more friendly, less messy. They are sometimes tidily arranged in the library, easily accessed, consistently organized internally. Sometimes they are fairly static, historical sources. In such disciplines, knowing the sources requires learning one fundamental system and seeing how all parts fit within it. Developing strategies to use those sources thus may also have differed from legal strategies. You may have researched separately, exhaustively collected all possible sources, studied them, and then developed your thesis. You may have selected an organizational scheme as you wrote, reorganizing the document several times until you had it right. Or you may have researched several possible topics for a graduate paper, selected one, changed your mind, re-researched, then postponed your paper as you discovered an original thesis. You may even have used these techniques to do a successful scholarly paper in law.

Such strategies suffer in law practice. Court deadlines, multiple assignments, and client demands limit your timetable. A sequential, heavily recursive writing process is simply impractical for the practitioner. Your work is rewarded for speed and accuracy, not just the latter. Legal materials are organized for quick, not tidy, access. Law sources change constantly because time is of the essence. They are as varied as the topics they profess, and the means for accessing them are fitted to the topic. There is always an index of some sort, but each source puts it in a different place, geared to the source itself. For annotated statutes, the index is usually at the end; for digests, the schema for a topic is at the beginning; for looseleafs, the "how to use" section is sometimes in the middle. These differences reflect both the nature of the source and its primary users, so learn as much as you can about both. Researching is such a rich experience for lawyers precisely because sources continue to change, multiply, and intersect with each other.

Your means of finding primary sources, for example, begins your architectural design process. You can go directly to the United States Code, for example, and just read the statute to discover the pure elements needed to analyze this question, or you can go to the United States Code Service and begin to read the annotations after you have paused for a moment to interpret the statute itself. Your reading will modify your understanding of the elements and may indicate how they relate to each other, such as which element is more prominent or whether all elements are treated equally. If you are looking for a recent law, you may find yourself in a specialized looseleaf that carries that law and the most recent versions of its interpretation, or if you are reading a recently passed regulation, you may find yourself on line, reading only its language in the Federal Register. Your very strategy and the interaction with primary sources that it generates begin your decision-making process on what to use and discard, what emphasis to give to certain sources, and how many sources you will have to include.

Finding primary sources for drafting contracts follows a similar, though often less official, process. You can go to standard forms books, using an index, but your primary sources are more likely to be inside your law office. If your law library has a database of contracts, you can target that. If the assigning attorney suggests some models from her files, you can use those. You may, however, be searching without indexes or advice. In that case, it is even more important to create a research strategy that allows you to discover good primary authority: the files of the assigning attorney, the files of attorneys who have created these kinds of contracts before, and the files of those attorneys who have designed contracts for the assigning attorney. You can similarly sort through examples that respond to your issue statement (*How does our client get what he wants?*). You will choose those contracts that provide a sound legal foundation for this transaction, that most closely match your facts, and that offer the best terms for your client.

Knowing your sources well enhances your strategic thinking and your understanding of the relationship among the parts of your document. This perspective allows you to see your analysis and your document design. Your ability to create a strategy that both anticipates your document design and incorporates your time and expense objectives should make your document easier to construct. As you plan a research strategy, consider how to tailor it for each project. Generally, no two research strategies should be alike because of the unique combination of factors discussed above. If you have a lot of experience in the topic, your research strategy may take you to a familiar source and an updating source and you may be finished. If you have very little experience in the topic, you may use secondary sources to get some background, then going to the primary sources, updating, and comparing with other jurisdictions. Having less time available usually means starting with primary sources; having fewer resources available may mean using a specialized secondary source as a finding tool; having access to a large library may yield an esoteric source that directly addresses your main issue. Each research decision you make is analytical because each decision reflects your understanding of your theme and design.

As you research, you cull materials in relation to your theme and in response to what you are reading. Your challenge is to make accurate decisions on the spot. In other fields or sometimes in longer legal projects, it may be possible to do a lot of research and think about it later, to read and reread enough times until you are sure of your sources. At some time in your education, someone has encouraged you to wait, to put off inventing even a preliminary theme until you have gathered all of your research. If you are doing scholarly work, you may choose to do a lot of research before you establish your thesis. But if you are negotiating a time–sensitive agreement, you may find such an approach unwieldy. You usually need to decide quite rapidly.

To do so, you can design a research strategy that fits the occasion, rather than use a method that is merely habitual. Without a specific strategy, you may find that your material or the library itself casts a spell on you, drawing you into many sources that may not be pertinent or valuable to your effort. Think first about what you expect to find. What is the range of possible materials to fit your theme? What are the possible jurisdictions or sources in which you could look? What possible ways of analyzing this problem occur to you before you read anything? List them and then put them in some kind of order, an order that helps you to develop your topic. If, for example, you are researching a brief, identify the jurisdiction and the substantive issues, as indicated in the previous chapter. Put those issues in some order, preferably one related to the result. Then, for each issue, list possible sources for finding authority on that topic. You may decide to try the bull's eye first, which is the primary law or statute. You may then want to look at annotations under the statute and then you may wish to update that statute, which will sometimes complete your research on that issue. If, however, you are working on an issue for which there is no direct precedent, such as an international law issue or a white paper on international transactions, you may list in–house sources on similar topics, newspaper articles, looseleafs, or your own files or collections of resources on that topic. Your first source may be finding the local expert on that topic and asking her questions. Thus your research strategy can take into account factors discussed in the next section.

At the end of each researching project, evaluate what worked and what did not. Make notes about where you can be more efficient, any short-cuts you discovered, and any techniques that helped. Then file your research results in a place where you can access them for future, similar projects. You may want to start your own electronic files that keep the most important notes and documents; you can then send the boxes to storage without losing your investment in the subject.

RESEARCH STRATEGY ELEMENTS

Cost, Time, and Duration

Theme and Related Issues

Available Resources

Project's Scope

Experience Level

Available Information

Preferences for Resources

Updating

Cost, Time, and Duration: the Practical Questions

You will most likely be accountable for your time, whether recorded in hours for your supervising attorney or billed to your client directly. Clients are becoming increasingly skeptical about the ways in which lawyers spend their time, whether in private or public sectors. Occasionally, clients give no limits, but quite often they will ask that you use the least amount of time and expense possible. Determine this either by asking directly or by researching the client's preferences. What has been the pattern in the past? How serious is the matter? Will research on this subject be the foundation for many topics of interest to the client or is this too esoteric to justify much time?

It simply takes too much time to research the project as though it were a scholarly paper, especially if you gather numerous sources, read them, and then select the issue, organize and write. Such a research strategy broadens your thinking but also broadens your time frame and may endanger your design. The more materials you gather, the more possibilities you have, and your design choices increase geometrically. If you are an expert and your client can afford it, you can gather enough to build a Gothic cathedral. If you have limited time and resources, however, you may rather want to gather only  the essential materials and design a useful home from them.

You can calculate how much time it will take to fold in each new project with all of the others on your desk. To decide accurately, check with both your client or supervising attorney and check your own schedule.

Something due three weeks from now may take you twenty hours or three. Be honest about the time frame and immediately identify when and where you will do the research. Beware of being too optimistic: what should take three hours may take ten. Look at your pattern from previous projects and factor in extra time if being overly optimistic is your tendency. You rarely know when you start exactly how much time the project will take, but you often know how much time you have. Match the two. In fact, the best researchers use this variable to design effective strategies. They find the cleanest, fastest way to the sources rather than hope later to re-research.

Your Theme and Related Legal, Factual, Policy, or Political Issues

Knowing your theme or the likely results speeds up your research and helps you create a direct, swift strategy. If you know, for example, that you are going to draft an opinion for the judge favoring one party, you can check the research submitted by that party and supplement it with any of your own. If you know that you are drafting a policy statement created by attorneys who supervise you, your research strategy will emphasize sources that support that statement. If, however, you do not yet know your results, you need a research strategy that gets you to them. You may create a strategy that puts in order the possible issues, facts, or policies and creates a possible schema into which they will fit. As you read, test your hypothesis: how does this source prove or disprove the theme? Read the sources not only for their intrinsic content but also for their relation to your theme.

Your research strategy follows the theme's related issues. However you frame them, you begin your strategy. Determine the most effective path for discovering answers and outcomes. Every lawyer determines a research strategy based on facts and issues, but not every lawyer always listens to the directions dictated by these sources. Be careful. Often lawyers begin researching the issue they like, not the issue that may, for example, dispense with the others. Some lawyers get fixated on certain facts or issues, which seem obvious, only to find later that other issues render these unimportant or unnecessary. Stand back, as described in Chapter 3, and see all possible issues and connections among them; see all facts, even the ones you have not yet accumulated. Arranging these in a few possible ways helps to determine a strategy.

You may, for example, be researching the restrictions placed by NASA on a private litigant who approaches a former NASA official for testimony or information. You may think to begin with the NASA regulations themselves; but, stepping back, you may determine that it is more effective to look at analogous regulations in other government departments, such as the Department of Defense, of the Navy, or of the Army, because they are more established and may have more specific, established regulations. Or you

may be researching the definition of a term under a statute, only to determine much later that the statute does not apply. Or you may want to immediately create a lengthy factual chronology and only much later stand back enough to realize that the plaintiffs did not preserve the case for appeal.

Use your theme to cull the information most effectively. How does this source help me answer this question? How does this source advance my theme? Look very carefully at the verb in your theme or your preliminary issue to see if that actual word or idea is addressed in the document that you are reading. If it does relate, determine how closely. You may decide that it is extremely important and central to your document, or that it will

be helpful only to give you one illustration, or that it is oblique and, while interesting, not that pertinent to your document. You may see it as a weakness, so include it as material that must be accounted for. Try throughout your culling process to put value on each of the sources that you research. Once you have done that, your analytical decisions help you to shape the overall document. If you stand back, look at the nature of the facts and issues, and try to determine a possible schema into which they will fit, your research strategy can track that schema efficiently. Use your issues before you go to the library to sharpen the appropriate strategy for your document.

TECHNIQUES

• *Use your preliminary issue to cull appropriate materials.* In law practice, you often need to find the right answer right away. You need to go directly to the source. Whether you are searching indexes to annotated statutes and constitutions or your office's collection of international transactions, you can often get to your primary materials quickly. That is, you can gather only what you need, nothing extraneous. With a research strategy focused on primary sources, and with a reading method based on deduction, you may quickly gather just enough to design your document.

Few of the problems you are being asked to solve have only one primary source, that is, only one contract or statute. You often need to sort through piles of primary sources to select what is appropriate for your client's needs. To sort while you search, rather than gather while you daydream, you can use your written, preliminary issue statement to take you directly to a constitution, statute, regulation, or primary contract.

Example 4.1.   Preliminary Issue Statement for Memo.

Issue: Under Nevada law, can the spouse of Frank Rizzo, a deceased local television sportscaster, recover damages for the unauthorized use of his image in a casino's advertisements when the spouse just noticed the advertisements, the spouse registered her husband's right of publicity after his death, and the commercials have been shown for close to a year now?
Possible primary sources: Nevada statutes, Nevada Constitution, Nevada cases.

Example 4.2.   Preliminary Issue Statement for Contracts.

Under Ohio and Illinois contract law, can our client set up a limited liability corporation when two parties practice psychology in Ohio and three practice psychology in Illinois?
Possible primary sources: Partner Smith's previous three LLC contracts; one interstate LLC contract, conflict of laws contracts cases in both states.

As discussed in Chapter 3, using your preliminary issue allows you to go directly to primary sources; using primary sources allows you to uncover specific language; specific language allows you to hone your analysis precisely from the start. For example, the general law segment of your issue should help you designate the foundation for your analysis. The legal question segment may define your topic and take you to a similar provision in a previous contract or the section within the digest where you can find the cases most related to yours. And the legally significant fact segment may help you sort through and find those primary authorities that fit with your facts. Your preliminary issue statement should provide a strategy for finding your analysis' foundation, its topics and sub-topics, and those authorities most closely related to your facts.

As you gather your materials, then, you are gauging their usefulness for your document. Just as an architect assesses the strength and durability of materials, the manner in which some materials may work together or even bond with each other, and the features they have in common, so you analyze your sources' validity, strength, and versatility. You are "researching the research." Whether you are looking at possible contract forms, sections that should be included in a lease, or agency opinions that must be accounted for in your letter to the agency, you are assessing the value of a source; that assessment in turn begins to show the proportion that source may have in relation to others in your document. You are reading critically, as described in Chapter 2, and you are often analyzing the reasoning used by the author. Because deduction so often lurks behind legal reasoning, you may be able to use its inherent structure, the syllogism, to assess the possibilities for your document.

In Chapter 3, you began inventing your theme, using your preliminary issue statement and a sense of direction that gave you a working conclusion. The facts you have gathered give you a minor premise. You can formulate possible major premises, which can be checked during research. And as the major premise requires a particular conclusion, given the minor premise, the conclusion (your theme) is re-invented as the research yields major premises that differ from the first guess. The process requires you to revise constantly until your theme is set.

YOUR AVAILABLE RESOURCES

The secret to swift and sure culling is knowing all available resources. Legal research is constantly changing so that, no matter what level your experience, you must always stay updated on valuable resources. Work with your librarian, whose knowledge is current. Do your own research on research so that you are aware of what new possibilities you can use. Many lawyers developing an area of expertise organize their own private libraries of cites and sources. Your office's library may be limited, so you need to know if the sources you need are at your fingertips or if you must go outside your office to find them. You also may assume that you can use on-line sources, but in fact you may have a client who limits or even forbids it. Sometimes you will be dealing with a single statute throughout your agency, but resources on the statute will be scattered throughout colleagues' offices rather than located in one place. Other times, your office may have created its own specialized databank on a particular topic or series of resources.

Know what is available and be willing to use it. One of the most time-wasting problems in law offices is the unwillingness of veteran lawyers to adapt to new sources, insisting on using the old, more time-consuming means of researching. While those means may be reliable, they may be slower, and the office may request all lawyers to adapt to using new resource banks. Keeping abreast of the changes will keep you flexible, versatile, and swift.

"The architect is a servant, a tailor, who cuts and measures the thin chap or the fat chap and tries to make him comfortable. He is not a reformer."

-Basil Spence

THE PROJECT'S SCOPE

Your research strategy is not automatically to make an exhaustive search. While you may prefer to exhaust all possible sources, your client may want only a discrete, interim answer. Many legal researchers assume they should look at everything, a mistake that costs them time and yields a long, unwieldy document. If, for example, you know that the document is to be a five-page brief for a trial judge, you limit your research to what can be included in that space. If you must look at all possible angles for a business negotiation, you may be limited only by jurisdiction. If you are doing a research paper that will address several clients' concerns nationally, then you are covering fifty states. Determine as precisely as you can the project's scope and tailor your research strategy to it.

YOUR EXPERIENCE LEVEL

You simply need more time if you are new to the topic. You may need to do more background reading or be brought up to speed on the facts. You may need to know more about the genre if you are switching from government contracts into food and drug law. If an experienced attorney suggests

that it will take you five hours, you know it will be at least ten. Be honest with yourself about your expertise and allow yourself more time and more traversing of sources in your research strategy. This is no excuse to dawdle, of course. You may choose to get up to speed on your own time, to spare your client the expense, or to develop strategies that bring you up to speed quickly. Whatever your choice, factor it in to your strategy.

AVAILABLE INFORMATION

You may have a wealth of information at your fingertips, either because the office specializes in a certain, narrow practice or because it has developed complete research banks. If so, you need not go far in determining your strategy because most cases tie in to these valuable, predetermined strategies. You may, however, get very little information from your client and you may not yet know what questions to ask. Try to glean as much information as possible in initial interviews by asking some of the questions suggested in Chapter 3. Your research strategy will have to account for going back to the sources multiple times if what you begin with is sketchy.

Preferences For Resources

Selecting what sources to use is risky. You may want to go to favorites, to sources that have given you success before. The positive reinforcement you received on the last successful project breeds a kind of affection for certain research sources, an affection that may not be repeated in your current project. Fight this temptation. Prefer those sources most pertinent for this topic and the other factors listed above. For example, while the American Law Reports Annotated might have previously yielded a perfect annotation that helped you explain to your client how successful he would be in four jurisdictions, it will likely have no annotations on an esoteric, new topic your next client wants an answer for. Similarly, printing cases off of Lexis may have been comfortable and easy for the last client, but cost and time prohibitive for this one. Consider your possibilities and add to your repertoire as you develop strategies for new projects.

> No person who is not a great sculptor or painter can be an architect. If he is not a sculptor or painter, he can only be a builder.
>
> -John Ruskin

To see all the possibilities, you can diversify your researching. Rather than depending on one strategy, you can invoke strategies appropriate to your client's situation. Oddly, some lawyers use only electronic research, and others only book research. Use both. To avoid the lawyer's nightmare (*No, your honor, I was not aware of that case*), you can create research strategies that depend not on habit or favorite sources but on the document's setting and the client's needs. While it is tempting to research and write your document without getting up from your desk, your client may object to the cost and narrowness of that approach. Think of your motivation for doing so: is it in the client's best interests or yours? You may be unable to understand the larger context if you do not see the subject's schema laid out in a book. You can update faster on the computer. Treatises are not all on-line, but the Web offers new sources barely accessible before. Your client probably wants a lawyer who is versed and versatile enough to find the best materials the best way. Increase your researching repertoire and diversify your strategies so that you can call upon the appropriate sources for the job.

Updating

Even updating the law can take on various strategies. You may decide to update as you go, to update at the end of your first run of researching, or to update only when you know exactly what sources you think you are going to use. You may go on-line, use Shepard's, or use the looseleaf services for your specific topic. Updating is also an integral part of your strategy because it leads you to other sources. For example, once you find pertinent statutes, your updating may give you the family of law you need to answer a narrow question.

As you research, then, you often need to hit the bull's eye of your sources as soon as you can. Instead of finding all precedents, you may be looking for all arguments, using a sampling technique. Each argument is a proxy for something else, and you begin to see patterns. You may sometimes have time to explore the outer circles of your research, but that is something to estimate according to the circumstances. In many busy law practices, you cannot treat a document as a term paper or scholarly treatise. You must give practical advice quickly. Again, most of us do not want to know the history of architecture if we are asking someone to design and build our dream house. Instead, your ability to create strategies appropriate to the situation may make the process engaging and stimulating. As your sources talk to you, they reveal not only raw materials for use in your document, but also ideas for the design itself. What you found at the center of your target may indeed be the foundation. Where will you place it? Automatically at the beginning? Or will you place it strategically throughout the document, a little bit at the beginning of each section? As you match the materials to your theme, look for ideas on form and proportion, too.

"What burns me up is that the answer is right here somewhere, staring us in the face."

TECHNIQUE

• *Create a research strategy and write it out.* You may think that you can keep your research strategy in your head. But, as with many of these techniques, they do not stand alone. Your process with one project intersects with your processes for others. Writing out a strategy, even if it is a small list of abbreviations, also gives you two advantages for one task. Before you begin, consider all relevant research elements as discussed above.

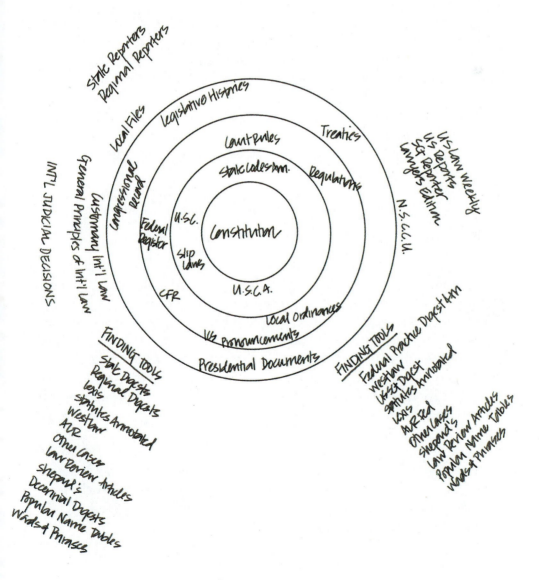

TECHNIQUE

Example 4.3. Research Strategy #1:
A Ten–Step Research Strategy

adapted from MARY B. RAY & JILL J. RAMSFIELD,
THE LAWYER AS WRITER: GETTING IT RIGHT AND GETTING IT
WRITTEN 311-14 (3d ed. 2000).

1. Collect the facts, using *who*, *what*, *where*, *when*, *why*, and *how* or a checklist or interviewing document or something similar that you have designed for your purposes.

2. Analyze the facts, using *parties*, *places*, *objects*, *basis*, *defense*, *relief*, the system of the main publisher you will use, or some brainstorming technique that allows you to generate search terms, including synonyms, antonyms, and terms that make the concept narrower or broader.

3. Write out your theme or message as clearly as possible. This can be your preliminary issues, put in order, or a statement of your theory or theme. It should have a verb. Put all issues in an analytical order that outlines a possible analytical sequence.

4. Verify any jurisdictional questions, including the "jurisdiction" of forms.

5. Force yourself to consider the research possibilities, rather than automatically going to the same source. If you train yourself to design your strategy to fit your project, you increase your research power—and your efficiency. List possible sources and put them in order so that you have a plan that both conforms to the topic and keeps you organized as you hunt through sources. Create a plan that you can remember, no matter how many interruptions you get. You were not just "in the library," you were halfway through source #3. You should be able to eliminate a lot of start-up time. So take a few minutes to map out a strategy that saves you retracing time later.

6. Find the law or policy or forms or facts. Start collecting sources, but read them with your issue statement in mind. Ask the Wiz. Approach each book as a sleuth, "interviewing" it the way you would a human source. Get what you need and get out of there.

7. Read the sources. Using your issue, message, or theme, decide how any source helps your answer the question or design the document. Look for cues here as you take notes (step 9). Are there patterns to the analysis? Are there consistencies? Threads of themes or ideas that connect seemingly disparate aspects of the analysis? Can you see groups emerging, such as contract provisions that can come under one overall heading? Subissues that fall under one issue? Point headings that unite law and your theory of the case?

8. Update your sources. Depending on how much time you have for the whole project, set aside periods for updating sources, whether you are checking back with clients on developments in a transaction, shepardizing cases, or incorporating an agency's policy decisions.

9. Take effective notes. Depending on the size of the project and your knowledge of the area, you may need to use your hand to teach your brain. Any time invested here is in "owning" the information, analogous to the classical rhetoric element, memory. If you cannot speak about the source without rereading it, you may not own it enough to use it in your document. See the section below on note-taking.

10. Ask, call, or get out of the way. Sometimes sources will not cooperate. Your best efforts yield nothing. Sometimes you start in the wrong place, trying to do scholarship rather than asking the local expert. When the nature of your research is esoteric, non-traditional, or cryptic, find the right person to ask. Your research may need to start here.

Example 4.4. Research Strategy #2: The Contract

1. Collect the information through interviewing document or checklist.

2. Find out if someone else in the office has created such a contract. If your office has established a library of documents, check it to find samples or previous documents that are similar.

3. Research the forms. Find at least three samples, if you can, so that you have a basis for comparison and can choose the best of all. You may want to get both the forms used in the office and one or two standard forms from form books.

4.   Sketch out a possible scheme for the contract, putting in unquestioned provisions and determining those that are unusual.

5.   Brainstorm issues. What other possible provisions are necessary? If you were the client, what would you want in there? Then switch: if you were the other party, what would you want? Think of every aspect of the transaction.

6.   Write out issues and put them in order. Decide what legal issues you must research, or any policy, fact, or logistical questions. Write them out and put them in some order, most important to least, hardest to easiest, or slowest to fastest, for example. You may want to put them in the order of the contract itself.

7.   Find the sources.

8.   Read the sources.

9.   Take notes.

10. Incorporate.

Example 4.5.   Research Strategy #3: Exploration.
An Individual's Approach
Josef Mrazek

1.   Pose a clear question as briefly as possible. Make this a hypothesis of what you think the answer should be.

2.   Test the hypothesis. Seek an answer from the best sources readily available.

3.   • Ask questions constantly:
          • How authoritative is this source?
          • Does this information raise important collateral questions?
          • Are there any useful analogies to be made from this?
          • Can I persuade a court that this argument must prevail?
          • Does it stand up to common-sense analysis?

A Word on Using Forms

Our legal writing culture has developed guidelines to make documents and performances consistent, careful, sometimes even predictable. Those guidelines are sometimes forms invented over time, conventions developed within the culture, or rules and customs for using authority. To the novice, some of these are saving graces, and some are maddening, unexplained rituals. To the experienced attorney, some are second nature, but some foster fossilized, unthinking imitation. To make the most of these guidelines, you may want to explore beyond their surface features. You can outsmart them by understanding their origins, and you may create new ways of using them.

Using Forms at All

To maneuver the world of legal writing, you can use forms to guide some of your decisions. Many experienced attorneys refer to form contracts, complaints, discovery documents, and wills. Someone, somewhere has created a form for most standard legal documents. What works about them is that they offer you something besides a blank screen when you are creating a document for the first time. What does not work about them is that they are not always current, complete, or comprehensive. Remember to allow yourself enough time to research the forms themselves. Even if you are accustomed to using them or another attorney has strongly recommended them, make sure they are accurate, appropriate, and analytically sound.

DO	DON'T
◆ Look at several choices	◆ Pick the first form you see
◆ Compare form with actual documents	◆ Take the form at face value
◆ Check the analytical validity	◆ Assume the form is legally accurate
◆ Update the form	◆ Assume the form has been updated
◆ Use a point of departure	◆ Just fill in the blanks
◆ Read carefully	◆ Skip over sections
◆ Rearrange parts	◆ Assume the arrangement is fixed
◆ Remove irrelevant parts	◆ Include irrelevant parts
◆ Add particular language	◆ Assume everything is there

One of the problems with using forms is that they perpetuate the traditional legal register. (*See* Chapter 6). Worse, they can create mistakes when a lawyer assumes they cover all of the provisions needed by the current client. It is a bit too easy to skip over sections, assuming they are correct. Try to find the correct balance between the time-saving aspect of using forms and the danger of lazy writing.

Using In-House Forms

Within your law office, other lawyers have developed forms that you can use to create a draft of your document. If you are in an office where these forms have been catalogued, either in hard copy or on-line, use that library as part of your research. As you select the forms that most closely resemble the document you are assembling, remember to consider this part of your research. You need to set aside time to select and compare the forms so that you choose the one closest to your situation and needing the least repair.

If the forms are not catalogued, you can assemble your own library of in-house forms. Start by collecting examples from in-house experts. You can ask them directly, research through their secretaries, or ask permission to read through files. Add to these your own forms. You might want to save the penultimate version of the last sales contract you prepared, not the final one, so that it is not too specialized for future use. You might want to save a complaint in its most general form, or convert it to a more generic model before you put it in your form file. The few minutes you take to do so when it is fresh in your mind may save you several minutes when you prepare your next similar document. Catalogue the forms according to their type and substantive area, e.g., sales contracts for one product, complaints for assault in Tennessee, or Interrogatory for Contract Breach. Date the titles, as well, so that you know how much something needs updating. Also include the name of the author—even if it is yourself—so you know the source to check if you have any questions. Delegate these filing tasks if you can.

Once you have selected a form, download it onto your computer, type it in, or use it as a mark-up. Any way you choose, you

can continue to check its validity as you research. Use your
research not only to answer your analytical questions but also to fill
in the form's blanks. Alternate filling in the easy ones with completing the research on the hard ones. That way, you can make sure
each research step counts twice: once to find answers and once to
verify and fill in the form. Most in-house forms are specific and
very useful if properly annotated and updated.

Using Published Forms

Published forms are often more generic than in-house forms,
but can sometimes be quite helpful. Published forms sometimes try
to cover a great range of information so that they are useful in
numerous settings; they sometimes are so general as to need extensive modification. Check to see what forms your library carries.
You may find a complaint for wrongful discharge or an interrogatory for breach of a sales contract.

These forms need two major adjustments: the first is to your
jurisdiction; the second is to your in-house rules. Give the form a
quick glance to assess the extent of the changes. If you must
change too much, you may decide not to use the form. If you find
it helpful as a starting point, then make sure you do the following.

1. Find the form before you begin your substantive research.

2. Check the form against any other sources that match the
   form, such as jury instructions, practice texts, or currently
   published summaries of the law.

3. As you research, adjust the form, accounting for all
   substantive points in your jurisdiction.

4. Update the form as you update the law.

5. Make sure you understand every word of the form.

6. Add any parts not covered; omit extraneous parts.

7. Rearrange the form to suit your purpose, audience,
   and stance.

8. Make sure the form conforms to in-house practices.

By the time you are finished, you have created a document to add
to your own library or to your office library. Remove the names,
give it a subject and date, and file it for future reference.

In the Laffon case, your strategies on what sources you use could vary as follows:

Choice A: Minimal time, lots of time pressures: U.S.C.A, related cases, shepardizing.

Choice B: Extensive resources, first time on this topic: Nimmer on ©, statutes annotated, cases, ALR annotations, law review articles, newspaper articles, shepardizing.

Choice C: Frightened, rich client: statutes annotated; cases; shepardizing; other states; cases shepardizing; secondary sources; Nimmer on ©.

Then work smart. Keep the issues in front of you as you read. Match legal language to the language you created in your issues, and turn to what may be the most time-saving investment you make: taking notes.

Taking Effective Notes

You may blanche at this idea. Taking notes does not seem to speed up your process, but to require excessive time. Yet many successful legal writers have found that the opposite is true. What they invest early in note-taking can cut down drastically on multiple drafts, which are much more unwieldy. They fight the temptation, whatever the circumstances, to assume that they will remember and know what they read after reading it once. Unless you are truly an expert in the field and know most of its definitive work, you may need to prepare as thoroughly as you did for exams. Those were fake. These are real. Invest early in the same way.

Many good legal architects do this. No matter what age or experience level, these writers gather information in a detailed, careful way. They do it once, they remember it, and they are able to translate it into the best results. They understand that, to design a document that works, they have to create a schema for thinking about the information and categorizing its parts. They have to pluck the salient language and see the connections among cases that use similar language or sources that suggest similar themes. They may translate similar ideas into a common language as they gather information, but each goes beyond highlighting pertinent text.

Highlighting is a form of selection. You select some segment of text that seems relevant. What informs your decisions? Your issue statement. You ask, *"How does this source help me answer that question?"* You select text that is relevant. But simple selection leaves that language in the voice and form used by that author for that purpose, neither of which may be an appropriate match for your document. While you are there, while you are selecting: translate. Create some system for studying the information and recording it for future use.

Many good writers often go beyond highlighting and use different systems for taking notes. These systems have in common two things: a schema for remembering the information and a translation for the purposes of this document. Such systems assist you to do the following:

a. remember the information,
b. maneuver the information,
c. hone the issue statement into a message,
d. see the design possibilities for your document,
e. select terms of art and subthemes for your document,
f. use the information in future projects, and
g. reduce or eliminate "start-up" time after interruptions.

By creating a note-taking system, you are able to remember the information because you have placed it in a schema of your own design. Similar to preparing for exams, your note-taking system allows you to prepare for writing your document. You are able to see not only the significant details of your sources or ideas, but also their connection to your issues. You can remember them in the rhetorical sense intended by the classicists. Only by memorizing could an orator have the confidence to interact effectively with his audience. The classical rhetoricians believed that this kind of ownership of the information was essential to effective argumentation.

For legal writers, who need not memorize the information, the task is easier but no less important: use notes to remember the details of your analysis. Time invested here is time saved in rewriting, redoing, revising, rethinking. Your recording of the information you are selecting and your creating a schema for presenting that information are, together, your analysis. Just as architects or engineers or scientists record significant information as they gather it, so must you. Your building of the analysis is often an inductive process, a discovering of details that you translate into an overall presentation. If you do nothing more than pile up the details, you will present your audience with a stairway to nowhere. If you gather them with specific goals in mind, if you allow the information to help you visualize a document, you will remember the information and be more likely to use it to its best purpose.

Many successful legal writers have created their own systems, from case charts to software. What each system has in common are two things: attention to detail and linkage to a grander scheme. For the first, the attention to

detail, these writers come back to the issue statement, to invention, which in turn dictates the notes they record. If, for example, a section of a case reads, *Defendant is liable for the gift tax for the tax year beginning six months after the death of his father...*, you may record, *Son paid gift tax because...* Or, if a medical record reads, *Injury to spinal column during Vietnam war*, you may tab that place in the medical history and record on a separate sheet of paper: SPINAL INJURIES, with columns on dates and terminology. Each time, the language, the details are related to the legal question framed in the issue presented, whether or not this is done formally. Good note-taking allows you, once again, to own the information, to commit it to your memory, and to compare analytical forms. Consider developing a range of systems, depending on the scope of the project. What follows are descriptions of some note-taking systems that you can refer to in building your own.

TECHNIQUES

- *Write down the date.* Either to keep a record of your research or to observe the development of your thinking, the date keeps you honest about how your analysis is unfolding.

- *Write down the full citation in whatever form you will use in your final document.* If your document does not require citations, you may want to record them anyway for future use.

- *Create a system for taking notes.* You may prefer note cards or their software equivalent; computer files for each source with citation at the top and your notes on valuable ideas or quotes; color-coded post-it notes with corresponding highlighters; or legal pads divided by columns into source, relevant information, where it will go in your document, and your comments. Whatever system you create, make sure that it permits you to 1) remember the information, 2) see where it fits into your document, and 3) use it in the future if needed. Some possible systems:

  - *Create files on a disk.* Use one disk per project and establish a file for each source. As you create the file, put the source's cite in Bluebook form. Then type in any notes from the source, including quotes and page numbers. Add your own notes about the source. Then note where it might fit in the document. In a separate file, start your overall plan by indicating where the single file might fit.

  - *Use separate legal pads for separate topics.* Rather than taking continuous notes and sorting later, sort while you read. Take one legal pad per topic. You may also want to divide the pad into three columns: source, what it says, where it might fit. Record the citation form, including the page number for each source. Note also where the source might be significant in the document.

- *Color code.* Take notes using different color ink or paintbrushes on the computer. Use black when indicating a neutral bit of information, green when indicating information that will be information to the client, red when indicating information that may be difficult or contrary to client's purposes. Create other colors for any technical information, dicta, or emotionally significant information, for example.

  - *Use a pyramid to organize information.* You may find that the visual organization of materials helps you to see their relationships to each other.

- *Be meticulous: filter, translate, paraphrase, quote.* As you read, translate your source into a form that will be most useful to you. If your preliminary issue statement read, *Does my client have to pay a gift tax....?*, then your notes can incorporate such points as *X paid gift tax when..., Y did not pay gift tax because...* rather than repeating quotes that do not show the source's relation to your document.

- *Record specific page and document numbers.* Whatever your source, make sure you know exactly where you found it. You are there; record it so that you do not have to hunt it up again.

- *Record your own thoughts about the source.* If you interviewed a witness, make your own comments about reactions, assessment of credibility, relation to the case. If you are looking at several contracts, note your reactions to their differences and similarities.

- *Allow for development of your theme or message—and record it.* You may initially have thought that the sources would yield X and now they are yielding X – 10. Adjust. Use your notes to reshape your hypothesis until you have gathered all of your "proof."

- *Record connections and sketch an overall design.* As you see connections among sources, as the possibilities emerge, start to sketch possible designs. Your sketch may take the form of a tree, with branches showing the relationship of sources to your message; of intersecting circles, with the intersections showing how subthemes overlap; of a traditional outline, with Roman numerals and subparts. Sketch, because you can see more than one possibility in order to choose the best one. Allow your sketches to change as you read more.

- *Keep track of sources, showing their relative importance.* As you read, develop markings that indicate the relative importance of your sources. If something is very important, mark it so, or rate it, say, from 1 to 10. Such a system begins to reveal the proportions each part will take in the final document. You can use a general system that uses a star for very important materials, check for good ones, squiggle for unsure ones, and an X for useless ones. Or rate them

  √ = probably   * = yes!
  § = don't know   X = no, don't reread

- *Write out Purpose, Audience, Scope, Stance; prioritize.* You may have done this at the beginning of your process. You can check it again now because it may have shifted or because your research has suggested that you redefine these rhetorical aspects of the document.

- *Write memos to intermediate readers.* As you develop your contract, you may want to keep a written conversation going with your client or supervising attorney so that your thinking does not go too far afield. Sometimes the researching itself makes you stray from your client's original objectives.

- *Create your own macros for recording and sorting information.* You can create a personalized system of note-taking or create a different one for each project. The macros get you started, give you something to fill in.

Example 4.6 Sample Note-Taking Chart.

Jurisdiction	Acme Argument	Service Argument
	Interest on WPT deficiencies accrues in the year in which the tax accrues	**Because all of Acme's WPT deficiencies are subject to the contest rule, deficiency interest should be deducted in the year in which the contest was resolved -- 1990.**
Federal Circuit	Hollingsworth, 568 F.2d 192 (Ct. Cl. 1977), considered whether a TP was contesting state income tax deficiencies and interest thereon. In Hollingsworth, the Service conceded that if the TP's in 1962 and 1963 taxes were not contested, then interest was deductible in those years. Thus, the interest on Acme's uncontested WPT deficiencies is deductible in the year to which the deficiencies relate.	Hollingsworth, 568 F.2d 192 (Ct. Cl. 1977).The RAR (p.1375) acknowledges that Hollingsworth held that absent a contest, interest on additional state taxes was deductible in the years to which the deficiencies related. Since Acme contested all of its WPT deficiencies, however, the interest does not accrue until the year of settlement -- 1990.
	Alexander Proudfoot, 454 F.2d 1379 (Ct. Cl. 1972), was cited in the protest for the proposition that deficiency interest and the underlying deficiency are inextricably linked: "[D]eficiency interest has been so closely braided to principal that it has been deemed an integral part of the tax. . . . The hair is to go with the hide."	Alexander Proudfoot, 454 F.2d 1379 (Ct. Cl. 1972). The RAR argues that the court's statement about the linkage of tax deficiency interest to the related tax was limited to the determination that the same statute of limitations governed both the tax and the TP's refund claim for interest related to that tax. Accordingly, the decision was narrow in scope and is not relevant to when deficiency interest accrues as a deduction for WPT purposes. Thus, it does not apply to Acme's case.

9th Circuit		
Tax Court	Burton-Sutton, 3 T.C. 1187 (1944), held that the contest rule, as announce in <u>Dixie Pine</u>, also applies to "the interest items in question." The court concluded that where the contest rule prevented additional state income taxes from being deducted in the years in which the taxes were originally assessed, interest amounts likewise did not accrue and were not deductible in those years. Thus, the interest on WPT deficiencies that Acme in fact contested does not accrue until the contest is resolved (1990). The holding of <u>Burton-Sutton</u>, however, does not apply to the interest amounts on the WPT deficiencies that Acme did not contest.	Burton-Sutton, 3 T.C. 1187 (1944). The RAR agrees that this case held that the contest rule, as announced in <u>Dixie Pine</u>, also applies to "the interest items in question." Since Acme contested all of its WPT deficiencies (under the RAR's reading of <u>Doug-Long</u>), Acme cannot carry back any of the interest amounts to the years to which the deficiencies relate. The interest amounts must be deducted in the year in which the contest was resolved -- 1990.
	<u>H.E. Fletcher</u>, 10 T.C.M. (CCH) 1025 (1951), held that in the absence of a contest, the interest on federal income tax deficiencies accrued in the year in which the tax accrued. The court concluded that, with respect to an interest liability on a tax deficiency, the all-events test is met once the tax deficiency has accrued, since all "facts necessary for the determination of the additional tax in the years to which they related." Thus, the deficiency interest on the uncontested amounts of Acme's additional WPT liabilities are deductible in the year to which the additional liabilities relate.	<u>H.E. Fletcher</u>, 10 T.C.M. (CCH) 1025 (1951). The RAR concedes correctness of Acme's statement of <u>Fletcher</u>, but argues that <u>Rev. Rul. 70-560</u> is the Service's position.

Other Authority (S.Ct. Opinions, other circuits, Service's positions)	Rev. Rule 70-560, 1970-2 C.B. 37, is an incorrect statement of law. As G.C.M. 38172 states, the ruling is contrary to <u>Anderson</u>, <u>Dravo</u>, and <u>H.E. Fletcher</u>, which collectively support Acme's position that for uncontested WPT liabilities, interest on deficiencies accrues in the year in which the tax accrued. [Moreover, the ruling is limited to interest on federal income tax deficiencies and does not affect the accrual of Acme's WPT deficiency interest. (Do we want to argue this, given our reliance on <u>H.E. Fletcher</u>, which deals with federal income tax deficiencies?)].	Rev. Rule 70-560, 1970-2 C.B. 37, involved a TP who, in 1970, contested in the Tax Court a federal income tax deficiency for the year 1966 that was asserted against the TP in 1968. The ruling held that the entire interest on the contested deficiency accrued in 1970, the year in which the contest was resolved. The ruling further held that, had the deficiency been uncontested, interest on the deficiency would have accrued in 1968 (the year in which he deficiency was agreed to by the TP) and not in 1966 (the year to which the deficiency related). Thus, any interest on Acme's contested 1980-85 WPT deficiencies is deductible in 1990, the year in which their contest was resolved in appeals. To the extent any WPT deficiencies are uncontested, they are also deductible in 1990, the year in which the WPT deficiencies were agreed to.

The point in creating your system is to, once again, get several benefits from one task. As you take notes, you are giving each bit of information a possible home. You may indeed start switching the information around, eliminating some of it, or even misjudging its value at first. But, by recording, beginning to create a schema, and thinking about the source's relevant importance, you are already writing. As you choose what sources seem important, you start to decide how much space they will have in the written document. As you choose those which are unimportant, you decide whether they will make it into the document at all and, if so, how lengthy their presentation will be. When you compare sources, you begin to structure sections, paragraphs, answers. Think in the past (where did the source come from?), present (what does it say that is pertinent to my question?), and future (where will I put this and how much will I say about it?). That readies you for your design techniques, and helps you to discover form and proportion.

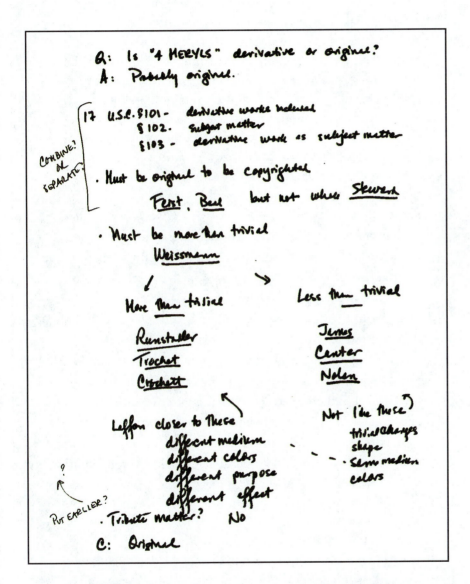

Many legal writers skip this step of translating and connecting as they read. They move from their own reading and simply dump that reading into their writing. That means that there are a lot of quotes, a lot of footnotes, a lot of single-spaced repeated information that comes directly from legal sources and stays in the same traditional turgid language. In other words, the legal writer has not done the work for the legal reader. Instead, you need to translate. One way to think about this stage as a kind of outlining for an

TECHNIQUES

- *Connect all subparts to the whole.* Create a schema that shows how each smaller part relates to the whole so that you could show the *definition* of the term; the *comparison* of one source to another; the *relationship* of one source to another, such as *cause and effect, antecedent and consequence, contraries,* or *contradictions;* the *circumstances* of each situation; or the *testimony* given by each source, such as *testimonial, statistics, precedent,* or the *law* itself. Use other categories than these classical rhetorical ones, but categorize the source in such a way that you can characterize it for a reader.

- *Paraphrase a source so it means something to you; then translate for the reader.* Rephrase the information in your own words. Doing so will reveal any analytical questions or discrepancies. If necessary, return to the source to clarify its meaning until you can translate it effectively. This paraphrasing make take several forms. You may write it out in prose form as a kind of note or letter to yourself, using the plainest and simplest, even colloquial, language so that you are sure that you understand exactly what it means. Another thing to do is to imagine—or use—a real audience, such as your spouse, child, or friend, and explain to them exactly what this source says and how it relates to the question. Or dictate the paraphrase with an imaginary setting in mind. Or actually talk it through with someone, paraphrasing while the dictaphone is on; then have those notes transcribed.

- *Tape record a summary of the document's content.* As though you were explaining it to a friend, dictate the document's message and how you will explain it. Have the summary typed up or do it yourself to prepare yourself for drafting possible designs for the document.

exam. You are using the outlining to own the information so that you can answer any question about it. You do the same thing as you research the relationships among the sources: so you can explain why you are reaching a certain conclusion on the topic, why you are recommending something to a client, or why you are choosing certain contract provisions. Your translation primes you for deciding on the document's design.

SEEING THE DESIGN POSSIBILITIES

The architect has some vision of what he is building as he starts to think through the materials he will use. Under normal circumstances, he does not first gather wood, concrete, and whatever else he can find, and then decide what to build. Instead, he uses his knowledge of physics, engineering, and math to consider possible architectural forms; he assesses materials according to their properties and appropriateness to the building and climate; he searches for configurations that suit the setting.

You can do the same. You have already considered the rhetorical and design possibilities, discussed in Chapter 3. You can use your well-designed research plan to write the document. By selecting search terms, framing to the theme, establishing jurisdiction, you can actually begin to construct a written document before you go to the library. Using this simultaneous model, you can select language to use in prominent places by selecting the search terms, design the document by framing the theme and ordering the related issues, and allow the design to develop by seeing form and the proportion of one part to another.

That is, you can design before and during your time in the library. To own the materials, you can be aware of what language is being used, what questions are being asked, what forms are being used to analyze similar questions, and what variations on those *forms* and *proportions* might be used to present this information. While researching a question in practice, you do not need to leave 100% of your thinking to the time after you gather too many sources. You can in fact

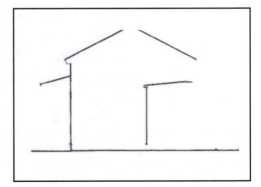

prepare a map of what you expect to find. By doing so, you can respond openly to what you find and alter the design accordingly, rather than wait to discover the entire picture.

The time you invest to create search terms, issues, strategies, and notes should result in a strong document. As you begin this intellectual process of researching and problem-solving in the law, you are designing the document. Each decision you make, whether to begin with one source or another, to use one source or another, to copy one source or another, furthers your analysis. Culling the relevant law or facts is the first step in your journey through the complex series of sources your project presents to you. These may be legal or factual sources, previous transactional documents, discrete statutes, or vague areas of international law. They may be medical

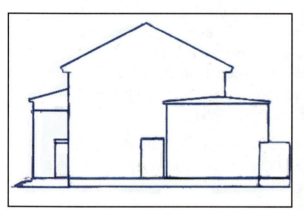

records, psychological reports, or a series of conflicting policy statements. You need to consider where to begin, how to search, how to remember your sources, and how to capture the appropriate sources for whatever kind of document that you are producing. Tailor your strategy to your situation.

Once an architect has researched the materials' possibilities, she may draw up several sketches for her client to inspect. Before doing so, she must be prepared to translate her findings in a way that is accessible to the client or to her supervisor. To translate, she must understand what she has gathered. Similarly, before you begin to decide on your document's design, while you are taking notes, you are moving from writer-based writing to reader-based writing. Your preliminary message, your notes from your intake memo, your recording of your ideas—all were focused on yourself as the audience. You are explaining things to yourself, learning them, taking them in, owning them. You are formulating the questions and connecting the resources to those questions. If necessary, you are reformulating the question in response to the resources you find, to information that you gather along the way, or to a discussion you have with a colleague. Ultimately, this is a recursive process, a process of discovery, a generative and creative process that allows you to talk to yourself about the sources and the answers. Once you own the information and have completed the research, however, you must release your inward focus. As you begin to build the document, your focus can now shift to the reader.

You can begin that shift in your note-taking as you translate and interpret the materials you uncover. To reach all of your readers—experts, non-lawyers, corporate counsel, opposing counsel, or law clerk—create techniques that pull you out of your initial perspective. See the document as they will see it. All of the following techniques elevate audience to 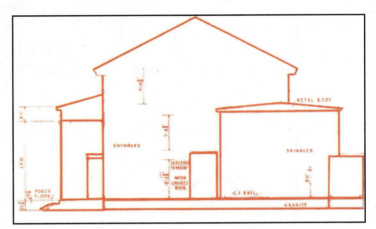 the particular prominence it has in legal writing. As writer, you leave behind yourself as audience. From this point in prewriting, you are the architect seeing the building as your clients see it. Consider their expectations for content, design, expression, perfection as you translate your materials into an appropriate design.

To translate effectively requires you to interpret your sources as you read them. While you take notes to determine, shape, or modify your message, you are interpreting. Your theme dictates your selection and your note-taking system connects each source to the theme and gives each source a place in the larger scheme of your document. Your research and your evolving analysis during the research process indicate to you possible choices for designing the document. The hierarchy that you select may be informed by the relationship among the authorities, or it may follow a series of arguments you have created as you have studied gaps in the reasoning of cases. It may simply follow traditional norms in your law office, conforming to a standard contract or standard boilerplate language in a letter to an agency.

As you gather your materials, as you select your sources from the rich array of possibilities, you can also imagine how they will fit. Part of the recursive nature of legal analysis is being able to see the details and the larger picture all at once. You may have found a case that is interesting, powerful, very much like your client's situation. That case may, however, be the eleventh such "powerful" case. Such information tells you at least two

things at once: that your point is a strong one and that you need not use all eleven to prove it. You are selecting the details in relation to the whole.

Exactly what comprises that whole is probably the most exciting part of document design. To select intelligently, to consider possible permutations and combinations of information, to create proportion and shape—these are your decisions as architect. These are the decisions that call upon your most creative and sensitive vision.

You have seen in this chapter how a research strategy and note-taking can themselves yield design possibilities. Because research is analysis, you should have a sense of where certain sections might fit before you go to the library. That sense comes from your knowledge of traditions and analytical forms, from your experience, and from your theme. You can use your knowledge of traditions and forms to measure the strength of a source; you can use your experience to assess materials for their appropriateness; you can use your theme to decide on a form with correct proportions to the setting. You can also create a unique document that transcends what your research yields.

This section discusses using classical models to read and analyze your document's design possibilities; Chapter 5 suggests more modern rhetorical models for designing your own documents, including those unique approaches. You can, of course, also use those models, or forms, for reading your sources. While modern lawyers rarely use the pure deduction and induction, you can use them to read, to assess a source's validity. As such, you may find basic rhetorical models to be indispensable points of departure.

USING CLASSICAL MODELS TO READ

USING INDUCTION

USING DEDUCTION

Classical models in law borrow heavily from classical rhetoric, although modern law practice has modified them to suit common law analysis. As architectural models, perhaps at their most rudimentary, the classical reasoning models of induction and deduction may reveal how to make separate sources fit with each other and whether or not there is more than one way to put the puzzle together. Using induction and deduction, you may discover enough possibilities for putting together the analytical puzzle, without getting too fancy for your client. Induction and deduction often force you to consider all basic aspects of your project, whether a contract or a brief. As a way of seeing the possibilities, induction and deduction force you to identify premises and fit all the pieces together. In other words, classical rhetorical models can not only give you a method of reading sources, but they can also reveal starting points for creating your form.

You are familiar with many forms, such as those that follow the chronology of a deal to structure a contract, those that present a client's argument deductively, or those that use induction to present a client's options. Sometimes you can anticipate that you will structure a document exactly as judges have structured their opinions, sometimes as a previous contract suggests, and sometimes according to the elements of a statute. You cannot, however, assume those forms will automatically transfer to your setting. You observe the general form, the proportion of parts in relation to each other and to the whole, and possible ways to derive an analytical pattern, dissect its parts and subparts, and match and differentiate among the segments. Using the design elements, you discover the best way to put your client's analytical jigsaw puzzle together.

Both rhetorical models and your experience tell you that certain materials or forms can be slightly modified to work in another setting, and others cannot. Your theme is your test. Set among your rhetorical elements, it helps you decide whether or not a certain source is valuable, whether or not a certain form will work. In some cases, your research will modify the theme itself, as you learn from your research what works for this kind of document.

Your sources fall basically into two categories: primary and secondary. Primary sources yield your essential materials; secondary sources offer background information. Similarly, your research strategies are either direct or indirect, moving from inside primary sources to less and less related sources, or moving from general topics and terms to the specific materials you will use in your document. As you research over time, become intimately familiar with the primary sources in your field, yet open to their changes, their infirmities, and their relationship to all other sources. As discussed below, use rhetorical models to read: pull from your sources the appropriate materials, see possible forms, and note possible proportions of materials within those forms.

##

Your research often yields many sources. Even when you find primary sources, such as statutes, constitutions, and contracts, they in turn lead you to examples of primary source construction, namely cases or other contracts. From these examples, you often extract the major premises

relevant to your analysis, what amounts to a "common law statute." You also begin to compare and contrast. Both of these processes, finding a general principle from examples and comparing, are inductive. You can use inductive principles as part of your strategy or part of your design.

Induction: Using Examples to Reach a General Conclusion

Inductive proofs proceed from a series of observations to a general principle. Law is often taught this way in the first year. You read a number of cases, each of which held something about an area of a doctrine; from those cases, you abstracted a general principle or theory about that doctrine. In contrast, had he taught deductively, your law professor would have handed out Emanuel's Outlines the first year and then shown you how the rules work in the cases. Of course, one of the reasons the first year is taught inductively is because your clients do not walk in with Emanuel's and tell you where their case fits. You are required to collect the specific facts, which may include many incidents, and to create a general theory under which you can rescue your client. Your very research process occurs in the same way: you gather

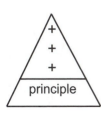

specific sources and synthesize them into a general analysis that fits the facts. You need to use induction to solve problems.

Example 4.7.   Induction to Reach General Principle.

Your research may reveal the following points as you study a number of dogs:

1. Rex is barking and has four legs.
2. Pierre is on a leash and is barking and has four legs.
3. Rover is running through the park on four legs.
......
55. Reggie is lying in the back yard and has three legs.
56. Sparky is wagging his tail and has four legs.

Therefore: Most dogs have four legs.

Induction does admit of contrary examples that correspondingly weaken, but do not necessarily destroy, the conclusion. You are using induction to reach your major premise, and your research reveals that almost all dogs have four legs and that perhaps one of the dogs had four and was injured so now has only three. While your conclusion is weaker, that is, you are not 100% sure from your research that Piotz has four legs, it nevertheless stands as probably true. And you can later distinguish the three-legged dog and other contrary examples, which may turn a weakness into a strength. The syllogism is valid, but the major premise is not proved to be true. The idea in classical models is that, structurally, arguments are more persuasive when the means of arriving at the conclusion are more likely to yield a true conclusion. In this way, deduction has the highest rational force in classical thought because the premises, if true, guarantee a true conclusion. Induction is the next strongest, followed by analogy.

As you collect several cases from which you are presenting the current law, then, you draw general conclusions from the specific cases. If you have six cases, all of which have characterized, though not outlined explicitly, a valid tender offer as having three elements, you can write a sentence that summarizes those three elements into a major premise.

1. Argentina will tax at a high rate any profits that remain on shore made from doing business in Argentina.

2. Brazil will tax at a high rate any profits that remain on shore made from doing business in Brazil.

3. Chile will tax at a high rate any profits that remain on shore made from doing business in the Chile.

Therefore, companies who do business in Latin America will pay high tax for any profits that remain on shore. (Advice: our client corporation, who does business in Latin America, would be wise to keep profits offshore.)

From this conclusion, you can form a major premise that builds a deductive presentation for your overall analysis or argument. You can begin with your statement, then explain the pieces that led you to the statement, then fit your case into that situation. Most arguments have both an inductive and deductive moment, as the bottom-up processing clicks with the top-down. For example, to determine your dog's status in this class, you can create a deductive argument as follows:

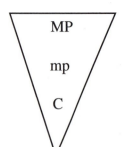

MAJOR PREMISE:	All dogs have four legs.
Minor Premise:	Piotz is a dog.
Conclusion:	Therefore, Piotz has four legs

Your syllogism reveals the premises; now you can test their truth as you continue your research. And when you use similar cases, comparing your client's case to those cases, then reach a general conclusion, you are testing by using induction. The more examples you get, the more they reveal a common theme. Even odd examples can strengthen your theme because the more regular examples you gather, the odder the others appear.

You also use induction when you assemble a number of contracts that have been negotiated in similar situations. Each situation differed somewhat from yours, however, so you must collect the common factors and reject the differences to build a contract that works in your client's situation.

The power of using induction when you construct your document lies in its dramatic impact. Whether you are writing a memo to a supervising attorney synthesizing a series of actions on the part of your client, or writing a summary of disparate cases that lead to a new theory within an old doctrine, or demonstrating to an appellate court that a series of mistakes on

the part of the trial court requires a new trial, you are using induction to build to your point. You are pulling the reader through an accumulation of separate elements that lead to a conclusion. This accumulation requires the reader's patience, something legal readers are not always willing to lend. For this reason, induction is often underused. Giving the history of your research, case by case, takes too long and leaves the reader to synthesize cases into the current rule. There, induction does not work. But reconsider its impact in constructing an argument or building a transaction. If the nature of your project lends itself to this classic form, use it. It can be a hearty part of your design repertoire. Explore within induction the various methods that you can use in researching and building legal documents.

Example 4.8   Inductive Point Headings

II.   SUPERVISORS WHO COMMIT ACTS OF SEXUAL HARASS-MENT MAY BE HELD LIABLE FOR THEIR DISCRIMINA-TION UNDER TITLE VII.

     A.   Title VII Should Be Construed Broadly in Light of Its Humanitarian Goals.

     B.   Title VII Authorizes Recovery From an Employer or Agent.

     C.   This Supervisor Committed Several Acts of Sexual Harrassment.

         1.

         2.

         3.

         4.

     D.   Under the 1991 Civil Rights Act, This Supervisor May Be Held Liable for These Acts of Discrimination.

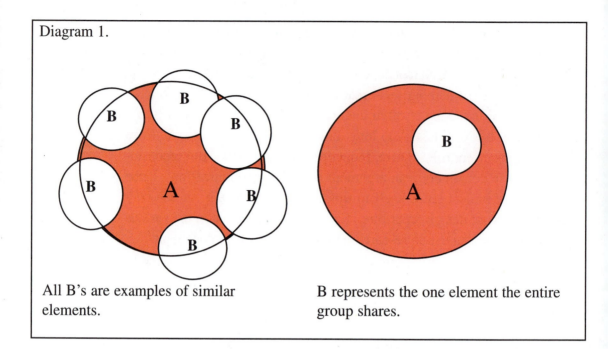

Diagram 1.

All B's are examples of similar elements.

B represents the one element the entire group shares.

Induction: Using Examples to Define

Using examples to give morals or define rules is a common form of induction. By giving examples, you can define entities, terms, abstractions. "The *exemplum*, an anecdote or short tale with a moral, once played a prominent part in literature. Aesop's *Fables* and Chaucer's *Pardoner's Tale* are just two instances of this genre." CORBETT, at 42. From examples, which are fictitious in this strict definition, these authors suggested that readers should extrapolate a general moral. In law, the example similarly appears as illustrated below, where Justice Scalia uses an anecdote to illustrate his point that going back and forth is no way to distribute justice.

Example 4.9. Personal Anecdote.

Justice SCALIA, dissenting.

The story is told of the elderly judge who, looking back over a long career, observes with satisfaction that "when I was young, I probably let stand some convictions that should have been overturned, and when I was old, I probably set aside some that should have stood; so overall, justice was done." I sometimes think that is an appropriate

analog to this Court's constitutional jurisprudence, which alternately creates rights that the Constitution does not contain and denies rights that it does. <u>Compare</u> <u>Roe v. Wade</u>, 410 U.S. 113, 93 S. Ct. 705, 35 L.Ed.2d 147 (1973) (right to abortion does exist), <u>with</u> <u>Maryland v. Craig</u>, 497 U.S. 836, 110 S. Ct. 3157, 111 L.Ed.2d 666 (1990) (right to be confronted with witnesses, U.S. Const. amend. VI, does not). Thinking that neither the one course nor the other is correct, nor the two combined, I dissent from today's decision, which eliminates a very old right indeed.

<u>Riverside v. McLaughlin</u>, 500 U.S. 44, 59-60 (1991) (Scalia, J. dissenting).

Legal documents are often rich with examples, usually in the form of hypotheticals, which make a legal principle concrete. The Restatements give examples of how the restated law might be applied, and courts may give hypotheticals to show how a principle could be applied. Your client letter may offer examples of possible actions a client may take, or your memo may give examples of what the courts might do if your case goes that far. You may also use examples in modern law to define general principles specifically. These are not fictitious.

Example 4.10. Example in a Judicial Opinion.

In Wisconsin, expert testimony is generally admissible if the person testifying is qualified and if the testimony will help the trier of fact to understand the evidence or to determine a fact in issue. <u>See</u> Wis. Stat. § 907.02 (1993–94); <u>Kerkman v. Hintz</u>, 142 Wis. 2d 404, 422–23, 418 N.W.2d 795, 797 (1988). A circuit court's decision about admission of expert testimony is largely a matter within the discretion of the circuit court. <u>See</u> <u>Kerkman</u>, 142 Wis. 2d at 422, 418 N.W.2d at 798; <u>State v. Friedrich</u>, 135 Wis. 2d 1, 15, 398 N.W.2d 763, 766 (1987).

The court has long recognized that certain kinds of evidence are difficult for jurors to evaluate without the benefit of expert testimony. <u>See</u> <u>Cedarburg Light & Water Comm'n v. Allis–Chalmers</u>, 33 Wis. 2d 560, 567, 148 N.W.2d 13, 20 (1967). When confronted with such a case, "the trial court may decline, upon motion, to permit the case to go to the jury in the absence of expert testimony. . . ." Id.

But the court has simultaneously emphasized that requiring expert testimony rather than simply permitting it represents an extraordinary step, one to be taken only when "unusually complex or esoteric issues are before the jury." White, 149 Wis. 2d at 960, 440 N.W.2d at 562. See also Netzel, 51 Wis. 2d at 7, 186 N.W.2d at 261; Cedarburg Light & Water Comm'n, 33 Wis. 2d at 567, 148 N.W.2d 13. Before expert testimony is required the circuit court must find that the matter involved is "... not within the realm of the ordinary experience of mankind. . . ." Cramer v. Theda Clark Mem. Hosp., 45 Wis. 2d 147, 150, 172 N.W.2d 427, 429 (1969).

Thus, for example, we have required expert testimony in many cases involving medicine, precisely because medical practice demands "special knowledge or skill or experience on subjects which are not within the realm of the ordinary experience of mankind, and which require special learning, study, or experience." Cramer, 45 Wis. 2d at 150, 172 N.W.2d at 431 (collecting cases requiring expert testimony).

Even in the medical realm, however, courts have limited the application of a requirement of expert testimony to those matters outside the common knowledge and ordinary experience of an average juror. Thus the Cramer court, for example, reversed a directed verdict for the defendant and held that the injured person need not introduce expert testimony regarding the hospital's alleged negligence and breach of its standard of care because the question of whether the injured person was properly attended and adequately restrained was not "so technical in nature as to require expert testimony." Cramer, 45 Wis. 2d at 153–54, 172 N.W.2d 427. "Consequently," wrote the court, "the trial court should have allowed the issues which could be determined by common knowledge to go to the jury and instructed them on such reasonable care." Id. at 154, 172 N.W.2d 427.

Weiss v. U.S. Fire & Cas. Co., 197 Wis. 2d 365, 541 N.W.2d 753 (1995).

This use of example further defines the general principle by showing examples of where expert testimony has been required and where it has been limited. In this way, specific holdings, presented as examples, set boundaries for general rules.

Induction: Using Analogies to Compare

Analogy is a variation of *example*, comparing a current situation to a "true" story or precedent. It is usually considered another kind of induction. Where the example refers to either fictitious situations that carry a message or holdings that set parameters of rules, analogy refers to actual circumstances in the past for the purposes of making a more explicit comparison to the circumstances being discussed. We use analogy extensively in common law to prove our analytical results.

Under the *stare decisis* principle, U.S. classical legal thought claims that like situations should be treated the same. Thus analogy becomes a centerpiece of legal analysis. Comparing your client's situation to the situations revealed in past cases puts you in the position of analogizing and distinguishing those previous cases. The nature of your inductive, analogical proof, then, is to make your case look more like previous favorable cases and to distinguish it from previous unfavorable ones. When you select contracts segments to use or have to explain choices to a client, you are similarly analogizing a current situation to previous ones, and using analogy.

The difference between analogy and general induction is that analogy offers many fewer pieces of data from which to draw a rule. Where a scientist uses induction when observing hundreds or even thousands of cases, a lawyer may have only a handful of previous illustrations. From those, she is drawing a "rule," a generalization that does not rely on so much data. For this reason, the classical rhetoricians considered analogy one of the weakest forms of induction. But analogy does offer a more explicit framework for putting the data into context. Because the examples are not fictitious and because the circumstances are very specific—not a general theory—analogy allows the reader to make specific comparisons and contrasts.

Example 4.11. Analogy in a Memo.

Challenges of pretext for arrest in the case of open-container law violations will fail if the facts establish probable cause for arrest. See Alvarez v. United States, 576 A.2d 713 (D.C. 1990). In Alvarez, the police made a custodial arrest of the defendant when they saw him in possession of an open container of alcohol on the street. Though "a warning or a citation might perhaps have been a more proportionate police response to the incident," these facts established probable cause for arrest. Id. at 714. Where there is an objective basis for the arrest, "the officer's subjective motivation is generally deemed irrelevant." Id. at 717. Similarly, the police had probable cause to arrest Mr. Jones when they saw him with an open container of alcohol. Even though his custodial arrest may have been a pretext for the police search which revealed his possession of narcotics, this will not affect the validity of the search. Thus, Mr. Jones' arrest and subsequent search cannot be challenged even if it was pretextual.

Example 4.12. Analogy in a Brief.

This brief addresses a statute that increases punishment for various crimes if they were motivated by racial hatred.

The State attempts to distinguish this Court's recent opinion in R.A.V. on the ground that R.A.V. dealt with "speech," albeit "unprotected" speech, and this case deals with "conduct." Contrary to the State's position, the principle underlying R.A.V. applies with equal force to Section 939.645. Government may not punish viewpoint and belief, even when they are associated with punishable acts. Whether those acts are speech or nonspeech is irrelevant.

In R.A.V., this Court held that even racist "fighting words," although "unprotected" speech, may not be treated more severely than other fighting words on the basis of their content or viewpoint. The same is true, said this Court, for "expressive conduct": "We have long held . . . that nonverbal expressive activity can be banned because of the action it entails, but not because of the ideas it expresses. . . ." 112 S. Ct. at 2544. See also Texas v. Johnson, 491 U.S. 397 (1989); United

<u>States v. Eichman</u>, 496 U.S. 310, 314-17 (1990); <u>Tinker v. Des Moines Indep. Community Sch. Dist.</u>, 393 U.S. 503, 505 (1969).

Government may not punish or regulate "pure speech" because of its disapproval of the ideas expressed. <u>R.A.V.</u>, 112 S. Ct. at 2542. <u>See also</u> <u>Simon & Schuster, Inc. v. Members of N.Y. State Crime Victims Bd.</u>, 112 S. Ct. 501, 508 (1991). The same principle logically applies to conduct, even criminal conduct. It may not be punished more severely solely because it carries a government-disapproved message or because of the content or viewpoint of the actor's thoughts. Thus, this Court's decision in <u>R.A.V.</u> is not distinguishable on the ground that the ordinance at issue in <u>R.A.V.</u> dealt with "speech" as opposed to "conduct."

Similarly, the area of disagreement between the <u>R.A.V.</u> majority and the Justice White concurrence, whether strict scrutiny is ever applicable in traditionally "unprotected" categories, is not at issue in the present case. Even under Justice White's view of the categorical approach, a law punishing thought and belief, as Section 939.645 does, is subject to strict scrutiny. The entire taxonomy of "pure speech," "unprotected speech," "expressive conduct," and "pure conduct" is simply not at issue here because the State's power to punish the underlying acts, whether "conduct" or "speech," is not disputed, despite any incidental impact on First Amendment rights.

Strict scrutiny is not invoked by the character of the underlying acts, but by the protected character of the single factor triggering the imposition of the additional punishment: a bigoted motive. The defendant's disfavored thoughts and beliefs are unquestionably within a protected category under the First Amendment, even when the defendant has also committed a crime. The question, therefore, is not how speech may be treated differently from conduct, or "protected speech" differently from "unprotected speech," or "expressive conduct" differently from "nonexpressive conduct."

Rather, the threshold question is this: within any of these categories, may bigoted motive be separately punished, in addition to the punishment for the underlying act? Even in a completely regulable category, not every possible added factor would be constitutionally punishable. For example, in punishing theft, the state may increase penalties based upon the value of the property stolen or use of a dangerous weapon, but not based upon the race or political affiliation of the defendant or the social prominence of the victim.

Some "pure speech" can be treated differently from other "pure speech" based upon factors such as time, place, and manner, but not based upon its content or viewpoint. R.A.V., 112 S. Ct. at 2544–45; Simon & Schuster; Collin v. Smith, 578 F.2d 1197, 1201–02 (7th Cir. 1978), cert. denied, 439 U.S. 916 (1978). Some "unprotected speech" may be treated differently from other "unprotected speech" based upon secondary effects, R.A.V., 112 S. Ct. at 2546–47, 2549, but not because of its content and viewpoint. Some "expressive conduct" may be treated differently from other "expressive conduct" because of its "non–communicative aspect." United States v. O'Brien, 391 U.S. 367, 376 (1968), but not because of its content and viewpoint. Texas v. Johnson 491 U.S. 397 (1989); Eichman, 496 U.S. at 315-17. By the same token, government may not treat even otherwise punishable conduct differently from other punishable conduct solely because of its content and viewpoint— not because the conduct is protected by the First Amendment, but because the content and viewpoint are.

Respondent's Brief at 7-10, Wisconsin v. Mitchell, 508 U.S. 476 (1993).

These forms of induction, then, offer you both a method for reading sources and for constructing your design. As you collect your materials, read for examples that yield general principles, definitional parameters, or sources for comparison. Line up the sources as you read, seeing what general forms begin to emerge. Decide what you will use to 1) build a rule by synthesizing cases, 2) define a rule by using examples to give parameters, or 3) prove a case by using analogies. You may have to be explicit about how you have done each of these. Often, though, you may find a more distinct deductive form taking shape.

USING DEDUCTION

Deduction is the perfection of classical legal thought. Like the design of the Parthenon, deduction promises order, reason, and enlightenment. The hallmark of logic, its form is tidy and its expression reveals truth and validity. If laws and institutions could establish "true" rules, then, using deductive logic, society would be orderly, situations predictable, and problems avoidable. No wonder that classical legal thinkers admired it.

Deduction moves from general principles to specific results. Starting with a general major premise, proceeding through a more specific minor premise to a very specific conclusion, deduction is classical reasoning at its purest. To test and analyze this deductive reasoning, Aristotle invented the syllogism. His explanation of deductive reasoning via the syllogism has been criticized subsequently as reductionist and oversimplified. It nonetheless offers an important reference point in studying U.S. legal architecture. Classical legal reasoning relied on it. As a starting point, then, the syllogism is useful; as an ending point, it may be too simplistic for constructing complicated legal documents. The syllogism is like the physics of architectural engineering. By knowing how it works, you can use it to unravel some of your sources' strengths and evaluate your design possibilities.

A Word on "Classical Legal Thought"

Classical legal thought, or formalism, is the school of thought associated with U.S. judicial opinions from the late nineteenth century through the mid-1930's. As with many schools, formalism defies a generic definition, but it resembles classical rhetoric on many levels. Its foundations were based on democratic ideals such as personal freedom, government nonintervention, and natural rights. The law, as such, consisted of determinate rules. These rules, like those in classical rhetoric, followed strict western logic, and judges were expected to follow the rules and the logic whether or not they agreed with either on policy, equity, or economic grounds.

For the classical thinkers, law was based on reason, rather than force; it was objective, rather than subjective; and it produced outcomes any reasonable and disinterested person would come to. In a sense, law was like geometry. "Each doctrinal field revolved around a few fundamental axioms, derived primarily from empirical observation of how courts had in the past responded to particular sorts of problems." William Fisher, et al., *The Bridge Project* (visited Nov. 23, 1999) <http://www.lexis.com/xchange/content/Bridge/R2/LegalRealism/essay2.htm>. The process of deriving such axioms was, of course, by using classical inductive thought. Such axioms then acted like the major premise of a syllogism: "From those axioms, one could and should deduce—through uncontroversial, rationally compelling reasoning processes—a large number of specific rules or corollaries." *Id.* While the formalists admitted that U.S. law did not yet conform to the ideal, they felt that purging fields of rules or decisions that did not conform to the conceptual order of a particular field was all it would take. Then, they argued, "the law would be 'complete' (capable of providing a single right answer to every dispute) and elegant." *Id.*

This, of course, was Aristotle's argument, and the allure is strong. Order. Predictability. A happy democratic society. Individuals have freedom, freedom of contract, freedom to enjoy property, freedom to decide morality for themselves. The government should not interfere. Rather, according to the formalists, courts should protect one person's rights against another's. They do that best by preferring form to substance, that is, by categorizing something as private or public, tort or contract, legislative or judicial. The formalist movement owed its origins certainly to Aristotle and also to the works of such writers as Locke, Montesquieu, and

Dicey. *See The Bridge, supra,* at 5. Their ideal kept government at bay, saying it could impose its will only through promulgation of laws by law-makers, who did not know the identity of those affected, and through enforcement of laws by judges, who were unbiased and immune to pressure. *See id.* Those laws were "clear, well-publicized rules that [were] capable of being obeyed." *Id.* Other propositions in that logic included treating similar cases similarly, saying no person is above the law, prevent-

ing rules from being retroactive, and ensuring that everyone has a day in court. *Id.* Such principles, argued the classicists, fostered activity and individual liberty and reduced arbitrariness and inequality.

When the formalists used classical reasoning and all the methods that accompany it, outcomes were fair, reasonable, and predictable. In fact, according to these classical thinkers, judges were better positioned than legislatures to reach the right conclusions because legislatures are political bodies and judges are reasoning people. Law became a science, taught as a science in law schools.

Such classical thought, unlike Aristotle's forms of argumentation, often ignored policy-based rationales. Judges turned to precedent to derive general principles that could be brought to bear on the cases before them, invoking policy only as an aid to establishing a strong rule. The practical result was that legal decisions in this era strongly favored businesses, including monopolies and entities who wanted to prevent strikes and collective bargaining.

Then came the Great Depression. Society changed. Economics changed. And other theories seemed to address these changes more effectively: philosophy became more pragmatic, Einstein's theories emerged, as did non-Euclidean geometry and new approaches in psychology and anthropology. They "all seemed to cast doubt on the utility of systems of axioms and theorems, the value of inductive and deductive reasoning, and the power of formal rules to organize human affairs." *See The Bridge*, *supra* at essay2. Formalism had no answer for these theories. They did not fit. Legal thought and the laws themselves underwent a transformation that has continued throughout the twentieth century.

Nevertheless, classical legal thought still percolates through some legal documents. *Seegenerally, e.g.*, RUGGERO J. ALDISERT, LOGIC FOR LAWYERS: A GUIDE TO CLEAR LEGAL THINKING (1992). Modern libertarianism is sometimes seen as another form of classicism. And some of what Aristotle labeled as logical processes are so natural as to be helpful in both reading and writing legal documents.

DEDUCTION: USING THE SYLLOGISM

The syllogism has three propositions that move from general to specific information: a *major premise*, which contains the *major term* (e.g., "All dogs"); a *minor premise*, which contains the *minor term* (e.g., Spot), and the *conclusion*, which is *deduced* from the two premises.

Syllogism 1. Standard Syllogism.

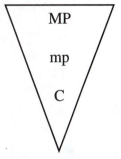

MAJOR PREMISE: **A dog is a being with four legs.**

MINOR PREMISE: **Spot is a dog.**

CONCLUSION: **Spot is a being with four legs.**

More technically, the *major term* is the *predicate term* of the conclusion, "four legs." The *minor term* is the *subject term* of the conclusion, "Spot." And the *middle term* is the term that appears in both of the premises but does not appear in the conclusion, "dog(s)." In a syllogism, the conclusion contains both the major and minor terms, but not the middle term.

Such reasoning appears in legal documents, though the premises are not labeled, of course. By analyzing a syllogism's major, minor, and subject terms, you can begin to see whether or not any deductive reasoning there is *valid*. Validity is a matter of form, not content, in classical terms. If the terms are properly drawn, the reasoning is valid, whether or not the premises are true. That link is, of course, essential in testing the reasoning in a legal source: a syllogism can be valid without its premises being true. Conversely, the premises may be true but the reasoning invalid. And a conclusion may be true even if the syllogism is invalid or if the premises are false; there is just no way to test whether or not the conclusion is true.

To test the validity, not necessarily the truth, of a proposition, ask the following five questions:

1. Does the syllogism use three and only three terms at a time? (It must)

2. Does the middle term apply to all cases in at least one of the premises? (It must)

3. If the term is distributed in the conclusion, is it distributed in the premises, that is, is the subject (A) of the major premise the predicate (B) of the minor premise? (It must be)

4. Does the argument have two negative premises? (It can't)

5. If either premise is negative, is the conclusion negative? (It must be)

Cooley at 292.

Further, each syllogism has a subject (A) and predicate (B). And each subject and predicate are joined by some form of the linking verb, *to be*. There are, then, four possible forms for any proposition:

All A's *are* B.	universal and affirmative
No A's *are* B.	universal and negative
Some A's *are* B.	particular and affirmative
Some A's *are* not B's.	particular and negative

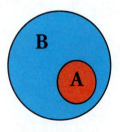

All A's are B.

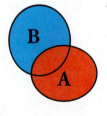

Some A's are B.

No A's are B.

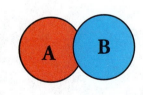

Some A's are not B's.

Each syllogism has three propositions, so there are 43, or 64 possible combinations of A and B, 256 possible syllogistic forms. Only twenty-four of those are valid. (*See Cooley* at 294).

For example, consider the following syllogism:

Syllogism 2. Invalid Syllogism Because of Undistributed Middle.

	A B
MAJOR PREMISE:	**All beagles are dogs.**
	C B
MINOR PREMISE:	**All French Poodles are dogs.**
	A C
CONCLUSION:	**All beagles are French poodles.**

This syllogism uses three terms: the major term is *dogs*, the minor term is *beagles*, but the middle term must be applied to all cases at least once. Nowhere here does it state that *All dogs are* .... Here, the premises are true, but the conclusion is invalid because the middle term is undistributed, that is, the subject (A) of the major premise is not the predicate (B) of the minor premise. That violates the second test of validity.

In Syllogism 1, the premises are true and the reasoning is valid, but look at the following:

Syllogism 3.   Untrue Syllogism Because of False Premise.

MAJOR PREMISE:	**All dogs have five legs.**
MINOR PREMISE:	**Spot is a dog.**
CONCLUSION:	**Spot has five legs.**

This argument is valid because it meets all five tests. But it is not true because the major premise is false. This happens in the law all the time: good reasoning with bad results. Trial courts reason well and appellate courts overturn them. Controversial, well-reasoned opinions like <u>Buck v. Bell</u> look bad in retrospect.

You can see where this is heading. Using the syllogism, you can read critically. You can assess the positions on each side of a transaction; you can assess the validity of a judge's decision; you can test your own reasoning as you build your document. As you read, be aware that a further complication arises when the conclusion is difficult to identify. When it has the word "therefore," it is easily identifiable. But the conclusion is not necessarily the statement that contains both the major and the minor terms but not the middle term. It may be a statement that looks very much like a major premise. To reconstruct a syllogism in law, you must be able to identify the conclusion. You cannot determine the major and minor premises unless you know the major term and the minor term, and you cannot determine the major and minor terms unless you know which proposition is the conclusion.

In the following syllogism, any of the statements could be the conclusion, but there is a maximum of one valid arrangement. Without knowing in which direction the syllogism is moving, it is impossible to know its validity, and this can happen in legal reasoning, too.

Syllogism 4.   Reversed Syllogism.

                    A   B
        All Spots are beings with four legs.
                    A   C
        All Spots are dogs.
            C   B
        Dogs are beings with four legs.

This syllogism is invalid in the direction shown, but valid if the first line is the conclusion.

As you analyze legal arguments, you can use syllogisms to test the validity of the arguments if you want to examine pure reasoning. Even when the model is not classical, such an examination can expose what role reasoning plays in the design. As you design your own document, you can use the syllogism in the same way. Assume, for the moment, that the reasoning is valid and that there are three propositions. Put the propositions in "A is B" form. Find the distributed term. The proposition without the distributed term in it is the conclusion. The proposition with the distributed term as its subject is the major premise. The term with the distributed term as its predicate object is the minor premise. And if there is no distributed term, or if there are other structural problems, such as more than three terms, then the syllogism is invalid and can be attacked in a variety of ways. Take for example, the following legal argument:

Syllogism 5. Valid Syllogism in Law.

MAJOR PREMISE: **Delay between the commission of an offense and the initiation of prosecution is a violation of defendant's due process rights.**

MINOR PREMISE: **The conduct of the State is a delay between this defendant's commission of the robbery and the State's initiation of prosecution.**

CONCLUSION: **Therefore, the conduct of the State is a violation of defendant's due process rights.**

This syllogism meets all five tests of validity: three terms at a time (*due process rights*, *State* as the major and minor terms, respectively, and *Delay* + its modifying prepositional phrase, *due process rights*, as the middle term); the middle term applies to all cases; the term distributed in the conclusion is distributed in the premises; the argument does not have two negative premises; and neither premise is negative, so we do not have to worry about the conclusion. The same is true of this syllogism:

Syllogism 6. Valid Syllogism in Law.

MAJOR PREMISE: **A party entitled to judgment as a matter of law is a party who can receive a directed verdict.**

MINOR PREMISE: **This party is entitled to judgment as a matter of law.**

CONCLUSION: **Therefore, this party is a party who can receive a directed verdict.**

In each example, the syllogism moves the reader from the general information to the specific conclusion. Of course, few legal propositions present themselves so neatly. Instead, the premises in legal arguments are themselves in dispute, depending on how they are stated.   Compare Syllogism 5 with the following:

Syllogism 7. Invalid Syllogism in Law.

> **MAJOR PREMISE:**   **Delay between the commission of an offense and the initiation of prosecution raises due process concerns.**
>
> **MINOR PREMISE:**   **There was a delay between this defendant's commission of the robbery and the State's initiation of prosecution because of investigative, not tactical, delay.**
>
> **CONCLUSION:**   **Therefore, the State did not violate defendant's due process rights.**

Huh? Ah, the major premise is really, *Some delays violate defendant's due process rights,* but this is not stated as such. As stated, the syllogism violates some of the tests. First, the argument deals with more than three terms: *due process rights* and *due process concerns* (are these the same or different?); *delay*; *State*; *investigative;* and *tactical.* Second, the repeated term, *delay,* is not applied to all cases because it is modified, which turns A into a subset of A, or the limited area in A that intersects with the modifier set. The syllogism collapses two syllogisms into one. This is *equivocation.* An argument equivocates when it uses the same term with more

than one meaning. If the meaning of a term in the argument shifts, that argument cannot be valid: A is B; B + 1 is C; therefore A is C. (See also the more detailed discussion of fallacies below.) The building begins to crumble.

TECHNIQUES

- *Test the validity of the syllogism in an argument, opinion, or memo.* Derive the major premise for the set of rules presented. Look at the facts of the case to derive the minor premise, and then see if the conclusion is valid, using the tests described above. The syllogism reveals steps in the logic, or lack of them. You can, in turn, decide how strong the source is and whether or not it can transfer into your document.

- *Make your hypothesis the conclusion; then use the primary sources to discover the major and minor premises.* Use the facts as the minor premise and the conclusion as itself (who wins and why? why this contract instead of another?). Then investigate the major premise. What is the foundation for the argument or the deal, the most general principle? You can test your hypothesis as you read to discover the general law that applies. From that term, you can match it to your facts to discover the minor premise. If this works, you may have at least one rudimentary model for your analysis: deduction.

- *Observe the similarities and differences among the syllogisms in all documents you are researching; is there a pattern?* Does it suggest a "logic" for your document? If your sources all use the same pattern, you may decide it is unwise to deviate. If they vary from each other, discover why; in turn, you may see the strengths and weaknesses of each case and the general strength of that area of the law.

- *Extract and synthesize your major premise from your resources.* Once you have read all of your resources, combine them to create your major premise. What parts do they have in common? What parts are updated and change the law? What is the law now? Create that major premise for your readers.

> *Test the validity and consistency of a contract by combining all parts into a syllogism.* Reconstruct the deal as a syllogism by starting with a major premise about the deal itself. (Deals that balance A with B work; this deal balances A with B; this deal works).

As you research, you can use the syllogism to test both the validity of your document and its relationship to similar documents. The hypotheses becomes the conclusion. Once you have a semi-refined conclusion, using the syllogism, you are then able to go to the library, where you may or may not find the same terms. The sources will provide the major and minor premises. This process may work best in reading opinions, but its principles may transfer to any research.

Example 4.13. Syllogism in Judicial Opinion.

While researching the procedures for the Voting Rights Act pre-clearance of voting changes, you come across <u>Young v. Fordice</u>, 520 U.S. 273 (1997). The procedural twists of this case are sorted out by gleaning the logical arguments. The Supreme Court ultimately goes with the Attorney General's logic. Testing the Attorney General's syllogism and comparing them with your own case can show you what procedures your client needs to follow.

We shall consider Mississippi's two important arguments to the contrary.

The first set of arguments concerns the effect of the Attorney General's preclearance letter. Mississippi points out that the Department of Justice wrote to the State on February 1, 1995, that the Attorney General did "not interpose any objection" to its NVRA changes. App. to Juris. Statement 17a. Hence, says Mississippi, the Attorney General has already precleared its efforts to comply.

The submission that the Attorney General approved, however, assumed that Mississippi's administrative changes would permit NVRA registrants to vote in both state and federal elections. The submission included a pamphlet entitled The National Voter Registration

Act, App. 26-43, which set forth what Mississippi's submission letter called the State's "plan to administratively implement NVRA on January 1, 1995." Id. at 110. The submission included legislative changes; indeed, Mississippi enclosed in the packet the proposed legislation that would have made a single NVRA registration valid for both federal and state elections. See id. at 86-104. The submission also included forms to be provided NVRA registrants, forms that, by their lack of specificity, probably would have led those voters—and the Attorney General—to believe that NVRA registration permitted them to vote in all elections. See id. at 44-50. These forms—perfectly understandable on the "single registration" assumption—might well mislead if they cannot in fact be used to register for state elections. Cf. City of Lockhart, 460 U.S. at 131-132, 103 S.Ct. at 1002 (requiring city to submit "entire system" because "[t]he possible discriminatory purpose or effect of the [changes], admittedly subject to § 5, cannot be determined in isolation from the 'preexisting' elements . . ."). Furthermore, the submission included no instructions to voter registration officials about treating NVRA registrants differently from other voters and provided for no notice to NVRA registrants that they could not vote in state elections.

Mississippi replies that, as a matter of logic, one could read its submission, with its explicit indication that the state legislation was proposed, but not yet enacted, as a request for approval of the administrative changes whether or not the state legislature passed the bill. It tries to derive further support for its claim by pointing to Department of Justice regulations that say that the Attorney General will not pre-clear unenacted legislation. See 28 C.F.R. §§ 51.22, 51.35 (1996). As a matter of pure logic, Mississippi is correct. One could logically understand the preclearance in the way the State suggests. But still, that is not the only way to understand it. At a minimum, its submission was ambiguous as to whether (1) it sought approval on the assumption that the state legislature would enact the bill, or (2) it sought approval whether or not the state legislature would enact the bill. Although there is one reference to the possibility of a "dual registration system" in the absence of legislation, App. 72, the submission simply did not specify what would happen if the legislature did not pass the bill, and it thereby created ambiguity about whether the practices and procedures described in the submission would be implemented regardless of

what the legislature did. The VRA permits the Attorney General to resolve such ambiguities against the submitting State. <u>See</u> <u>McCain</u>, 465 U.S. at 249, 255-257, 104 S.Ct. at 1045-1046, 1048-1050 (burden is on the State to submit a complete and unambiguous description of proposed changes); <u>Clark v. Roemer</u>, 500 U.S. 646, 658-659, 111 S.Ct. 2096, 2105, 114 L.Ed.2d 691, 700 (1991) (relying on "presumption that any ambiguity in the scope of the preclearance request must be construed against the state") (internal quotation marks and citations omitted); <u>see</u> <u>also</u> 28 C.F.R. § 51.26(d), 51.27(c) (1996) (requiring preclearance submissions to explain changes clearly and in detail). Hence the Attorney General could read her approval of the submitted plan as an approval of a plan that rested on the assumption that the proposed changes would be valid for all elections, not a plan in which NVRA registration does not qualify the registrant to vote in state elections. We find nothing in the Attorney General's regulations that forces a contrary conclusion.

<u>Young v. Fordice</u>, 520 U.S. 273, 286-88 (1997).

Comments: Here the court actually invokes strict logic—and rejects it. The Attorney General's argument can be outlined as the following syllogism:

> MAJOR PREMISE: The attorney general's approval for Voting Rights Act changes is approval for both national and state elections.
>
> MINOR PREMISE: Mississippi's voting rights changes that have the attorney general's approval.
>
> CONCLUSION: Therefore, Mississippi's changes are for both state and national elections.

The state's argument, as a matter of pure "logic," is different:

> MAJOR PREMISE: The attorney general's approval for Voting Rights Act changes is approval for only enacted changes.
>
> MINOR PREMISE: Mississippi submitted voting changes have the attorney general's approval.

CONCLUSION: Therefore, the attorney general approved
                           only the enacted national changes.

The problem with the state's argument is in the major premise. They are
building into the premise a condition that is ambiguous and, according to
precedent, is resolved against the state. You may derive different syllogisms from this discussion, showing that either the premises are untrue, as
here, or that there is invalid reasoning, as in the following:

MAJOR PREMISE: The attorney general's approval for Voting
                           Rights Act changes is approval for what is
                           explicitly stated in a proposal.

MINOR PREMISE: Mississippi explicitly stated that the Legislature
                           had not enacted the proposed changes.

CONCLUSION: Therefore, the attorney general approved
                           only the state changes.

Here, the state's argument has an undistributed middle. The subject of the
major premise is not the predicate of the minor premise. Either way, the
state's "logic" failed.

Deduction: Using the Enthymeme

Omitting the major premise or assuming the reader knows the major premise is called the *enthymeme*. Considered in classical rhetoric as the rhetorical equivalent of the syllogism, an *enthymeme* is a syllogism with an implied major premise: Since the officers' presence in the house was unlawful, they could not rely on defendant's consent to search. The syllogism is as follows:

Syllogism 8. Syllogism Using Enthymeme.

[MAJOR PREMISE: (Unstated)	All officers who are in a house unlawfully cannot search the house, even if a defendant consents.]
MINOR PREMISE:	The officers were in the house unlawfully.
CONCLUSION:	Therefore, the officers cannot search the house.

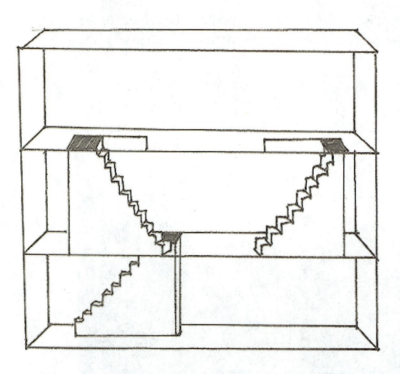

The enthymeme omits the major premise. You can use enthymemes to read as you discover omitted premises, and you may use them in you own writing.

In your memo, for example, you often have to infer major premise from a case or cases to use it as a foundation for your reasoning. You also use enthymemes in everyday conversation when you say such things as, "I'm going to be fired because I'm filing this brief late." The corresponding syllogism is as follows:

Syllogism 9. Syllogism Using Enthymeme.

[MAJOR PREMISE: (Unstated)	All people who file late briefs are fired.]
MINOR PREMISE:	I'm filing a late brief.
CONCLUSION:	Therefore, I am going to be fired.

If all traditional legal documents honored the standard syllogism, rather than using the enthymeme, they would be either infinite or incomplete. They would be infinite because the reasoning could still be valid but of dubious truth. That is, if what is true is proved only by true premises in a valid syllogism, then the premises themselves must be conclusions of syllogisms.

But those syllogisms in turn also rely on premises whose truth must be shown. The progression backward is infinite. While the syllogism exposes weaknesses in a source's structure, then, it has its own weakness. Namely, the major premise of the syllogism may itself depend on induction. As such, it is incomplete and needs informal logic to complete it. Alternatively, if the chain of syllogisms is truncated, the premises at the top are not proved; therefore, while the syllogism may be valid, the truth of the conclusions is dubious, uncertain. For the syllogism to be useful, then, it must admit of alternate means of finding truth, in logicians' terms, such as the enthymeme.

The modern audience is not patient enough for such formal, detailed logic. Neither was the classical audience, for that matter. Many links in the chain of an argument are apparent to the experienced reader; most writers will also assume a kind of intelligence in the reasoning process. That is, most writers omit some of the links because they give their audiences credit for being able to supply those missing links. These omissions become implied premises in the syllogism.

This truncated syllogism, the *enthymeme*, offers two possibilities to you as legal researcher and writer. First, when you read, remember to identify the unstated premises and question their truth. A judicial opinion may be based on an assumed premise that is simply not true, such as all people believe "A deal is a deal" in contract law. Second, when you write, you may wish to make explicit the source of questionable premises. That is, you may want to explain your premises, reveal more of your sources, or offer more detail in explaining the foundation of your argument.

Enthymemes are the lawyer's tool and delight, because anything left unsaid leaves room for other interpretations, which are the makings of counter arguments. Simply remember, as the writer and designer, to make explicit what you do not want questioned.

Example 4.14. Syllogisms and Enthymemes in a Judicial Opinion.

People v. Haven, 59 Cal. 2d 713, 381 P.2d 927, 31 Cal. Rptr. 47 (1963)

Summary from headnotes 5–8:

[5] Where defendant was suddenly confronted by five police officers who had entered his house unlawfully, without right or permission, the officers could not rely on defendant's consent to a search of his person; the substantial probability that the unlawful entry was essential to securing consent and the inescapable uncertainty whether the consent was voluntary precluded treating the consent as an independent valid basis for the ensuing search of defendant's person.

[6] A search and seizure made pursuant to consent secured immediately following an illegal entry or arrest is inextricably bound up with the illegal conduct and cannot be segregated therefrom, and is therefore invalid.

[7] A search of a hotel room, the key to which was found in defendant's pocket during a search of him at his home, was not justified as incidental to defendant's arrest, whether such arrest took place at his house or at the hotel room, where the hotel room was at a distance from defendant's house, and where the officers did not take defendant to the hotel and enter the hotel room to arrest him but to conduct a search, the arrest, which was made after marijuana was found in the room, thus being at most an incident of the search and not available as a pretext to justify it.

[8] When it appears that a search and not an arrest was the real object of officers in entering on premises, and that the arrest was a pretext for or at the most an incident of the search, the search is not reasonable within the meaning of the Constitution.

Enthymeme:	MP	[Entries into a home without evidence establishing a consent are entries into a home without consent.]
	mp	The officers' entry into defendant's home was entry into a home without evidence establishing consent.
	C	Therefore, the offers' entry into defendant's home was entry into a home without consent.

Syllogism:	MP	Entries into a home without consent are illegal entries.
	mp	The offers' entry into defendant's home was entry into a home without consent.
	C	Therefore, the officers' entry into defendant's home was an illegal entry.

Syllogism:	MP	Consents to searches given after illegal entries are consents that are not reliable.
	mp	[Defendant's consent was consent to search after an illegal entry.]
	C	Therefore, defendant's consent was a consent that was not reliable.

Syllogism:	MP	Searches made pursuant to consents that are not reliable are searches that require warrants.
	mp	The officers' search was a search made pursuant to consent that was not reliable.
	C	Therefore, the officers' search was a search that required a warrant.

Syllogism:	MP	Searches that require warrants that are conducted without warrants are illegal searches.
	mp	The officers' search was a search that required a warrant conducted without a warrant.
	C	Therefore, the officers' search was an illegal search.

Syllogism:	MP	Evidence gathered pursuant to an illegal search is evidence that cannot be admitted into court.
	mp	The evidence gathered by the officers was evidence gathered pursuant to an illegal search.
	C	Therefore, the evidence gathered by the officers is evidence that cannot be admitted into court.

We use enthymemes in the law, but they may cause trouble when they assume too much. The enthymeme follows all the rules and the questions for the syllogism. The validity of the twenty-four combinations is still true and the fallacies all apply. You must draw out the major premise to test the truth of all of the premises and the validity of the reasoning. Whereas the pure syllogism leads to a necessary conclusion from universally true premises, the enthymeme leads only to a tentative conclusion from probable premises. That is to say, truncating the syllogism automatically leaves open the possibility of untrue premises, which in turn invalidates the reasoning.

As you research the possibilities for your document, then, remember that bad reasoning often works—as does bad architecture. At least for a while. Be careful. A common fallacy used in law is the personal (*ad hominem*) argument, such as *Plaintiff is wasting the court's time with unfounded arguments*. Such tactics may catch a reader's attention but can damage the writer's credibility. A contract negotiated by using the straw man approach (*You want this, but that is unreasonable; you want that, but we don't like it*) may damage the negotiation's success and the negotiator's reputation. Choose your "logic" carefully. And define your terms.

A Further Word on Using Classical Syllogisms and Fallacies for Reading and Designing

The study of classical rhetoric will absorb you for years if you let it. This section allows you to indulge yourself a bit more, though it is rather long. As a foundation for American legal thought, it may be worth exploring because what follows is often a reaction against it.

So, as much as we do not formally follow it in U.S. legal discourse, we do harken to it from time to time. Its clean approach helps us to see sometimes how far away from it we have moved. These moves are revealing of both the validity of other kinds of logic and of our own assumptions. In that spirit, this section delves a bit deeper into both the syllogism and logical fallacies. Knowing these well may both sharpen your reading during research and rescue your design from logical pitfalls.

Some Structure Problems in Syllogisms

The attraction in using deduction as a means of assessing materials is the certainty of being able to identify these terms and identify a syllogism's validity in this rather mathematical way. Of the twenty-four valid forms, none can have a false conclusion if the premises are true, which provides the link between validity and truth.

Other structural problems occur in syllogisms, such as *Affirming the Consequent* and *Denying the Antecedent*. The first occurs in hypothetical or conditional arguments when the minor premise affirms the second part of the major premise: If A then B; B; Therefore A, as in the following syllogism.

Syllogism 8.   Invalid Syllogism: Affirming the Consequent.

MAJOR PREMISE:	Tactical delay between the commission of an offense and the initiation of prosecution violates a defendant's due process rights.
MINOR PREMISE:	The State did not create a tactical delay between this defendant's commission of the robbery and the State's initiation of prosecution.
CONCLUSION:	Therefore, the State did not violate defendant's due process rights.

In this syllogism, no valid conclusion can be drawn because other situations might also violate defendant's due process rights. (A is B; C is not A; but D, E, and F are also B). Proving the negative only allows the validity of the contrapositive, not the opposite proposition. (No A is B; therefore, B is not A). But in the following, a valid conclusion can be drawn. (A is not B; C is A; therefore, C is not B).

Syllogism 11. Corrected, Valid Syllogisms

MAJOR PREMISE: Investigative delays between the commission of an offense and the initiation of prosecution do not violate due process rights.

MINOR PREMISE: The delay between this defendant's commission of the robbery and the State's initiation of prosecution was investigative.

CONCLUSION: Therefore, the State did not violate defendant's due process rights.

This collapse is related to the enthymeme, discussed above, because it assumes the original separate premises and combines them into one.

Syllogism 12.   Invalid Syllogism: Denying the Antecedent.

MAJOR PREMISE: If the value of Sludgeco's common stock drops below 18, Mega Corp. will withdraw its takeover bid.

MINOR PREMISE: Mega Corp. withdrew its takeover bid.

CONCLUSION: Therefore, Sludgeco's common stock must have dropped below 18.

Similar to Affirming the Consequent, Denying the Antecedent occurs when the minor premise denies the first part of the major premise: If A then B; Not A; .re not B.

Syllogism 13. Corrected, Valid Syllogism.

MAJOR PREMISE: If Spumco delivered the goods after April
                       15, then they breached the contract.

MINOR PREMISE: But Spumco delivered the goods on April
                       13.

CONCLUSION: Therefore, Spumco did not breach the con-
                       tract.

Breaking the arguments into syllogisms helps call into question the
reasoning behind the major premises. Why this distinction between
delays? If delay is a problem, why isn't all delay a problem? Putting a
legal argument into this form shows its holes, controversial premises,
assumptions, bald assertions, and so on. Once you use the syllogism as a
means of testing deduction, you get used to its advantages and disadvan-
tages.

Fallacies

You must also be aware of logical fallacies. To present a sound analysis, you must anticipate and account for arguments against your client's
position. To design a document using traditional logic, you must be aware
of fallacies in reasoning, spot them when you are reading, and build around
them–just as an architect accounts for weaknesses in the land on which he
is constructing his building. So use traditional fallacies to anticipate counter arguments and to check the soundness of your own reasoning. You have
heard these terms enough among lawyers, but they are sometimes used too
loosely to be helpful. Add these to your growing repertoire.

a) Fallacy of the Undistributed Middle

This fallacy is caused by a failure to link the subject (S) of the
major premise to the predicate (P) of the minor premise. A is B; C is B;
therefore, C is A.

Syllogism 14.

MAJOR PREMISE:	Bank robbers violate federal statutes.
MINOR PREMISE:	Defendant violated a federal statute.
CONCLUSION:	Defendant is a bank robber.

b) Tautology

In a tautology, the second premise does not contain any more information than the first. This type of argument is circular because it merely restates the same claim in different words.

Syllogism 15.

MAJOR PREMISE:	Bank robbers violate federal statutes.
MINOR PREMISE:	Bank robbers break the law.
CONCLUSION:	Defendant broke the law.

c) Begging the Question

This fallacy is closely related to the tautology. Begging the question means that the argument assumes what it is trying to prove: "My client could not have broken the law because he is an upstanding citizen."

Syllogism 16.

MAJOR PREMISE:	Upstanding citizens do not break the law.
MINOR PREMISE:	My client is an upstanding citizen.
CONCLUSION:	My client did not break the law.

d) False Dichotomy (Either/Or Fallacy)

A false dichotomy occurs when a proposition is couched in "either/or" fashion in a situation where there are more than two possible alternatives or where the two alternatives are not mutually exclusive: If A, then B, but C also exists or B and C overlap. "If Mr. Gladstone was negligent by driving after drinking two beers (A), then Mr. Rodriguez (C) bears no liability for the automobile accident.(B)" Mr. Rodriguez's situation also exists, but the oritinal proposition does not address that. In the following, there are more than the two choices suggested in the major promise, such as a sentence of ten years.

Syllogism 17.

MAJOR PREMISE:	Either bank robbers should receive life sentences or community work..
MINOR PREMISE:	Defendant did not receive a life sentence.
CONCLUSION:	Defendant should do community work.

e) Straw Man

The straw man argument occurs when an argument is set up and then knocked down. This argument is fallacious when the original argument is mischaracterized. The argument fails to defeat the real claim. Even when the argument is stated correctly, the argument has no cohesion because it resembles a shooting gallery: up and down, up and down.

Syllogism 18.

ARGUMENT:	They say that upstanding citizens break the law.
COUNTER ARGUMENT:	But upstanding citizens do not break the law.
CONCLUSION:	My client is an upstanding citizen and did not break the law.

f) Slippery Slope

The slippery slope is an attack on analogical reasoning that suggests that, if one position prevails, it will give way to an endless series of bad positions when in fact there is a reasonable limitation on the first position.

Syllogism 19.

ARGUMENT:	If marijuana is legalized, this will lead to the legalization of cocaine, heroine, crack, and all other drugs.
Counter Argument:	A reasonable line can be drawn at marijuana without legalizing all drugs.
Conclusion:	Legalize marijuana.

g) Post Hoc, Ergo Propter Hoc (After this; therefore because of this)

An argument committing this fallacy mistakes temporal coincidence for causality. In other words, because A happened before B, A caused B. This causal link may be false for several reasons: there may be more than one cause, the listed cause may not be necessary or sufficient, the listed cause did not operate in this particular instance, and so on. "On the day that Ms. Mifune switched to Clean toothpaste, she suffered a seizure. Therefore, Clean proximately caused the seizure, making Clean Co. liable for Ms. Mifune's injuries."

Syllogism 20.

MAJOR PREMISE:	A car broke a dog's legs two days ago.
minor premise:	Spot has a broken leg.
Conclusion:	Spot's leg was broken by that car two days ago.

h) Ad Hominem

The ad hominem fallacy occurs when an argument addresses the character of those arguing instead of the issues involved. While questions of personal character may be relevant to some arguments, they are fallacious when they are used to divert attention from other issues. "Ms. Lincoln is an outspoken member of the NRA, which goes to prove that she is just the type of person who would commit an assault."

Syllogism 21.

MAJOR PREMISE:	Defendant robbed a bank.
MINOR PREMISE:	Defendant is mean, dishonest, and unfair.
CONCLUSION:	Defendant robbed this bank.

You may consider this fallacy as you consider ethos and pathos, as described in Chapter 5. Your design decisions may be affected by the character and emotions of your audience–as well as your own.

i) Red Herring

Similar to the ad hominem fallacy, the red herring fallacy is an irrelevant line of argument intended to divert attention away from the initial issue. "My client did not commit the murder. The victim lived an unsavory lifestyle, and was probably killed by Columbian druglords." This fallacy affects structure because it may add arguments or points that should not be included.

Syllogism 22.

MAJOR PREMISE:	Defendant robbed a bank.
MINOR PREMISE:	Banks do not have proper security.
CONCLUSION:	Defendant should have robbed the bank.

j) Hasty Generalization

This is an inductive fallacy, where an argument jumps to a conclusion based on inadequate evidence. The evidence may be inadequate in quantity, scope, or source. "In U.S. v. Lopez, the Supreme Court struck down the Gun–Free School Zones Act of 1990 as an invalid exercise of the Commerce Clause, on the grounds that gun possession in schools does not substantially affect interstate commerce. This shows that the Court will begin to actively protect the Second Amendment right of the people to keep and bear arms."

Syllogism 23.

MAJOR PREMISE:	Bank robberies have increased.
MINOR PREMISE:	Six banks have been robbed this year.
CONCLUSION:	All banks will be robbed; it's just a matter of time.

As you enjoy the syllogism's tidiness, be careful not to be seduced into designing documents that too literally replicate classical syllogisms. The syllogism may be more helpful for reading than for writing. It may reveal more as an extracting process than as a building one. You may find strictly syllogistic designs to be either too simplistic or too mechanical. The law school's IRAC (Issue/Rule/Application/Conclusion) or CRAC (Conclusion /Rule/Application/Conclusion) formulas reveal a general-to-specific approach, but often unnecessarily reduce analyses to inelegant and inaccurate patterns whose cues come more from the formula than the situation or the law. Both formulae suggest that the writer set forth all applicable law, then "apply" it to the facts, then reach a conclusion.

Overall, this sometimes works, but what lies in the "Application" sections might benefit from more explicit explanation, as discussed below and in Chapter 5. Rather than using the syllogism to test the validity of an argument, these formulae may suggest that you reduce your analysis to a general syllogism, oversimplifying the premises and omitting subtle details. Traditional legal forms borrow from the wealth of formal logic in reaching the so-called "rule," or major premise, and in creating the minor premise. The architecture will be too uniform.

TECHNIQUES FOR USING BASIC RHETORICAL MODELS TO READ AND DESIGN

1. Identify what root "logic" is being used: deductive or inductive.

2. Test the validity of the syllogisms within your source. Also, test the truth of the premises.

3. Identify definitional terms of art. Select phrases and terms of art for continuing your research.

4. Identify examples and analogies.

5. Handwrite the language of the sources so as to understand it yourself.

6. Translate or paraphrase the source into language that makes sense to you, remembering that it is your paraphrase. Use a similar technique with contracts.

7. Diagram the source so that you can understand the relationship of the language in syntactic terms.

8. Read the source aloud several times so that you can hear what it means.

9. Study the source's organization for content and consistency; outline or diagram it.

Moving to Design

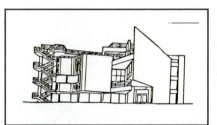

Classical legal thought offers at least two advantages to you as you research: a way of reading and a way of designing. Because so much classical thought still permeates legal writing, particularly opinions, you can impose inductive and deductive forms to expose a source's strengths and weaknesses. You can read to see how the reasoning proceeds, where it falters, where the possible comparisons and contrasts are. These classical forms allow you to read critically and closely, to take notes carefully, and to separate cases or contracts and resynthesize them for your perfect use.

The perfect syllogism is, of course, rare. The enthymeme raises questions about unstated premises. Fallacies abound. These problems that accompany infinite or incomplete formal logic highlight the need for imperfect but practicable, rather than perfect but impossible, reasoning. The common law system also had to create its own rules, example by example. Thus inductive reasoning, or the legal discourse community's modifications of it, became more prevalent in U.S. legal reasoning. Your researching of the possibilities of your document must incorporate induction, too.

Statutes may have explicit definitional sections that offer terms that courts will interpret. Contracts may also have lengthy definitions of terms that assist you in identifying those terms in cases and other contracts. And regulations will supply terminology for analyzing factual situations. The terms you extract from statutes, contracts, and regulations—and the impossibility of finding the perfect syllogism—offer a combination of classical deduction and induction.

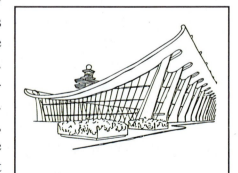

Then, from closely reading your sources and testing their forms according to classical models, you can discover possible designs emerging for your document. As you observe the premises used in constitutions, statutes, and contracts, you begin to find the common terms that blend them into a coherent whole. You begin to forge your own major premise for your own document, to hear what terms of art are most useful for your document, and to structure your document itself based on the premises you have been reading. This process of assembly is inductive and moves you into your own document's design. As you continue to design, the cases may offer not only evidence of deductive organizations, but also of inductive process of analogy and distinction. You begin to compare.

These comparisons form the bases of your design possibilities. You may wish to use a classical rhetorical model. This chapter has offered you a short course in classicism. By using the classical models, you may be better prepared for analyzing your materials' strengths and weaknesses, seeing how they fit together, and placing them in the proper landscape.

More likely, however, you will choose features from several sources, seeing a more sophisticated modern model emerge. You may see that classical models do not account for policy, efficiency, or social change. They may restrict, rather than liberate, your negotiations or arguments. You may itch for something based less on reasoning and more on rights. Or you may simply want an updated version of classicism. You are getting ready for more complicated forms. You are getting ready to design your space.

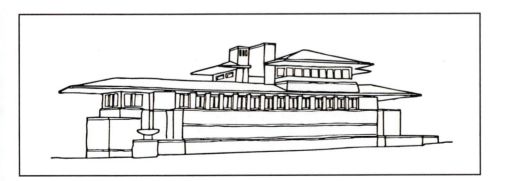

CHAPTER 5

DESIGNING THE SPACE

We shape our buildings: thereafter they shape us.

– Sir Winston Churchill

When you approach the National Gallery's East Wing in Washington, D.C., you are introduced to it by the pyramids that anticipate those at the Louvre. Those triangles anticipate the building's geometric concept of the triangle set on a trapezoid. On the right is the famous "touching" perspective, a fusion of marble that forms a triangular wall so tightly connected that you have to touch its perfectly smooth fusion to believe it. The marble is stained by the hands of casual visitors who hold on to the three-dimensional triangle as they look up the line formed by the two marble walls to the collision of triangle and blue sky. When you stand in the atrium, you stand under a giant Calder mobile that moves gently with the wind created by the gallery's visitors. You look up at a ceiling of glass triangles; you stand on a floor of marble triangles, and you see a gallery of triangular forms. One geometric concept. One gigantic space that holds hundreds of powerful pieces of art.

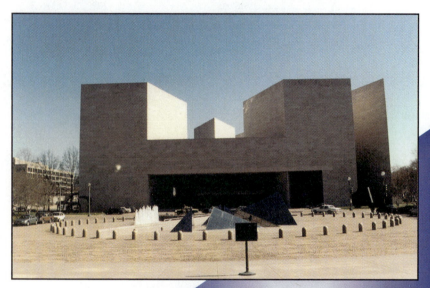

When I.M. Pei considered the East Wing, he designed the building's space in such a way as to suit a host of practical considerations: the landscape, an odd trapezoid of flat land; the building's function, to display modern works of art; the clients' needs, to host the art in a way that drew people in and kept them there; the appropriate size, perspective, and cost, among other things. He shaped several models before deciding on his final version, a version simple in its concept—the triangle upon the trapezoid—but complex in its execution. The design is unified, powerful, and highly successful in establishing the building's relationship to the main building, which is a neo-classical, domed, wisteria-trimmed monument to traditional art. You know immediately what the East Wing is, how it contrasts to its partner, and what to expect when you move throughout the gallery.

A reader likes to know the same things when she moves throughout a legal document. The essence of legal writing is its architecture, the arrangement of analytical space, its form. The first impression the reader takes is not of the first sentence but of the whole document. The reader asks, *What am I reading? What is this document—a memo, letter, list, part of brief, contract?* Then, *how long is it?* And, more analytically, *How is it put together? How many rooms are there? In what order are they presented? Why?* By answering these questions, you create in the reader's mind a design or form through which she absorbs your analysis and assimilates it with what she already knows. Your document becomes a companion to another she already knows. The two fit into a larger pattern of all the documents she's read.

As a reader begins reading a legal document, she should be able to recognize the document's form at a glance and, as she reads, she should see its proportions sharply. *How big is each room? Why? What is each room's relationship to the others?* Together with the document's overall form, its proportions give definitive messages about its function and how each part works analytically with the other parts. The legal architect's decisions reflect the fusion of form and function, the analogue between analysis and arrangement, and the partnership between proportion and purpose. Form and proportion are the architectural elements that substantively define the document, that embody the rhetorical elements, that place each smaller part into a coherent whole.

In other words, what comprises legal writing is not only the sentences, phrases, and vocabulary, nor is it only the law, arguments, or facts. It is their fusion into a particular form with particular proportions serving a particular purpose for a particular audience: its analytical architecture.

To meet all of your clients' demands, you may often create a unique form, an arrangement of your materials that suits the particular setting. Among the many possible design choices that can work, you select the one that coincides best with the situation. You may, in fact, need to negotiate with your client or others the document's form, proportion, and even interior design. As non-lawyers, but users of the document, some clients are often concerned about matters that lawyers have either overlooked or reduced in importance. As lawyers, other readers see aspects of the design that need to be emphasized or reconnected to other parts. Your ability to draft with a legal architect's expertise and flexibility is essential to your success.

> I don't think of form as a kind of architecture. The architecture is the result of the forming. It is the kinesthetic and visual sense of positions and wholeness that puts the thing into the realm of art.
>
> —Roy Lichtenstein

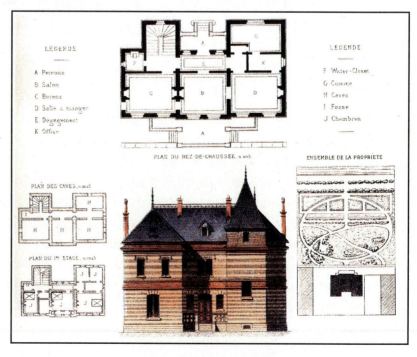

Think, then, about what you are building as you approach your drafting board. Is it a cathedral, with flying buttresses, gargoyles, stained glass windows? *The treatise.* Is it a Frank Lloyd Wright prairie home made to fit into the landscape and to cost very little? *The winning brief or elegant contract.* Or is it tract housing? *The form letter.* As a legal writer, you can design a variety of documents; clients select you to do the work according to your expertise and your ability to create documents that are appropriately functional and pleasing.

Just as good architectural form follows function, so does good document form follow its function. To design a document well, like any architect, you begin with the most fundamental concepts of design and then elaborate as you gain experience and expertise. In Chapter 2, you examined the architectural elements of legal documents. You saw several factors contributing to a document's form, such as historical practices, traditions, specialized creations for certain settings. The older judicial opinions based upon oral rhetorical practices, the traditional form contracts pasted together from hundreds of cases, and the agenda item created for use by an agency—all reveal architectural forms following legal functions, that is, fitting into particular circumstances and relaying contextual messages. You saw how the proportion of parts to each other also indicated the relationships among ideas and their relative importance.

The law, like architecture, lends itself to the drafting board. You can sketch three circles representing three elements to be discussed in a statutory analysis; scales representing a balancing test with indications about which factor will be discussed first and which outweighs the other; a web demonstrating the relationships among authorities with the discussion beginning at the center; or a standard outline indicating major topics and subtopics. Sketches of legal documents may

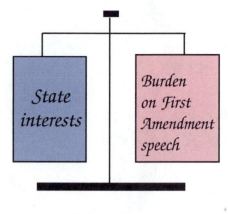

Balancing Test

use trees to indicate the *if...then* nature of a tax problem or flow charts that show elements of a transaction and their place in the formal contract.

Some pieces are more central, some are larger, and some are connected to others in surprising ways. It is this very peculiar "puzzle" nature of legal problem-solving that attracts lawyers and befuddles their clients. As a legal architect, you can translate your business transaction or legal analysis into a form with appropriate proportions that, by its design, explains the nature of the legal problem.

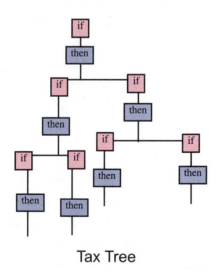

Tax Tree

You can also design the document's form to signal its accessibility. You may design it so that it can only be read from front to back: one entrance only. You may instead allow readers to enter your analysis in several places, such as through headings, an executive summary or statement of purpose, a conclusion, or a Table of Contents: several entrances with lots of internal movement. You may make three distinct breaks to three parts of the document, or even tab them: three entrances. You may need to rearrange the design to suit rhetorical purposes or a client's fears.

If you invest some time drawing and evaluating these form sketches before you write the document, you can avoid committing yourself to writer-based decisions that are hard to reverse. You are not the client. If you consider several possible ways to construct the document to suit your clients, you may save yourself from choosing a singular version that ends up to be too expensive, large, or confusing. Thus the time you invest sketching and evaluating possible forms can be time saved from redoing the document because you can use your sketches, not your extensive text, to figure out what to say.

By investing time in considering possible forms, you also build a rich repertoire from which to select your design, classical forms such as *deduction*, *induction*, or *enthymeme*; neo-classical forms such as *analogy-within-deduction, balancing test, element-by-element, elements-within-induction, elements-within-deduction, enthymeme*; or modern forms such as *inversion*, or *reverse order*. These possibilities enable you to identify and manipulate your design elements. Using principles of classical rhetoric, you can sharpen argumentation. Using historical knowledge, you can choose from many perspectives. Using the principles of modern rhetoric, you can sharpen your ability to meet your audience's needs. Using the experience of colleagues, you can avoid beginners' mistakes. And using the design elements discussed in Chapters 1 and 2, you can develop efficiency in designing legal documents, whether they are standard contracts or ground-breaking briefs, form letters or complicated transactional documents.

This chapter's theme is *Design a form that advances your document's purpose and matches its theme*. The analytical "space" you design guides your reader's thinking as much, if not more than, the words. The arrangement of concepts, negotiating positions, or arguments shapes your reader's reactions. Your anticipation of those reactions helps you design the space.

This chapter suggests that you use the elements discussed in Chapters 1 and 2 and the preparatory methods developed in Chapter 3 to build on the basic architectural shapes discussed in Chapter 4. This chapter adds shapes to your repertoire by exploring three approaches to building legal documents: 1) using neo-classical, traditional designs; 2) customizing modern designs to fit specific settings; and 3) creating unique designs that shape legal thinking itself.

Architecture is the art of creating a space.

- Yoshinoba Ashihara

As you design, you might want to think about guiding your reader through a museum collection. The exhibits must be arranged with some larger goal in mind, such as informing the viewers about Picasso's swift and stunning rise as a painter, not just showing several small pictures. If you group different painters together or place their paintings separately, if you use subject or chronological arrangement, you are guiding the manner in which your viewers will see and learn. As a legal designer, your goal may be to achieve a successful negotiation or to edu-

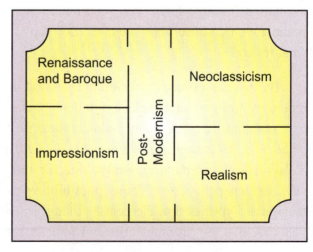

cate the court; it may be to construct a unique theory of law or to send a firm message to a client. Remember that your floor plan itself sends a message. To design effectively, revisit both rhetorical and architectural elements in a more specific document design setting.

Remembering Rhetoric

As you see your theme emerging, as you complete your exploration of the topic so that you understand it well, as you commit to memory your knowledge of the subject, you begin to see various designs for presenting that information. But according to what? How do you decide what order is best? How do you usher your readers, who may or may not read sequentially, through the document? How do you keep your various readers engaged? By revisiting your rhetorical questions and refining your answers, you can see architectural choices starting to emerge.

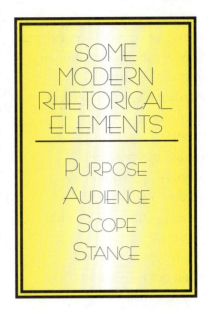

SOME MODERN RHETORICAL ELEMENTS

PURPOSE
AUDIENCE
SCOPE
STANCE

Purpose

Your document's purpose is a primary element in choosing which design works best. Knowing what you now know, what design will make the document most useful, ensure that it fulfills its function? Having researched the document's possibilities, you are aware that it can serve several purposes, so the possible combinations of its parts increase. By deciding the relationship among the possible purposes, you may begin to decide what parts of the document precede others. These complex purposes in legal writing make your design choices difficult and time-consuming; they are also at the root of design disagreements between writers and supervisors. You may find negotiating the hierarchy of purposes the most essential factor in deciding what design to use.

Some Possible Purposes for Legal Documents

To persuade
To inform
To settle
To find out what the court will do
To determine if the client is breaking the law
To intimidate
To reassure or instill confidence
To lay out the facts politically
To protect the firm
To update a specific project
To position
To settle
To avoid malpractice
To analyze potential risk
To create a paper trail
To create a transmittal letter
To build business
To convey property
To find out information
To bind parties

To set out duties, rights, and responsibilities
To get parties to agree
To deny
To convince a client to sue or not to sue
To focus a lot of people on a topic or issue
To structure the end of a transaction
To make the other side look bad
To satisfy a client's internal reporting requirements
To have someone take action, e.g., not ask any more questions
To cover yourself
To ask for something
To support a decision or a position
To discuss problems in proposed actions
To harass, annoy, placate

Fundamental to designing your document's form, these possible purposes help you to articulate your design choices. As discussed in Chapter 3, put your purposes in order so that your small-scale design decisions are also consistent with the overall hierarchy you select. For example, if you are writing a brief, your purposes include both informing and persuading. You may design a brief on family law that prioritizes persuading by putting your client's strongest argument first, or you may design a patent law brief that prioritizes informing by orienting the judge to the problem's technical parameters. You will also be trying to assist the judge's clerk, so you may design a brief that persuades by its interconnected purposes, such as to make arguments accessible and citations perfect. Keep reviewing your decisions on purposes—and remember them as you select your design.

If you are designing an employment contract, you may be trying to do at least two things: protect your client's interests by putting in a covenant not to compete and convince a renowned doctor to join the practice. If the first purpose is more important, you may arrange the contract by putting your client's requirements first; if the second purpose is more important, you may arrange the contract by showing the prospective doctor the benefits provided by joining the practice. Whatever the type of document, your decisions on purpose will directly affect your design.

AUDIENCE

Your audiences deserve the same treatment. By the time you have gathered all of your materials and learned more about your audiences' needs, you should have a better sense of scope and proportion. You may need large sections that are immediately accessible to both experts and nonexperts, or you may want smaller sections for the uninitiated to explore on their own. You may be designing a contract for a stubborn client who wants very specific sections omitted; but you must also keep your eye on the court who may eventually examine the document and question the omissions. Again, write down all of your possible audiences and decide who is most important on your list.

If you are new in an office, your first priority may be your supervising attorney. She will inform your decisions on design, and you may take your design cues from some of her previously written documents. If you are working in a federal agency, your supervisor's supervisor may be your highest priority, the person who makes the final decisions. If you are handling your own clients, your client may be your first priority because you are concerned with keeping his business. Or if you are drafting legislation, the public may be your first priority because the legislation is controversial and far-reaching.

SOME POSSIBLE AUDIENCES

• Judges	• Law clerks	• Consumers
• Supervising attorney	• Law students	• Federal agencies
• Other lawyers	• The public	• Journal editors
• Opposing counsel	• Congressional staff	• Friends and peers
• The client	• The board of directors	

You may sometimes have the luxury of a commission from a rich client: a contract that you can draft by hand, afresh, designing the transaction in your own language. More often you will have a commission for a "public building," that is, a document accessible to many members of the public, who have neither the experience nor the expertise to navigate a complicated document. So the first person on your *audience* list may help you make tough decisions about order, size, and detail; but the sum of your *audiences* will help you make final decisions on your overall design.

Your research may have revealed very interesting choices on your document's scope. What you had thought was a short contract now has 137 sections; what you thought was a large brief has boiled down to ten pages. Some scopes are dictated by rules within a jurisdiction; others are created by developing a strategy or negotiating with your audiences. When you are ready to make final design decisions, make sure the scope takes into account not your concerns (*But I found all of this research—I just have to use it!*), but your reader's concerns (*Give me only what I need to complete the transaction and keep me out of court*).

Your decision on scope may rest on an external restraint, such as a page limit, or may flow from the document's purposes and audiences. You can carefully cull the essentials. If you are including a boilerplate section or a source or a fact, your audiences assume it is essential to the document's purposes. If you include it and never use it again, your audiences will likely be confused. *What is this? Why do I have it? What am I supposed to do with it?* Use only those materials the document actually needs.

Scope applies not only to the materials you choose to include in your document but also to how much detail you use in implementing them. You can choose to elaborate on a case or capture only its holding; you can choose to use six different verbs to account for possible obligations in a contract—or two. You can choose to lengthen paragraphs to give additional information or omit that information altogether.

Scope is also affected by practical considerations you have probably decided on at this point in your design process, such as how long you expect the document to endure, how many future audiences may use it, or how local culture limits how much you can expect to be read. If you expect the document to have a long life, you may want to give more context and background, more detail for those who will not be familiar with the document's original setting. If you know that the document will be short–lived, you may be able to omit details familiar to all audiences. Select your scope creatively to make the most use of your materials.

SOME POSSIBLE SCOPES

External considerations

- Everything that comes up in the transaction, past, present, future
- Ten pages
- Limited number of jurisdictions
- All jurisdictions

Internal considerations

- Major negotiated points, boilerplate, general reference to the rest
- Outline of the cases in bullet form
- One page "executive" summary
- Detailed reference document with table of contents and tabs
- Chart of relevant sources

STANCE

Having researched your document's possibilities, you now choose a stance. *From what angle do you want to present the information?* You can think of stance as the architect thinks of perspective: how the building looks from the client's height and how the angles, shadows, and curves pull the client into the building and give the client a consistent sense of calm, awe, comfort, or power. Your decisions about stance sharpen the contours of your analysis by making them consistent, unified, and directed.

Again, you have many possibilities. You may choose to be blunt in a letter discouraging a client from asking so many questions, or you may choose to be cautious in responding to a settlement letter. You may want to be crisp and businesslike in your contract provisions. Of course, these choices are not always so singular. The combination of possible stances within one document may sometimes seem contradictory. If so, try to resolve those conflicts. You may wish to take a neutral stance but find yourself persuading as you explain your analysis to a client. You may wish to be aggressive in collecting a bill only to find yourself apologizing for taking so long to get back to your client. You may instead prefer to be passive when allowing your client to determine what direction to take in the transaction, yet you see yourself pushing as you compose the letter. Untangle these stances, decide which should predominate, or find another that gives the document the consistent stance that will accomplish your purpose and reach your reader.

Your stance also leads directly to internal design choices, such as voice and tone. Once you choose a consistent point of view, your voice will emerge more strongly and your word choices will build the appropriate tone. Again, it is worth your time to consider your choices and place them in a hierarchy. Then you can begin to create your architecture from a focused point of view.

Your answers to the questions of purpose, audience, scope, and stance form the rhetorical foundation for your design decisions. Because legal writing is a socially-situated act, you will always be deciding among many choices, some of them defined explicitly by supervising attorneys or forms, some of them defined implicitly by office traditions, and some

SOME POSSIBLE STANCES

• Aggressive	• Bemused
• Conciliatory	• Business-like
• Patient	• Determined
• Kind	• Weary
• Firm	• Impatient
• Apologetic	• Exasperated
• Cautious	• Calm
• Witty	• Concerned
• Helpful	• Indignant

of them inexplicable. Design your document to fit into its dynamic setting, to move most gracefully from user to user, and to preserve both legal and ethical integrity.

As you design, then, you may realize that the integrity of your explanation, argument, or mode of negotiation might call upon not just the "logical" possibilities explained in more detail below, but also on other matters, such as process, equity, policy, or economics. You may base your design decisions not on so-called legal reasoning, but on the effect your narrative will have on your audience or on the raw fairness of the situation.

Your ability to clarify or negotiate the deeper rhetorical concerns of the writing will lead to clearer decisions about its architecture. Some of your decisions are easy; they have been standardized for you by years of tradition and practice, as discussed in Chapter 4. Others are more complex, yet traditional; these are choices among neo-classical approaches to legal architecture. Other decisions ask you to use modern designs to fuse current law with current circumstances. And yet other decisions call on your most sophisticated notions of design; these postmodern choices break with tradition and allow you to formulate unique documents based on your synthesis of situation and rhetoric. What follows are some of the most traditional, reliable, and easily recognizable legal architectures.

A Word on Design Repertoire

Whether your purpose is to inform or persuade, to predict or prevent, you have available to you scores of traditional, though non-standard, designs. Both the classical and modern rhetoricians categorize and label traditional forms of negotiating and arguing. Both recognize that these designs are points of departure, within which the writer must arrange materials to suit the document's purpose. The classical rhetoricians recognized that law was a special discourse, some of which drew upon the principles of argumentation used in classical rhetoric. Law's evolution since that time, particularly in the U.S. system where *stare decisis* principles have created a specialized kind of reasoning, has spawned a rich, traditional repertoire of document design possibilities. These traditional legal document designs include classical deductive and inductive reasoning. In the United States, neo-classical designs also include the embedding of analogical reasoning—the comparing of two seemingly like entities for the purpose of concluding that they should be treated the same way—within deduction. These three combinations of the triangle are the fundamental forms of most traditional legal document designs.

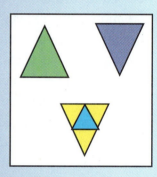

If you choose the classical or neoclassical school of design, your document's form may resemble the classical *Proof* or *Refutation*. The classical rhetoricians created three categories of *artistic proofs* that have survived some traditional legal documents, even contracts: *pathos*, a pres-

entation based on anticipated audience response; *ethos*, a presentation based on the authority or character of the speaker; and *logos*, a presentation based on text or reasoning. The *non-artistic proofs*, such as witnesses and oaths, used by classical lawyers accompany these *artistic* proofs (see below). The difference between the two is that the *artistic proofs* require more work than the "non-artistic" proofs, which simply find what is there. *Artistic proofs* require you to explore all three possible *proofs*, none of which is mutually exclusive or stands alone. This exploration directly affects your design decisions.

The traditional school of document design uses three related modes: *equity*, based on the audience's sense of fairness; *policy*, based on the audience's sense of the societal norms that drive the law; and *logic*, based on text or reasoning. Traditionally, legal documents based on text or reason have received more attention, perhaps because of choices made in law school design over a century ago. Then, "the scientific method was adapted as an instructional model for legal education. It was directed by logic and the systematic study of precedent as a means of rationally discovering legal rules. The case method viewed law as an empirical science and rejected all non-rational persuasion and judicial decision-making." Linda Levine & Kurt M. Saunders, *Thinking Like A Rhetor*, 43 J. LEGAL EDUC. 108 (1993).

This approach, still alive in law today, places reason at the center of legal problem-solving, sometimes to the exclusion of *ethos, pathos, policy,* or practicality. Thus many of the designs lawyers use owe their origins in patterns of reasoning set in the last one hundred years. You may find this comforting or upsetting; in either case, putting reasoning in a larger context gives your designs more possibilities.

SOME TRADITIONAL PROOFS

CLASSICAL "ARTISTIC" PROOFS

Logos: based on text or reasoning

Pathos: based on anticipated audience response

Ethos: based on authority or character of the speaker

TRADITIONAL LEGAL PROOFS

Logic: based on text or reasoning

Equity: based on fairness

Policy: based on context and values

LOGOS AND "LOGIC"

Within our legal community, we have developed peculiar forms of reasoning that spring from the law itself, the traditions of practice, and the particulars of clients' situations. In classical rhetoric, legal argument had its own form of rhetoric, *forensic rhetoric*, which was concerned with justice and injustice, accusation and defense. The lawyer's tools, again, were often the *non-artistic proofs*, the witnesses, contracts, oaths, and so on. And the lawyer did not always have to invent his topic because his clients did that for him. Nevertheless, the classical lawyer invoked argumentative principles in presenting a defense. As he developed the art of legal oratory, he also developed the particular form of *logos* that worked in the courtroom, making sure his premises were true and his reasoning valid.

In Chapter 4, you examined that traditional Western logic, the formal deduction and informal induction used in western societies since Aristotle identified them. As a tool for testing the possibilities for the materials you gather, the syllogism forces you to test the truth of the premises and the validity of the reasoning. Formal reasoning can be incomplete when premises are missing or their origin is unclear. Induction gives you the means for filling in the gaps. Together, they help you test the validity of the reasoning in cases, opposing briefs, letters, and negotiation tactics. You can examine the assumptions behind contract provisions and plan your strategies accordingly. This ability to dissect reasoning is a key to your design decisions.

Be aware, however, that you are working within the boundaries of very traditional western civilizations, whose concept of "logic" may differ from what others consider "logic." A lawyer from the United States may approach negotiations with a lawyer from Japan by setting out each step in a transaction, literally taking the lawyer through every possible argument. The path those arguments take seems sensible to someone from the United States—"logical." In fact, the U.S. lawyer may be making two large mistakes in his "logic," both cultural and analytical. Being literal about each step may insult a Japanese lawyer, who expects to understand the contours of the transaction but not to be led like a child through each step. And the approach to the transaction may not conform to the Japanese lawyer's sense of what should come first, second, and so on. Another Japanese lawyer might respond differently yet. Similarly, a Mexican lawyer may be put off by the direct, short, dry approach of U.S. legal thinking; an Indonesian lawyer may find the approaches to statutory interpretation in sharp contrast to those written into the Indonesian code.

Such clashes occur within the U.S. culture, too. One lawyer may draft a brief, feeling that his arguments are quite "logical," only to have the brief rearranged by a supervising attorney, who sees another "logic." Thus the term "logic" may be too general or too complex to be the final justification for designing your document. You may find it more useful to understand the various types of traditional Western "logic" that we use in the law, then to customize that "logic" to your client's needs.

Your design decisions must account for these differences. Traditional Western "logic," based on the classicist perspective outlined in previous chapters and in this one, offers you a large-scale arrangement that covers the ingredients of a legal argument in the United States. This traditional "logic" also offers cues about arranging other documents, such as letters explaining a situation, but subtly trying to dissuade a client from a potentially harmful course of action; memos reporting on unfavorable law; or negotiations that lead to a particular transaction. Your large scale organizational choices fall basically within *deduction* and *induction*. In fact, we have developed a peculiar hybrid, *analogy within deduction*, discussed more completely below under Neoclassicism.

Remind yourself of all aspects of your traditional presentation, aspects that inform your decisions on overall strategies, approach and tone, sentence structure, and word choice. These are the less explicitly treated aspects of design because they flow from less well-articulated traits, such as *character*, *judgment*, *morals*, and *societal norms*. Some modern commentators scorn them, but you, as designer, can incorporate them as you choose. As you design the document to suit your audiences' needs, you are also building your own reputation as a problem solver, dispute preventer, international arbitrator, or businessperson. Therefore, consider several schools of design as you select a model: neoclassicism, which focuses on reason; modernism, which focuses on what will be most appropriate, ethical, and practical in the circumstances; or postmodernism, which combines the personal with the political.

Designing your document is creating a schema for your reader to follow, a plan that is at once coherent and accessible. As you make your design decisions, then, you can explore all of the modern rhetorical elements of purpose, audience, scope, and stance to design your document. Weave into those the more classical concepts of your audiences' emotions if you are arguing, your own credibility as you present your analysis, or the fairness of your situation if you are negotiating. Then begin to design. You may choose *narrative* arrangements, as dictated by *pathos,* or an appeal to the audience's passions; *anecdote*, as dictated by *ethos*, or an appeal to the audience's sense of the speaker's character; or *deductive* or *inductive* arrangements, as dictated by *logos*.

Some design choices are discussed in detail below, but the best design is often your own, based purely on these rhetorical considerations. Consider both the outer contours of your presentation, the form and the inner contours, the size and relationship of the document's rooms—the proportions.

CHOOSING NEOCLASSICISM: ANALOGY WITHIN DEDUCTION

In modern U.S. practice, we have developed a peculiar blend of deduction and induction that is a popular traditional form: Analogy within Deduction. This form is a descendent of classical rhetoric, an unusual hybrid that combines our propensity for deduction with our need to account for common law decisions. In the U.S. system, the combination of statutory and common law allows you to present your major premises by stating statutory language, a deductive process, or to synthesize your major premise from several cases, an inductive process. In addition, you might use example to make your point practical. In a strictly common law system, you use induction to fashion the rules that apply to this situation; by reading similar cases, you infer from the cases' respective outcomes what the rule is for those situations. You then compare your client's situation to the others and to the rule derived from the others.

What occurs between the rule—whether derived deductively from statutes or inductively from cases—and the conclusion in this overall deductive organization is often analogical reasoning. You use this between the rule and conclusion in our common law system because *stare decisis* requires you to compare a situation to previous law. At one time, argumentation in the U.S. legal system was almost exclusively analogical, requiring inductive arguments that pulled comparisons to other cases with no overriding, explicit principles against which to judge or predict the outcome. Our legal system has now codified most of those resulting principles, and thus, from a neoclassical perspective, combines statutory and common law analysis in a peculiar hybrid of induction and deduction.

ANALOGY WITHIN DEDUCTION

1. DEFINE THE RULE BY STATING THE STATUTE OR SYNTHESIZING PRECEDENT. THIS IS THE MAJOR PREMISE.

2. IN UNCERTAIN AREAS, DEFINE TERMS.

3. PRESENT THE CLIENT'S SITUATION AS THE MINOR PREMISE.

4. PROVE THE MINOR PREMISE BY ANALOGIZING IT TO PREVIOUS CASES.

5. DISPROVE THE COUNTERARGUMENT MINOR PREMISE BY DISTINGUISHING IT FROM PREVIOUS CASES.

6. ONCE THE MINOR PREMISE IS PROVED, PUT BACK IN SYLLOGISTIC FORM TO REACH CONCLUSION.

This traditional form is generally used to define the terms of the major premise in such a way that it will show that the minor premise falls inside—or outside, as the case may be—the rule. In the following example, the analogy to previous, similar cases demonstrates that like cases are being treated in a like manner. Note that steps 2 and 3 are often interchanged. Whatever order you chose, the details are necessary because the U.S. reader expects to see the precise comparison with previous cases. In this example, the comparison is factually identical. Here, the comparison may be not just to facts, but to the policies behind the reasoning or the reasoning itself.

The mechanics of this neoclassical traditional form of U.S. legal proof go something like this:

Example 5.1 Analogy Within Deduction I: Using the Syllogism

> 1. Define the rule by stating the statute or synthesizing precedent. This is the major premise.

Syllogism 24.

> MAJOR PREMISE: In cases of gifts of payment for medical expenses, where payment is made by a qualified transfer, people are exempt from gift taxes.

> 2. In uncertain areas, define terms.

> ANALOGOUS CASES:
>
> a) A case similar to the client's case, where a gift was determined to be for medical expenses;
>
> b) Another case similar to the client's case, where a gift was determined to be for medical expenses;
>
> c) A case in which payment to the doctor by bank check was determined to be a qualified transfer for the purposes of the tax code;
>
> d) Another case in which payment to the doctor by bank check was determined to be a qualified transfer for the purposes of the tax code;
>
> e) Another case in which payment to the doctor by bank check was determined to be a qualified transfer for the purposes of the tax code.

> ### 3.　Present the client's situation as the minor premise.

MINOR PREMISE:　Our client's payment was a gift for medical expenses and was made by a qualified transfer.

> ### 4.　Prove the minor premise by analogizing it to previous cases.

ANALOGIZING:　　My client's case is one of a gift of payment for medical expenses, where payment was made by a qualified transfer, just like cases a) – e).

> 1.　This gift was for medical expenses, just like the ones in a) and b).
>
> 2.　This payment to the doctor was by bank check just like the payment in c) – e).

> ### 5.　Disprove the counterargument minor premise by distinguishing it from previous cases.

You may have not only cases a) – e) to account for, but you may also have the following cases:

> f)　A case different from client's case, where a gift was determined to be not for medical expenses;
>
> g)　A case similar to the client's case, where a gift was determined to be not for medical expenses;
>
> h)　A case in which payment to the doctor by personal check was determined to be not a qualified transfer for the purposes of the tax code;
>
> i)　Another case in which payment to the doctor by cash was determined to be not a qualified transfer for the purposes of the tax code.

Now you must account not only for the contrast to these cases, but for the counter-arguments that weaken your client's case. This is just comparing and contrasting, but such a requirement offers several permutations and combinations for your design. So, you may need to establish the counter-arguments and why your minor premise is the appropriate choice.

> DISTINGUISHING: My client's case is not like the cases where a gift was not for medical expenses or paid by bank check.

> 6. Once the minor premise is proved, put back in syllogistic form to reach conclusion.

> CONCLUSION: My client does not have to pay the gift tax.

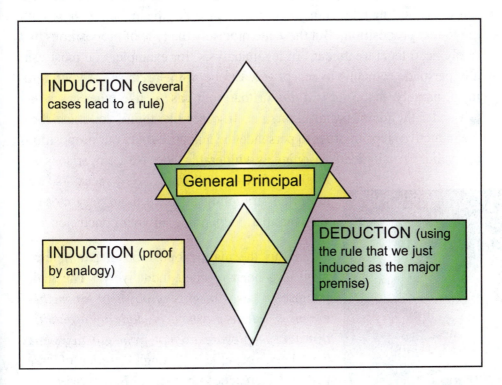

As a design matter, your deductive approach bulges while you make the comparisons. Then, within the section on comparisons, you have several choices: summarize all similar cases and compare in one large analogy; summarize some cases and compare to those small groups, such as demonstrated above; compare to each case; and so on. You may wish to revisit your rhetorical elements to decide the best way to present these comparisons. A busy audience with a scope defined by page limits may require you to synthesize your analogy more succinctly. If your purpose is to win by drawing a fine distinction between your case and all the rest, you may wish to do several smaller comparisons.

Neoclassical argumentation is still popular, but there are a number of problems that call the truth of the premises into question. Legal arguments almost always contain propositions or premises that are in dispute or are uncertain. Consequently, in legal arguments you frequently must "show your work" by making explicit the inductive, analogical reasoning used to reach your premises. For example, in Example 4.7, the proposition *All dogs are beings with four legs* was, at some point, reached by induction. We are not born with an innate knowledge of dog anatomy, but we experience it during our lives, and so have generations before us. After a while, the proposition becomes so uncontroversial, so much a matter of common sense, that we do not feel the need to recount all of the inductive steps leading to that proposition. But these are precisely the type of propositions that rarely need legal treatment. In legal analysis, for example, you must usually persuade someone to accept at least one of the premises of your argument, namely, that *Spot is a dog* or that your case is like other cases that fall under the major premise, or rule. In cases like these, you must show the inductive steps in order to persuade the audience that your propositions are valid. Analogical reasoning is vulnerable because comparisons are rarely perfect—on all fours, so to speak—so you are often struggling to make them very close or very far apart, depending on your conclusion.

Thus the main proposition in Example 5.1 may have been reached inductively. The major premise *In cases of gifts of payment for medical expenses, where payment is made by a qualified transfer, people are exempt from gift taxes* may have been formulated through a series of cases that finally reached that rule. Some cases may have occurred where there was a controversy and, after a series of decisions, the stated major premise may have become the law. The history may or may not be significant to your design. If the premise is new or still controversial, then you may want to explain what led to it. If it is old and uncontroversial, simply stating it may be enough.

In legal writing, you create the same kinds of categories. You look at a group of cases with similar characteristics and pick out what you think are the most crucial ones. For example, from the <u>Miranda</u> cases, courts have decided that such things like the place, duration, and tone of interrogation are important features, worthy of being the things you analogize your own cases to. (*See* Example 5.3).

In neoclassism, you are "proving" your conclusion by using the reasoning methods described above. To make sure that your premises are "true," you are often "proving" your premises by demonstrating their sources. Increasingly, statutory texts and prescriptive judicial opinions give you less room to maneuver your major premise. Instead, you are often "proving" your minor premise by using analogy. This combination of deduction and induction is the architecture peculiar to neoclassicism.

This neoclassical approach to reasoning occurs frequently in legal practice. That is, an analysis, discussion, explanation will move from the general to the specific, carrying the reader through top-down thinking that applies a more abstract rule to a specific situation, as in the following examples.

Example 5.2. Analogical Reasoning in a Judicial Opinion.

A. <u>Motions for Directed Verdict and Judgment N.O.V.</u>

> Define the rule by synthesizing precedent.

"A directed verdict and a judgment n.o.v. are justified only if, after looking at the evidence and all reasonable inferences in a light most favorable to the nonmoving party, 'the trial court concludes that there is no competent evidence which would support a verdict in his favor.'" <u>DeBry v. Cascade Enters.</u>, 879 P.2d 1353,1359 (Utah 1994)(quoting <u>Gustaveson v. Gregg</u>, 655 P.2d 693, 695 (Utah 1982)). If reasonable persons could reach differing conclusions on the issue in controversy, then the motion should be denied. <u>Id.</u>; <u>Management Comm. of Graystone Pines Homeowners As'n v. Graystone Pines, Inc.</u>, 652 P.2d 896, 897–98 (Utah 1982). Thus, a motion for a directed verdict or judgment n.o.v. can be granted only when the moving party is entitled to judgment as a matter of law. <u>Hansen v. Stewart</u>, 761 P.2d 14, 17 (Utah 1988). In reviewing the trial court's denial of a directed verdict and a judgment n.o.v., this court applies the same standard.

> **Present the situation as minor premise.**

Wilcox asserts that the trial court erred in not granting his motion for a directed verdict and a judgment n.o.v. because reasonable minds could not conclude that Wilcox ever had "exclusive possession and control" of the cattle. Plaintiffs' cattle were grazed for an extended period of time on public land to which the general public had access. Plaintiffs also had a key to access Wilcox's range and did so a number of times for various purposes. Thus, Wilcox contends, he did not have the legal right to exclude either members of the public from the public lands or plaintiffs from the entire rangeland. He argues that because plaintiffs failed to prove his exclusive possession and control of the cattle, they were not entitled to the presumption of his negligence under an agistment theory. Lacking any direct evidence of his negligence, Wilcox concludes that the jury's verdict is not supported by any competent evidence. We disagree.

> **In certain areas, define terms.**

The court of appeals has held that "exclusive possession and control"

> does not mean that the bailee must be the only one who has access to the property. <u>The bailee may allow others to access the property without destroying the bailment</u>. The requirement is only that the bailee have the right to exclude all persons <u>not covered by the agreement</u> and to control the property.

<u>McPherson</u>, 830 P.2d at 305 (emphasis added); <u>see also</u> 8 Am. Jur. 2d <u>Bailments</u> §78 (1980)(explaining that bailee is ordinarily entitled to exclude others "within the terms of the bailment"). In <u>McPherson</u>, a landlord assured his vacating tenants that their furniture would be safe if they left it in his condominium. 830 P.2d at 303. The landlord's son moved into the unit. The furniture was subsequently stolen, and the landlord denied any liability, claiming that he did not have exclusive possession and control of the furniture. The court applied the negligence presumption against the landlord and held him liable under a

bailment theory because access by the third party had been contemplated in the bailment agreement. <u>Id.</u> at 305.

> Prove minor premise by analogizing it to previous cases.

This case is like <u>McPherson</u> because in both instances, the parties to the bailment envisioned that others would have access to the bailed property. Here, both plaintiffs and Wilcox were ranchers and knew that when the cattle were on public land, third persons would have access to them. The parties also agreed that plaintiffs, as owners of the cattle, should have limited access to them for a few narrow purposes such as administering vaccines and medicine. This access, fully contemplated by the parties when the agistment contract was formed, should not destroy the presumption of the agistor's negligence when it was discovered that the property was missing.

> Disprove the counter-argument by contrasting it to previous case.

This case is very different from <u>Staheli</u>, where stored grain was destroyed by a fire of unknown origin. 655 P.2d at 681. This court refused to give the bailor the benefit of a presumption of negligence on the part of the bailee because (1) the bailor had unlimited access to the warehouse where the grain was stored, (2) there was evidence of the bailor's negligence, (3) the bailee was not primarily responsible for controlling the conditions that led to the fire, and (4) the lack of control and precautions arose through an emergency situation to find storage for the grain. <u>Id.</u> at 684. . .

> Once the minor premise is proved, put back in syllogistic form to reach conclusions.

[I]n this case, plaintiffs are entitled to the presumption of negligence because Wilcox was the one entrusted with the care of the cattle and was in a better position than plaintiffs to control the conditions of loss or damage. Thus, the burden is upon Wilcox to proffer sufficient evidence to show an absence of negligence on his part or to show the circumstances surrounding the loss and why it was not due to his negligence. The jury heard Wilcox's evidence as to the care he gave the cattle but was unconvinced that it rebutted his presumed negligence. We find sufficient competent evidence to support the verdict.

<u>Cornia v. Wilcox</u>, **898 P.2d 1379, 1383-1385 (Utah 1995).**

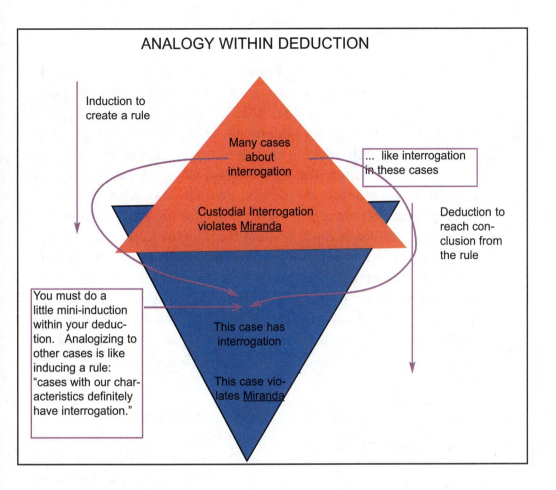

Example 5.3. Analogy Within Deduction in a Brief.

I.   THE SUPERIOR COURT ERRED IN DENYING DEFENDANT'S MOTION TO SUPPRESS HER STATEMENT BECAUSE THE STATEMENT WAS MADE SHORTLY AFTER DEFENDANT HAD INVOKED HER RIGHT TO COUNSEL AND IN RESPONSE TO THE FUNCTIONAL EQUIVALENT OF POLICE INTERROGATION.

When a defendant is in custody, "If the individual states that he wants an attorney. . . interrogation must cease until an attorney is present." **Miranda v. Arizona,** **384 U.S. 436, 473 (1966).** The State concedes that the defendant was in custody and had invoked her **Miranda** right to counsel at the time she made the statement that she seeks to suppress. The only issue, then, is whether the police conduct that prompted defendant's statement constituted "interrogation."

> Define the rule.

* * *

The police may violate Miranda's proscription on interrogation without engaging in direct questioning. <u>State v. Graham</u>, 441 A.2d 857, 186 Conn. 437 (1982).

<table>
<tr><td>Define terms.</td></tr>
</table>

"<u>Miranda</u> inhibits not only police encounters of the third degree kind; it also precludes all types of questioning and psychological ploys, calculated or reasonably likely to produce the desired result." 441 A.2d at 860. In <u>Graham</u>, the defendant was under arrest for narcotics violations. A policeman who knew the defendant from junior high school engaged the defendant in conversation, and the defendant invoked his right not to discuss the current situation. After 45 minutes of conversation, the officer said "Roger, it's too bad that this had to happen. It's a shame. You have a beautiful wife and a beautiful child." The defendant replied with an incriminating remark. The court held that the officer's statement constituted interrogation under <u>Rhode Island v. Innis</u>. <u>Id.</u>

<table>
<tr><td>Present client's situation as minor premise and prove by analogizing to previous cases.</td></tr>
</table>

Just as in <u>Graham,</u> the officer here wove his eliciting remark, which did not take the form of a question, into 45 minutes of conversation. Alvarez and Maxwell also avoided overt questioning. Instead, they resorted to a subtle scheme of upsetting the defendant by questioning "whether [Penny] was really sick," suggesting that she was getting involved with drugs, and finally manifesting an intention to bring her in for questioning. (T.12). Such schemes are not permissible, specifically those which exploit the defendant's concern about the possible negative consequences that the episode might entail for the defendant's loved ones, equally with direct questioning. 441 A.2d at 869, citing <u>Innis.</u>

Further, "[a]ny knowledge the police may have had concerning the unusual susceptibility of a defendant to a particular form of persuasion might be an important factor in determining whether the police [engaged in the functional equivalent of interrogation]." 446 U.S. 301. That the officer had prior knowledge of the defendant's family situation seems to be a key element underlying its holding. Thus, Maxwell and Alvarez' knowledge of defendant's concern for her daughter and the traumatic effect of Maxwell's previous arrest of Penny supports a finding of interrogation.

Disprove by distinguishing from previous cases.

Whether the police have engaged in the functional equivalent of interrogation "focuses primarily upon the perceptions of the suspect, rather than the intent of the police." 446 U.S. 301. The subjective motivation of the police officer in making his statement does not matter. See id. In Graham, the Court instead based its holding on the fact that this was a defendant who was obviously concerned about his family and whose emotions had been engaged by the officer's evocative statement. In this case, though, the officers' statements were a deliberate scheme to elicit a statement from the defendant, so the subjective motivation of the officers' statements is actually irrelevant to whether they engaged in interrogation. The relevant facts supporting such an outcome are the "perceptions of the suspect," essentially the defendant's belief that the policeman whom her sick daughter already feared was going to drag her to the police station for questioning, and that the only way to avoid such an occurrence was to make the statement that she made. (T. 23) . . . .

While such syllogisms are useful once specific categories, such as *interrogation* or *dogs*, are classified, they do not really help to create those categories. Remember that analogy is the process by which items are decided to be of one category or another; deduction flows from this categorizing. So, elements may have characteristics, some of which matter to categorizing them, or establishing "rules," and some of which do not matter.

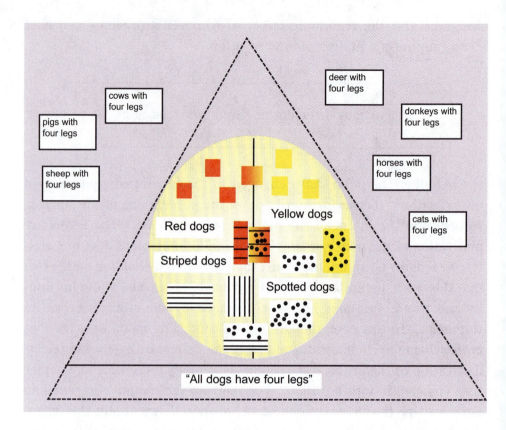

For example, the general rule in this illustration is *All dogs have four legs*. Within that category, there are many different kinds of dog characteristics—spotted, striped, yellow, red, for example. The categories are drawn around these characteristics to further separate the dogs. In this, a dog being yellow, red, striped, or spotted makes a difference. But who is to say that the texture of the dog's fur or the loudness of the dog's bark are not more important characteristics? Neither neoclassicism nor modernism is clear about the rules by which characteristics are determined to be relevant for the purposes of drawing analogy. Your choices create your design.

TECHNIQUES

• *Sketch or outline.* Try to create a blueprint that reflects the theme and shape of your document. You may sketch a diagram, as on these pages, or a web that connects ideas to each other. You may use something resembling a blueprint, or you may use traditional outline form. Whatever you choose, try to decide why each segment belongs where it does, how it relates to segments surrounding it, and how big it should be. Keep an open mind and allow the shape to change as your thinking evolves.

• *Don't get it right, get it written.* Free write. Put your thoughts on paper to get them translated from your mind. Let the design evolve from those thoughts — once you are done. You may generate ideas as you write, or you may finish writing, then see what you have and what design possibilities you have discovered. Don't call this a draft; call it "notes." Then open a new file and put in it only those ideas that fit your design.

Neoclassicism offers other designs, all of which flow from deductive and inductive forms. These designs are still popular in legal writing, as in the examples that follow.

Eample 5.4 Neoclassical Design: Induction to Form a Rule in a Memo

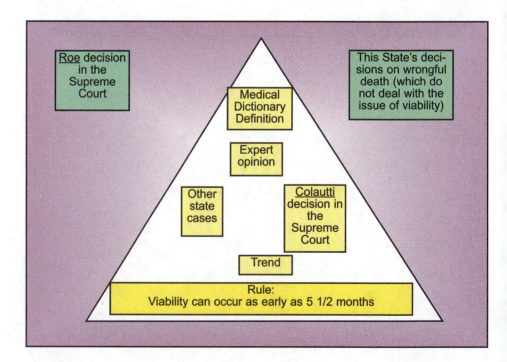

Because the viability of the fetus in <u>Moen</u> was implicitly acknowledged by the parties (the baby being expected in 30 days), the court refrained from defining or delimiting what it meant by viability. <u>Id.</u> at 266. Moreover, the court reached no conclusion as to whether a cause of action exists for injury to a nonviable fetus. <u>Id.</u> at 268. Generally, the word viable refers to the stage of prenatal development at which the fetus would be capable of independent existence if removed from its mother's womb. Shapiro, Right to Maintain Action or to Recover Damages for Death of Unborn 84 ALR3d 411, note 72, (L.Ed. 1978). [Hereinafter Damages]

Viability can occur before or at 5 fi months. For example, <u>Stedman's Medical Dictionary</u> 1556 (5th Unabridged L. Ed. 1982) defines viability as usually occurring when the fetus has reached 500 grams in weight and 20 gestational weeks. Moreover, in <u>Obstetrics</u> (10th ed 1950), Professor N. Eastman of John's Hopkins University writes that the smallest and youngest fetus to survive independently of the mother was 20 weeks and 400 grams—and that was back in 1950. Finally, in a recent Connecticut case, a 5 fi month old fetus was held to be viable and hence capable of maintaining an action for an alleged act of police brutality. <u>Douglas v. Town of Hartford</u>, 542 F. Supp 1267 (1982).

> Medical Dictionary Definition

> Expert Opinion

> Case Example

> Another Case Example

Despite these sources' endorsing the viability of Mrs. Hemings' fetus, most states have held that the fetus is not viable for the purposes of wrongful death actions until the 6th or 7th month of development. See Damages, at 432, note 72. Moreover, the U.S. Supreme Court has said that viability occurs between the 24th and 28th weeks of gestation. <u>Roe v. Wade</u>, 410 U.S. 163 (1973).

<u>Roe</u> can properly be distinguished from the Hemings case since that case was based on the balancing of the state's interest in regulating abortion with the pregnant woman's right of privacy, whereas the Hemings' wrongful death action would not involve such a conflict of interest. Also, the court later struck down a state attempt to incorporate that generalization into the abortion statute and held that viability must be determined on a case by case basis by the attending physician. <u>Colautti v. Franklin</u>, 439 U.S. 391 (1979).

> Colautti: Another Case Example

The **Collauti** decision typifies a burgeoning trend in wrongful death cases to extend the notion of viability to more than just the number of gestational weeks. <u>See</u> <u>e.g.</u> <u>Chrisafageorgia v. Brandenburg</u>, 55 Ill. 2d 368, 304 N.E.2d 88 (Ill. App. 1973). ("Viability is a relative matter, depending on the health of the mother and child and many other matters in addition to the stage of development"); <u>Renslow v. Mennonite Hospital</u>, 67 Ill.2d 348, 10 Ill. Dec. 484, 367 N.E.2d 1250 (Ill. App. 1977)(viability also depends on the weight and race of the child and the available life sustaining techniques). The Illinois Supreme Court has held that the viability of a 14 week old fetus is a question for the jury. <u>Green v. Smith</u>, 71 Ill.2d 501, 377 N.E. 2d 35 (1978).

> Trend
> Described with
> Other Case
> Examples

Therefore, although the majority of courts have circumscribed viability as beyond the 6th month, the Hemings could urge the court to follow recent trends as evinced by the Illinois' courts to hold their 5 fi month old fetus viable.

> Rule
> Induced

Example 5.5. Neoclassical Design: Deduction Using Example.

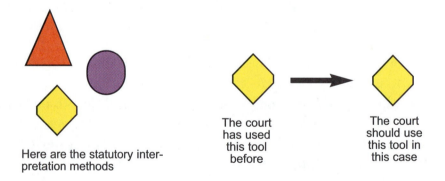

Here are the statutory interpretation methods

The court has used this tool before

The court should use this tool in this case

B. <u>Wisconsin Statutes Sections 632.32 and 631.43 Do Not Prevent Insurers From Limiting Their Liability By Contractual Reducing Clauses.</u>

The automobile insurance statutes of this state do not explicitly prohibit reducing clauses. In fact, "a policy may provide for exclusions not prohibited by sub. (6) or other applicable law. Such exclusions are effective even if incidentally to their main purpose they exclude persons, uses or coverages that could not be directly excluded under sub. (6)(b)." Sec. 632.(5)(e). (See Appendix A).

Section 632.32(6) and its notes do not prohibit reducing clauses. Further, section 632.32(4)(a) requires only that all insurance policies contain a provision for uninsured motorists of $25,000 per person and $50,000 per accident. No language in any of these statutes requires insurers to go beyond the limits of their policies once the insured has been indemnified up to those limits.

The dispute in this case arises from the language in sec. 631.43, Stats., which states as follows:

When two or more policies promise to indemnify an insured against the same loss, no 'other insurance' provisions of the policy may reduce the aggregate protection of the insured below the lesser of the actual insured loss suffered by the insured or the total indemnification promised by the policies if there were no 'other insurance' provisions. (Emphasis added).

Appellant claims this provision allows her to stack the indemnity coverage of the uninsured motorist provision of her policy with the liability coverage of American family's policy. Respondent says that its reducing clause is permissible and prohibits this double recovery.

The threshold question, then, in construing the statute, is whether the statutory terms are ambiguous. State v. Wittrock, 119 Wis. 2d 664, 669, 350 N.W.2d 647 (1984). Statutory terms are ambiguous if reasonable persons could disagree as to their meaning. Id. However, in cases like this, where parties disagree as to the term's meaning, the court will look to the language of the statute itself to determine whether well–informed persons should have become confused as to a term's meaning. Aero Auto Parts, Inc. v. Department of Trans., 78 Wis. 2d 235, 283 N.W. 896 (1977); Kollasch v. Adomany, 104 Wis. 2d 552, 313 N.W.2d 47 (1981); State v. Wittrock, 119 Wis. 2d 664, 350 N.W.2d 647 (1984).

When the language is clear and unambiguous, the statute must be interpreted on the plain meaning of its terms. Wittrock, 119 Wis. 2d at 670; Aero Auto Parts, Inc., 78 Wis. 2d at 238–39. When the language is ambiguous, the court must consider it in relation to its scope, history, context, subject matter and object to be accomplished or remedied. Kollasch, 104 Wis. 2d at 562. In any case, a statutory subsection may not be considered in a vacuum, but must be considered in reference to the statute as a whole and in reference to statutes dealing with the same general subject matter. Aero Auto Parts, Inc., 78 Wis. 2d at 239.

For example, the language of the eminent domain statute was found ambiguous and therefore required judicial construction to clarify it in light of prior law, the general chapter in which it was contained, and the remainder of the subsection. Id. at 239–246. Similarly, where definitions of "retailer" and "seller" were circular between two sections, the Court corrected the circularity by looking at legislative intent and the context of the Retail Sale Tax Statutes. Kollasch, 104 Wis. 2d at 561–568. But the Court looked no further than the plain meaning of the words in the Sentence Credit Statute when that interpretation gave the only reasonable result. State v. Gilbert, 115 Wis. 2d 371, 340 N.W. 2d 511 (1983).

The Court need look no further here than the plain meaning of section 631.43. The language addresses only indemnity coverage, not liability coverage. Even if the Court finds the statute ambiguous, the statute's scope and purpose still prevent stacking liability coverage with indemnity coverage.

Example 5.6. Modern Design: Deduction Using Elements.

In this example, the analysis proceeds according to three elements in the statute. There is no local case law available, so the arguments proceed on a plain meaning theory.

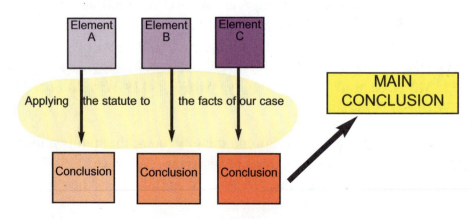

I.   The Crime

The crime of assisting suicide is "intentionally advising, encouraging, or assisting another in the taking of his own life." Kan. Stat. Ann. § 21–3406 (1991). Assisting suicide is a class E felony that is punishable by 3–5 years imprisonment. Id. The crime of assisting suicide, then, is comprised of three elements, all of which must be proved beyond a reasonable doubt before our client can be convicted. First, a suicide must have occurred as a matter of fact. Second, the accused must have actually advised, encouraged, or assisted the person committing suicide. Finally, the person who indeed assists another in committing suicide must be proved to have intended to do exactly that.

According to Kansas statute § 21–3409 (1991), a defendant is presumed to be innocent until the contrary is proven. When there is reasonable doubt as to her guilt, she must be acquitted. State v. Lovelace, 227 K. 348, 354, 590 P. 2d 1027. Thus, the prosecution's failure to prove any of the three elements beyond a reasonable doubt means our client maintains her freedom. She is likely to do so because the State cannot prove any of the elements beyond a reasonable doubt.

A.   The Existence of an Actual Suicide

The State cannot prove that Mr. Pernitz committed suicide. Although he may have intended and desired to commit suicide, there is no evidence of his actually doing so. Specifically, no one was in the room with Mr. and Mrs. Pernitz when he died, and there are currently no autopsy results that determine his cause of death. Mr. Pernitz had been suffering from lung cancer, a terminal disease, and may easily have died from the disease itself. However, evidence either way is presently lacking.

Here, Mrs. Pernitz may have the corroborating testimony of hospital personnel who may have also heard Mr. Pernitz express his desire to commit suicide and who may have witnessed his depressed state of mind while in the hospital. Friends and other family members may be able to attest to his more positive state of mind out of the hospital as compared to when he became hospitalized.

The only other evidence is circumstantially provided by the nurse who witnessed Mrs. Pernitz run out and then back into her husband's hospital room. The nurse never saw the switch turned off nor did she note that Mr. Pernitz' tubes were out. However, she did see that Mr. Pernitz was no longer breathing when she entered the room just after Mrs. Pernitz ran back into the room. Such circumstantial evidence, however, says nothing about whether Mr. Pernitz actually committed suicide; it goes only to Mrs. Pernitz' behavior at the time of her husband's death.

Because there are no witnesses nor any physical evidence to indicate otherwise, the State will not be able to prove beyond a reasonable doubt that Mr. Pernitz committed suicide.

B.   "Assisting"

Kansas has considered only once the element of "assisting" a suicide. State v. Cobb, 229 K. 522, 625 P.2d 1133 (1981). In Cobb, a woman claimed to have assisted a friend in committing suicide in accordance with explicitly stated wishes by pushing the plunger to a needle filled with an overdose of cocaine into each of his arms, and later by shooting him in the head to be sure he was dead.

As in Cobb, the focus of prosecutorial inquiry here will undoubtedly be on Mrs. Pernitz's actions in determining whether she assisted her husband's suicide. The court in Cobb adopts Oregon's interpretation of the word "assist" as used in the Assisting Suicide statute:

> [T]he statute does not contemplate active participation by one in the overt act directly causing death. It contemplates some participation in the events leading up to the commission of the final overt act, such as furnishing the means for bringing about death—the gun, the knife, the poison, or providing the water—for the use of the person who himself commits the act of self–murder.

State v. Bouse, 199 Or. 676, 264 P.2d 800 (1953). Here, Mrs. Pernitz's actions consist of reaching over and turning off the power switch to the main respirator after which she ran out of the room, immediately ran back in, and turned the switch back on. In light of the fact that a respirator is designed to help patients breathe, an essential activity for maintaining life, Mrs. Pernitz's actions could very well be the cause of her husband's death. To fall under the Assisting Suicide statute, Mrs. Pernitz only could have assisted her husband while he took his own life. If Mrs. Pernitz was the cause of her husband's death, she is liable for a different crime.

On the other hand, there are two other explanations that raise a reasonable doubt. First, the question remains as to whether Mr. Pernitz succeeded in committing suicide on his own if he was indeed attempting suicide. Moreover, Mr. Pernitz was suffering from the advanced stages of lung cancer, a terminal illness. It is therefore easily possible that the disease itself claimed his life. Thus the State cannot prove this element beyond a reasonable doubt.

C. The Requisite Intent

Intent is the third requirement that the State must prove for Mrs. Pernitz to be guilty of assisting suicide. Kan. Stat. Ann. § 21–3201 (1991) provides that a criminal intent is an essential element to every crime. Criminal intent may be established by proof that the conduct of the accused person was willful. Willful conduct is defined as purposeful and intentional, not accidental. Clinkingbeard v. State, 6 K.2d 716, 717, 718, 634 P.2d 159 (1981).

Mrs. Pernitz's state of mind arises twice in the facts. First, her husband's repeated desire to commit suicide tore Mrs. Pernitz between her beliefs about living until the very last moment possible, and the torture of watching her husband endure such pain and suffering. As a result, she began attending meetings of the local euthanasia chapter for about three months. Hence, the evidence shows that she was at least considering the notion of mercy killing. However, considering such a profound departure from her moral system is a far cry from physically committing the act. Furthermore, Mrs. Pernitz's attendance at these meetings is not dispositive of whether she was actually considering euthanasia; the possibility remains that she was merely trying to understand her husband's position.

Secondly, her motives come from her own words. In what Mrs. Pernitz described as "a moment of overwhelming sympathy," she turned off the power switch. This moment signifies the unlikelihood that Mrs. Pernitz acted with the purpose of helping to bring about her husband's death.   Rather, she merely sought to relieve herself of enduring the painful ordeal of seeing him suffer and wish for death for possibly another six months.

Because of the ambiguity of these feelings, the State cannot prove beyond a reasonable doubt that she intended to help her husband end his life.

CONCLUSION

We can cast a reasonable doubt over all three elements of the crime. The most difficult element to defend Mrs. Pernitz from appears to be whether her actions assisted her husband if the State proves he was committing suicide. Yet, it should be next to impossible for the prosecution to prove that Mr. Pernitz was indeed in the process of successfully committing suicide. Weakly pulling at his tubes does not qualify as committing suicide if Mr. Pernitz was unable to disconnect them. Moreover, even if they did come undone, the prosecution still must show that Mr. Pernitz would have died from that almost immediately thereafter. Thus, assisting suicide, if any, is not the appropriate crime under the Kansas statutes with which to charge Mrs. Pernitz.

Example 5.7. Neoclassical Fallacy: Straw Man to Leave No Law in Responsive Brief.

The Straw Man appears often in respondents' briefs. Respondents cast their opponents' arguments in such a way that they can be knocked down, rather than constructing respondents' own argument. The problem is, this approach leaves no law, no reasoning, no basis for constructing anything in the future. While such an objective may sometimes be attractive, remember that this is generally considered a weak defensive approach. (*See* A Further Word on Using Classical Syllogisms and Fallacies for Reading and Designing, Chapter 4).

Plaintiff's memorandum in opposition to the government's motion to dismiss relies on a misapprehension of the effect of the compliance policy guide (CPG) at issue in this case, CPG 7132.16. The CPG does not declare all compounding by pharmacies illegal, as plaintiff contends. The CPG explicitly states that it is not intended to interfere with the traditional practice of pharmacy, that is, the compounding of drugs in reasonable quantities upon receipt of a prescription for an individually identified patient from a physician or other licensed practitioner. See CPG 7132.16 at 1. Nor does the CPG require that pharmacies submit a new drug application ("NDA") for all medications they compound, as plaintiff asserts. Rather, the CPG sets forth circumstances in which compounding by pharmacies may amount to manufacturing and thus may be subject to regulatory action by the Food and Drug Administration ("FDA") under the adulteration, misbranding, and new drug provisions of the Federal Food, Drug, and Cosmetic Act ("the Act"). The CPG is intended both as internal guidance to FDA personnel, see CPG 7132.16 at 6, and as notice to the industry of what the agency will consider in deciding whether to initiate enforcement action against pharmacies that engage in compounding, see id. at 4.

Plaintiff argues the merits of the case extensively in what purports to be its Statement of Facts. See Plaintiff's Memorandum in Opposition to Defendants' Motions to Dismiss and to Stay Discovery and in Support of Plaintiff's Motion to Compel Discovery ("Pl. Mem.") at 5–8. As discussed in the government's opening brief and below, defendants believe that the court need not reach the merits because the case can and should be dismissed on ripeness and standing grounds; however, to explain why those grounds warrant dismissal, it is necessary to discuss some issues that intertwine with the merits, such as whether the policy expressed in the CPG is new.

These neoclassical, reason-based approaches may form the basis of your design repertoire. Such approaches may seem simple enough, but the variations on the syllogism alone offer you many choices. Once you embed analogy into your document, you have created many permutations and combinations from which you can mold an effective document. Return to your theme for guidance.

TECHNIQUES

- *Decide on your document's theme.* You may have had several ideas about your theme. Once you experiment with a few designs, your theme should "click" with a design. If you are having trouble, it may be that your theme has too many parts and needs a more overarching idea or that you have too many rooms to be united under one theme. Step back, discuss it with someone else, and then write out your final theme in one sentence if you can.

- *Check the headings to make sure that each advances the theme.* Once you feel comfortable with your theme, make sure that each section advances that theme. You can check that by rereading headings in one sitting. Make sure they connect with each other and relate in some way to the theme. The headings are what your reader may check early on to make sure he understands the general idea and the relationship among the parts.

- *Use a descriptive, or reverse, outline to make sure you can justify each paragraph and its place in your analysis.* Check the paragraphs to make sure that each advances the theme or sub-theme. Then look at each paragraph to see if it is doing the same thing. It may advance a sub-theme, provide a transition, or remind the reader of the overall theme. Make sure it has an appropriate function. Your "reverse outline" can be constructed either by marking in the margins how each paragraph functions or by making a separate outline from the paragraphs and comparing it to your original plan. Then merge the two by referring to the theme and purpose, audience, scope, and stance.

- *Fill in any holes you left or omit any repetitive parts.* This may be the hardest task in rewriting: making sure the scope is appropriate to the theme, audiences, and purposes. Often you have much more than you need, and it seems like too much work to pare. But your reader will be grateful that you have done the work.

• *Check the first sentences of each paragraph to make sure they are connected to each other.* This technique allows you to see if your main sentences really carry the document. Like a traveler looking at a map, a reader often skims the writing to get the gist, to see where he is going. Your topic sentences provide nicely drawn boundaries and street names or vague hills and meadows. Try for the former.

• *Rearrange the text if necessary.* This may be the most critical thing you do in rewriting. While it may seem like an upheaval, such rearrangements may be the key to a unified, elegant whole. Be strong. Look critically, and try to put sections in an order that enhances the overall effect, advances the theme, and demonstrates the proper proportions. Often it is this step that moves a document from merely OK to really good.

• *Avoid making small-scale changes simultaneously with writing or re-designing.* Try to keep your editing pen away during this critical architectural stage. Why worry about the furniture when the rooms are not settled yet? In writing terms, why are you fixing a sentence you are going to get rid of? Such adjustments distract you from your main task: setting the architecture a final time.

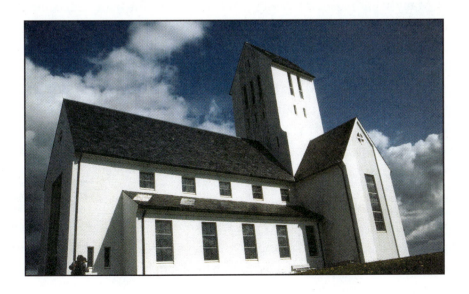

As powerful as the neoclassical models can be, however, you may question the validity of the classical logician's own premise, which is that induction and deduction are the only two ways to gain knowledge.

Syllogism 25.

MAJOR PREMISE:	**All knowledge not gained through deduction or induction is invalid.**
MINOR PREMISE:	**I gained my knowledge through experience.**
CONCLUSION:	**Therefore, my knowledge is invalid.**

Many legal reasoners criticize the syllogism for being unnecessarily reductionist. "All" statements are hard to come by in the law; so many exceptions abound that stating an all-inclusive rule is sometimes impossible, so the major premise is flawed. Similarly, the predicate of the minor premise is hard to show: is experience a kind of induction? deduction? Rarely can we state for certain the predicate of the minor premise; it is usually proved by analogy, as described above, and reason rarely stands alone, even in traditional legal documents. You are likely to consider the roles of policy and passion, which take you into modern design.

The combination of so many components gives you the design possibilities. In the modern setting, you are likely to be dealing with nuances that suggest a particular change here, an adjustment there. You may indeed have a basic floor plan for a four-bedroom home, but you may have a client that wants to convert one bedroom to an exercise room or move a wall to accommodate an elderly parent. You may need to put in a fire lane for fire departnment access. You may have contracts that, together, form an industrial complex of a transaction, but you may need to rearrange the buildings, add a small warehouse, or shift the order in which the parts are put together.

This is where designing legal documents becomes interesting. You do not have to be a philosopher or mathematician to practice law, but you can be aware of the many possibilities for presenting your information, for demonstrating your proof. You can explore even a half dozen possibilities to test which best respond to the rhetorical questions of purpose, audience, scope, and stance reviewed at the beginning of the chapter. You can create a checklist to test whether or not your document is correct, complete, or coherent, as in the next technique box.

You quickly discover that if you are representing the unusual client, if you are creating international transactional documents, or if you simply like to win, classical and neoclassical designs are not enough. Whether you are constructing a transaction or arguing a motion, you can still consider how such matters as policy and pathos affect your decisions. You must find a more modern way, create a new approach, or write a new law. To do so, consider modern schools of legal architecure.

TECHNIQUES

• *Create a rewriting checklist.* You may need to test your design and your reasoning once you have drafted the document. If you have followed classical or neoclassical designs, you need to test the reasoning. Construct checklists for each type of document, form, and overall approach.

SAMPLE REWRITING CHECKLIST

1.   ARE THE ISSUES ACCURATELY SUMMARIZED?

2.   ARE UNNECESSARY ISSUES OMITTED?

3.   HAVE I COORDINATED SUBSTANTIVE AND TECHNICAL ISSUES? IS THE DOCUMENT ACCURATE?

4.   ARE THERE ANY UNSTATED ASSUMPTIONS?

5.   HAVE I PROVIDED REASONS FOR ACTIONS OR PROPOSALS?

      IS THERE ANY UNSTATED REASONING? DO I USE "CLEARLY" RATHER THAN STATE THE REASONS FOR EACH STEP IN THE ANALYSIS?

6.   HAVE I CONSIDERED THE DOCUMENT'S IMPACT ON OTHERS? IN THE OFFICE? OUTSIDE THE OFFICE?

7.   HAVE I USED THE NECESSARY AUTHORITY? IS IT ACCURATE? WHAT DID I USE? WHERE DID I USE IT? WILL ANY LEGAL READER UNDERSTAND IT?

8.   DID I ARTICULATE THE PARTIES' ARGUMENTS? HAVE I ACCOUNTED FOR ALL SIDES OF THE ISSUE?

9. HAVE I INCLUDED ALL RELEVANT, SPECIFIC FACTS?

10. DOES THE ORGANIZATION MATCH THE THEME?

11. DOES ORDER OF ISSUES MAKE SENSE?

TOPICAL?

MOST IMPORTANT -> LEAST?

MOST CONTROVERSIAL -> LEAST?

LOGICAL - BY ISSUE - I.E., ONE ISSUE DISPENSES WITH ANOTHER?

MOST GENERAL -> SPECIFIC

CHRONOLOGICAL WHERE CHRONOLOGY IS LEGALLY SIGNIFICANT?

ELEMENT BY ELEMENT?

BALANCING TEST, TWO SIDES, THEN THE BALANCE?

12. HAVE I RECHECKED MY USE OF AUTHORITY?

UPDATED DOCUMENTATION?

USED CITES AS REQUIRED IN THIS CONTEXT?

CONFORMING CITATIONS IF CHANGED?

13. HAVE I "UNIFIED" THE DOCUMENT AFTER ANY EDITS?

14. DO THE FINAL PARTS OF THE DOCUMENT CONCLUDE, RECOMMEND, DISPOSE OF EVERYTHING, OR ADVISE AS APPROPRIATE?

MOVING TO MODERNISM

SOME MODERN DESIGNS

LEGAL REALISM: POLICY AND PURPOSE

LEGAL PROCESS: THRESHOLD QUESTION FIRST

LAW AND SOCIETY: GUIDELINES

LAW AND ECONOMICS: EFFICIENCY

Modernism in legal thinking and design began to take shape in the 1930s when the classical ideals began to break down. Working conditions in post-nineteenth century United States were difficult, and neoclassical legal thinking broke down. As a result, four major modernist schools of thought emerged from the 1930s to the 1970s: Realism, which asserts that hunches, not doctrine, determine outcomes; Process, which asserts that outcomes are determined by process, not substantive rights; Law and Society, which asserts that outcomes are determined by external influences, like power, history, and cultural influences; and Law and Economics, which asserts that outcomes are determined by comparing costs and benefits.

These modern movements departed from neoclassicism, changed the way law was taught, and changed the way institutions reached decisions. Or, depending on how you look at it, these movements reflected societal and institutional changes, which were results of a rapidly changing modern world.

The same had already occured in architecture. Eighteenth century neoclassicism had given way to neo-gothic, romantic, and art nouveau architecture, then finally to modernism. Beginning around the same time, the 1930s, architecture responded to the modern world by incorporating modern materials, such as iron, glass, concrete, and plastic. These changes were internal at first, iron structures with masonry fronts, for example, but then took over the outer structure as architects brought iron outside. For some modernist architects, "ornament was crime," and, like the Legal Realists, they eliminated excess dressing of legal elements and went to the core of results and functionalism.

Each movement has had a concomitant impact on legal architecture. Bursting from the confines of reasoning, legal thinking took on new shapes to fit a changing society. As form follows function, so legal forms shaped themselves to these new schools. Briefs took on new dimensions, contracts followed transactions and anticipated alternative dispute resolution, and outcomes were predicted from new vantage points. For leverage, document design moved into a new realm: modernism.

Modern legal design incorporates a mixture of elements that explore law from perspectives beyond reasoning. Those perspectives account for other materials to be used in design, modern materials such as the structure of legal institutions, the inequities among social classes, the procedural basis of legal transactions, the philosophical bases for decision-making, and the diversity of people who bring, argue, and resolve disputes.

These perspectives inform design by offering a rich variety of choices on which to base transactional stances, arguments in litigation, or approaches to alternative dispute resolution. Incorporating modern design concepts expands your repertoire of design choices; it also makes them more complex because of the very nature of the concepts themselves.

LEGAL REALISM: POLICY AND PURPOSE

In the United States, the first assault on Classical Legal Thought came from a group now known as the Legal Realists. They asserted that there was more to law than rules, deductions, and inductions. Law was instead only meaningful if it was put in the context of social conditions. Thus, the purposes of the law should be examined as well as the policies behind it. According to the Realists, law was based on experience more than logic, on economics, sociology, and statistics, not on abstract legal principles. Law was a matter of degree, and interests had to be balanced against each other. The point was to look at what effect the law actually had.

Thus modernism was born. And it is still with us. Policy arguments are often invoked by parties who seek to move beyond the rules, who seek to balance one interest against the other. Modernism may have emerged most dramatically or memorably when one man imported realism to brief writing.

Example 5.8. Example of Realism breaking from Neoclassicism: the "Brandeis Brief."

The model for brief writing was forever altered when the case was built not on legal doctrine or traditional logic, but on social science. The appeal here was not to intellectual notions of keeping within the law, but to social notions of changing it. The very materials out of which the document was built changed its form and redefined brief writing. The case was <u>Muller v. Oregon</u>, 208 U.S. 412 (1908).

TABLE OF CONTENTS

Laws of the Several States in Force Limiting the Hours of Labor of Adult Women

ARGUMENT

FIRST PART—*Legislation Restricting the Hours of Labor for Women*

I.   THE FOREIGN LEGISLATION

II. THE AMERICAN LEGISLATION

SECOND PART—*The World's Experience upon which the Legislation Limiting the Hours of Labor for Women is Based*

I.   THE DANGERS OF LONG HOURS

   A. <u>CAUSES</u>

      1) Physical Differences Between Men and women

      2) The New Strain in Manufacture

   B. <u>BAD EFFECT OF LONG HOURS ON HEALTH</u>

      1) General Injuries from Long Hours

      2) Specific Evil Effects on Childbirth and Female Functions

   C. <u>BAD EFFECTS OF LONG HOURS ON SAFETY</u>

   D. <u>BAD EFFECT OF LONG HOURS ON MORALS</u>

   E. <u>BAD EFFECT OF LONG HOURS ON GENERAL WEL-FARE</u>

      1) State's Need of Protecting Woman

      2) The Effect of Women's Overwork on Future Generations

II. SHORTER HOURS THE ONLY POSSIBLE PROTECTION

III. THE GENERAL BENEFITS OF SHORT HOURS

   A. <u>GOOD EFFECT ON THE INDIVIDUAL HEALTH, HOME LIFE, ETC.</u>

   B. <u>GOOD EFFECT ON THE GENERAL WELFARE</u>

IV. ECONOMIC ASPECT OF SHORT HOURS

   A. <u>EFFECT ON OUTPUT</u>

      1) Shorter Hours increase Efficiency, and thus prevent Reduction of Output

      2) Long Hours result in Inferior Quality of Product

ARGUMENT

The legal rules applicable to this case are few and are well established, namely:

First: The right to purchase or to sell labor is a part of the "liberty" protected by the Fourteenth Amendment of the Federal Constitution.

Lochner v. New York, 198 U.S. 45, 53.

Second: This right to "liberty" is, however, subject to such reasonable restraint of action as the State may impose in the exercise of the police power for the protection of health, safety, morals, and the general welfare.

Lochner v. New York, 198 U.S. 45, 53, 67.

Third: The mere assertion that a statute restricting "liberty" relates, though in a remote degree, to the public health, safety, or welfare does not render it valid. The act must have a "real or substantial relation to the protection of the public health and the public safety."

Jacobson v. Mass, 197 U.S. 11, 31.

It must have "a more direct relation, as a means to an end, and the end itself must be appropriate and legitimate."

Lochner v. New York, 198 U.S. 45, 56, 57, 61.

Fourth: Such a law will not be sustained if the Court can see that it has no real or substantial relation to the public health, safety, or welfare, or that it is "an unreasonable, unnecessary and arbitrary interference with the right of the individual to his personal liberty or to enter into those contracts in relation to labor which may seem to him appropriate or necessary for the support of himself and his family."

But "If the end which the Legislature seeks to accomplish be one to which its power extends, and if the means employed to that end, although not the wisest or best, are yet not plainly or palpably unauthorized by law, then the Court cannot interfere. In other words, when the validity of a statute is questioned, the burden of proof, so to speak, is upon those" who assail it.

Lochner v. New York, 198 U.S. 45, 61.

Fifth: The validity of the Oregon statute must therefore be sustained unless the Court can find that there is no "fair ground, reasonable in and of itself, to say that there is material danger to the public health (or safety) of the employees (or to the general welfare), if the hours of labor are not curtailed."

Lochner v. New York, 198 U.S. 45, 61.

The Oregon statute was obviously enacted for the purpose of protecting the public health, safety, and welfare. Indeed, it declares:

> "Section 5. Inasmuch as the female employees in the various establishments are not protected from overwork, an emergency is hereby declared to exist, and this act shall be in full force and effect from and after its approval by the Governor."

The facts of common knowledge of which the Court may take judicial notice——

See Holden v. Hardy, **169 U.S. 366.**
Jacobson v. Mass, **197 U.S. 11—**
Lochner v. New York, **198 U.S. 481.**

establish, we submit, conclusively, that there is reasonable ground for holding that to permit women in Oregon to work in a "mechanical establishment, or factory, or laundry" more than ten hours in one day is dangerous to the public health, safety, morals, or welfare.

These facts of common knowledge will be considered under the following heads:

Part I. Legislation (foreign and American), restricting the hours of labor for women.

Part II. The world's experience upon which the legislation limiting the hours of labor for women is based.

Using policy arguments also allows you to step outside the stringent confines of traditional Western logic and look at the law's context. Policy is a foundation for logic, a step up from deductive application of rules. Policy arguments are based on the law's context, societal norms, and the reasons behind passing laws. Policy perspectives allow you to question the truth of the premises themselves, to advocate changes in your client's situation or in the law itself. You can look at the intentions of a government agency, at consistency, and at plans for the future.

Policy arguments also allow you to put strict reasoning in a larger context, to decide what proportions arguments might have to each other. As you weave policy into your design, you may find that it refines the order of your analysis, the general direction of your reasoning. Each part of your design is related to every other part. Policy can unite your theme with your form, can designate the proportions of the parts of the analysis to each other. Law alone is usually too raw for changing issues; reasoning alone reduces those issues to syllogistic nonsense in the face of changing mores or social demands. Using policy to cast your analysis can move a reader to change his mind or can explain an otherwise paradoxical situation.

Example 5.9. Opinion Using Policy To Set Tone for Argument

This opinion discusses whether or not one juror's post-trial testimony that other jurors abused alcohol and drugs during the trial can be used to impeach the jury's verdict.

Defining terms: Internal and external influences

By the beginning of this century, if not earlier, the near-universal and firmly established common law rule in the United States flatly prohibited the admission of juror testimony to impeach a jury verdict. . . Exceptions to the common-law rule were recognized only in situations in which an "extraneous influence" . . . was alleged to have affected the jury. In <u>Mattox</u>, this Court held admissible the testimony of jurors describing how they heard and read prejudicial

Sources of Authority: Common law and federal statute

information not admitted into evidence. The Court allowed juror testimony on influence by outsiders in <u>Parker v. Gladden</u>, 385 U.S. 363, 365 (1966) (bailiff's comments on defendant) and <u>Remmer v. United States</u>, 347 U.S. 227, 228–30 (1954) (bribe offered to juror). . . .[more cites] . . . . In situations that did not fall into this exception for external influence, however, the Court adhered to the common law rule against admitting juror testimony to impeach a verdict. [Cite]. . . .

Most significant for the present case . . . is the fact that lower federal courts treated allegations of the physical or mental incompetence of a juror as "internal" rather than "external" matters . . . .

There is little doubt that post-verdict investigation into juror misconduct would in some instances lead to the invalidation of verdicts reached after irresponsible or improper juror behavior. It is not at all clear, however, that the jury system could survive such efforts to perfect it. Allegations of juror misconduct, incompetency, or inattentiveness, raised for the first time days, weeks, or months after the verdict seriously disrupt the finality of the process. . . Moreover, full and frank discussion in the jury room, jurors' willingness to return an unpopular verdict, and the community's trust in a system that relies on the decisions of lay people would all be undermined by a barrage of post verdict scrutiny of juror conduct. . . . [P]etitioners argue that substance abuse constitutes an improper "outside influence" about which jurors may testify under Federal Rule of Evidence 606(b). In our view the language of the Rule cannot easily be stretched to cover this circumstance. However severe their effect and improper their use, drugs or alcohol voluntarily ingested by a juror seems no more an "outside influence" than a virus, poorly prepared food, or a lack of sleep. . . .

POLICY ARGU-MENTS

The dissent emphasizes the value of the jury process over the finality of verdict.

Dissent: Marshall, joined by Brennan, Blackmun, Stevens

REFUTATION
OF
POLICY
ARGUMENTS

I readily acknowledge the important policy considerations supporting the common-law rule against admission of jury testimony to impeach a verdict, now embodied in Federal Rule of Evidence 606(b): freedom of deliberation, finality of verdicts, and protection of jurors against harassment by dissatisfied litigants. (references). It has been simultaneously recognized, however, that "simply putting verdicts beyond effective reach can only promote irregularity and injustice." (ibid). If the above–referenced policy considerations seriously threaten the constitutional right to trial by a fair and impartial jury, they must give way.

In this case, however, we are not faced with a conflict between the policy consideration underlying Rule 606(b) and petitioners' Sixth Amendment rights. Rule 606(b) is not applicable to juror testimony on matters unrelated to the jury's deliberations. By its terms, 606(b) renders jurors incompetent to testify only as to three subjects (i) any "matter or statement" occurring during deliberations; (ii) the "effect" of anything upon the "mind or emotions" of any juror as it relates to his or her "assent to or dissent from the verdict"; and (iii) the "mental processes" of the juror in connection with this "assent to or dissent from the verdict." Even as to matters involving deliberations, the bar is not absolute . . . .

Petitioners are not asking for a perfect jury. They are seeking to determine whether the jury that heard their case behaved in a manner consonant with the minimum requirements of the Sixth Amendment. If we deny them this opportunity, the jury system may survive, but the constitutional guarantee on which it is based will become meaningless.

<u>Tanner v. United States</u>, **483 U.S. 107 (1987).**

Example 5.10. Modern Design: Balancing Test.

Balancing test is introduced.

Although the criteria for determining the validity of state statutes affecting interstate commerce have been variously stated, the general rule that emerges can be phrased as follows: Where the statute regu-

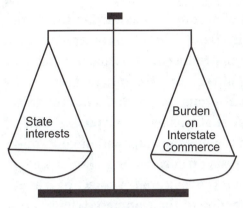

Balancing Test

lates even-handedly to effectuate a legitimate local public interest, and its effects on interstate commerce are only incidental, it will be upheld unless the burden imposed on such commerce is clearly excessive in relation to the putative local benefits (cites omitted). . . .

> State interest is identified.

At the core of the Arizona Fruit and Vegetable Standardization Act are the requirements that fruits and vegetables shipped from Arizona meet certain standards of wholesomeness and quality, and that they be packed in standard containers in such a way that the outer layer or exposed portion of the pack does not 'materially misrepresent' the quality of the lot as a whole. [cite] The impetus for the Act was the fear that some growers were shipping inferior or deceptively packaged produce, with the result that the reputation of Arizona growers generally was being tarnished and their financial return concomitantly reduced. It was to prevent this that the Act was passed in 1929. The State has stipulated that its primary purpose is to promote and preserve the reputation of Arizona growers by prohibiting deceptive packaging.

> State interest is analyzed.

We are not, then, dealing here with 'state legislation in the field of safety where the propriety of local regulation has long been recognized,' [cites] or with an Act designed to protect consumers in Arizona from contaminated or unfit goods. Its purpose and design are simply to protect and enhance the reputation of growers within the State. These are surely legitimate state interests. [cite] We have upheld a State's power to require that produce packaged in the State be packaged in a particular kind of receptacle. [cite] And we have recognized the legitimate interest of a State in maximizing the financial return to an industry within it. [cite] Therefore, as applied to Arizona growers who package their produce in Arizona, we may assume the constitutional validity of the Act. We may further assume that Arizona has full constitutional power to forbid the misleading use of its name on produce that was grown or packed elsewhere. And, to the extent the Act forbids the shipment of contaminated or unfit produce, it clearly rests on sure footing. For, as the Court has said, such produce is 'not the legitimate subject of trade or commerce, nor within the protection of the commerce clause of the Constitution.' [cites]

> Appellant's burden is analyzed.

But application of the Act through the appellant's order to the appellee company has a far different impact, and quite a different purpose. The cantaloupes grown by the company at Parker are of exceptionally high quality. The company does not pack them in Arizona and cannot do so without making a capital expenditure of approximately $200,000. It transports them in bulk to nearby Blythe, California, where they are sorted, inspected, packed, and shipped in containers that do not identify them as Arizona cantaloupes, but bear the name of their California packer. [cite] The appellant's order would forbid the company to pack its cantaloupes outside Arizona, not for the purpose of keeping the reputation of its growers unsullied, but to enhance their reputation through the reflected good will of the company's superior produce. The appellant, in other words, is not complaining because the company is putting the good name of Arizona on an inferior or deceptively packaged product, but because it is not putting that name on a product that is superior and well packaged. As the appellant's brief puts the matter, 'It is within Arizona's legitimate interest to require that interstate cantaloupe purchasers be informed that this high quality Parker fruit was grown in Arizona.' [cite]

> Burden is weighed against the state interest.

Although it is not easy to see why the other growers of Arizona are entitled to benefit at the company's expense from the fact that it produces superior crops, we may assume that the asserted state interest is a legitimate one. But the State's tenuous interest in having the company's cantaloupes identified as originating in Arizona cannot constitutionally justify the requirement that the company build and operate an unneeded $200,000 packing plant in the State. The nature of that burden is, constitutionally, more significant than its extent. For the Court has viewed with particular suspicion state statutes requiring business operations to be performed in the home State that could more efficiently be performed elsewhere. Even where the State is pursuing a clearly legitimate local interest, this particular burden on commerce has been declared to be virtually per se illegal. [cites] . . . .

> Conclusion is formed.

While the order issued under the Arizona statute does not impose such rigidity on an entire industry, it does impose just such a straitjacket on the appellee company with respect to the allocation of its interstate resources. Such an incidental consequence of a regulatory scheme could perhaps be tolerated if a more compelling state interest were involved. But here the State's interest is minimal at best—certainly less substantial than a State's interest in securing employment for its people. If the Commerce Clause forbids a State to require work to be done within its jurisdiction to promote local employment, then surely it cannot permit a State to require a person to go into a local packing business solely for the sake of enhancing the reputation of other producers within its borders.

The judgment is affirmed.

Pike v. Bruce Church, 397 U.S. 137, 142-144 (1970).

Legal Process: Threshold Questions First

Those believing in Legal Process agreed with the realists that law was not a matter of rules and reasoning. In that sense, they are modernists who reject classical legal thought. They did not, however, share the skepticism of the realists about how disputes could be resolved. They invented the notion that even those who are disagreeing with each other can agree on the procedure or process by which the dispute should be resolved. Thus the law has an internal, process morality, rather than an external reasoning morality.

In this sense, the process theorists and practioners are formalist. They have simply redrawn the categories of rules and syllogisms into sequences of events. Their overall modern impact has been to restructure analysis along process lines. Many lawyers win cases today because procedure has not been properly followed, as in the next example.

Example 5.11. Opinion Using Process.

2. Insufficiency of service

The defendants moving for dismissal have done so in part on the ground that they have never been properly served with the complaint in this matter. Fed.R.Civ.P. 12(b)(5) provides for dismissal of actions for "insufficiency of service of process." The Dahls have filed with the court copies of the "green cards" or return receipts from their certified mailings of the complaint to the defendants showing who signed for receipt of each complaint. However, the court concludes that certified mail return receipts do not prove effective service of process for a number of reasons.

First, the Eighth Circuit Court of Appeals ruled that under former Fed.R.Civ.P. 4(c)(2)(C)(ii), which authorized service by certified mail if the defendant returned an acknowledgment of service, that "the signing of the 'green card' was not sufficient to evidence acknowledgment of receipt of the summons and complaint and consequently did not satisfy the requirement of Rule 4(c)(2)(C)(ii) that service be acknowledged in order to be effective." Gulley v. Mayo Foundation, 886 F.2d 161, 165 (8th Cir.1989); . . . It is clear that under former Fed.R.Civ.P. 4(c)(2)(C)(ii), the Dahls did not effect proper service on any of the defendants, because they received no valid acknowledgment of service.

When the Federal Rules of Civil Procedure were revised in 1993, the provisions for service by certified mail with acknowledgement

were extensively revised and were moved to subsection (d) of the Rule. Fed.R.Civ.P. 4(d). The Advisory Committee noted the following:

> The former text [of Rule 4(c)(2)(C)(ii)] described this process as service-by-mail. This language misled some plaintiffs into thinking that service could be effected by mail without the affirmative cooperation of the defendant. E.g., Gulley v. Mayo Foundation, 886 F.2d 161 (8th Cir.1989). It is more accurate [now] to describe the communication sent to the defendant as a request for a waiver of formal service.

Fed.R.Civ.P. 4(d), Notes of the Advisory Committee on 1993 Amendment. Thus, Fed.R.Civ.P. 4, as currently amended, provides for mailing of a complaint to the defendant with a request for waiver of service. Fed.R.Civ.P. 4(d)(2). [FN12] The newly amended rule provides a number of conditions, including receipt of a waiver of service, before mere mailing of a complaint to a defendant effects proper service. Id. [FN13] The Dahls plainly have not met the conditions for effective service in this case, because nothing in the record indicates the mailing of a request for waiver of service, and certainly the Dahls have not filed with the court any waiver of service obtained from any defendant. Under the former rule, the plaintiff was responsible for obtaining proper service on defendants. See Lee v. Armontrout, 991 F.2d 487, 489 (8th Cir.) (per curiam) (plaintiff was responsible for obtaining proper service, including providing marshal with proper address for service on defendant), cert. denied, 510 U.S. 875, 114 S.Ct. 209, 126 L. Ed. 2d 166 (1993). The court finds nothing in the newly-amended version of the rule that relieves a plaintiff of that responsibility, even though defendants are now required to be more cooperative in waiving service. The court therefore concludes that the Dahls have not obtained effective service on any of the defendants in this matter.

Dahl v. Kanawha Investment Co., 161 F.R.D. 673, 679-680 (N.D. Iowa 1995).

Example 5.12. Legal Process: Putting the Threshold Question First.

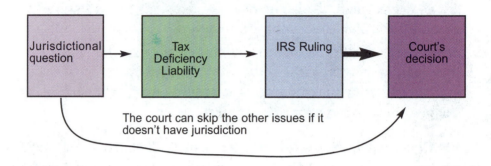

In a notice of deficiency issued on February 24, 1986, the Commissioner of Internal Revenue notified taxpayers Earl and Donna Cole that they were liable for a tax deficiency of $5,651 and additions to tax for the taxable year 1982. In response to the notice of deficiency, the Coles filed a petition pro se in the Tax Court for a redetermnation of their liability. The petition stated that the petitioner elected to have the case proceed as a "small tax case" and that such cases are not appealable to higher courts.

The Coles subsequently retained counsel, and the case was assigned to Special Trial Judge John J. Pajak as part of a group of cases known as the "U.S. Mining and Manganese cases." The Coles did not request removal of the "small tax case" designation from their case, nor did the Tax Court order the designation removed.

*   *   *

The Coles signed a petition stating that they elected to have the case conducted under the "small tax case" procedures and that a decision in the case could not be appealed to this court.[1] Hence, unless the case's "small tax case" designation was removed, we lack jurisdiction to hear this appeal.

The Tax Court Rules allow the Tax Court, on its own motion or that of a party, to enter an order removing the "small tax case" designation of a case. Tax Ct.R. 172(c), 173; see also 26 U.S.C. § 7463(d). When the Court redesignates a small tax case to a regular tax case, it orders the letter "S," used to designate small tax cases, dropped from the docket number. See <u>Horvat v. Commissioner</u>, 37 T.C.M. (CCH) 679, 680 n. 1 (1978); <u>Reiss v. Commissioner</u>, 37 T.C.M. (CCH) 298, 299 (1978); <u>Williams v. Commissioner</u>, 35 T.C.M. (CCH) 1591, 1591 (1976).

There is no procedure by which a small tax case can become a regular tax case by any means other than an express court order. The Tax Court Rules provide that a case is a "small tax case" if the petitioner has so chosen and "[t]he Court has not entered an order in accordance with Rule 172(d) or Rule 173, discontinuing the proceedings in the case under Code Section 7463." Tax Ct.R. 171.

In the present case, neither party made a motion and the Tax Court never entered an order to remove the "small tax case" designation from the case and the "S" from the docket number. Throughout the proceedings, the docket number of the case continued to end in an "S." Furthermore, the Coles never claimed that the amount in question exceeded $10,000. Hence, the case was at all times a small tax case and cannot be appealed to this court.

CONCLUSION

We lack jurisdiction to review the Tax Court's decision in this case. The appeal is DISMISSED.

[1] Above the Coles' signatures, the petition reads: "Petitioner(s) request(s) that this case be conducted under the 'small tax case' procedures authorized by Congress to provide the taxpayer(s) with an informal, prompt, and inexpensive hearing at a reasonably convenient location. Consistent with these objectives, a decision in a 'small tax case' is final and cannot be appealed to higher Courts (the Courts of Appeals and the Supreme Court) by the Internal Revenue Service or the Petitioner(s)."

<u>Cole v. I.R.S.</u>, 958 F.2d 288, 289-90 (9th Cir. 1991).

LAW AND SOCIETY: GUIDES

According to those in the Law and Society movement, law does not operate in a vacuum, removed from the rest of the world. It is, in fact, an "external" product of values, culture, history, and religion as opposed to an "internal" product of reasoning, as in classicism and neoclassicism. By studying the remedies actually allowed by courts, proponents of Law and Society noted the unintended consequences of the law, the way that the legal system affected people and institutions. As a sociological phenomenon, law often responded to situations rather than creating rules that could govern them. This movement suggested the mediating role of lawyers, then, people who could guide people through legal situations, knowing all elements of the circumstances.

Example 5.13. Example of Results of an Arbitration.

SUMMARY AND AWARD

We are of the opinion that all aspects of this discipline have been proven and justified except that the agency did not consider or apply the agreed requests of the contract that the "discipline imposed by employer will be designed to correct the unit employee's behavior." The employer will exercise reasonable judgment to ensure the disciplinary action taken is in proportion to the nature of the offense and consistent with the concept of progressive discipline.

Here, applying the Douglas factors, the other statutes and regulations pertinent and the sense of the contract, we must find that straight discharge does not recognize the progressive punishment. There were mitigating facts and there is a chance the grievant will learn the nature of her misconduct. She should be able to correct her ways with regard to going armed and with regard to failure in judgment to understand why a school system cannot indulge guns, which are dangerous and threatening.

In terms of the discipline decreed by the agency, we here hold that the misconduct was grievous but that to recognize the contract, we also hold:

1. The termination is set aside.

2. The disciplinary punishment will be suspension from the date the suspension was declared, December 5, 1997 until the first work day in September, 1999.

3. There is no back pay or lost benefits to be paid by the agency to the grievant.

4. Grievant, at that time, if she wishes, may ask and receive return to work to Fort Knox School System.

5. She will be provided the same or an equivalent job, but the administrator of the school system is granted the freedom that grievant need not be returned to this particular job or this particular school, but may be placed in an equivalent job anywhere in the Fort Knox system.

6. This will be considered a first step in progressive punishment.

It is hereby provided that the grievance is granted but only to the extent as stated above.

<u>In re Fort Knox Community Schools</u>, 112 Lab. Arb. Rep. (BNA) 1073 (1999).

Law and Economics: Efficiency

The proponents of Law and Economics suggest that law operates as a result of transactional costs and distribution. Rather than emphasizing fault, as some perspectives on law have done, Law and Economics suggests that, when empirically studied, law can be seen as a series of transactions in which cost and benefit are measured and certain outcomes become predictable from those measurements. By using economic theory to analyze such matters as negligence, proponents of this field suggest that certain costs can deter certain behaviors. Legal rules can then be created to foresee these costs and thus regulate behavior.

Example 5.14. Law and Economics Analysis in an Opinion.

We have suggested in previous cases, such as Davis v. United States, [cite], that one way to make sense of comparative negligence is to assume that the required comparison is between the respective costs to the plaintiff and to the defendant of avoiding the injury. If each could have avoided it at the same cost, they are each 50 percent responsible for it. According to this method of comparing negligence, the jury found that Susan could have avoided the attack at a cost of less than one thirty-second the cost to the Adamses. Is this possible?

It is careless to open a motel or hotel door in the middle of the night without trying to find out who is knocking. Still, people aren't at their most alert when they are awakened in the middle of the night, and it wasn't crazy for Susan to assume that Michael had returned without telling her, even though he had said he would be spending the night at the base. So it cannot be assumed that the cost - not to her (although her testimony suggests that she is not so naïve or provincial as her lawyer tried to convince the jury she was), but to the reasonable person who found himself or herself in her position, for that is the benchmark in determining plaintiff's as well as defendant's negligence, [cites] - was zero, or even that it was slight. As innkeepers (in the increasingly quaint legal term), the Adamses had a duty to exercise a high degree of care to protect their guests from assaults on the motel premises. [cites] And the cost to the Adamses of warning all their female guests of the dangers of the neighborhood would have been negligible. Surely a warning to Susan would not have cost the Adamses 32 times the cost to her of schooling herself to greater vigilance. . . .

The only one of these omitted precautions for which there is a cost figure in the record was the security guard. A guard would have cost $50 a night. That is almost $20,000 a year. This is not an enormous number. The plaintiff suggests that it would have been even lower because the guard would have been needed only on busy nights. But the evidence was in conflict whether the Sunday night that Susan was attacked, was a busy night. And the need for a security guard would seem to be greater, the less busy rather than the busier the motel; if there had been someone in the room adjacent to Susan's she might have been saved from her ordeal. In any event the cost of the security

guard, whether on all nights or just on busy nights -- or just on unbusy nights--might be much greater than the monetary equivalent of the greater vigilence on the part of Susan that would have averted the attack.

Once you have analyzed the rhetorical elements and researche the possibilities for your modern design, you have enough information to begin designing. You have considered who is going to use your document, why they are going to use it, how large the document is going to be, and from what angle it will be viewed. You have also gathered your materials, sorting out what accomplishes your purposes and satisfies your audiences. Just as an architect decides all of these matters, so can you. One of the causes of bad legal writing is a failure to recognize that each document is unique. Some documents will be used over and over again, like the designs used in tract housing; their uniqueness is only in their different paint color. Others must be designed from scratch for their specific audiences and purposes, and they will never be used again. Having answered the rhetorical questions, you can decide why something goes first, second, or at the end; why more elaboration is appropriate; and why less authority is necessary, for example.

At this point, you pivot from writer-based writing and thinking to reader-based writing. You design and build a structure for your audience. The newer you are to a certain topic, the more writer-based it is; but the sooner you think about it rhetorically, the more reader-based it is.

TECHNIQUES

• *Do several designs.* To design effectively, try writing out your choices and seeing at least three ways of building the document. If you simply choose the first design that comes to your mind, you may design a writer-based document, one that makes sense to you, but not to your audiences. If you simply choose the last traditional design used for this type of document, you may build something that does not suit the landscape or the current users. Instead, try at least three basic designs before selecting one to fill out in detail.

The following example offers varied architectural schemes for the same document.

Example 5.15. Example of Doing Three Possible Designs.

Memorandum of Points and Authorities in Support of a Motion for Permanent Restraining Order.

STATEMENT OF THE CASE

On June 22, 2001, Mrs. Washington filed a petition for dissolution of marriage along with a temporary restraining order prohibiting Mr. Washington from removing the children from Mrs. Washington's custody. Mr. Washington filed an answer asking that he be granted custody of the children. The temporary restraining order was granted with an order to show cause. Mr. Washington filed a motion for temporary custody. Hearing for cause will be held October 2, 2001.

STATEMENT OF FACTS

Dennis and Proveena Washington were married in 1990. They have two children, nine-year-old Jackson and seven-year-old Nicole. After eleven years of marriage, Mr. Washington moved out of the house on April 16, 2001, without discussing his departure with Mrs. Washington or making arrangements for the children. Mrs. Washington believes that Mr. Washington had been having an intimate relationship with a business associate for some time.

Mr. Washington is a successful business person who has worked ten or more hours each day during the period of the marriage, often during the evenings. According to a psychiatric evaluation of the family procured in August by Mrs. Washington, Mr. Washington is achievement–oriented, compulsive, and leads a routine and scheduled life. Although he has the potential to be nurturing and sensitive with the children, the psychologist characterized him as rigid and overly consistent, authoritarian and uncompromising. In addition, he is uncomfortable with and refrains from expressions of emotion but has not been abusive toward the children. Mr. Washington is concerned for the children's welfare and plans to hire a full time housekeeper if he is awarded custody.

After Mrs. Washington was married, she stayed at home and cared for Mr. Washington and the two children for over five years. Five and a half years ago, she took a job as a teacher and Mr. Washington began to perform some of the household tasks. Mrs. Washington has remained at the same job and has developed a good relationships with her co-workers. She has a good working relationship with her principal and has been comfortable requesting his aid dealing with children who have discipline problems. Her work schedule also coincides with the children's school hours and vacations.

According to the psychiatrist who evaluated the family, Mrs. Washington is warm, outgoing, and appropriately emotional. She has knowledge and experience in dealing with children, and responds to the individual needs of her own children. The evaluation further states that Mrs. Washington is comfortable with expressions of emotion by others and is herself appropriately expressive.

As Mr. Washington directed more of his energies toward the business, the marriage began to deteriorate and the marital tensions increased. Mrs. Washington occasionally relaxed with a drink to cope with these tensions. Upon realizing that drinking could become a problem, she sought the help of her family physician, who suggested that she try to contact Alcoholics Anonymous. Mrs. Washington stated that she removed alcohol from the house; she has not used alcohol in the past year except for an occasional glass of wine with dinner.

Mr. Washington sees Mrs. Washington's problem as more serious. He alleges that she drinks to excess. The evaluations note that Mrs. Washington is somewhat insecure and has a tendency to cope with stress by use of alcohol. The evaluation notes, however, that Mrs. Washington is capable of regrouping when she becomes aware of a problem; she reasserts control appropriately. The experts note, on the basis of interviews and testing, that Mrs. Washington controlled her drinking since she became aware of the problem. Mr. Washington, however, has alleged that Mrs. Washington has continued to drink to excess. At their daughter's birthday party in May, he stated that she drank to excess and caused embarrassment. In addition, Mr. Washington has felt uncomfortable with her expression of feelings, which sometime involve anger or crying. These episodes have increased to once a week as the marital problems intensified.

The children both show appropriate range of emotion for their ages and interact well socially. Both children are active and involved in a variety of activities. Neither child has expressed a preference for the custodial parent. The psychiatrist recommended that Mrs. Washington be granted custody of the children because of her warm, loving, and nurturing relationship with children.

You represent Mrs. Washington and are preparing a brief for the trial court. You have researched the law, discovered a statute applies, found several useful cases from before and after the statute's enactment, and taken notes. So far, you have sketched the following preliminary outline as you simultaneously took more detailed notes:

- Custody disputes
  statutory—five factors + 1
  (court can consider anything else relevant)
- Apply here—Mom wins on all
- Conclusion

You have written and prioritized your rhetorical questions as follows:

PURPOSES	1. help the trial judge account for all parts of the statute, which she must. 3. inform of law, arguments for mom. 4. raise arguments against father 2. get the kids for mom
AUDIENCES	2. judge 1. judge's clerk 3. the mom 4. opposing counsel, father
SCOPE	15 pages, double-spaced
STANCE	helpful firm concerned

You may them fill in your outline as follows. _See_ Mary B. Ray & Jill J. Ramsfield, <u>Legal Writing: Getting it Right and Getting it Written </u>at 239-40 (3d ed. 2000).

Design A.

Custody disputes – general background information

Factor 1–Wishes of parents
    both want, both will give visitation rights
Factor 2–Wishes of child
    nothing expressed
Factor 3–Interrelationship of children w/parents
    mother drinks (<u>Johnson</u> mom drank too–distinguish)
    father strict (<u>Pines</u>–father got son–same?)
    mother stable? (see–<u>Schwartz</u>–not as crazy as this woman: distinguish)
Factor 4–Child's adjustment to home & community with mom now,   no adjustment
    father will live in same city, but move required
Factor 5–Mental and physical health
    mother stable? (see <u>Schwartz</u>; distinguish this mother, not that
        crazy)
    father unemotional
Other factors–adultery, moral character
    father having an affair, missed meeting with kids
    cf. <u>Hilderbrand</u>–doesn't mean he can't "mother"

 Conclusion

    Mom probably gets them because she is more responsive to their needs, has them now, hasn't missed any time with them.

    Any legal reader will not misunderstand this architecture. Having designed it as such, you may feel you are finished. It tracks the statute, a standard choice for design, one that respects both the law and the judge's duty to account for all factors outlined by the statute.

You are in a hurry yourself and this design will do, you think. But will you get the children for Mrs. Washington? You know that three factors are not in dispute. Suppose you take just a few more moments and reconsider your rhetorical points as follows:

PURPOSE	4. help the trial judge account for all parts of the statute, which she must. 2. inform of law, arguments for Mom. 3. raise arguments against father. 1. get kids for the mom.
AUDIENCE	1. judge 2. judge's clerk 3. the mom 4. opposing counsel, father
SCOPE	7 pages, double-spaced; court won't read much more.
STANCE	aggressive professional

In just a few minutes, you may redesign your document as follows:

Design B.

I. THE TRIAL COURT SHOULD AWARD CUSTODY TO MRS. WASHINGTON BECAUSE IT IS IN THE CHILDREN'S BEST INTERESTS TO STAY IN THEIR FAMILY HOME.

Factors not in dispute

A. Interrelationship
B. Mental and Physical Health
C. Other Factors

II. THE TRIAL COURT SHOULD NOT AWARD CUSTODY TO MR. WASHINGTON BECAUSE HE CANNOT DEVOTE ENOUGH TIME TO THE CHILDREN.

A. Interrelationship
B. Mental and Physical Health
C. Other Factors

III. CONCLUSION

Or, if you feel you want the brief to gain momentum, you might design as follows:

Design C.

I.   THE TRIAL COURT SHOULD NOT AWARD CUSTODY
TO MR. WASHINGTON BECAUSE HE CANNOT
DEVOTE ENOUGH TIME TO THE CHILDREN.
Factors not in dispute
A.   Mental and Physical Health
B.   Other Factors
C.   Interrelationship

II. THE TRIAL COURT SHOULD AWARD CUSTODY TO
MRS. WASHINGTON BECAUSE IT IS IN THE CHIL-
DREN'S BEST INTERESTS TO STAY IN THEIR FAMILY
HOME.
A.   Interrelationship
B.   Mental and Physical Health
C.   Other Factors

III. CONCLUSION

In just a few minutes, you have created three designs for this document, a document crucial to your client. You did not commit to the first, although it would have functioned. It would also have been longer and might have taken longer to write. By standing back, analyzing your rhetorical direction, and being creative about solutions, you have generated a more concise document that meets all your goals. Choose which one you prefer. Even if you return to the first, you will know why.

Designing a document like this absorbs much discussion, sooner or later, in the law office. Unfortunately, it is too often after you have written your draft. Then your own thinking, and the comments of other attorneys, focus on second guessing your intentions. Why not think ahead? By asking why you are using a design; by connecting your answer to specific notions of purpose, audience, scope, and stance; by discussing the possibilities—you design documents that work. If you can work with your colleagues to get to the *why* of a certain architecture, your design will take on a new luster. Many legal writers choose a design that is simply familiar, or one that helps them understand the problem better, a writer-based choice. Or they may choose one that is essentially a research report. These designs can work in a limited way; they may not meet all of the audience's needs, serve all of the possible purposes, or present the appropriate stance appropriate for this document. Consider these questions, and your job as designer-writer will not only go more quickly, but it will be also be more productive and creative.

Add to those classical forms of thinking any patterns dictated by the law itself, such as the balancing test and the element-by-element approach, and you have a repertoire from which to choose for most documents. Some forms you choose will imitate similar documents; each can be customized to fit your client's situation. And each can bear your "hand" in the design, which is the combined influence of your credibility, creativity, and critical eye.

Review your techniques at this point. You may have been able to make these design decisions before you wrote, or you may be rewriting the document to better match purpose with architecture. Then, once you have examined your negotiation, analysis, or argument through the lenses of both neoclassical and modern legal rhetoric, you may find that your analysis re-forms itself into an original design that is even more suited to the circumstances than modern architectural designs.

You may find that you are stepping into the most creative world of legal document design: the post-modern, epistemic architecture that molds new documents uniquely created for special situations. You may even design such an original document from the start.

TECHNIQUES

• *Let the document sit for a while.* This is always good advice, not always easy to do. In a busy schedule, it sometimes seems impossible. Nevertheless, you can let a document sit while you make phone calls, attend a meeting, or work on another project. Eventually, you can plan your writing process so that the draft is done earlier, leaving you more time to evaluate it from several perspectives. The more time away, the more you will look at the document's architecture from the client's perspective, not from yours. Then you can see what works and what does not.

• *Write the document as your last task of the day, then rewrite it first thing in the morning.* One way to let the document sit is to plan your day so that you compose a document by the end of the day, sleep on it, then return fresher in the morning.

• *Change the medium.* This, too, allows you to see your work in a different form. Most people print the document rather than read it on the screen. They look at it as the readers will. You can also use a tape recorder, reading it in, then listening to it. Or you can have your secretary, colleague, or paralegal read it while you listen.

• *Read aloud.* You can often hear what you cannot see. As you are redesigning your document, listen to its progression and make sure that it conforms to the form you intend, that it is internally consistent, that themes and sub-themes are carried through, and that you hear yourself guiding the reader through the building that is your document.

• *Change your environment to get a new perspective.* It sometimes helps to change your physical surroundings so that you can break out of the writer mode and into the reader mode. You may simply go to the other side of your desk and be the client as you read. Or you may want to reserve a conference room to reread your test or even go outside.

- *Pretend that the document has already been turned in.* Some people can create the kind of concentration that seems to come only after a document is filed: then you see the mistakes. If you can trick your critical reader into thinking that has been done, then you may see some of them before you turn it in.

- *Delegate the rewrite to someone else.* This takes trust. But once you have a close working relationship with a colleague, it can be the most powerful tool in your repertoire. Your read hers and she'll read yours. As intelligent readers, you can see if the theme appears concretely, if the order makes sense, if the proportions are appropriate, and so on. Commenting on each other's work breaks open a dialogue about writing and makes not only the document better, but also each other's general architectural techniques.

- *Literally cut and paste.* Ah, the old way. It works pretty well. This entails taking two hard copies of your document and spreading one out on a conference table to see the entire blueprint. Mark what it is doing, how the sections are connected, and whether or not they are working. If you see sections, paragraphs, or sentences that need moving, number them in the original, then start cutting and pasting. Literally lay out the document so it flows well, just as an architect moves parts of her models. This technique will serve you well by giving you a tactile feel for flow in legal writing.

- *Synthesize comments from others.* All comments are reader feedback. As such, they are valuable information about reactions from users of the document. Remembering that you are building it for them, try to incorporate their suggestions into your unified whole. Don't just tack on another room or stick something in the basement. Make sure the adjustment works with you overall theme. This may mean there is a chain reaction in the document, something that requires a number of adjustments. Dive in and make them. The integrated whole will serve the ultimate users better.

CREATING INNOVATIVE ARCHITECTURE

Do you have the strength to "destroy every institutional model"? To "break free from idolatry"? Can you become the architect of unique documents that change the law, recreate the concept of transactions, or solve unusual disputes? Can you defy the habits of those around you?

Much of legal practice also lends itself to creative imagination. As problems become more complex, so do the vehicles we use for solving them. Contracts have become longer, more detailed, more complex as the law itself helps to define the parameters of agreements. International transactions and the growing body of international law have reinformed U.S. document design, forcing us to consider intercultural ways of analyzing situations. And international clients are asking us to anticipate and address situations for which there is no precedent. Federal lawyers are handling more complex problems for a wider audience than before. Even the solo practitioner faces more complex litigation requirements and a swiftly changing body of law from which she must pull her sources.

Indeed, with tremendous effort and immense joy, we must strip away the cultural taboos we have inherited. We must track them down one by one in our minds and desanctify them. For the modern architect, the paralyzing taboos are dogmas, conventions, inertia, all the dead weight accumulated during centuries of classicism. By destroying every institutionalized model, he can break free from idolatry. He can reconstruct and relive the whole process of man's formation and development, realizing that more than once in the course of the millennia, architects have wiped the slate clean and erased every grammatical and syntactical rule. In fact, genuinely creative spirits have always started from scratch. The modern revolution is not unprecedented or apocalyptic. There has been a recurrent struggle against repressive bonds throughout the ages.

—Bruno Zevi
The Modern Language of
Architecture, 7–8

To operate successfully, comfortably, and creatively within this evolving world, you can develop your imagination. Your ability to understand the needs of your clients, to anticipate situations that have not yet happened, to fit your client's situation into a quickly evolving legal system will all make you more useful to your client and more comfortable with your job. You can then design documents that will move into a new mode of practice, even set the tone. This requires you to be flexible, energetic, and bold, even visionary.

You can use materials and methods in a way not used before. You can have, in a sense, a philosophy of lawyering, an approach that distinguishes you from others. You may believe that language can be adapted as lines in drawing. You may believe that deduction is the enemy, just as architect Philip Johnson believes the straight line is the enemy. You may feel that language is to law as light is to inspiration, as many architects believe. You may adamantly believe that writing less is saying more. Or you may believe that paper is obsolete and electronic and graphic communication is the new legal writing.

Many practices lend themselves only to the occasional creative touch, the occasional departure from tradition. Even if this departure occurs only once in your career, spot it and stretch your imagination to create something useful and unique. Be watchful, ready, willing. And, because you may be situated in a setting that does not often lend itself to creative imag-

ination—as distinguished from selfish insistence on a personal "style"—prepare your colleagues by researching the deeper rhetorical questions surrounding the client's situation.

The questions are the same: purpose, audience, scope, and stance. Your analysis of these elements in turn drives your choices of theme, materials, form, proportion, and interior design. But now the possibilities begin. What will you draw? What has no one drawn before? Your creativity here is not a matter of style, but of philosophy. What is the role of legal writing? How will your document not only serve a function but also make a statement? Some clients will not want a statement, but some will. Suppose you are preparing a white paper on international issues. This is your opportunity to use graphics, invent a new arrangement, catch your readers' attention by flipping their traditional expectations. Suppose you must draft a contract for an international transaction that involves three countries' laws. You need to pull far enough back from those laws to get beyond contrast to unity, to see what they have in common as the centerpiece of your document, and their contrasting characteristics as integral, but non-central, detail. Suppose you are writing a speech for a partner on a controversial topic. Who says you have to use traditional order? Create an order that rivets listeners by its creative energy: a metaphor, a mysterious buildup, or a riddle.

SOME INNOVATIVE IDEAS

Work outside traditional legal boundaries: use social science, psychology, or empiricism to establish your theory of the case.

Turn traditional "logic" inside out.

Infuse your structure with your personal perspective—narrate.

Reject binary approaches—allow for simultaneous possibilities.

Use metatext—write about what you are writing.

Use visual images.

Deconstruct—and reconstruct.

Use humor.

Write poetry.

Be assymetrical.

Parody.

A real building is one which the eye can light and stay lit.

Ezra Pound

Be prepared to think of new solutions. You can connect the following dots using six lines or more, a traditional approach. Can you use five? Or four?

Do not abandon creativity in legal writing; recreate creativity itself. You may master so much in this complex field that you stop with traditions. Yet the lawyers who break with tradition are often the most successful, distinguishing themselves as creative masters.   Redefine your approach. Stretch. Design a unique document.

Like the actor who "breaks the plane" between him and his audience, you can walk up the aisles of legal writing. As you are communicating, you can write about what you are communicating. I did that in Chapter 3 as I described how the introduction had changed in the process of writing it. This is a book about writing. You can do the same to illustrate your very point. If you have a recalcitrant client who wants you to make an absurd argument to a federal agency on her behalf, you can lead her through an argument that to her will seem absurd, then show her that she is making a similar argument that the federal agency will find absurd. If you are arguing that your client's silence is being used against him, you can begin your oral argument with a full minute of silence. Or if you are trying to illustrate a point: draw it. Innovating requires bold approaches, as in the following examples.

Example 5.16. Example of Minimalism: The Short Brief.

Less may be more. If you want to send a message that the court needs to do minimal work to dispense with the case, make the brief minimal. Carve from it only the absolute essentials, as is done in the following brief filed with the U.S. Supreme Court.

**RESPONDENTS BRIEF IN OPPOSITION TO
PETITION FOR A WRIT OF CERTIORARI TO
THE UNITED STATES COURT OF APPEALS
FOR THE SIXTH CIRCUIT**

QUESTION PRESENTED

Whether the court below correctly held that the City of Cleveland could constitutionally charge Park Place, Inc., a higher permit fee than

other businesses which make less use of and have fewer privileges in their use of City airport facilities?

STATEMENT OF THE CASE

Petitioner Park Place, Inc. ("Park Place") is in the business of providing an off airport parking site for Cleveland, Ohio's, city airport. As is necessary to the operation of such a business, Park Place employs a fleet of shuttle buses to make frequent and continuous passenger trips between the airport and Park Place's parking facility. In addition, Park Place also has greater parking and phone privileges than do hotels, motels, and cab companies that provide less frequent and casual airport service.

For this greater use and additional privileges, the Respondent City of Cleveland (Cleveland), by ordinance, charged Park Place a higher permit fee than was charged the more casual users.

Park Place objected to the higher fee.

On the stipulated facts the trial court entered summary judgment for Cleveland. The Court of Appeals for the Sixth Circuit agreed that this higher permit fee was constitutionally permissible.

REASONS FOR DENYING THE WRIT

All judges who have reviewed the stipulated facts in this case have unanimously concluded that there is no denial of equal protection or violation of the Commerce Clause. These judges are correct. New Orleans v. Duke, 417 U.S. 297 (1976); Toye Bros. Yellow Cab Co. v. Irby, 305 F. Supp. 911 (E.D. La. 1969), aff'd, 417 F.2d 806 (5th Cir. 1971).

The constitutional principles of business regulation arising in this case were settled long ago and were correctly applied by the courts below.

CONCLUSION

The petition for writ of certiorari should be denied.

Example 5.17. Example of Critical Race Theory Used in a Brief.

Critical race theory suggests that, despite any kind of reasoning or examination of policy or economics, people are denied legal rights based on their race. This theory is derived from Legal Realism and admits there are no absolute rules. It goes further, however, expanding to the postmodern idea that, among other things, outcomes are based on subjective prejudices, not any reasoning. Documents following this theory, then, can derive their forms from factual evidence and personal stories of racial-based discrimination.

Thus, Congress has expressly included "Native Hawaiians"-- which it has repeatedly defined since the 1970s to mean any descendant of the Islands' inhabitants prior to 1778, without regard to blood quantum [footnote omitted]--in scores of statutory programs benefiting indigenous people across the Nation. See 42 U.S.C. s 11701(19)-(20) (listing statutes); 20 U.S.C. s 7902(13)- (16)(same); Jon M. Van Dyke, The Political Status of the Native Hawaiian People, 17 Yale L. & Pol. Rev. 95, 106 n.67 (1998).

In 1993 Congress passed a Joint Resolution signed into law "apologiz[ing] to Native Hawaiians" for the United States' role in the coup, and "the deprivation of the rights of Native Hawaiians to self-determination." 107 Stat. at 1513. The law specifically acknowledged that

"the health and well-being of the Native Hawaiian people is intrinsically tied to *** the land," that land was taken from Hawaiians without their consent or compensation, and that indigenous Hawaiians have "never directly relinquished their claims *** over their national lands." Id. In other recent acts, Congress has expressly affirmed the "special"-and "trust"--relationship between the United States and Hawaiians, and has specifically recognized Hawaiians as "a distinct and unique indigenous people." 42 U.S.C. s 11701(1), (13), (15), (16), (18); accord 20 U.S.C. s 7902(1), (10).

In light of Hawaii's unique historical and geographic circumstances, it is perhaps not surprising that Congress chose to delegate to the State authority to manage the public trust for Native Hawaiians. The pulls of federalism are particularly strong in the case of the most isolated land mass in the world, some 5000 miles from our national Capital. No other State has been given such responsibility with respect to an indigenous people. The people of Hawaii were required to accept this responsibility as a condition of statehood, and did so. See Ahuna v. Department of Hawaiian Home Lands, 640 P.2d 1161, 1168 (Haw. 1982); 20 U.S.C. s 7902(10); 42 U.S.C. s 11701(16).

In 1978 Hawaii--reaffirming the "solemn trust obligation and responsibility to native Hawaiians"--amended its constitution to establish OHA, to better "address the needs of the aboriginal class of people of Hawaii." Haw. Rev. Stat. s 10-1(a). OHA was empowered to receive a share of the revenues generated by the lands conveyed to the State pursuant to s 5(f) of the Statehood Act, manage those and certain other assets on behalf of indigenous Hawaiians, and, more generally, promote Hawaiian affairs. See Haw. Const. art. XII, ss 4-6; J.A. 35 (Comm. Rep. No. 59). OHA also receives federal funds and helps to administer federal programs for indigenous Hawaiians. See 42 U.S.C. s 2991b- 1..

OHA's overriding purpose is the "betterment of conditions of native Hawaiians" and "Hawaiians." Haw. Rev. Stat. s 10-3 (1)-(2). "Native Hawaiian" means "any descendant of not less than one-half part of the races inhabiting the Hawaiian Islands previous to 1778, as defined by the [HHCA]." Id. s 10-2. "Hawaiian" includes "any descendant of the aboriginal people inhabiting the Hawaiian Islands *** in 1778." Id. The latter definition was added to bring state law "in line

with the current policy of the federal government to extend benefits for Hawaiians to all Hawaiians regardless of blood quantum." J.A. 46 (Comm. Rep. No. 59) (emphases added). See note 4, supra.

Example 5.18. Example of Feminist Theory in a Brief.

In 1989, an amicus brief was filed in the case of <u>Webster v. Reproductive Health Services</u>, 492 U.S. 490 (1989) which has been since been called the "Voices Brief." The brief was entitled "Women Who Have Had Abortions, et al." and it included testimonials of women who had endured illegal abortions. This brief may be the "Brandeis Brief" of feminist jurisprudence.

Since this time, other briefs have incorporated emotional appeals by the people most affected by the case. In this example, we hear voices in another situation: physician assisted suicide. The amicus writers here cite the "Voices Brief" as authority for the unusual form of their brief. <u>See Brief for Amicus Curiae of Surviving Family Members</u> at 5, n.2, <u>Washington v. Glucksberg</u>, 1997 WL 348037 (S.Ct. 1996) (No. 96-110).

Attorneys for Amicus Curiae Surviving Family Members in Support of Physician-Assisted Dying

TABLE OF CONTENTS

VII.   CONCLUSION ... 29

1   Declaration of Roberta Lau

2   Declaration of Patsy McLaughlin McGeorge

3   Declaration of Leanne Gallison

4   Declaration of Kay Beck

5   Declaration of Elvin O. Sinnard

6   Declaration of Patty Rosen

7   Declaration of Jeff (Joseph) Halsey

8   Declaration of Tania Bloom

9   Declaration of Gail Bereny

10   Declaration of Dorothy B. Hoogstraat

11   Declaration of Gosta Pearson

12   Declaration of Keith William Green

13   Declaration of William F. Meyer III

14   Declaration of Steve Knipp

15   Declaration of Jinny Tesik

A WORD ON POSTMODERNISM

The word "postmodernism" was first coined by architects in the 1970's, who were rebelling against modernism, also known as the international style of architecture. The word is, of course, self-contradictory, because any style of the present age is "modern." Gothic style was "modern" in 1165. The very notion of coining the word suggests the nature of postmodernism: evocative and arresting in architecture, startling and disconcerting in the law, perhaps.

MODERNISM

In architecture, modernism, or the international style, suggested that the principles used were "volume (space enclosed by thin planes) rather than mass, regularity as opposed to symmetry, elegant materials; technical perfection, and fine proportions in place of applied ornament." HILARY FRENCH, ARCHITECTURE: A CRASH COURSE 108 (1998) (citing PHILIP JOHNSON & HENRY-RUSSELL HITCHCOCK, THE INTERNATIONAL STYLE: ARCHITECTURE SINCE 1922 (1932)). Details and ornamentation were not used; instead, the style was characterized by "white flat walls with no extra applied decoration, severely cubic forms, large areas of glazing, and open planning." *Id.* The movement removed frills, concentrated on the essence of design, and eschewed classical forms. Motivated by social concerns, the modernists analyzed functional and social concerns in designing forms.

The same was true to some extent in law. Legal Realism broke with classical legal thought and, also based on social concerns, introduced the notion of policy and a deeper evaluation of rules and rationality as a useful means of solving problems. Legal Process tried to return some order to law, but not in classical ways; instead, the clean lines of process were used for "seeing" the law. Law was opened to view, its basest lines laid bare, the merits saved until last. Law and Society resurrected the merits, but in light of new sciences, and Law and Economics replaced classical rationality with practical formulas that wove together motivations of the parties with legal predictability.

Postmodernism

Modernism dominated the twentieth century in both architecture and law but, around the 1970's, both began to shift. In architecture, a sustained attack on modernism was initiated in 1966, when architects began to tire of the puritanical quality of modernism. *See* IRVING SANDLER, ART OF THE POSTMODERN ERA 5 (1996) (citing ROBERT VENTURI, COMPLEXITY AND CONTRADICTION IN ARCHITECTURE (1966)). This reaction called for eclecticism, complexity, ambiguity, and decoration. Understandably, this meant a variety of styles. Postmodernism, then, "has become a term of convenience, an umbrella term for a pluralism of architectural styles of the late twentieth century. . . . [M]uch of what was originally labeled 'Post-Modernism' was conceived and/or viewed as a reaction against aspects of the International Style, the high profile, influential style that profoundly affected mid- and late-20th century design concepts." Memorandum from Karin M.E. Alexis, Ph.D., Art & Architectural Historian, The Smithsonian Art History Series, to Jill J. Ramsfield (Nov. 16, 1999) (on file with author). By rejecting the modernists, the postmodernists could base their movement on criticism, not on any unified principle, and certainly not an international one.

Critical legal theory took a similar path. First a reaction against modern movements, it incorporated many elements of realism and Marxism, though never returned to either. To some extent, the modern movements, like the architectural movements, had hoped for neutral, objective means for solving problems. Clean lines. The critical legal theorists claimed that no such neutrality could exist, that results depended on subjective matters, such as who was asking the question, what social situation the problem-solvers came from and were in, and how society preferred certain outcomes.

Such theories opened up legal architecture. Personal voices became important in such fields as feminist legal theory and critical race theory. Arguments were constructed not just on reasoning or objective data, but on contradictions themselves. Rather than using abstract principles to solve problems, postmodern lawyers analyzed social situations, accounted for prejudices, and factored in ugly facts. Beyond that, the movement became too eclectic, itself espousing a principle of postmodern architecture. Basing the movement on criticism means, by definition, there are no universal, coherent qualities. Those may not emerge until historians use the next movement to define postmodernism by contrast. Until then, your design possibilities are extraordinary; you can help define the legal architecture of this age.

The preceding briefs represent critical legal studies, a part of post-modern legal architecture. These designs eschew the pure reasoning of classicism and neoclassicism and owe their origins to Legal Realism. Rules are reference points, often for tyranny, for the critical theorists. What lies behind the law are prejudicies, irrational assumptions, and faulty procedures. The design key is in the stories and situations of those most affected.

Voices, narratives, and ancedotes become a powerful form of proof. Thus, if you design your document using these innovative theories, you may be drawing from personal stories, constucting one large narrative from several individual ones, or using facts to define the abstract, asserted "rules" and "outcomes" described by courts.

As usual, analyze your situation to assess the appropriateness of your innovative design. You need not be a proponent of critical theories to be innovative. You may simply liberate your own voice in a creative way.

Example 5.19. Poetry in a Judicial Opinion.

We close with the following "Ode to Conway Twitty":
Twitty Burger went belly up
But Conway remained true
He repaid his investors, one and all
It was the moral thing to do.
His fans would not have liked it
It could have hurt his fame
Had any investors sued him
Like Merle Haggard or Sonny James.
When it was time to file taxes
Conway thought what he would do
Was deduct those payments as a business expense
Under section one-sixty-two.
In order to allow these deductions
Goes the argument of the Commissioner
The payments must be ordinary and necessary
To a business of the petitioner.
Had Conway not repaid the investors

His career would have been under cloud,
Under the unique facts of this case
Held: The deductions are allowed.

Jenkins v. Commissioner, T.C. Memo 1983-667, 1983 WL 114653 at
668 n.14 (November 3, 1983).

Example 5.20. Musical Reference in Judicial Opinion.

In light of the "abstruse, intensely technical [scientific] standards
involved," Hopkins v. State, 579 N.E.2d 1297, 1303 (Ind.1991), courts
are well advised not to pick sides in scholarly controversies between
eminent scientists about molecular biology or population genetics. As
one scholar has observed, "[t]he theory and technology of DNA far
surpass everyday knowledge. In fact, only those specifically trained in
molecular biology and chemistry [and population genetics] can even
begin to understand the concepts involved." Norman, DNA
Fingerprinting: Is It Ready For Trial, 45 UNIV.MIAMI L.REV. 243,
243-44 (1990). We, therefore, elect instead to heed Lord Mountararat's
musical commentary on the House of Lords:

    And while the House of Peers withholds

    Its legislative hand,

    And noble statesmen do not itch

    To interfere with matters which

    They do not understand,

    As bright will shine Great Britain's rays

    As in King George's glorious days!

    WILLIAM GILBERT & ARTHUR SULLIVAN, IOLANTHE, ACT

    II (1882).

    The hereditary peerage is not the only branch of government which
    can benefit from his lordship's counsel.

United States v. Porter, 618 A.2d 629, n.14 (D.C. 1992).

In every writing situation, you can determine your choice of neoclassical, modern, or innovative architecture by examining the contextual, rhetorical, and architectural elements discussed in Chapter 1. The process by which you create a document is by making a series of highly informed decisions. As your clients call, analyze the design possibilities even as you listen to the first suggestions of the problem. Be alert to the prospective document's landscape and build your repertoire of design possibilities which each project. Use your office's local conventions as a challenge to your creativity: create within convention. Build a town house that fits in the country or a skyscraper that's flat. Adapt throughout your career to the situation in which you are writing. That ability to adapt should make you flexible, creative, and quick.

Innovation is so rare in legal writing that it will draw attention immediately. Some readers find it refreshing; others feel threatened. Be persistent and willing. Whether you parody existing norms (_See, e.g., The Common Law Origins of the Infield Fly Rule,_ 123 U. PA. L. REV. 1474 (1975)) or allow the text to change the meaning of itself (_See, e.g._, Pierre Schlag, _Missing Pieces: A Cognitive Approach to Law,_ 67 TEX. L. REV. 1195 (1989)), you are creating new models for the future. If you innovate well, others will follow, and legal writing will itself evolve. The legal community as "target culture" is changed by the very people who come to it, just as countries are changed by immigrants and cities by creative architects. When you can, be bold in your creative design and change the very community in which you write.

Here, then, is one way to connect those dots:

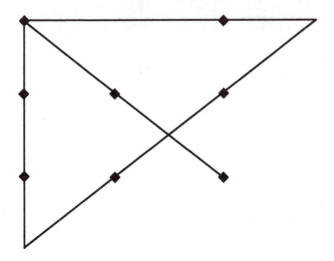

Whether you design within the box or outside, your choices carry over from outside to inside. As you move into your documents, paragraphs, and sentences, you manifest those choices in the interior of your design.

CHAPTER 6
DESIGNING THE INTERIOR

Writing has laws of perspective, of light and shade,
just as painting does, or music.
If you are born knowing them, fine.
If not, learn them.
Then rearrange the rules to suit yourself.

Truman Capote

You know when a building's design works. From your outside perspective, you can identify the building's type and its outer contours. You know its function, its users, its size. As you move from outside to inside, you see that the building's structure, proportions, then lighting, colors, and even art all harmonize. You may be conscious or

unconscious of this harmony. Perhaps it is so subtle that it simply washes over you; you just know you like it and you want to come back. Sometimes a building appeals to you because of its no-nonsense simplicity, its pure functionality. Sometimes it appeals because it integrates unlikely pieces into a whole. Sometimes you simply appreciate its unusual use of ordinary materials. However the architectural and interior design elements are combined, they have created a specific effect on you.

As you move from the outside of your document to the inside, you continue to use the design elements to affect your readers. You have studied so far the laws of perspective and form in legal writing. You saw in Chapter 3 how to anticipate possible themes for your document. You experimented in Chapter 4 with ways of seeing your materials' possibilities and for choosing the perspective that best suits your purposes and audiences. In Chapter 5, you explored ways to design your document's form to follow its function and to create the proper proportions for each segment. This chapter explores some methods for designing the interior once your theme, materials, form, and proportion are established. Architect meets interior designer here: in the interior of your prose. Your interior choices can reinforce your exterior choices. You can use the laws of interior design to create a specific effect, whether comfortable, brazen, unusual, or stark.

Inside a document's form reside its accoutrements: paragraphs, sentences, phrases, graphics, words, punctuation. Together, these give the document color and texture, internal shape, character, and harmony. Together, these allow a reader to see how the document's pieces work together, to experience the connections between one section and another, to remember the document in detail. This is where the reader resides, too, among your sentences and phrases, a guest in the building you have designed. But whose choices are these? Are you the kind of designer who leaves his mark, no matter what the client wants? Do you send the message that the designer is more important than the client (who must have bad taste, by the way)? Or do you take into account the client's needs and harmonize them in a way that looks professional, yet is uniquely the client's? Are you in a situation where someone else is the architect and you the interior designer, and vice versa? Will there be harmony or dissonance between the document's exterior and interior?

Your audiences' needs vary here, too. Sometimes you have the resources and the time to design a unique interior, such as a tailored letter to a CEO who has asked for a detailed analysis of his personal tax situation. Often, however, you are in the business of designing interiors to be used by multiple consumers: offices or passageways through which many eyes will pass. You then find a kind of universal interior design that rises above your personal tastes. You may be able to create an interior whose character is so artful that it is appreciated by nearly all of its users.

As an interior designer in the law, you distinguish yourself and your documents, then, not only by your structural designs but also by your small-scale designs, from sections to paragraphs to sentences to terms. You collect ideas and furnishings for the interior from the law itself, from the sections, paragraphs, sentences, and terms used by legislatures and judges. At times, these furnishings are cumbersome, large, or outdated, but you are stuck with them because they have been used repeatedly to build legal doctrines. In some cases, they are the law itself. In turn, you are aware when you draft legislation, contracts, letters, opinions, or briefs, that your legal writing may also become law; you can correspondingly "stick" someone else with unclear, unuseful, or unwieldy structure or language. Therefore, be particularly sensitive in selecting how to design and furnish the interiors of your sections, paragraphs, and sentences. You can preserve specialized terms, yet make them accessible to your readers; you can use specialized syntactic devices to maneuver through complex strategies and reasoning, yet make your prose readable. You can choose from a repertoire of possibilities.

As with form, you are operating within three general modes of interior design: traditional, modern, and innovative. Traditional interior design is derived from British and U.S. common law, statutes, regulations, and documents used within the legal community. Wills, contracts, leases, lending agreements, and sales documents were created from the law itself and designed to cover all contingencies. They captured the structure, phraseology, and terminology pertinent at the time and remained the same for many years. Some designers and clients, of course, still have a taste for the traditional.

Modern interiors, like modern forms, have emerged in this century, creating a design repertoire that accounts for traditional elements (*the living room has a couch*), but transforms them into sleeker, more streamlined presentations. Lawyers following this modern school of interior design consider their audiences as consumers, customers who must be able to use the document comfortably. These consumers often prefer one walk through the document and expect with that to be able to decide on business transactions, to activate expenditures, to sue or not, to get remedies when wronged, to comply with regulations and statutes.

Innovative interiors are rare, but they do exist. Minimalist briefs are filed, poetic complaints are drafted, and pictures sometimes replace words. To be innovative in this generally traditional profession is to be bold. But your repertoire can include some unusual interiors: rearrange the rules to suit the circumstances.

The more versatile you are with these three modes, the more comfortable you are in the interior of your prose. You may develop a specialty, but you usually begin by studying traditional interiors and fitting your designs to please two primary audiences: your supervising attorney and your client. You can know the baroque style of old opinions, the classical style of Holmes, and the florid style of Cardozo. You

can be equally at home with terse and elaborate prose, with curt sentences and thick paragraphs. You may not choose to adopt these patterns into your own writing, but, as a master designer, you should probably understand them and their place in legal history. You can then render your interiors with powerful versatility. Most importantly, you can master the interior design of your prose so that each element harmonizes with your architecture.

Once you have decided on the overall form of your document, including the relative proportions of its sections, you are ready to decide on the document's interior design, namely, its paragraphs and sentences. To harmonize these details with your architecture is to make your message clear, to achieve elegance and harmony. Here you decide on the rhythm of the smaller parts of your document, on the texture of the sentences and the color of the words. You may choose to be modern, using simple, uncluttered sentences to fit a direct message. You may choose to be baroque, using complex sentences and illustrious words to send a more formal, ornate message. You may dare to be innovative, using language to shape ideas more abstractly. Whatever your choice, your reader reacts with the least confusion when you choose consistently and intentionally.

A Word on the Legal Register

Linguists use the specific term *register*, rather than style, to refer to a discourse community's use of the language and instruments of communication themselves. Linguists refer to register as that organization of language used in a special group or field of expertise. All groups have a kind of register for communicating to each other, groups such as business people, scientists, gangs, knitting specialists, politicians, architects, musicians—and lawyers. They use English for a specific purpose, inventing terminology specific to the field, phrases that capture certain concepts in the field, shorthand that allows experts to communicate more efficiently.

Studies in register have typically examined such matters as the verb forms in scientific English; sentence length, voice, and vocabulary in certain discourse communities; and genre in a target language. *See* JOHN SWALES, GENRE ANALYSIS 6 (1990). That target language could be scientific English, business English, or medical English, for example. Those studies of register in target communities also showed how different influences, such as changing communicative purpose, can operate within a single spoken or written discourse of a particular type, such as between sections of research articles or paragraphs of newspaper articles. *See id.* at 3. Thus the rhetorical elements of purpose and audience were seen to affect the communicator's choice of vocabulary, syntax, or form. For example, scientists use technical terms to summarize results for knowledgeable colleagues, doctors use medical shorthand and charts to communicate with other doctors who may treat the same patient, and sports announcers use abbreviated terms and elliptical syntax in announcing events in action.

Technically, a register incorporates the *lexicon*, or specialized terms created by the community, and *phraseology*, or specialized strings of terms embedded within the sentences; the *syntax*; and the *genres*, or instruments, used by the community. Register can also be described as the *functional variety* of a language, a contextual category that correlates linguistic features with recurrent situational features. *Id.* at 40. In the socially-situated act of legal writing, we correlate language with legal situations. In fact, these aspects of our legal register are our elements of interior design, explained more metaphorically in this chapter.

Lexicon and Phraseology

Lexicon, or vocabulary, and its combination into phraseology is specialized within a field. We call them terms of art. For example, in law, lexicon and phraseology includes such terms of art as *nuisance, holder in due course, defendant, destination contract, shifting the burden of proof,* and *due process*. Certain phrases appear in some texts, such as *Enclosed please find* in the openings of some business letters or *Now comes the plaintiff* in traditional complaints. Lawyers must acquire this lexicon and phraseology not only generally but also for specific areas of practice. Acquiring the

lexicon and phraseology, like acquiring any language, requires more than reading the dictionary or rules definitions; it also requires an understanding of usage in the legal context. The following example, from a brief, offers context.

Example 6.1. Example of Lexicon in Context, from a Brief.

Plaintiff argues that its letter dated February 4, 1997, constituted a request for rulemaking whose denial is final agency action subject to judicial review. It is true that the denial of a citizen petition is reviewable final agency action, <u>Upjohn Mfg. Co. v. WWHT. Inc.</u>, 520 F. Supp. 58, 62 (W.D. Mich. 1981), <u>aff'd</u>, 681 F.2d 480 (6th Cir. 1982), but plaintiff submitted no such petition. "Citizen petition" is a term of art; to qualify as a citizen petition and to be treated like one, a request must comply with the requirements of 21 C.F.R. § 10.30. Plaintiff submitted an ordinary letter, not a citizen petition. Moreover, the letter did not request formal rulemaking; it merely requested "public comment and participation" in the development of FDA's 'guidelines' regarding pharmacy compounding. Pl. Mem., Ex. 22.

In this example, the writer defined "citizen action petition" by explicitly referring to the regulation that defines it, a source that the reader needs. The writer has assumed that the reader understands the phrase of art, "final agency action," and includes no definition. Such usage of the term assumes that the reader has an understanding of administrative procedure. The writer also assumes that the reader understands the contrasts between "formal rulemaking" and "public comment and participation." The writer also assumes, of course, that the reader understands how to find the sources and what the abbreviations mean. The language and phraseology are peculiar to not only administration law, but also to specific questions used by one agency, the FDA. As a legal writer, you must gauge your reader's level of familiarity with the technical terms used in the discussion.

Syntax

In register, *syntax* refers to the arrangement of the language in the sentence. Different specialty areas use particular syntactic devices, such as passive voice in scientific writing and conditional clauses in tax law. Business memos use short, direct sentences, and instructions use the imperative. Both the traditional and the modern legal registers use identifiable and imitable syntactical patterns. For example, fact sections in opinions often use subject–verb–object order, preceded by a phrase identifying the dates. The traditional legal register uses passive voice, nominalizations, complex conditionals, and intrusive phrases, as elaborated upon below. The modern legal register uses active voice, simpler sentence structure, fewer dependent clauses, and closer proximity of subject and verb, also as elaborated upon below.

Two basic interiors—or registers—dominate legal writing now. One is the traditional interior, which is most frequently caricatured as typical of what lawyers write: it is marked by doublets, passive voice, Latinisms, and nominalizations, among other features. The other is the more modern interior, which uses plainer language, simpler syntax, strong headings and topic sentences, and less clutter. Many variations exist on these two interiors; some attorneys mix them freely. A third choice lies beyond these modes, an innovative interior that you can make uniquely yours.

It may help to understand the features of these various interiors. Each uses the elements of balance, shape, texture, color, rhythm, and light differently. Each collects accoutrements particular to its design.

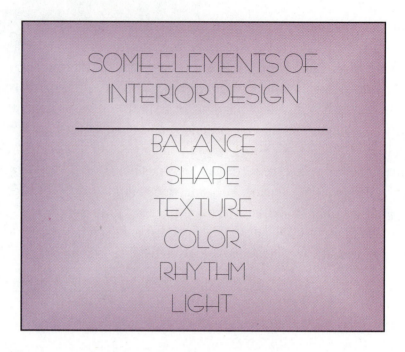

Just as the parts of the document fit the whole in proportion to their relative importance to the document's theme and purpose, so the smaller parts can reflect their relative importance. Shorter paragraphs can work as transitions or quick expositions of less important points; longer paragraphs can offer more detail for a more important point. If a less important point is nevertheless technical, several short paragraphs may move the reader quickly through the technical material rather than one long paragraph that stops him and makes him reread. In modern legal writing, readers generally prefer more small paragraphs to one large one, transitional paragraphs to hidden sentences, graphics or headings that give directions to long stretches of unbroken text. What follows are six elements of interior design that you can analyze as you harmonize the document with its structure.

BALANCE

Readers respond well to balanced text, that is, text that is neither concentrated at the beginning or end—neither too long nor too short, neither too ornate nor too simple. Once you have used your rhetorical elements to decide on form and proportion, you can concentrate on balance within each portion of the document. You can achieve balance by being aware of it:

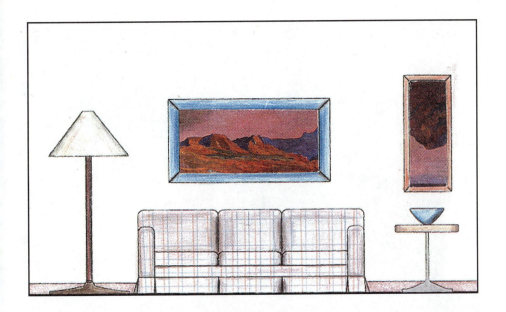

shaping sections, paragraphs, and sentences so that they work in balance with each other. Many traditional forms suggest an overall balance. For example, most scholarly papers begin with an introduction and end with a conclusion, each of which is much shorter than the middle sections. Briefs begin with a Summary of the Argument and end with a Conclusion, each of which is also shorter than the middle sections. Legislation can begin with a preamble and end with shorter procedural sections. Contracts can similarly use shorter sections to build to the more complex part of the document by describing the transaction itself, for example, or conditions necessary for completion of the transactions, and then close with shorter boilerplate sections.

All of these approaches give a bell-curve to the writing, a balance between the shorter "bookends" and the longer books in the middle, something you can emulate within sections, paragraphs, and sentences. You can, for example, open a section with a two-or three-sentence introduction that summarizes the section and relates its sub-message to your theme. You can end with a paragraph of similar length, which concludes and connects to the next section. At the paragraph level, your first and last sentences can similarly shape the paragraph, and your sentences can begin and end with similar phrasing or words. This paragraph begins with a long sentence that gives a theme of connecting large-scale design to small-scale design and ends with this sentence, of about the same length, that demonstrates the point.

You can invert this traditional balance, creating long opening sections, short middle sections, and long closing sections. Or you can alternate short and long. Should you get particularly artistic, you can follow a kind of *rondo* form within your sections, repeating points after expositions of new information; or a *sonata* form by introducing a sub-theme and then modulate to another, using the same proportion of elements but with new facts or cases; or you can do a theme and variations by repeating certain key words and phrases while introducing new materials that give the theme a stronger impact. Should these classical forms be too balanced for your taste, you can design according to the document's substantive sub-parts by bunching sub-parts together to make one larger whole so that the document has three equivalent sections; alternating short and long information; or putting four smaller parts at the beginning that balance two longer parts at the end.

The idea in achieving balance is to engage the reader without tiring her, to raise just enough expectation that surprises are memorable, and to present an equilibrium within the section that directs her to the document's essence. The following examples show balance at the section, paragraph, and sentence level, respectively.

Example 6.2. Balance within a Section of a Brief.

B.   <u>**Plaintiff does not have personal jurisdiction even when she alleges that defendant engaged in tortious conduct that caused injury within Colorado.**</u>

In rare circumstances in Colorado, negligent conduct in a foreign state that culminates in injury to a plaintiff in Colorado can amount to tortious conduct in Colorado within the meaning of the long-arm statute. <u>See</u> <u>McAvoy v. District Court</u>, 757 P.2d 633 (Colo. 1988). However, in some cases, even if a plaintiff sustains an injury in Colorado, the defendant's tortious acts are so remote as to preclude personal jurisdiction. <u>See</u>, <u>e.g</u>, <u>Fleet Leasing v. Armoir, Inc.</u>, 949 P.2d 1078, 1080 (Colo. 1998); <u>Cambridge Bridges v. Coyote Cables, Inc.</u>, 999 P.2d 109 (Colo. 1999). Then, courts require a closer nexus between the defendant and the state to satisfy due process requirements. <u>See</u> <u>id.</u> That closer nexus did not occur here.

In cases where the defendant is alleged to have committed a tortious act in Colorado, courts undertake a minimum contacts analysis in order to determine whether due process requirements would be met in asserting personal jurisdiction over the defendant. See Fleet Leasing, 949 P.2d at 1084-88. In Fleet, the defendant was alleged to have negligently repaired a truck in Washington, causing injuries in Colorado. Id. at 1089. The court concluded that it had no basis for personal jurisdiction over the defendant because there was no indication that the defendant had been trying to serve a market broad enough to encompass Colorado. Id. at 1080. The nexus was not close enough.

In fact, the United States Supreme Court has specifically limited the idea that plaintiffs can sue defendants in a court of any forum where its product was alleged to have caused injury. See World-Wide Volkswagen, 444 U.S. at 297 [citations omitted]. Foreseeability for a due process analysis "is not the mere likelihood that a product would find its way into the forum State. Rather, it is that the defendant's contacts in connection with the forum State are such that he should reasonably anticipate being haled into court there." Id. Defendants must have some degree of predictability. That is, "[t]he Due Process Clause, by insuring the 'orderly administration of the laws,'. . . gives a degree of predictability to the legal system that allows potential defendants to structure their primary conduct with some minimum assurance as to where that conduct will and will not render them liable to suit." Id. Defendants must be able to structure their conduct so that they can anticipate—and therefore even avoid—suits.

D Corporation could not have done that here. There is no close nexus between D Corporation's allegedly negligent acts and XYZ Corporation. D Corporation at no time anticipated dealings with XYZ Corporation. D Corporation did not attempt to serve a market broad enough to encompass Colorado because the cost of doing business in the western region of the United States is prohibitive for D Corporation. Less than one percent of D Corporation's product has been sold through a trading company to one Colorado entity. Since D Corporation's primary conduct—99 per cent of its product distribution—occurs east of the Mississippi, D Corporation could not have reasonably anticipated that it would be haled into court in Colorado.

Thus, while XYZ Corporation's allegations of negligence may be tortious acts under the Colorado long-arm statute, they are not constitute tortious acts under the Fourteenth Amendment. This Court should dismiss this action as to D Corporation for lack of personal jurisdiction.

Comment: This section achieves balance by placing the main points at the section's opening and closing—tortious acts under long-arm statute v. tortious acts under the Fourteenth Amendment. The opening paragraph sets forth the intersection between the two, and the closing brings them together again, though more succinctly. The paragraphs in between are devoted to the long arm statute, Fourteenth Amendment, and an analysis of this situation, respectively. The balance occurs between opening and closing, with a reminder just over half-way through.

Example 6.3. Balance within the Paragraph of a Memo.

To show that a landlord's breach of duty was the legal cause of the tenant's injuries, the key standard has been whether the criminal activity was reasonably foreseeable. See Haley v. Mt. Olive Apartments, Inc., 555 So. 2d 41 (Fla. App. 1999). Thus, when a tenant was raped and murdered in her apartment, the criminal activity was reasonably foreseeable because of the landlord's negligence. See id. at 44. Also, when a tenant was sexually assaulted on the premises of an apartment building, the criminal activity was reasonably foreseeable because of previous crimes on the premises and in the neighborhood. See Crisinski v. Sunset Condominiums, 666 So. 2d 200, 203 (Fla. App. 2001). In Crisinski, the history of crime in the area and a previous sexual assault on the premises four years earlier were relevant factors in determining foreseeability of potential criminal acts. Id. at 204. Here, the mugger's actions were reasonably foreseeable because the tenant's apartment is in a high-crime area, muggings in the area have increased within the last two years, and another woman was almost mugged two months earlier. This mugging was reasonably foreseeable, and the landlord's breach of duty in not repairing the broken lock was the legal cause of the tenant's injuries.

Comment: Here, the opening and closing sentences mirror each other. The first starts with "legal cause" and ends with "reasonably foreseeable." The last reverses the order, giving a mirror quality to the paragraph. The examples setting up the analogy are balanced to a point about two-thirds through the paragraph, when the focus shifts to this case.

Example 6.4. Balance within the Sentence from a Brief.

To dismiss the case because of insufficient evidence is warranted, but to warrant evidence gained from insufficient sources is illegal.

or

The issue is not whether Congress was using the term "discard" in its ordinary sense, but whether the term "ordinary sense" has been discarded by Congress.

Comment: This is the most integrated form of balance, *antithesis*. The second part of the sentence inverts the first part.

You choose certain types of syntactical furniture for the interiors of your sections and paragraphs. These shape your prose. These syntactical devices might be angular—sharp sentences, short paragraphs—or soft and fluffy—inviting pillows on which your reader can rest his weary head. In writing terms, these are the paragraph and sentence structures, the syntactical choices that make a statement in themselves. Because you may want to make your reader wait a while to get the main point of your sentence, you can choose elaborate curves by constructing long sentences with long, introductory dependent clauses, rather like this sentence, which takes you through several phrases and asks you to hold one thought while reading another that is just now being introduced, namely, that of shaping your sentence by putting the main point at the end.

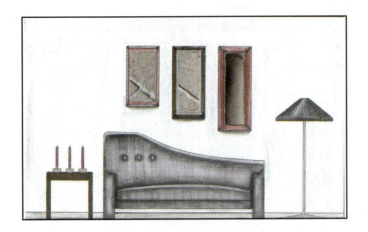

You can be blunt. That choice forces short sentences. No nonsense. Sharp angles. Or you can blend together the shapes of your headings and sentences by creating gentle curves in the internal structure of your sentences. To blend in such a way is to concentrate on where in the sentence your main message falls. The last two sentences blended by emphasizing the beginning and the ends of the sentences, respectively, using the term *blend* to unite them in subtheme, but deliberately shifting the reader's attention from beginning to end of the sentences. You may want to think of shape as a kind of emphasis; you build sentences to draw the reader's attention to particular points.

The following example chooses rather traditional sentences shapes. It uses the subject/verb/dependent clause order in almost every sentence, with the dates inserted via prepositional phrases, adjective strings, or participial phrases.

Example 6.5.   Similar Sentence Shapes, from a Board of
                 Veterans' Appeals Decision.

A discharge summary of an April to May 1983 hospitalization of the veteran noted that he had been living with the appellant until recently since their divorce in 1975. Similarly, a discharge summary of a September to November 1985 hospitalization documented the veteran's report that he and his "present wife" had problems, and were then "separated." A July 1986 discharge summary indicated that the veteran was married. A similar document reflecting a hospitalization of the veteran from November 1987 to January 1988 reported that he had "family problems," and experienced murderous impulses towards his ex-wife. A discharge summary of a June to July 1988 hospitaliza-

tion noted the veteran was experiencing marital problems with his separated wife while an August 1989 discharge summary noted that he would stay with his grandmother for several months, but lived in Houston.

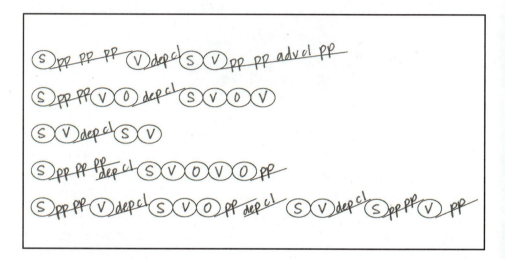

You can choose to accent even traditional shapes by using a repetitive phrase structure within sentences. This example's pattern accents dates by using prepositional phrases at the beginnings of sentences and as intrusive phrases within sentences. These shapes are alternately angular (pp) and smooth (s/v/o).

Example 6.6. Repetitive Sentence Shapes, from the fact section of an FCC Agenda Item.

Here the intrusive phrases, surrounded by commas, create a rough, bumpy texture.

Summary of Proposed Action: Slimfone, Inc. implemented, in October 1994, an experimental air/ground interconnected telephone service under Part 5 of the Commission's Rules on a limited number of commercial aircraft. QQM, Inc., in 1995, purchased Slimfone, and the experimental air/ground service had, by early 1997, expanded to include several hundred aircraft. Owing to the success of the experimental service, the Commission, on February 25, 1997, adopted a Notice of Proposed Rule Making (Notice) that proposed. . . .

You can also shape your document's interior by creating complex sentences. The following example uses formal openings, the royal *we*, passive voice, long sentences, and cautionary language in the traditional legal register.

Example 6.7.   Example of Elaborate, Velvety Textures, from an Opinion Letter.

Enclosed please find our analysis regarding a potential copyright action against George Ikopi. According to our conversation last week, a work by the architect Ikopi **was recently profiled** in Architectural Digest, a prominent architectural magazine, and the work resembles one of Soren International Sites' (SIS) designs. You stated in our conversation that it was your belief that Ikopi's work was a copy of one of SIS's designs, a copy of which is also enclosed herewith. **We** have examined the matter as carefully as **we** can without seeing the actual works, and **we** feel that, barring any major departure from the enclosed designs, you may have a claim against Ikopi, depending, of course on your relationship with ProTech. It seems that the relationship you established with ProTech was such that you should own the copyright to your work, and it appears from our preliminary discussions that Ikopi had access to your work before producing a similar work that he marketed as his own. **We** must caution you, however, that **we** cannot be certain of this opinion until the two works **have been**

examined in person, the details analyzed, and expert opinions rendered on each.

To modernize your shapes, to make them a bit cleaner and less curly, you can shorten the sentences, shift to the first person for the writer, the second person for the reader, and use the "because" connector to indicate the reasons, as in the following example.

Example 6.8. Example of Modern Sentence Shapes, from an Opinion Letter.

When we spoke last week, you asked me to advise you about a potential copyright action against George Ikopi. When you saw one of his works profiled in Architectural Digest, you were concerned that Ikopi had copied one of your designs. As this letter explains, you probably can make a claim against Ikopi because your relationship with ProTech was such that you should own the copyright to your work, and because Ikopi had access to your work before producing a similar work that he marketed as his own. I cannot, however, be certain of this opinion until I have seen the two works myself.

To shape your document's interior, you can choose from the rich variety of syntactical structures that are appropriate for your theme and your form. You can also use your phraseology to give texture to those shapes.

TEXTURE

You can create texture in your writing by designing paragraphs and sentences that give the reader a feel for thick, rich texture, or clean, sparse lines. You may want to underscore the complexity of a matter by offering rich paragraphs for a sophisticated reader to digest. Or you may want to downplay another matter by drawing it in short, memorable, staccato points. You may wish to impress a reader with the roughness of the circumstances by using several simple sentences, or you may want to consciously design your document to vary in texture: short, bumpy introductions; smooth transitions; and velvety conclusions; with multi-textured paragraphs explaining the details of the analysis or transaction.

Readers sense whether or not a document is too rich for their tastes, or too simple for the complexity of the transaction. While your readers cannot necessarily shop for their choices, you may be able to design for theirs. Some readers expect the velvety textures of traditional legal prose; others want the same elements presented in clear, contemporary lines. Try your hand at several variations on each, again remembering that you may have readers with varied tastes. You may decide that your interior design should be, simply, comfortable. Note the textures of the examples below.

Example 6.9. Example of Rich Texture, From a Judicial Opinion.

This example gains its rich texture from long sentences that include multiple prepositional and intrusive phrases, among other constructions.

Mr. Justice Cardozo delivered the opinion of the Court.

The rates chargeable by the appellant, the Ohio Bell Telephone Company, for intrastate telephone service to subscribers and patrons in Ohio are the subject-matter of this controversy.

Appellant was reorganized in September, 1921, by consolidation with the Ohio State Telephone Company, till then a competitor. Soon afterwards it filed with the Public Utilities Commission of the state schedules of new rates to be charged in those communities where an increase was desired for the unified service. Except in the case of toll charges, the rates were not state-wide, but were separately stated for each of the company's exchanges, of which there were many. By the statutes then in force (the Robinson law, passed December 19, 1919, 108 Ohio Laws, p. 1094, as amended by the Pence law, passed April 4, 1923, 110 Ohio Laws, p. 366), the operation of an increase might be suspended for 120 days, at the end of which time the rate was to go into effect upon the filing of a bond for the repayment to consumers of such portion of the increased rate as the Commission upon final hearing should determine to have been excessive, with interest thereon. Construing these statutes, the Ohio courts have held that a refund must be limited to rates collected under a bond, jurisdiction being disclaimed when that condition was not satisfied. City of Lima v. Public Utilities Commission, 106 Ohio St. 379, 386, 140 N.E. 146; Great Miami Valley Taxpayers Ass'n v. Public Utilities Commission, 131 Ohio St. 385, 386, 2 N.E. (2d) 777. Some of the new exchange schedules were the subjects of protests, and in proceedings to revise them (known as Pence Law proceedings) were made effective by bonds, a separate one for each exchange. Protest was also aimed at the new schedule for toll service which was to apply throughout the state. On the other hand, schedules for other exchanges became effective without protest and therefore without bond, and are not now at issue.

Ohio Bell Tel. Co. v. Public Utils. Comm'n of Ohio, 301 U.S. 292, 293 (1937)

Example 6.10. Example of Smooth Texture, from a Brief.

The following interior is more contemporary, using smoother textures of short sentences, active verbs, close proximity of subjects and verbs, and direct words.

B. **Wis. Stats. Secs. 632.32 and 631.43 Do Not Prevent Insurers From Limiting Their Liability By Contractual Reducing Clauses.**

The automobile insurance statutes of this state do not explicitly prohibit reducing clauses. In fact, "a policy may provide for exclusions not prohibited by sub. (6) or other applicable law. Such exclusions are effective even if incidentally to their main purpose they exclude persons, uses or coverages that could not be directly excluded under sub. (6)(b)." Wis. Stat. § 632.(5)(e) (1977). (See Appendix A).

Section 632.32(6) and its notes do not prohibit reducing clauses. Further, section 632.32(4)(a) requires only that all insurance policies contain a provision for uninsured motorists of $25,000 per person and $50,000 per accident. No language in any of these statutes requires insurers to go beyond the limits of their policies once the insured has been indemnified up to those limits.

The dispute in this case arises from the language in section 631.43, Stats., which states as follows:

> **When two or more policies promise to *indemnify* an insured against the same loss, no 'other insurance' provisions of the policy may reduce the aggregate protection of the insured below the lesser of the actual insured loss suffered by the insured or the total *indemnification* promised by the policies if there were no 'other insurance' provisions. (Emphasis added).**

Appellant claims this provision allows her to stack the indemnity coverage of the uninsured motorist provision of her policy with the liability coverage of American family's policy. Respondent says that its reducing clause is permissible and prohibits this double recovery.

The threshold question, then, in construing the statute, is whether the statutory terms are ambiguous. See State v. Wittrock, 119 Wis. 2d 664, 669, 350 N.W.2d 647, 650 (1984). Statutory terms are ambiguous if reasonable persons could disagree as to their meaning. Id. However, in cases like this where parties disagree as to the term's meaning, the court will look to the language of the statute itself to determine whether well-informed persons should have become confused as to a term's meaning. See Aero Auto Parts, Inc. v. Department of Trans., 78 Wis. 2d 235, 283 N.W. 896 (1977); Kollasch v. Adomany, 104 Wis. 2d 552, 313 N.W. 2d 47 (1981); State v. Wittrock, 119 Wis 2d 664, 350 N.W.2d 647 (1984).

When the language is clear and unambiguous, the statute must be interpreted on the plain meaning of its terms. Wittrock, 119 Wis. 2d at 670; Aero Auto Parts, Inc., 78 Wis. 2d at 238–39. When the language is ambiguous, the court must consider it in relation to its scope, history, context, subject matter and object to be accomplished or remedied. Kollasch, 104 Wis. 2d at 562. In any case, a statutory subsection may not be considered in a vacuum, but must be considered in reference to the statute as a whole and in reference to statutes dealing with the same general subject matter. Aero Auto Parts, 78 Wis. 2d at 239.

For example, the language of the eminent domain statute was ambiguous and therefore required judicial construction to clarify it in light of prior law, the general chapter in which it was contained, and the remainder of the subsection. Id. at 239-246. Similarly, where definitions of "retailer" and "seller" were circular between two sections, the Court corrected the circularity by looking at legislative intent and the context of the Retail Sale Tax Statutes. Kollasch, 104 Wis. 2d at 561–568. But the Court looked no further than the plain meaning of the words in the Sentence Credit Statute when that interpretation gave the only reasonable result. State v. Gilbert, 115 Wis. 2d 371, 340 N.W. 2d 511 (1983).

The Court need look no further than the plain meaning of section 631.43. The language addresses only indemnity coverage, not liability coverage. Even if the Court finds the statute ambiguous, the statute's scope and purpose still prevent stacking liability coverage with indemnity coverage.

Example 6.11. Example of Comfortable Texture, from a Judicial Opinion.

You can also create a comfortable, homey interior as in the following example, by using plain language and parallel structure.

We deal [here] with a right of privacy older than the Bill of Rights— older than our political parties, older than our school system. Marriage is a coming together for better or for worse, hopefully enduring, and intimate to the degree of being sacred. It is an association that promotes a way of life, not causes; a harmony in living, not political faiths; a bilateral loyalty, not commercial or social projects. Yet it is an association for as noble a purpose as any involved in our prior decisions.

Griswold v. Connecticut, 381 U.S. 479, 486 (1965) (Douglas, J.).

COLOR

Color resides in words and phrases. Some words carry vivid, intense colors from the nature of their connotations; others are neutral, fading into the background. Still others flicker with hues of unexpected colors, those coming from outside a text's predominant palette. You may choose to use a neutral palette, writing in shades of beige to quiet a client's temper. You may wish for primary colors, to paint a bold, clear picture of your analysis, or you may wish to combine two or three hues to achieve a particular effect. No one assigns actual colors to words, but you, as designer, can create color schemes that in turn create an effect on the reader.

If you are trying, for example, to lull a reader into a comfortable sense that everything is going to be all right, you probably want to use common words, like those in this sentence, familiar, perhaps even over-used, but not too threatening. If you want, instead, to stun a client, one whose intended actions are grounded in virulent, vengeful, even violent emotions, then say so. If you want a court to remember your theme, that the defendant was negligent, weave the word *negligent* around those negligent actions, never missing an opportunity to demonstrate that, once again, the defendant was

negligent. Be bold in deciding what colors match your form, what words best reveal the intricacies of your theme.

Example 6.12. Color in an Appellate Brief.

Appellant and veteran divorced twice, but they lived, before and after these divorces, as husband and wife. Both divorces occurred because the family needed to protect itself from the veteran's abusive behavior. He used and abused alcohol and drugs repeatedly and extensively. While drugged or drunk, he was violent and often threatened appellant and the children. The children testified that he abused them; police reports document that he abused them; lay statements report that he abused them. Yet, when he was not drinking or using drugs, he lived in peace with his family, who welcomed him back for a new start each time. When he went for medical treatment, he consistently listed appellant as his wife.

Comment: The passage is tied together by two concepts: abusive behavior and alcohol and drugs. By selecting these phrases, which are strong in themselves, you allow them to take on bolder colors through repetition and placement in positions of emphasis.

RHYTHM

You can create an impression on your reader, invade her memory, and hold her attention with the rhythm of your document. By listening for the sound of the language and the cadence of your sentences, you can create an effect that enraptures your reader. This rhythm comes from two sub-elements: the rhythm of your sentences and the sounds of the words. Your sentences can be short and percussive, steady and mesmerizing, or themat-ic in their repetitious sounds. These uses of rhythm need not be ostenta-tious or obvious; in fact, your ability to create a rhythm that harmonizes with the document's architecture should make your art only subtly visible.

Between words' you can also create impact from the combination of sounds that resound from word to word. Your use of assonance, allitera-tion, onomatopoeia, or rhyme can make your phrases memorable or cap-ture your thought with double meaning. While some lawyers leave these devices to the poet, others have used them to their advantage.

Example 6.13.   Example of Short Rhythm to Long, From a Judicial Opinion.

Investigator James Miller's report was placed in evidence in the plaintiff's case in chief. The plaintiff testified that Miller had removed pieces of wire from the very two areas where Miller claimed that the fire had started. The plaintiff further testified that Miller's report to United Fire did not mention these wires, did not describe any testing of the wires, did not explain the conclusion that the fire was not electrical in origin, and did not explain why or how other accidental causes for the fire had been ruled out.

Weiss v. United Fire & Cas. Co., 541 N.W. 2d 753, 758, 197 Wis. 2d 365, 382 (1995) (Shirley Abrahamson, J.).

Example 6.14. Example of Periodic Rhythm, From a Brief.

Periodic rhythm takes the same idea and elongates it from one sentence to the next.

To remand this case for further proceedings would correct the three procedural errors. To reverse the trial court's decision granting

an injunction to respondent would free appellant to carry on his legitimate business. But to reverse with directions to lift the injunction, grant appellant relief, and charge all costs to respondent would be to satisfy both legal and equitable claims and return appellant to his rightful status as businessman and citizen.

Example 6.15. Example of Alliteration and Assonance to Create Rhythm.

Winner of the 1992 Legaldegook Award: The She-Sells-Seashells Award for Liltingly Luscious Alliteration

Shucking of Shellfish: Shellfish shall not be subjected to contamination while being held or processed. Shellstock to be shucked shall be stored . . . in such locations that contamination from standing water or splash from foot traffic does not occur. ... Only safe and wholesome shellfish shall be shucked.

25 Tex. Admin. Code § 241.70(a)(1), (a)(3) (West 1992).

The Legaldegook Awards: 1991-1992, 3 Scribes J. Legal Writing 107, 113.

LIGHTING

As you enter a room, you are usually aware of the lighting. Beyond light or dark, you become aware of how lighting guides your eye to certain features of the room: a light focused on a picture, a reading chair with a special light, a window left undraped to nurture a group of plants. Your page can be light or dark, too; you can move the readers' eyes to a certain place by the way you use just the shades of language. Long sentences packed one on top of the other, filling long paragraphs and sitting above long, single-spaced footnotes darken the page and give the reader a sense of a closed, cluttered interior. It's difficult to see. Shorter sentences in shorter paragraphs with headings and bullet points create white space on the page, a lighter interior.

Some writers use graphics to lighten their pages. Increasingly, lawyers use charts and diagrams to illustrate points, thus removing so much dark ink from the pages. Think about how you want to use the white space on a page to guide your audiences' eyes to specific places. Accentuate important places by making them easy to find.

Example 6.16. Example of Dark Interior, From an Exception to an Administrative Law Decision.

The Respondent, Sara's Pantry, by and through undersigned counsel, hereby files exceptions to the decision of the Administrative Law Judge issued on November 13, 2005, and states as follows:

The Administrative Law Judge (ALJ) has issued a proposed decision concluding that Respondent, insofar as concerns the advertisements extending from its March 2005 campaign, have violated the Consumer Protection Act. These conclusions of law are not supported by the evidence developed at the hearing, nor are they supported by the statutes or case law of Maryland. In discussing the facts, the ALJ takes discrete positions of a long ago concluded advertising campaign out of context and finds them deceptive, without considering all of the information provided to the consumers. Indeed, the Proponent's witnesses themselves are complaints taken out of context. Despite the existence of hundreds of thousands of satisfied customers, this proceeding was brought, and the findings based, upon the receipt of 11 complaints. While the existence of a complaining consumer may not be a legal requirement for a proceeding such as this, the wisdom of utilizing limited resources to undertake this investigation, hearing, and remedial action in the absence of widespread complaints, is subject to question. Moreover, the existence of so few complaints speaks volumes about whether the practices complained of were in fact deceptive.

The ALJ compounds the problem of a case built on 11 complaints from almost 400,000 satisfied customers by making findings of fact concerning Respondent's refund policy based on the testimony of three complaining individuals, and ignoring the testimony of Respondent's employees. The proposed decision contains findings and conclusions which are far greater distortions than anything complained of in Respondent's advertisements.

Example 6.17. Example of Light Interior: A Revision of the Exception.

The Respondent, Sara's Pantry, by and through undersigned counsel, hereby files exceptions to the decision of the Administrative Law Judge issued on November 13, 1999, and states as follows:

INTRODUCTION

Q. So, what we're saying is that when you saw the ad you understood perfectly what it meant.

A. Right.

Cross-examination of proponent's witness Mary Southers, Exhibit B at 10.

The Administrative Law Judge (ALJ) deceived us all when he decided that Sara's Pantry's advertising violated the Consumer Protection Act. This decision is unsupported by the evidence and the laws of Maryland.

First, the ALJ failed to consider all information provided to the consumers when he determined that Sara's Pantry's advertising campaign was misleading. He took discrete portions of these ads out of context and found them deceptive, even though witnesses like Mary Southers understood them correctly.

Second, there was no evidence that this advertising could deceive anybody. The ALJ based the findings of this proceeding on 11 complaints. The ALJ ignored, however, the satisfaction of over 400,000 Sara's Pantry customers. Though evidence of a complaint is not necessary to prove that advertising is deceptive, the lack of complaints suggests that the advertising was not actually deceptive.

A simple style is like white light. Although complex, it does not appear so.

-Anatole France

Finally, the ALJ should have relied on Sara's Pantry employees for information about their return policy, not three disgruntled customers.

In short, the ALJ's decision contains findings and conclusions which are far more distorted and deceptive than the most annoyed customer could ever claim Sara's Pantry's advertising to be.

A Word on Genre

Genre refers to the kinds of documents particular professions use to communicate with each other, such as medical charts, lab reports, or editorials. An architect's genre is the type of building she is designing: a home or a studio, a skyscraper or a barn. In law, genres are types of communicative events, such as briefs, contracts, or judicial opinions. These events have a shared set of communicative purposes, and the rationale behind each establishes constraints on a document's content, form, and interior design. Genres bring together what is sayable with when and how it is sayable. A genre, then, such as a judicial opinion or memorandum of points and authorities, constrains the combination of variables in the legal register. *See* John Swales, Genre Analysis at 45-46 (1990).

For example, memos inform quickly by defining issues and giving answers at the outset; contracts clarify a transaction's events by identifying parties and defining terms at the beginning; and briefs structure the argument for the reader by using point headings. Genres also give cues for analyzing

architectural form, or analytical paradigms, because they have a beginning, middle, and end. Your knowledge of the genre informs your interior design decisions. If you are writing a friendly informative letter, you may choose informal language and syntactical structures. If you are writing a contract, you may choose specific legal terms that accurately preserve common law contract principles and define the transaction.

Genre has particular power for lawyers. We have invented types of documents to serve specific purposes and refined them so much that our decisions about form, proportion, and interior design are intertwined. Linguist John Swales provides a working definition of genre that uses the following criteria:

1. *A genre is a class of communicative events*, which comprise "not only the discourse itself and its participants, but also the role of that discourse and the environment of its production and reception, including its historical and cultural association." SWALES, at 45-46 (1990).

The U.S. legal discourse community manifests itself in its genres. For example, the judicial opinion is a direct product of the common law system; its history and culture embody the traditions of judge-made law. Client letters, to meet ethical standards, should contain enough information so that the client can make his own decision about how to proceed. Motions follow rules of civil procedure, and interrogatories include questions that honor the discovery rules' requirements that information be exchanged before trial. Each genre reflects the discourse, its participants, and historical and cultural associations. The traditional register particularly manifests itself in genres whose history requires specific language, such as contracts.

2. *The principal criterial feature that turns a collection of communicative events into a genre is some shared set of communicative purposes.* Those purposes might be specific, such as in the genres of recipes or new stories, or quite complex, as in the case of poetry. *See Id.* at 46-49.

In the law, this shared set of communicative purposes is specifically defined. It includes informing, as in memos; persuading, as in briefs; assuaging, as in some letters; denying, as in responses; and encouraging, as in advice letters. These purposes, complex and rarely singular, are culturally specific and need clarifying if we are to make accurate and appropriate design choices.

3. *Exemplars or instances of genres vary in their prototypicality.* The elements that define this prototypicality might be communicative purpose, but also format, structure, and audience expectations. *See Id.* at 49-52.

Thus an in-house memo may require the same elements from firm to firm, but be arranged differently for different audiences or purposes. A brief written to a trial court will be less formal than an appellate brief written to a circuit court judge. And formal requirements for notice, pleading, and motions will vary from county to county within a state.

4. *The rationale behind a genre establishes constraints on allowable contributions in terms of their content, positioning and form.* "Established members of discourse communities employ genres to realize communicatively the goals of their communities. The shared set of purposes of a genre are thus recognized—at some level of consciousness—by the established members of the parent discourse community; they may be only partly recognized by apprentice members; and they may be either recognized or unrecognized by non-members. Recognition of purposes provides the rationale, while the rationale gives rise to constraining conventions. The conventions, of course, are constantly evolving and indeed can be directly challenged, but they nonetheless continue to exert influence." *Id.* at 52-53.

To understand genres within a discourse community or a subset of that community, then, you need to know the local rules. If you are new to the community or to a law office,you may find certain genres restrictive, overly formal, even stultifying. You may feel that legal writing has no creative aspects because the genres require such specific information and even the order of the information may be prescribed. A contract may contain boilerplate sections both at the beginning and the end; a law firm may further restrict the contract by creating its own conventions for contracts of a certain nature. The law itself further constrains the genre by requiring that specific information be included so that the contract, for example, complies with the state's contract laws. You need to know what is behind the genre's creation; you need to have a sense of the underlying logic or rationale. *See id.* at 54.

5. *A discourse community's nomenclature for genres is an important source of insight.* Those who routinely use the genre, or its active members, "give genre names to classes of communicative events that they recognize as providing recurring rhetorical action." *Id.* at 55.

Arbitration conferences, a form of spoken genre, indicate the purpose of the communicative event and the rhetorical action, as do *respondent's brief, contract, motion*, and *filing*.   Active members generate genre categories, as well, such as *Lexis search, key number search, client counseling*, or *book review*.

Genres differ greatly in rhetorical purpose and in the extent to which their producers are conventionally expected to consider their anticipated audience and readerships.   *See id*. at 62.   Thus, legal writers must anticipate their audiences.   "As I write, I make judgements [sic] about the reader's possible reactions, anticipate any difficulties that I think he might have in understanding and following my directions, conduct, in short, covert dialogue with my supposed interlocutor."   *Id*. (quoting H.G. WIDDOWSON, EXPLORATIONS IN APPLIED LINGUISTICS 176 (1979)).   And to anticipate effectively, we must incorporate into our writing processes a kind of second guessing of both the readers' "general state of background knowledge and . . . potential immediate processing problems."   *Id*.   There is a "reciprocity of semantic effort to be engaged in by both sides; a contract binding writer and reader together in reaction and counter-reaction."   *Id*. at 62-63.   But this contract is subject to fluctuations among local audiences and puts constraints on the writer's decision-making process.   The expert learns to shift quickly for these fluctuations; the novice moves more slowly and may produce writer-based prose.   More interesting, the expert may produce writer-based prose in a new genre.   *See id*. at 64.

Being aware of lexicon, syntax and phraseology, and genre allows you to identify patterns in a target community such as a federal agency, a corporate law division, or a judge's chambers.   Having identified the patterns acceptable both to the legal community at large and to a specific target audience, you make more informed decisions about language choice, placement, and structure of genre.   You move more quickly from novice standing to expert, you sharpen your expertise within a specialized community, and you make your writing more accessible to more readers.   Your knowledge of a genre's special features and the register choices within that genre also make you more adept at interpreting the traditional forms and interiors and translating or transforming them into modern ones.

WORKING WITH TRADITIONAL INTERIORS

THE TRADITIONAL INTERIOR

DOUBLETS

LATINISMS

NOMINALIZATIONS

PASSIVE VOICE

FORMAL INTRODUCTIONS

LONG, COMPLEX SENTENCES

LONG, COMPLEX PARAGRAPHS

COMPLEX CONDITIONAL VERB TENSES

INTRUSIVE PHRASES

The traditional interior, the legal register that is often referred to as turgid and impenetrable, is a form of fossilized English. Fossilization occurs when terms freeze, or fossilize, into a specific meaning, and remain in use despite natural evolution of the language. This fossilized traditional interior manifests itself in formal introductions, long and complex sentences, long paragraphs, latinate words, and complex conditional verb tenses.

The traditional interior also contains particular discourse markers, or particular uses of language, that are a shorthand for legal writers. For example, *whether*, not the standard English *whether or not*, precedes the formal issue statement, rendering it an incomplete sentence. The actor and the person acted upon are referred to by the traditional *-or* and *-ee* signals, such as in *offeror* and *offeree* or *lessor* and *lessee*. Notary notices accompany many documents, and some jurisdictions still require "boilerplate" language to introduce such documents as complaints or Notice of Motions or to outline certain contract provisions.

The traditional interior is most evident in judicial opinions, real estate documents, wills, contracts, statutory drafting, and some scholarly writing. It is also associated with certain extinct genres such as demurrers and bills of lading. Many novices in the legal discourse community consider the traditional interior the secret language of lawyers and may begin to emulate it. Experienced lawyers, adept at this elaborate interior, use it with ease and are sometimes reluctant to abandon it.

Both groups have their reasons. Language becomes the law. Once "set" as a definition or a term that embodies a doctrine, the language becomes a term of art and will only stubbornly give way to new terms. This phenomenon is probably more true in law than in some other disciplines, where invention easily overrides previous work and the terminology that accompanied it. Lawyers are more likely to hang on to language to fulfill the broadly defined goal of predictability than are, say, novelists, who may play with language and syntax to invent new texts.

Example 6.18. Example of Traditional Interior, from a Deed of Trust.

> **Borrower irrevocably grants and conveys to Trustee, in trust, with power of sale, the following described property located in the District of Columbia: which has the address of 1600 Pennsylvania Avenue, Washington, DC 20015 ("Property Address"); Together With [sic] all the improvements now or hereafter erected on the property and all easements, rights, appurtenances, rents, royalties, mineral, oil and gas rights and profits, water rights and stock and all fixtures now or hereafter a part of the property.**

District of Columbia, *Deed of Trust* (Form 3009 (1983)).

Comment: This paragraph is one sentence. The several ideas it contains are held together with a relative pronoun, prepositions, and four kinds of punctuation. The technical language (*easements*, *appurtenances*, *fixtures*) is undefined; the verb is a doublet (*grants and conveys*); many phrases intrude (*in trust, with power of sale, which has …, now or hereafter*); and the long list is archaically punctuated.

The following example demonstrates how traditional interiors require study, interpretation, and transformation to be used and appreciated.

Example 6.19. Example of the Traditional Interior: "The Most Incomprehensible Reg."

If the taxpayer's passive activity gross income from significant participation passive activities (within the meaning of section 1.469–2T (F) (2) (II)) for the taxable year (determined without regard to section 1.469–2T (F) (2) through 4) exceeds the taxpayer's passive activity deductions from such activities for the taxable year, such activities shall be treated, solely for purposes of applying this paragraph (F) (2) (I) for the taxable year, as a single activity that does not have a loss for such taxable year.

Bill McAllister, <u>Giving IRS The Prize for Gobbledygook</u>, The Wash. Post, Apr. 13, 1990, at A23.

Diagrammed, the regulation looks like this:

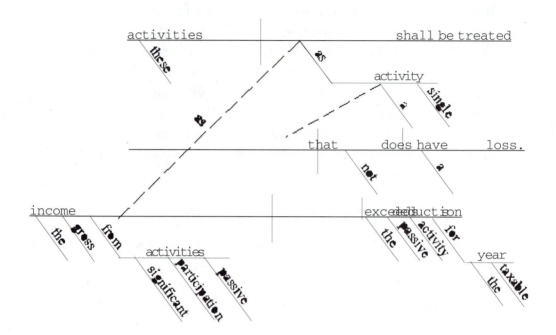

Some possible modern translations:

1. **If gross income from a significant passive activity exceeds the deductions from that passive activity for the taxable year, then the activity will be treated as a single one with no loss deduction allowed for that year. This regulation is subject to the following: 1) passive activity within meaning of §1.4692T (F)(2)–(4); and 2) activities that apply to ¶ (F)(2)(I).**

2. **A taxpayer's significant participation passive activities (SPPA) will be treated as a single activity that does not have a loss for the taxable year when all of the following conditions are met:**

    1) **The purpose is restricted to the application of this ¶ (F)(2)(I) for the taxable year;**

    2) **The taxable year is determined without regard to § 1.469–2T (F)(2) thru (4);**

3) **The taxpayers passive activity gross income from SPPA is within the meaning of §1.469–2T (F)(2)(II); and**

4) **The taxpayer's SPPA exceeds the taxpayers passive activity deductions.**

The terms and features of traditional interiors that are essential to legal work are probably limited, however. Out of habit and tradition, lawyers may have held on to the traditional interior design for too long. Under continuous criticism, particularly from the consumers of legal language, the traditional interior is giving way to more modern interiors. Like any good designer, you perform better when you are able to interpret, understand, and design traditional interiors. Some of your clients may want exclusively traditional interiors; others are likely to want only traditional touches in a modern interior.

A Word on "Clarity"

CLARITY

Form Matches Theme
Syntax Matches
Substance

The word *clarity* is often stated in relation to a legal document. What does clarity mean? And to whom? How, exactly, do you achieve clarity? Such an abstract concept eludes many legal writers, probably because it lends itself to so many interpretations. One possible definition is that a document is clear when 1) its form matches its theme, and 2) its syntax matches its substance.

Clarity occurs when the reader follows, unimpeded, your theme because your document's architecture consistently sends that theme by its form, proportions, and relationship among the parts. Each section advances the theme and shows the section's relation to preceding and following sections as well as to the whole. The reader comprehends the document on a large-scale level because its very structure sends the theme's message. "Unclear" writing confuses the reader with a structure that contradicts its message. For example, when a brief lists points, the fifth of which is the main point, the reader will probably miss its import. If a contract places parts of the transaction randomly, a reader will have trouble constructing the transaction. If a letter places the advice in the middle, the reader may miss it.

To achieve clarity, then, match theme with form and proportion by revisiting the document's rhetorical elements, purpose, audience, scope, and stance. If you are constructing a transaction, organize the document in a way that emphasizes what you find most important: the transaction's chronology, elements, or simplest to most complex parts. If you are writing legislation, organize the statute by worst to least heinous crime, by general to specific information, or by general purpose sections to specific actions sections, for example.

Once you have made your architectural match, move on to examine whether or not the syntax matches the substance. If a main idea occurs in a dependent clause, the reader may assume it is unimportant, whether consciously or not. If a list does not use parallel structure, the reader may assume that the elements are not of equal weight and may miss some of them. If the actor is missing in a passive voice construction, the reader may assume he is unimportant.

To match syntax with substance, consciously pair the two at both the paragraph and sentence level. Structure your paragraphs to indicate the relative importance of ideas: paragraphs of similar length imply similar importance; shorter paragraphs may be transitional or dramatic; long, complex paragraphs suggest long, complex ideas. At the sentence level, if you are making a list, use parallel structure, tabulation, or a series. If you are subordinating an idea, use a subordinate clause or put it in the middle of a paragraph. And if you are emphasizing something, put it in a heading, or at the beginning of a paragraph.

Clarity, like *style*, is an all-inclusive term, rarely clearly defined itself. The definition here simply suggests that clarity occurs when elements of your writing synchronize, rather than compete. You can use many variations to achieve clarity; choose those that build an immediately comprehensible document.

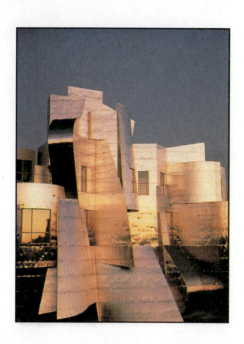

MOVING TO MODERN INTERIORS

The modern legal reader, expert or novice, lawyer or non-lawyer, often hopes you will translate traditional language to a more modern, accessible version, with active verbs, concise terms, and trimmed sentences. This translation has evolved into a modern interior design, a contemporary interior that feels familiar and acceptable to most readers. In linguistics terms, such an interior can be called the Modern American Legal Register, or MALR. This Modern American Legal Register accounts for terms of art created for traditional legal interiors, but brings them into a more contemporary interior. This modern interior arranges paragraphs, sentences, phrases, and language to clarify, rather than obscure, meaning. That clarification occurs when the structure and syntax actually reflect the text's substantive meaning.

THE MODERN AMERICAN LEGAL REGISTER

- Context-independent texts, with definitions, authorities, relevant excerpts of documents included in the text

- Fronting, or putting the most important information first, such as remedy sought, brief answer, or the answer to the client's question

- Headings, with verbs, to guide the reader

- Strong topic sentences, related to message, headings

- One general idea per paragraph, with emphasis on short paragraphs

- Simpler syntax that matches substance, with roughly one thought per sentence

- Variety in sentence length and structure, with more liberal use of short sentences

- More extensive use of paraphrase, fewer floating quotes

- Concrete subjects, verbs, and objects, rather than abstract ones

- Preference for active voice verbs over descriptive, abstract, or passive

- Close proximity of subjects and verbs

- Consistent use of terms of art

- Deliberate and frequent use of cohesive devices to guide the reader

- Deliberate use of rhetorical devices, such as antithesis or periodic structure

- Using Citations for Credibility and Conciseness

- Graphics, such as tabulation, bullets, and charts, to clarify points

- Absence of excessive nominalizations

- Few prepositional phrases

- Minimal use of footnotes, if any

In designing modern interiors, you do the work for the reader. The interior, in other words, is user-friendly. While the following features are common in these modern interiors, they are not absolute. Remember that each interior you design also honors the rhetorical elements that underlie it, the theme, form, and proportion dictated by the substance and the client's needs, and the history and context of the document itself. These interior design elements, like the rhetorical and architectural elements, are points of departure, parts of your repertoire.

For example, within MALR are discourse markers that have become a more accessible shorthand than those used in the traditional register. MALR's signals include use of graphics such as bullets to signal lists of equivalent points, boxes to outline comparative analyses, direct questions with question marks in framing issue statements, and the second person singular in writing to familiar clients. Such use of a modern interior design can translate the text in the previous section as follows.

Example 6.20. Example of Traditional Modern Interior Design Translated From Traditional Interior (cf. Example 6.18).

Borrower grants to Trustee in trust the property that is located at 1600 Pennsylvania Avenue, Washington, DC 20015. The property includes the following, whether or not they are a part of the property now or in the future: improvements; easements; rights; appurtenances; rents; royalties; mineral, oil, and gas rights and profits; water rights; stock; and fixtures.

Comment: The single sentence has been broken into two. The first describes the property and the transactions. The second describes the subsets of the property, moving the list to the end of the sentence for easier comprehension. This version is also shorter.

Similarly, the following text is in the traditional legal register, and MALR, respectively.

Example 6.21. Examples of the Default Provision in
              Traditional and Modern Interior Design,
              Respectively.

There are plenty of ruined buildings in the world but no ruined stones.

--Hugh MacDiarmid

Traditional: **In the event of default in the payment of this or any other Obligation or the performance or observance of any term or covenant contained herein or in any note or other contract or agreement evidencing or relating to any Obligation or any Collateral on the Borrower's part to be performed or observed, or the undersigned Borrower shall die; or any of the undersigned become insolvent or make an assignment for the benefit of creditors; or a petition shall be filed by or against any of the undersigned under any provision of the Bankruptcy Act; or any money, securities or property of the undersigned now or hereafter on deposit with or in the possession or under the control of the bank shall be attached or become subject to distraint proceedings or any order or process of any court, or the Bank shall deem itself to be insecure, then. . . .**

Modern: **<u>Default</u>. I'll be in default under either of the following conditions:**

1. If I don't pay an installment on time; or

2. If any other creditor tries by legal process to take any money of mine in your possession.

Adapted from SCOTT J. BURNHAM, DRAFTING CONTRACTS 272 (1993). To translate effectively, you can spot patterns in the text and invoke the features of modern interior design.

Context-Independent Texts

Legal readers are unlikely to want to go elsewhere to get information or ideas. They usually expect a text to provide all that is necessary for the circumstances. They are also suspicious of assumptions and omissions. Thus many genres are designed to be self-contained, even though the information may seem repetitive or unnecessary to some legal readers who will use it. Contracts include all aspects of a transaction, even though all parties understand that some aspects are routine or boilerplate and some sections of the contract will likely not be invoked. A trial brief contains a Facts section, even though the parties, the judge, and the judge's clerk have heard the record and been present as the case unfolded. Statutes have definitions so as to minimize unintended interpretations, and so on. Even office memos sometimes contain facts because cases last so long that different lawyers may be called upon to update the memos or convert them to briefs. Important sections of the record are often culled and presented in an appendix to a trial brief so that the reader does not have to remember them or go elsewhere to find them.

For documents that are targeted to both experts and non-experts, such as a memo to a corporate client or a brief on a technical subject, achieving context independence requires gauging all audiences' needs. The non-expert needs more background, definitions, explanations, and illustrations; the expert wants to move directly to the heart of the analysis. The document's design, therefore, must allow both to use the document accordingly, perhaps by designing a Table of Contents, by separating background information so as to make it easy for the expert to skip over, or by putting definitions in an appendix. Say *You had asked whether or not you should change the wording in your prospectus to accommodate a recent technical change in the law* rather than jumping in with *The text of your prospectus, page 13, states...* Say *You requested me to research three procedural issues before our meeting with Mr. Leraas on June 1* rather than *Mr. Leraas needs to disclose the information on Property X by June 15*, which is just stating the first issue.

FRONTING

Fronting is putting the most important information first, such as remedy sought, brief answer, recommendation, or stated purpose of the document. Legal readers do not want to search through the document to find the so-called bottom line. Even though the analysis is essential to justifying the outcome, and even though the writer wants the reader to understand all reasons for the final conclusion, the practice of legal readers is to search the document for the ultimate answer. Putting that answer at the beginning saves the reader time, allows the reader to take in the reasons with an idea of where they fit, and prepares the reader for the results.

Some of the old traditions are giving way to fronting. Judicial opinions, which usually had the outcome at the end of the opinion, now sometimes have it at the beginning. Briefs, which once drew the reader into the case by laying out the facts first and saving the remedy for the last page, now sometimes use the first page to ask for the remedy, and statutes, which did not always state their purposes explicitly, now do.

Fronting occurs not only at the macro level of the whole document, but within sections, paragraphs, and sentences. Theme statements occur at the beginnings of sections, topic sentences often begin paragraphs, and subject-verb combinations often lead sentences. None of these is mechanical or predictable or used in every sentence, but the tendency is to keep the reader from guessing, to explicitly guide the reader through the text, and to minimize ambiguity. Thus a court may begin an opinion with the following paragraph.

Example 6.22. Example of Fronting in a Judicial Opinion.

A jury found defendant guilty of possession of marijuana in violation of stats. Section 2345. He admitted a prior conviction of violating stats. Section 2343, and the trial court sentenced him to prison for the term prescribed by law. He appeals, contending that the marijuana introduced in evidence against him was obtained by an illegal search and seizure. It was. We reverse.

Similarly, a paragraph may begin with the main idea. Say *Plaintiff is an at-will employee* rather than *The next point to consider is whether or not plaintiff is an at-will employee*, a more descriptive sentence that forces the reader to wait.

TECHNIQUE

• *"Front" the main sentence in the document.* This may be a purpose statement in a contract or regulation, the theory of the case in a brief, or the answer to a client's question in an opinion letter. Uncover it and work carefully to arrange the language exactly as you mean it. Place it toward the document's beginning.

Headings, with Verbs, to Guide the Reader

Because legal readers use documents in so many ways, we have to make it easy for them to maneuver through the document. In longer documents, such as a long contract or prospectus, you can use a Table of Contents to assist the reader, and you may even tab the sections. In shorter documents, such as an opinion letter, motions brief, or memo, you can use headings to break up your analysis and assist the reader in understanding the overall structure.

Headings come in a spectrum of sizes. At one end is the label, *Section 43(a)*. The label is useful for identifying a section, but not for telling the reader anything about it. At the other end of the spectrum is the point heading for a brief.

> **I.   The Court Should Reverse the Trial Court and Grant a New Trial Because the Plaintiff Introduced Substantial Evidence of Defendant's Malpractice.**

Somewhere in the middle is a heading with a verb, *Cable Must Notify Its Customers by November 1 to Comply with Section 43(a)*. Headings with verbs allow the reader both to identify the section and to get some meaning from it without diving into the text. Skimming the document still gives answers; moving to one section in the document is also easier. Clients may have some question about a part of the transaction and can move to a certain section of an explanatory letter, or partners can refer to one section when on the phone with the client.

Strong Topic Sentences

Legal readers generally do not like surprises. They like to be sure about the topic of a paragraph. They like to speed read. Making the first sentence of the paragraph the topic sentence often helps them. Topic sentences potentially can do three things: state the topic of the paragraph, relate to the previous paragraph, and relate to the theme. You do not have to do all three things with each topic sentence, but you probably want to do the first. The second allows for cohesion, showing how the two ideas connect. The third, relating to the theme of the document, serves to remind the reader of both the message and this paragraph's part in that message. Thus a sentence such as *Despite that ruling, our client can still aggregate activities if the activities "constitute an appropriate economic unit"* introduces the theme of *appropriate economic unit*, relates to the previous paragraph about the ruling, and reminds the reader of the overall theme of *our client can probably aggregate*.

Example 6.23. Example of a Series of Strong Topic Sentences in a
Memorandum in Support of a Motion.

I. Summary

The most alarming characteristic of environmental liability is that it can reach far beyond the protection of the corporate shell and reach parent corporations and individual corporate officers, directors, and shareholders. Several courts have held officers, directors, and shareholders individually liable for violations of CERCLA. *The overriding theme in CERCLA liability cases, however, is consistent with traditional corporate law.* Personal liability under CERCLA is typically imposed only in instances where the shareholder was personally involved in or responsible for the CERCLA violation.

Corporate shareholders, whether individuals or parent corporations, are typically regarded as entities distinct from the corporation itself, and are protected from the corporation's liabilities by the corporate veil unless specific and unusual circumstances require that the veil be pierced. In CERCLA cases, courts make the same inquiries into the nature of the activities engaged in by officers, individual shareholders, or parent corporations as they do in other corporate cases; i.e., did he shareholders engage in acts that violated corporate formalities or that were likely to perpetuate an injustice to third parties? Did the corporate officers personally participate in tortious or illegal acts of the corporation? Of course, a corporate officer may also be a shareholder, but his or her individual liability in each instance is premised on different theories.

In the CERCLA context, courts have held individual shareholders or parent corporations liable under two legal theories: (1) "piercing the corporate veil," and (2) direct liability as an "operator" under CERCLA § 107(a)(2). Recent cases suggest that courts are taking a practical approach to the analysis of the extent of permissible parent involvement in the subsidiary's affairs, with due regard for the business realities involved in operating a subsidiary as well as for the mandates of CERCLA. Thus, a court will look at whether parent corporations or shareholders have the kind of direct responsibility that CERCLA contemplates as a basis of liability of "owners" and "operators" of hazardous waste sites.

The relevant inquiry in determining parent corporation or shareholder liability under CERCLA is not whether a particular parent or individual possesses 51% or more of the shares of a company. Rather, it is whether the corporate officer, because of the realities of the corporate power structure, has the authority and the ability to control the management of the company if he so chooses. Put another way, the relevant inquiry is whether the officer is a *managing* shareholder who, for some reason—whether by virtue of majority ownership or the agreement of the other shareholders, or the indifference or acquiescence of the other shareholder—can direct the overall operation of a corporation and, in doing so, has the authority to control the facility in question. While the ability to exert such control is more readily apparent when the defendant is a sole or majority stockholder, the broad, remedial purposes of CERCLA militate against restricting the scope of operator liability only to those shareholders.

As this memorandum will illustrate, application of various approaches to assess whether the owner or operator liability attaches to a parent corporation or shareholder requires a very fact-specific review. In undertaking this analysis, the factors listed in the cases below are merely guideposts for a court in making its decision. No one factor alone will cause a court to find a parent corporation or shareholder liable, nor must all of the factors be present.

ONE GENERAL IDEA PER PARAGRAPH

In the traditional interior, paragraphs can contain several ideas, be long, single-spaced, and take up one page or more. Maneuvering through these takes time and patience and may lead to multiple interpretations. In the modern interior, ideas are broken up more, visual breaks on the page are more frequent, and connections between paragraphs are stronger. Paragraph structure can still be classical: deductive, beginning with the topic sentence and moving from general to specific, or inductive, moving from the specific to the general. Paragraphs can also use more modern structures to list, compare, illustrate, define, or make transitions. Whatever their functions, their structure can follow them, but in the modern interior that structure tends to be discrete and narrowly defined. Thus, this message might work better in three paragraphs, rather than one long one:

Example 6.24.   Example of One Idea in Three Modern Paragraphs.

In the more recent cases, those factors indicating a "public use" are similar to the factual circumstances involving the proposed project by the Q Corporation. For example, in City of St. Joseph, the court held that the corporation was found to be a charitable corporation, executing the will of the General Assembly by providing homes for WINS under stats. Section 123. The reasons were twofold: the property was owned and used by the State, specifically CJS; and the benefit accrued to the general public in providing to WINS care, diagnosis, training, education, and rehabilitation.

Q Corporation's project allows a public right to enter, which should qualify as "public use." In Greensborough, a public right to enter upon or make use of the property implies a public use, according to the court, which found no "public use" in that case. However, this "right to enter" factor was de-emphasized in City of St. Joseph, which identified several situations where certain public facilities can curtail such a right, as in the case of a penal institution, a courthouse, the Comptroller's office, and other safety-sensitive facilities.

Similarly, another corporation's plans to operate an adolescent shelter was probably "public use." [Cite] There, the shelter was licensed by the Social Services Administration of the Maryland Department of Human Resources, governed by MOMAR 11.22.33, and coordinated with various county Departments of Social Services in the referral of needy children. The court there did not directly dis-discuss "public use" because the property was privately owned and therefore failed the "public use" test. Absent the private ownership, however, the use might have been "public," just as Corporation Q's project is.

This example was redesigned from the original, traditional version:

In the more recent cases, those factors indicating a "public use" are similar to the factual circumstances involving the proposed project by the Q Corporation. In <u>City of St. Joseph</u>, the corporation was found to be a charitable corporation, executing the will of the General Assembly by providing homes for WINS under stats. Section 123; the property was owned and used by the State, specifically CJS; and the Court held that the benefit accrued to the general public in providing to WINS care, diagnosis, training, education, and rehabilitation. In <u>Greensborough</u>, which did not find a "public use," the Court noted that a public right to enter upon or make use of the property implies a public use; however, this "right to enter" factor was de-emphasized in <u>City of St. Joseph</u>, which identified several situations where certain public facilities can curtail such a right, as in the case of a penal insti-tution, a courthouse, the Comptroller's office, and other safety-sensi-tive facilities. From <u>Madison</u>, one can conclude that although discussion of "public use" is absent from the opinion, it is probable that the private non-profit corporation which planned to operate an adolescent shelter license by the Social Services Administration of the Maryland Department of Human Resources, governed by MOMAR 11.22.33 and coordinated with various county Departments of Social Services in the referral of needy children would suffice as a "public use." The rationale here is that the Court affirmed the denial of exemption because the property was privately owned and not because it failed the "public use" test.

SIMPLER SYNTAX THAT MATCHES SUBSTANCE

When syntax and substance intersect, meaning becomes clearer. In the traditional interior, long sentences can confuse readers, sometimes losing them. Main ideas are submerged in subordinate clauses; important ideas are in intrusive phrases and parentheticals. By choosing syntax that matches your meaning, you give the reader two chances to comprehend the sentence. You can, for example, match subordinate ideas to subordinate clauses, lists to parallel structure or tabulation, main ideas to main clauses, and compound actions to compound verbs. Consciously call on syntax to carry meaning, as if you were selecting the most appropriate vehicle to travel somewhere.   Avoid stuffing too many ideas into a sentence, which is a fragile vehicle if overloaded.

TECHNIQUE

• *Reorder sentences to unify the paragraph.* Analyze sentences and their relationship to each other. These relationships carry your document's meaning. Is there an internal coherence to each paragraph? Is important information at the beginning or end? Try rearranging sentences to expose the paragraph's meaning. By doing so, you may expose unnecessary repetition, leaps in logic, or omissions of crucial parts. This is small-scale design, which directs your reader to use the paragraph a particular way.

Example 6.25.   Example of Syntax that Matches Substance in a Letter.

Further, a stop work order is probably inappropriate here, even though the town building code does authorize the mayor to issue stop work orders at his own discretion and without a prior hearing. As you know, King County Department of Environmental Protection inspectors have determined that the demolition of the structure on the subject property did not violate the County building permit. In fact, that permit was based on the same application and plans that formed the basis of the Town building permit.

This version argues directly, rather than forcing the reader to read between the lines, as in the following, original, version.

Example 6.26.   Example of Syntax that Fights Substance in a Letter.

Further, although I am aware that the town building code does authorize the mayor to issue stop work orders at his own discretion without a prior hearing, I suggest that such action would be inappro-

priate here in light of the fact that King County Department of Environmental Protection inspectors have determined that the demolition of the structure on the subject property did not violate the County building permit, which permit was based on the same application and plans that formed the basis of the Town building permit.

Variety in Sentence Length and Structure

Designing to keep readers interested requires variety. In traditional interiors, the burden is on the reader to interpret text. In the modern interior, the burden is on the writer to design accessible prose. Once the syntax matches the message, the writer has to evaluate it for variety and still maintain accuracy. This is hard. To construct an accurate sentence, to follow it with another, to make sure the transition between the two is smooth, and to test a series of sentences for variety is to design an accessible and useful text. For any idea, of course, there are many possible correct ways for expressing it. Choose not just the first way that comes to mind, but the way that offers the right combination of structure and length to keep the reader engaged.

Example 6.27. Example of Variety in Sentence Structure and Length.

We draw the same conclusion from those no action letters that did consider the 100-person test set forth in Section 3(c)(1) of the Act, even though those letters focused primarily on the 10% test set forth in that Section. For example, in Holstein, available June 15, 1999, the Staff considered the construction of the statutory provisions regarding beneficial ownership. They concurred with a no action request of a small business investment company.

That company's outstanding securities were owned by, among others, a limited partnership. That partnership held more than 10% of the potential investment company's outstanding voting securities. Counsel argued that neither

Section 3(c)(1) nor any other provisions of the Act, nor the rules and regulations promulgated thereunder "provide for attribution of beneficial ownership to the security holders of security holders" of a company owning 10% or more of the outstanding voting securities of the potential investment company. We disagree.

Example 6.28. Example of No Variety in Sentence Structure.

The same conclusion can be drawn from those no action letters which did consider the 100 person test set forth in Section 3(c)(1) of the Act, notwithstanding the fact that such letters focused primarily on the 10% test set forth in such Section. In Holstein, available June 15, 1999, for example, the Staff considered the construction of the statutory provisions regarding beneficial ownership and concurred with a no action request of a small business investment company, whose outstanding securities were owned by, among others, a limited partnership which held more than 10% of the potential investment company's outstanding voting securities. Counsel argued that neither Section 3(c)(1) nor any other provisions of the Act, nor the rules and regulations promulgated thereunder 'provide for attribution of beneficial ownership to the security holders of security holders' of a company owning 10% or more of the outstanding voting securities of the potential investment company, but we disagree.

More Paraphrasing, Fewer Quotes

Quotes are hard to read. As accurate as they are, as precise as their meaning is, legal readers tend to skip them. Legal writers love to write them. It avoids decision-making, thinking, translating. It also avoids mistakes. The secret is balance: accurate translation or some fusing of quoted language into the writer's text. The reason readers skip them is because they float in from another's text, like importing someone else's living room into your house. They are another's words, written in a different context, for a different purpose. They are, by definition, out of context, which draws suspicion from the legal reader's eyes.

By paraphrasing, translating, or carefully fusing the quote into your own text, you give the reader both accuracy and readability. You give the language a new context and account for the old. You explain the translation and make it work in your own analysis. Many readers do not want this translation by a novice because credibility, use of language, and analytical expertise are too new. Even then, the novice can quote and offer a paraphrase next to the quote that translates the information for the purposes of the document.

Example 6.29. Example of Quote Integrated into Text.

Plaintiffs contended that they were entitled under the ESA to an award of all of their reasonable legal fees and costs because 1) all of their claims were interrelated, and 2) they substantially prevailed on the major goals of the litigation. Variable levels of success, however, result in variable awards.

When a plaintiff fails, for example, to prevail on a claim that is distinct in all respects from his successful claims, "the hours spent on the unsuccessful claim should be excluded in considering the amount of a reasonable fee." [Cite] When a plaintiff achieves only limited success, he should be awarded "only that amount of fees that is reasonable in relation to the results obtained." [Cite] But when the claims are related, "a plaintiff who has won substantial relief should not have his attorneys' fee reduced simply because the district court did not adopt each contention raised." [Cite]

Example 6.30. Example of Unintegrated Quote in a Judicial Opinion.

Plaintiffs contended that they were entitled under the ESA to an award of all of their reasonable legal fees and costs, because all of their claims were interrelated and they substantially prevailed on the major goals of the litigation. The court stated that:

> **Where the plaintiff has failed to prevail on a claim that is distinct in all respects from his successful claims, the hours spent on the unsuccessful claim should be excluded in considering the amount of a reasonable fee. Where a lawsuit consists of related claims, a plaintiff who has won substantial relief should not have his attorneys' fee reduced simply because the district court did not adopt each contention raised. But where the plaintiff achieved only limited success, the district court should award only that amount of fees that is reasonable in relation to the results obtained. [Cite]**

USE OF CONCRETE, RATHER THAN ABSTRACT, TERMS

Using abstract terms in the law is convenient, but usually counterproductive. Lawyers deal in abstractions—the law—that must be made concrete in specific circumstances. Your job as a legal writer is often to make the abstract concrete. Your language should reflect the work you have done. Avoid terms such as *justice*, *fairness*, *provisions*, or *characteristics*; use terms such as *reversal*, *inconsistency*, *Code section 432*, or *business activity*. To say that *Justice will be served if this court decides in my client's favor* may not be as helpful as *This court should reverse the trial court's ruling and admit the gun as evidence*. Similarly, *The construction shall not last beyond the customer's satisfaction* may not be as helpful as *The contractor agrees to complete construction of the family room by July 1, 1997.*

PREFERENCE FOR ACTIVE VOICE VERBS OVER DESCRIPTIVE, ABSTRACT, OR PASSIVE

Such terms as *involves*, *seems*, *concerns*, and *might* raise questions, rather than answering them. This annoys most legal readers. If a reader asks, "What does that mean?" you are in trouble because he probably feels

TECHNIQUE

• *Read for one thing at a time.* Try reading your document for one revising matter, such as strong topic sentences or active verbs, at a time. That way, you improve the entire document with each reading, not just the part you read until you are interrupted or grow tired. You will also save time because you will be able to breeze through the document with a purpose. Finally, you will heighten your awareness of each aspect of the writing: if you focus on active verbs for the next twelve projects, you are likely to start using them more vividly in the draft of your thirteenth project.

he must go outside the text to understand the precise meaning of your text. Similarly, such descriptive verbs as *addresses*, *discusses*, *explains*, and *illustrates* describe the very functions the writing should be performing, but by doing so fail to perform them. This is a form of putting the reader off and avoiding answering questions. While all of these verb forms are grammatically correct, they make the document more inaccessible.

Unless such inaccessibility is your deliberate intention, use active, precise language, terms that answer questions instead of ask them. Verbs that state outcomes, answer questions, and anticipate action are more memorable and dynamic. *This memo recommends that our client file as soon as possible to avoid paying the fine* rather than *This memo discusses whether or not the client should pay the fine*. *Artists must register copyrights in order to collect damage*s rather than *The case involved an artist who did not register a copyright*.

CLOSE PROXIMITY OF SUBJECTS AND VERBS

Any more than seven words between the subject and the verb and the reader starts getting lost. Keeping the characters and the actions together promotes readability; it also encourages active verbs. More importantly, it allows the legal reader to keep straight who is doing what. In a contract,

Buyer agrees to pay Seller $40,000 for . . . is less ambiguous than *The Buyer, who will have the correct amount of consideration ready for the Seller, agrees to pay $40,000 for . . . .* In a letter explaining the transaction to the client, *You must prepare the enclosed materials for the transaction* is less ambiguous than *The enclosed materials, which have been prepared by our associates in response to discussions with you, must be completed by you by the first of the month.*

CONSISTENT USE OF TERMS OF ART

While elegant variation was the standard advice from our seventh grade teachers, we are not looking for that in most legal writing. In the modern legal interior, precision triumphs. Here, the legal reader attaches language to things, to specific notions. Changing the word for the sake of doing so may change the meaning of the sentence. Thus *agreement* cannot become *contract* without others mistaking them for two different documents; *plaintiff* cannot become *Mrs. Armstrong* for the same reason.

DELIBERATE AND FREQUENT USE OF COHESIVE DEVICES TO GUIDE THE READER

Lawyers are fond of lists and too often leave them as such: several points hanging around each other. Without connections, these points are less memorable, less meaningful. Cohesive devices keep an analytical paradigm glued together, making the shifts precise and somewhat obvious. Cohesion occurs when you connect your ideas explicitly, both within the overall structure and within a paragraph. In the traditional interior, for example, conditionals might be created with the word *whereas*, which introduces the reader to a series of clauses that sets up the proposition for a contract; the word *aforementioned* refers back to text before. In the modern interior, you can use more explicit cohesive devices, such as transitional words and dovetailing. You can use transitional words signaling similarity (*similarly, analogously, as*), contrast (*conversely, however, nevertheless, yet*), causation (*if . . . then, because, accordingly, therefore, thus*), or summarizing (*finally, in conclusion*). You can also use devices that are imbedded into the syntax, such as the following:

Example 6.31. Repitition and Reenforcement.

Reliance on a promise that lacks consideration is a means to equitable relief. Mill v. Corbett, 333 Wash. 2d 219, 204 P.2d 845 (1999). **That reliance** occurs under the following circumstances.

Example 6.32. Tabulation Using Text, Numbers, or Bullets.

Plaintiff can use promissory estoppel to avoid injury in two situations. First, he may use promissory estopped when parties have 'failed to properly form a contract but one party has acted in reliance on the promise of another.' See id., at 52, 667 P.2d at 111. Second, he may use promissory estoppel when a promise is supported by consideration and the contract fails solely because is falls within the statute of frauds. See Family Medical, Inc., v. Dept. of Social Services, 337 Wash. App. 655, 656, 766 P.2d 33 (2001).

Example 6.33. Dovetailing.

Plaintiff received damages for detrimental reliance when a plaintiff had an agreement with Famous Fried Chicken that they would issue him a franchise if he found a suitable site. See Klinke v. Famous Fried Chicken, 94 Wash. 2d 534, 312 P.2d 88 (2002). Klinke found that suitable site, then quit his job, changed his residence, and negotiated for property on which to locate the franchise.

Example 6.34. Tabulation and Parallel Structure With Mid-Level Schema.

Promissory estoppel may be used to avoid injury in two situations. . . .

The Wisconsin Supreme Court upheld damages for the first kind of detrimental reliance when a plaintiff agreed to establish a franchise, moved his family, and invested $50,000. . . .

The Washington Supreme Court upheld damages for the second kind of detrimental reliance when a plaintiff agreed to establish a franchise, quit his job, moved, and negotiated for property on the new site. . . .

Example 6.35. Substitution.

One who explicitly promises to make a written agreement to sat-isfy the statute of frauds and then breaks that promise is estopped from using the statute of frauds as a defense. Mr. Derieri explicitly promised to make a written agreement and broke that promise. He is therefore estopped from using the statute of frauds as a defense.

Example 6.36. Reference.

If, as in Hoffman, Mr. Derieri should have foreseen Mr. Carpenter's reliance, then a jury should hear the evidence.

TECHNIQUE

•   *Use cohesive devices.* You can make your document seamless by consciously using cohesive devices. The typical kinds of cohesive devices used in law, especially in the traditional register, are those that lead into paragraphs or sentences such as: traditionally, similarly, however, in contrast, furthermore, and so on. While these connectors can be effective if they are precise, you can use others that are more embedded in the text itself.

A Word on "Style"

Many lawyers use the word *style* to discuss register—and just about everything else in legal writing. When pushed, they attribute most writing strengths and weaknesses to *style*. Even composition theorists have had trouble defining style, yet lawyers use it generously. We use it to cover everything from content to expression. "It's just a matter of style," remarks the first-year student about her grade. "But you left out the statute," replies the professor. "Still, that's just a matter of style." Or the young associate remarks that the partner "just changed a couple of words" in the document, so "I must be a pretty good writer." Those words were key phrases that changed the document's import; the associate had misunderstood the law. We need more precise language than that in working with legal writing.

We bandy about the term *style* much more flippantly than the classical rhetoricians did. They suggested that style had to do with the way a person articulated his ideas. Cicero separated style into three kinds: the low or plain style, the middle or forcible style, and the high or florid style. Each style was suited to one of the three functions of rhetoric: *deliberative, judicial,* or *ceremonial*. The plain style was most appropriate for instructing, the middle for moving, and the high for charming. To create any of the styles, the speaker called on their components, such as word choice; arrangement of words; correct syntax; sentence patterns, such as parallelism and antithesis; proper use of conjunctions and other correlating devices, both within and between sentences; the euphony of sentences, secured through the artful juxtaposition of pleasing vowel and consonant combinations and through the use of appropriate rhythmical patterns; and tropes and figures. *See* Corbett at 26-27. And the classicists were concerned with the functional versus the embellishing character of style, asianism versus atticism, the written style versus the spoken, and the economy of words versus copia of words. *See Id.* We can use the same terminology in analyzing legal style, though many lawyers may find such terminology off-putting.

The new rhetoricians also discuss levels of language, but not in one word, *style*. They may refer to them as formal English, informal English, or technical English. These are not the same categories as Cicero's low, middle and high. Rather, the new rhetoricians analyze how language, or English in particular, adjusts to certain rhetorical situations. Formal

English is used in argumentation or literature, and the first person is avoided, as are contractions and other informal constructions. Informal English is used in personal essays and diaries, where the first person is emphasized, as are other conversational English constructions. Technical English is used by specialists, whose vocabulary is invented and defined by the field itself, such as biology or business or architecture.

The trouble is that even separating such discussions into a separate chapter suggests that a writer's considerations of style can be separated from the rhetorical level of her writing, from the document's purpose, audience, scope, and stance—from the content itself. In law, this is almost impossible. Each decision we make depends on the law and the circumstances in which we are writing, a theory known as *aesthetic monism*. The old theories of *rhetorical dualism*—"style is separate from substance"— and *psychological monism*—"style is the man"—are not so helpful for lawyers. *See* Elizabeth D. Rankin, *Revitalizing Style: Toward a New Theory and Pedagogy*, 14 English News 8, 11 (1985).

We cannot make arbitrary style decisions in a vacuum. We cannot base our decisions on suspended notions of style gained in other disciplines, nor can we base our decisions solely on personal taste. Our choices flow from the content itself, from the doctrine we invoke, the language used previously to discuss the doctrine, the language traditionally used in contracts, or the language of the statute or regulation we are analyzing. We also select style on the basis of local conditions, language preferences developed within a government agency, within a law office, or within a discipline, such as government contracts. This theory of *aesthetic monism*, that style and form are an inevitable consequence of content, forces us to analyze the language we use in terms of content, legal language, traditions, and setting.

And as lawyers, we must consider not only classical *style* but also *delivery*. We must choose a style that delivers our message. For the classicists, delivery was gained by practice and observation, not by reading about it. They were concerned that the speaker could manage his voice and gestures. They discussed proper modulation for pitch, volume, and emphasis, for pausing and phrasing. Body posture, and the management of the eyes and facial expressions were all part of delivery. Style and delivery may convert to register and use of graphics for the modern lawyer. We can distinguish these kinds of English, but can we reproduce them? Can we

construct different styles? Can we ghost write, write informally, imitate, use figures of speech? Can we gesture and modulate our voices on the written page though our sentence structure, graphics, and word choice? If so, we have begun to develop the appropriate repertoire of choices for designing the interior of any document.

So no legal composition is simply reduced to "my style" versus "your style." It is a complex series of decisions about how language carries specific meaning in specific rhetorical settings; how language reflects and defines purpose; how language can guide readers to a specific result; how readers may interpret the language, given the interpretive traditions within a specific practice area; how clients may understand language, given their level of expertise. We compose in context. We define our terms and place them in certain phrases and syntactical settings. We invent phrases that serve particular purposes. In short, we manipulate our registers, both traditional and modern. And we communicate best with our colleagues and audiences when we are highly aware of our choices.

Deliberate Use of Rhetorical Devices

Not all legal writing is persuasion, although some lawyers suggest that all language is. In the contexts where you are trying to make a point, even in a memo to a friendly supervisor or a letter to a feisty client, you can use rhetorical devices to frame your ideas. Such devices as antithesis, inversion, periodic structure, or parallel structure can add force to your message.

If you want your reader to remember your message, frame it using antithesis: *Our client can choose to merge with the new company, but the merger will preclude further choices* or *You must file your taxes by September 15 or your tax agent will file charges against you.*

If you want to end a brief with a powerful punch, use periodic structure. Instead of saying, *For the forgoing reasons . . .* , say *The plaintiff offers no facts that are in dispute. What the plaintiff offers are facts that she stipulated and with which the defendant agrees. What the plaintiff needs are facts that favor her case, change the circumstances, and allow a trial to take place, but she offers no new facts, no facts in dispute, and no facts that preclude summary judgment.* If you want to catch your reader's eye, use inversion: *Reversal we seek.* Such devices may refresh your presentation and revitalize your reader's memory.

Using Citations for Credibility and Conciseness

Your credibility often depends on how you use authority. Some audiences are less formal than others about authority, so adjust accordingly. For most readers, your credibility is linked to how you present your materials through your citations. To establish your credibility, cite after all propositions or all inferences from authority. For example, cite when you are stating a rule of law, when you are stating the holding, when you are referring to dicta, and when you are referring to any mandatory, persuasive, or secondary authority. If there is no citation after a statement, it will be understood as being your own.

Citations are a form of shorthand within the legal discourse community. Particularly when writing to each other, lawyers do not use much text to explain authority. The Bluebook's signal system offers a means to text economy. You can trim extraneous descriptive phrases from your text. As you know, when you cite a case directly, with no signal, you are saying that the cited case literally states that proposition. When you use *See*, you are saying that the point follows from the case, but that the court did not explicitly state it.

Look what happens when you remove descriptive phrases. That extraneous text drops away and important information moves to an important syntactical place in the sentence. You have a match. Instead of writing, *The court stated that the plaintiff's choice of forum. . .*, you can write, *The plaintiff's choice of forum should rarely be disturbed. <u>See</u> <u>Caldwell v. Wilsey</u>, 222 F.3d 999 (2005)* . Instead of writing, *Although the court did not explicitly state that Somalia was an adequate . . .*, you can write, *There, Somalia was an adequate alternative forum when the plaintiff had a close connection to the case and the court was familiar with governing law. <u>See</u> <u>Jones v. U.S.</u>, 444 F.2d 567 (2005).*

You can write more directly, more explicitly about the law. Your citations can help you to elevate to prominence the most essential parts of your analysis. Your subjects and verbs can carry important information about the subject matter, not about the courts. *Deposing an adverse attorney is appropriate when the information sought is relevant to the case's outcome* tells the reader more than *The court in Johnson recognized that deposing an adverse attorney is sometimes appropriate.* Legal readers are more concerned about legal points than descriptive ones in your text. They can understand and remember the law better when it is stated in main clauses than in dependent ones. Try to avoid cluttering your text with statements about courts having held, recognized, stated, suggested, or described. Replace the subject and verb with the information that is important to the reader and that relates to your theme.

Also try to avoid the clutter of too many parentheticals. While you can use signals as a shorthand, you are technically required to use a parenthetical to give the information represented by the signal. This device is used primarily in law review footnotes. But these are hard to read if used to excess. A proliferation of string cites followed by parentheticals seems to have moved up from the scholarly footnote into the text of briefs and memos. Check with your local audiences and their expectations, but be careful not to become so cryptic or choppy as to interrupt or disrupt the flow of your argument. By definition, this kind of technical block in an argument can be fatal to the flow of the piece even though it does establish credibility and depth of argument.

Instead, you may replace the signal with an introductory phrase. Writing *For example* instead of *E.g.* will make your text flow, give your reader the important use of the information and help you avoid using a parenthetical.

Example 6.37. Cohesive Devices to Connect Authority.

> **Generally, plaintiffs must prove they were wrongfully discharged. For example, one plaintiff proved her wrongful discharge by showing her excellent reviews up to the time of discharge. See Smith v. Jones, 888 Wis. 2d 488, 999 N.W.2d 22 (2006). Another plaintiff proved his wrongful discharge by presenting witnesses who testified to his excellent performance and his boss' continuous praise until the day of the incident. See Brown v. Green, 889 Wis. 2d 55, 999 N.W.2d 777 (2005). And a plaintiff proved she was wrongfully discharged when she received ten awards over as many years, was promoted three times, and then testified about a safety regulation. See Cue v. Bee, 889 Wis. 2d 102, 999 N.W.2d 891 (2006). . . .**

This example uses the citations to punctuate the authority, but leaves the essential language to the main text. The next text forces the reader to bump over parentheses and punctuation, by definition hard to follow for most readers.

Example 6.38. Citations That are Too Concise.

> **Plaintiffs must prove they were wrongfully discharged. See Smith v. Jones, 888 Wis. 2d 488, 999 N.W.2d 22 (1999) (holding that plaintiff proved her wrongful discharge by showing her excellent reviews up to the time of discharge); Brown v. Green, 889 Wis. 2d 55, 999 N.W.2d 777 (1999) (holding that plaintiff proved his wrongful discharge by presenting witnesses who testified to his excellent performance and his boss' continuous praise until the day of the incident); Cue v. Bee, 889 Wis. 2d 102, 999 N.W.2d 891 (1999) (holding that plaintiff proved she was wrongfully discharged when she received ten awards over as**

many years, was promoted three times, and then testified about a safety regulation). . . .

GRAPHICS TO CLARIFY POINTS

We need white space on the page. Too much of our writing becomes technical, thick, dense, unreadable. Some writers, still socialized into using the traditional interior, fill pages half with single-spaced text, half with footnotes. The reader tires. Consider using charts, graphs, tables, bullets, or just plain white space on the page to relieve the reader's eyes and heighten comprehension. These devices must match the meaning, of course, but we often have opportunities for doing just that: pie charts for showing how a whole is divided, such as revenue sources for a corporate client; bar graphs showing how the quantity of something is changing, such as number of international clients; stacked bar graphs to show comparison, such as how property tax rates compare between sections of a city; or tables to organize data, such as the kinds of products handled by a client.

Example 6.39. Graphics Used to Report Data in an Article.

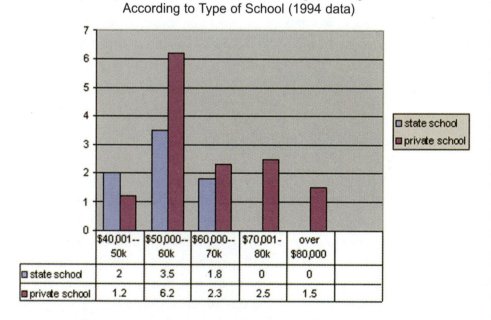

Salary Ranges of Full-Time Tenure Track Legal Writing Professors According to Type of School (1994 data)

	$40,001--50k	$50,000--60k	$60,000--70k	$70,001--80k	over $80,000	
state school	2	3.5	1.8	0	0	
private school	1.2	6.2	2.3	2.5	1.5	

Jill J. Ramsfield, *Legal Writing in the Twenty-First Century: A Sharper Image*, 2 LEGAL WRITING 64 (1996).

ABSENCE OF EXCESSIVE NOMINALIZATIONS

There is nothing grammatically wrong with a nominalization, which is a verb, adjective, or adverb turned into a noun. Look at them:

Nominalization	Root
statement	*state*
objection	*object*
causation	*cause*
explanation	*explain*
difference	*different*
quickness	*quickly*

They look perfectly innocent. But stack them up and you get stuffy.

I am in <u>receipt</u> of your letter of March 3, 2000. In <u>compliance</u> with your <u>request</u> for our <u>assistance</u>, I am asking for your <u>response</u> to some <u>questions</u>.

Traditional legal writing is full of these and they creep unsuspectingly into modern legal writing, too. It may be that lawyers categorize information by turning it into nouns, then keep those in the text. Some nominalizations are terms of art that should not be tampered with, such as *alienation of affection* or *offered no reasonable explanation*, but you can often change nominalizations back into verbs. By doing so, you preserve action and enliven your writing. So write,

I received your letter of March 3, 1999, asking our firm to assist you. Please answer the questions I have outlined below.

TECHNIQUE

• *Look for patterns.* View your writing differently. Look at the features of MALR or the features of your supervising attorney's writing. Compare yours with the other, noting the patterns. Here are typical patterns that weaken some lawyers' writing:

LEGALESE

WEAK TOPIC SENTENCES

TOO MANY LONG SENTENCES, PARAGRAPHS

EXCESSIVE QUOTES

EXCESSIVE FOOTNOTES

ABSENCE OF 'REMINDERS' TO READER

ABSENCE OF CLUES

STRING CITES AND PARENTHETICALS

WEAK PARAGRAPH ENDINGS

LACK OF THEME, THEORY

FEW PREPOSITIONAL PHRASES

For similar reasons, legal readers eschew prepositions: there is a noun at the end of them. Usually these nouns can become verbs, or the construction can be abbreviated in some way. *No one testified to the innocence of the plaintiff* can become *No one testified to plaintiff's innocence. The readiness of the defendant to testify on his own behalf* can become *Defendant was ready to testify. The court ruled that the facts in this case demanded a finding of negligence on the part of the defendant* can become *The court found the defendant negligent.* Try to spot prepositions and transform them into action, description, or possession.

MINIMAL USE OF FOOTNOTES

This topic will cost you many hours if you bring it up with any traditional legal writers. To them, footnotes are the saving grace of legal writing. When they cannot decide what to do with some information, they drop it in a footnote. When they are stuck on how to make something flow, they take the natty part out and drop it in a footnote. When they want to beat the page limit, they use footnotes. Yet, when asked if they like to read footnotes, they blanch. In most modes of legal writing besides scholarly writing, footnotes are unwelcome. Few legal readers like to read them because they distract from the text by making the reader decide whether or not to read them. If that doesn't interrupt flow, what does?

If you want to include something, include it. Decide: in or out. If your flow is being interrupted, rethink your small-scale organization and insert the idea at the end of a paragraph. If you like the idea, incorporate it into a sentence and bring the cite into the text. Legal readers are used to cites in text; they give the writer credibility. Properly used, that is as sentences or clauses, they do not upset the syntax of the text. Readers can easily skip cites when the text flows; they find it hard to skip footnotes that take text from the main body of the discussion. When the cites are removed from the text and dropped into a footnote that the reader can quickly identify as only a cite, they can work. But, generally, readers are distracted. Reading footnotes is like taking a trip to the basement. The modern interior keeps the reader on one level. As one tired judge said, "If God had meant us to read footnotes, he would have put our eyes one above the other!"

Example 6.40. Example of Brief Without Footnotes.

This Court has recognized that the sentencing provisions governing cocaine base offenses are rationally based and not in violation of the Equal Protection Clause. [Cite] The Sentencing Commissions' report and recommendations, therefore, cannot, absent congressional adoption, refute those provisions. The report shows that the distinctions between cocaine and cocaine base, as drawn by the legislature, are highly debatable, but not irrational or illegitimate. In fact, the Commission's report recognizes this Court's distinctions between

cocaine and cocaine base when it found the statute and related Sentencing Guidelines constitutional. For example, the Commission found that there is a greater likelihood of addiction resulting from the use of crack cocaine than from cocaine powder based upon the route of administration of crack cocaine (smoking). Report, pp. 45-47. The Commission also found that the available data shows that the marketing and distribution of crack cocaine is more prone to increased levels of criminal activity, including violence and weapon possession. Id. at 49-51. Finally, the Commission recognized that "the ease by which crack can be administered and its ability to be marketed cheaply have made it particularly appealing and accessible to a broader population, including . . . the poor and the young." Id. at 51-53, 60.

This Court has also already recognized that this statutory classification is debatable, and will likely continue to be debated, but the debate is not enough to require its invalidation. Jones v. U.S., 998 F.2d 555, 557 (1999). The provisions are constitutional. Therefore, this Court must reject, again, defendant's equal protection argument.

Example 6.41. Example of Brief With Footnotes.

The Sentencing Commission's report and recommendations, therefore, cannot, absent congressional adoption, serve to refute the clear recognition by this Court that the sentencing provisions governing cocaine base offenses are rationally based and not in violation of the Equal Protection Clause. The report, at best, shows that the distinctions between cocaine and cocaine base, as drawn by the legislature, are highly debatable, not irrational or illegitimate.[1] As this Court has already recognized in Jones, that this statutory classification is debatable, and will likely continue to be debated, is not enough to require its invalidation.[2] Jones v. U.S., 998 F.2d 555, 557 (1999). As a result, defendant's argument based upon equal protection must again be rejected by this Court.

_____

[1] Even the Commission's report continues to recognize the distinctions between cocaine and cocaine base relied upon by this Court in finding the statute and related Sentencing Guidelines constitutional.

For example, the Commission found that there is a greater likelihood of addiction resulting from the use of crack cocaine than from cocaine powder based upon the route of administration of crack cocaine (smoking). Report, pp. 45-47. The Commission also found that the available data shows that the marketing and distribution of crack cocaine is more prone to increased levels of criminal activity, including violence and weapon possession. Id. at 49-51. Finally, the Commission recognized that "the ease by which crack can be administered and its ability to be marketed cheaply have made it particularly appealing and accessible to a broader population, including . . . the poor and the young." Id. at 51-53, 60.

TECHNIQUE

• *Create your own revision list.* Build a revision checklist that focuses you on your own foibles. Are you *however* happy? Do you use too much jargon? Are your sentences consistently too long? Do modifiers dilute your arguments? Do you use too many empty connectors, such as *on the other hand* or *in that regard*? List those things that your readers consistently complain about, that you sense are unhelpful to your writing, or that do not conform to MALR. Then create your checklist.

You may, of course, do any of the things on this list at any time in your writing process. The one danger is that these interior design matters will distract you from questions of materials, form, and proportion. You can make the writing beautiful, but if the structure is weak or the space poorly designed, no amount of paint will fix it. The methods suggested here allow you to compartmentalize, that is, check—as your reader does—for accuracy in content and appropriateness of form before looking for the perfect word.

---

2 The debatable nature of this classification was most recently reflected in the House Judiciary Committee's vote to overturn the recommendation by the Sentencing Commission to equalize penalties for possession of cocaine base and powder cocaine. 1999 U.S. H.B. 789. Janet Lean, Equalizing Sentences for Cocaine Crimes, Wash. Post, August 20, 2002.

SAMPLE REVISION CHECKLIST

- Is theme or thesis accurately stated? Do subject and verb use precise terms of art?

- If used, do headings present the document's architectural plan?

- Do topic sentences lead the reader through the document? Are they *fronted*?

- Is paragraph structure internally consistent?

- Are topic strings set up that carry the sequence of ideas throughout the document?

- Does substance match syntax?

- Does sentence length and structure vary?

- Are verbs active, carry agency precisely through the document?

- Are nouns and verbs concrete rather than abstract?

- Are unnecessary words omitted?

- Do rhythms and words create subthemes and reminders?

- Is the language consistent, conforming to a defined tone and point of view?

A Word on Being Concise

An average English word is four letters and a half. By hard, honest labor I've dug all the large words out of my vocabulary and shaved it down till the average is three and a half . ... I never write 'metropolis' for seven cents, because I can get the same money for 'city.' I never write 'policeman,' because I get the same price for 'cop.' I never write 'valetudinarian' at all, for not even hunger and wretchedness can humble me to the point where I will do a word like that for seven cents; I wouldn't do it for fifteen.
— Mark Twain

As to the adjective: when in doubt, strike it out.

—<u>Id.</u>

    Legal readers put a premium on conciseness, mostly because of their time. They really do not want to read more than they have to. Being concise in legal writing, however, is much more than a habit or a "style." It is a matter of mastering the material so that you are able to glean from it the absolute essence necessary for your reader. It is also a matter of mastering grammatical material. The art of both matching your document's form to its theme and matching its substance to its syntax is the art of being not only clear but also concise.

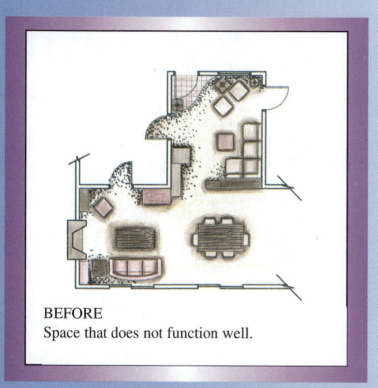

BEFORE
Space that does not function well.

As you rewrite, eliminate all sections of your document that are repetitive. Blend together similar sections and shorten. It is during that stage that you will likely make the biggest cuts in your document. If you are focused only on sentences, you will make small adjustments to shorten the document, but only by a bit. Your ability to see the overall purpose and to gauge you audience's needs enables you to create the most concise form. Train yourself to keep in mind at all times your document's purpose, audience, scope, and stance; more importantly, train yourself to stay open to shorter ways of saying the same thing. You might also create a practical challenge for yourself: never to go to the page limit. Or never to go over half of the page limit. That exercise alone will force you to decide what stays and what goes. Judges usually hate giving extensions in time or length; lawyers usually love them because they eliminate the difficult decisions on conciseness.

As you revise, work on the paragraphs and sentences. Never use two words where one will do. Never use five syllables where three will do. The architecture of your document should convey its message; the design of your sentences its meaning. A few guidelines for being concise:

1. Use apostrophes instead of prepositions: *corporation's* for *of the corporation*.

2. Use verbs instead of nominalizations: *stated* for *made the state ment that*.

3. Use shorter words: *omit* for *eliminated*.

4. Omit all adjectives and adverbs and make them fight to get back in.

5. Collapse long phrases into shorter ones: *his failure* for *the fact that he had failed*; *defendant, a restaurant owner* for *defendant, who is the owner of a restaurant*.

6. Use citations and signals instead of descriptive phrases like *The court held* or *Another example is....*

AFTER
Space that functions.

7. Omit verb phrases that are redundant: *she can protect her rights* for *she may be able to protect her rights*; *defendant said* for *defendant then went on to say that...*

Generally, conciseness cannot come at the expense of accuracy. For beginners, conciseness can be an enemy to a full understanding of the law; beginners sometimes omit the law itself in the name of conciseness. For experienced practitioners, however, conciseness usually means more work. For experienced readers, the writer's work is worth it.

TECHNIQUE

- *Rewrite and revise with modern interior elements in mind.* As you look at your text, make sure you have the law in place first; then make the syntax match the substance. Identify the patterns in the writing first; then harmonize the document's light, color, rhythm, texture, and balance.

The following example revises a portion of a brief according to interior design elements and the principles outlined in the sections on clarity and elegance. As you read the original version, actually filed in court, note some of the writer's patterns: nominalizations (blue), prepositional phrases (yellow), and passive voice (lavender).

Example 6.42. Example from a Brief.

This ruling also has support from other jurisdictions. The case of Moore v. The Atchison, Topeka and Santa Fe Railway Co., 28 Ill. App. 2d 340, 171 N.W.2d 393 (1960) demonstrates this. A train belonging to the defendant went through a red signal and had a head-on collision with another train. The Court in Moore ruled that '. . . a plaintiff is entitled to a direct verdict in a *res ipsa loquitur* case if the circumstances are so strong that reasonable men cannot reject it.' Id. at 363. At trial, the defendant offered no reasonable explanation for the accident and the Court ruled that the facts in this case demanded a finding of negligence on the part of the defendant. This is similar to the case at bar. At trial, the defendant was unable to introduce evidence that would offer a reasonable explanation for the accident absent his own negligence. A part introduced into evidence by Charles Hagberg set out a number of possible causes of the fire. The first two causes mentioned, improper or non-functioning controls and improper combustion, would occur due to negligent maintenance by the defendant. Number three, a gas line failure, can be ruled out as there was no smell of gas present which would indicate that failure. The defendant checked the burner orifice so if that could have been a cause, again negligence on the part of the defendant would be at fault. The Bastion Blessing control was ruled out as a possible cause as it was operating properly. The use of Soot Destroyer was not ruled out as a possible cause although it would be the misuse of this compound that would cause the fire. Mr. Hagberg stated that the pressure or temperature valve could not be the cause. Finally, it is asserted in Mr. Hagberg's report that an intervening cause occurred. (R-JJ, Tr. at 369, 373). The only reasonable explanation available is that the accident occurred due to the negligence of the defendant. The plaintiff introduced evidence showing that negligence was the probable cause of the fire. The defendant could not, and did not, rebut this. The only conclusion to be drawn is that the defendant's negligence was the cause of the fire. The Trial Court should have ruled that the defendant, as a matter of law, was negligent in his maintenance of the gas water heater and, following Wisconsin law, should have directed the verdict for the plaintiff. The failure to direct the verdict was error and this error should now be corrected on appeal.

Comment: Neither does the architecture match the message in this document, nor does the syntax match the substance. The doctrine is *res ipsa loquitur,* which requires that the plaintiff show what was not the cause of the accident, then who controlled what was left. The overall organization does not recognize this, but randomly lists points from both parties' points of view. You may have identified any of several patterns: nominalizations, passive voice at the end, active verbs that moved to linking and then passive verbs, overuse of ambiguous demonstrative pronouns, and too many prepositions. Try to revise the brief now, having identified those patterns.

POSSIBLE REVISION

Another jurisdiction supports this ruling. An Illinois court of appeals affirmed a directed verdict for plaintiff when defendant train company offered no reasonable explanation for its train colliding head-on with another train. See Moore v. The Atchison, Topeka and Santa Fe Railway Co., 28 Ill. App. 2d 340, 171 N.W.2d 393 (1960).

Similarly, defendant can offer no reasonable explanation here, and thus the court should have directed the verdict for the plaintiff. No smell of gas indicated a gas line failure, so that was not the cause. No failure of the Bastion Blessing control occurred, so that was not the cause. No failure of the pressure or temperature valves occurred, so those were not the cause. And no intervening cause occurred.

The only causes of the accident, then, could be improperly functioning controls, non-functioning controls, improper combustion, or misuse of the compound Soot Destroyer. Defendant controlled all of these; he negligently maintained and used the controls, the equipment, and the compound.

Defendant offered no reasonable explanation for his negligent maintenance of the gas heater and thus the trial court should have directed the verdict for the plaintiff.

As you design your interior, then, use the design elements to capture the overall effect. Then use the various components of traditional or modern interiors to create specific impact. Create light by using graphics on the page or more variety in sentence or paragraph structure. Use particular phrases in positions of emphasis to create color. Harmonize an entire section by placing key phrases in headings and topic sentences. Put rhythm into the interior by listening to the length and cadence of your sentences and the relative relationship of paragraphs to each other. Engage your readers by composing interiors that match exteriors.

Your research into rhetorical elements signals how to create the document's architecture; your use of architectural elements signals what interior is appropriate. You can design a simple document that explains a short answer to an often-asked question by keeping the form straightforward and the sentences contemporary. You can design a complex, traditional transaction using traditional form, proportion, and interior. You can also break the molds and design a modern, minimalist memo.

All of the elements can work with each other to keep your readers engaged and your creativity evolving. Be bold where you can, conservative where you must. Surprise your readers where appropriate. Once you have made all of your design decisions, built the document, and harmonized these elements, all that remains is your finishing.

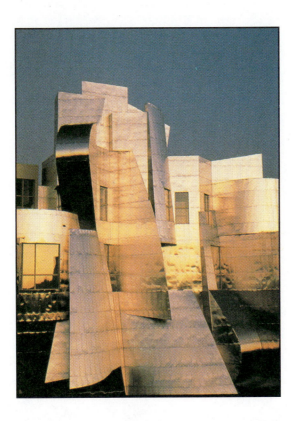

CHAPTER 7

FINISHING

When we build, let us think that we build forever.
John Ruskin

When the famous and controversial pyramids were finished at the Louvre, viewers were astonished at their stark contrast to the French palace. To some, the smooth, shiny surfaces seemed to mock the palace's soft, yellow stone. To others, the surfaces complemented each other: the warmth of the stone finish was set off by the bright sheen of the glass. Now the pyramids happily reside inside most Feng Shui books as an example of the fire element complementing the water element. The finishes in fact combine to enhance each other. The shocking combination works.

But the architects forgot to consider one practical aspect of the pyramids: how they would be cleaned. Once the dirt started collecting, the French government was stumped. No one had thought about keeping the

I think I did pretty well, considering I started
out with nothing but
a bunch of blank paper.

-Steve Martin

shiny finish sparkling. The solution: the pyramids are cleaned by mountain climbers.

As you draw to a close on your document, consider three aspects of finishing. First, review your document overall for its general impact and consistent sheen: sharp edges, shiny surfaces, or porous warmth. Look at its overall effect on the reader as you page through the document. Certain sections may not blend with others; certain parts may not be as finely finished as others. Second, review it for the finer finish of having no mistakes. Most legal readers are highly intolerant of any kind of error, from grammar to citations, from typographical errors to poorly placed commas. Third, reflect on what you have learned from building this document. Honor your achievements, learn from your mistakes, and note why some techniques worked and others did not. Remember that your design repetoire must serve many building situations, so it needs constant expansion and adjustment. As you finish, note how this document fits into your portfolio of all documents and how these techniques fit into your design repetoire.

By the time you reach this stage, you may be feeling quite weary of the subject and of the document itself. Try not to abandon it before it is truly perfected. It takes a lot of concentration to perfect and probably twice as much time as you think it should. Finishing properly is, however, crucial to your credibility and precision.

To finish your design, consider both the document's overall effect and its details. Be both a pragmatist and a perfectionist so that the document serves its purpose and stands on its own as a fine piece of architecture. Refresh yourself on your client's position, remember who is actually signing the document, and be ready to react to a sudden change of policy. Be alert to the document's uniformity, consistency, and overall harmony. To

finish your document so that it fits its situation, also be alert to legal conventions, local conditions, and your own management abilities.

CHECKING THE OVERALL EFFECT

Stand back from your document to get a picture of how it looks over-all. Check the perspectives, the mixture of theme and subthemes, the general impact on the reader. By this time, your mind may be fixed on margins, punctuation, and cites. First make sure you have captured the grand design. Then let your eye fall over the document to make sure nothing is too rough, too dense, too unmatched. There may be a section that is too detailed, too full of authority, or too lightly drawn. Most point headings may be three lines long, but one is six lines long—it stands out too much even though it is accurate. An opinion letter may begin and end with short paragraphs that comfort the reader, but the middle section is too technical, the paragraphs too long. You may need to make some slight adjustments to even out the document.

TECHNIQUE

- *Adjust appropriately for the document's context.* Most legal readers expect perfection, so allowing enough time to adjust satisfies both you and your reader. You may want to let your document sit for a while as you do other tasks. You can return, page through it, adjust, and finish. Sometimes you simply need to clean up.

Example 7.1. Example of Letter With Rough Finish.

PERKINS & PEABODY
P.O. BOX 6789
MADISON, WI 53701

ATTN: John Q. Peabody

RE: Legal File No. 93-11-0000

Dear John,

Enclosed please find a file which I would like your law firm to defend on behalf of our company. The file involves two separate claims by our insured; the first being a claim for a theft loss of some tools and the second being a fire loss. You will note that this file has been around for some time and we had retained Attorney John Moffatt of Baraboo to represent us. Attorney Moffatt filed a Motion for Summary Judgment on the basis that one claim had not been filed within one year as required by sec. 31.83 Wis. Stats. Plaintiff's defense was that we had been treating both claims as a single entity and that the second claim was timely filed. The Court has rendered an opinion that there are material factual questions and denied our motion. It is John Moffatt's opinion that he needs to make himself available to testify as to our good faith and the absence of any basis for waiver or estoppel by our treatment of the plaintiffs' claims. You will note the plaintiffs have claimed entitlement to punitive damages.

I will be monitoring this file on behalf of our company. I ask that you bill us periodically, such as quarterly or semi-annually.

Very truly yours,
Karl Kennedy

CAREFUL MUTUAL INSURANCE COMPANY

Comment: This letter has one very long paragraph, and one short one, odd proportions in a short letter. The overall effect is off-putting. With minor adjustments, the finish can be evened out so that the reader's eyes glide more carefully over the final product, as in the following revision, which has some short paragraphs that contrast with a long middle paragraph.

Example 7.2. Example of Letter With Smooth Finish.

PERKINS & PEABODY
P.O. BOX 6789
MADISON, WI 53701
ATTN: John Q. Peabody
RE: Legal File No. 93-11-0000

Dear John:

Enclosed is the file that Careful would like you to defend for the company. The file involves two separate claims by our insured: 1) a claim for the theft of some tools, and 2) a claim for fire loss.

Attorney John Moffatt of Baraboo has represented Careful thus far. He filed a Motion for Summary Judgment based on the plaintiff's failure to file one claim within the one year required by section 31.83, Wis. Stats. Plaintiff defended by claiming that Careful had been treating both claims as a single entity and that therefore the second claim was filed within the required time. The court denied the motion, stating that there are material factual questions to be resolved.

Attorney Moffatt suggests that he should testify that Careful acted in good faith and that there is therefore no basis for waiver or estoppel. You will also note that plaintiffs have claimed punitive damages, and that issue will have to be addressed in the defense.

I will be monitoring this file for Careful. Please bill us quarterly and let me know if you have any questions.

Very truly yours,

Karl Kennedy

CAREFUL MUTUAL INSURANCE COMPANY

NOTING CONVENTIONS

Finishing your document is not just a cosmetic check; it requires reviewing local conventions to make sure they are appropriate to the document and they have not forced you to ignore the document's content. You already investigated legal conventions as a part of your research. You gathered materials as needed for your document, including information about local conventions. You recognized more general conventions for the legal profession, as well, whether consciously or unconsciously. These local and general conventions helped frame some of the ingredients for your document's architecture.

Some conventions are probably not worth fighting. Using a local citation form, filing brief covers in a certain color, or organizing contracts as a partner has dictated, may be simpler left alone. Whether you are a lateral hire, a summer associate, or a newcomer to the jurisdiction, you simply need to be alert to local conventions, learn them, and use them. You will be more adept at judging their worth if you study them so that you understand their purpose. Be particularly aware if you are working internationally because any conventions may be culturally based, which require your deeper understanding of their purposes.

TECHNIQUES

• *Use the appropriate level of formality.* If you try to deal with this too early, you may never be able to find a consistent voice in the document. You may need to draft a document in an informal tone, for example, just to see your ideas. You can make the language more formal during revising and then adjust for a particular person's needs at the end. Try to see the difference between formality and the overly large "style" question (*see* Chapter 6); by adjusting positions of emphasis and topic sentences, you can sometimes shift the document's formality level at this finishing stage.

• *Review expected scope.* Unwritten conventions exist for the length and breadth of certain documents, such as contracts or complaints. Determine the nature of previous usage so that you can make sure the document conforms. You probably checked on this when you began the project; adjust at the end to refine any sections that have gotten too long or short, appear in unhelpful or surprising places, or call inappropriate attention to themselves.

• *Honor business practices.* Each law office has developed particular business practices, and these vary widely. Do not assume anything. Find the people who run the business and make sure that you know the protocol and procedure for completing documents, billing, filing, and preserving the document for future use. Most offices have developed a procedure, and your document may need to be catalogued accordingly before you release it.

• *Honor the office "stamp."* Be very clear about your role as you make your final adjustments. Is this a document for your signature only? For those of supervising attorneys? Is this a document that should have a standardized agency or firm "stamp" that makes its origins obvious? Does the audience expect certain appearances, such as covers, headings, or a predictable order of presentation? Make sure that you adjust for expectations besides your own, which means killing the little darlings you have invented if they do not fit appropriately into this document's format.

• *Check the use of jargon.* Some offices, some writers, some audiences prefer legal jargon, or very traditional interiors, to modern ones. You may need to draft your document in modern language first and then translate into traditional language during revising. If so, you need to adjust at the end for consistency. If you drafted using the jargon, check for accuracy and readability.

• *Check salutations and closings in letters.* Most lawyers and clients are sensitive about letters. Your office may have developed, over a long time, certain phraseology or tone for particular letters. Check any letters for these phrases, which may appear ordinary but have been carefully carved for specific purposes.

• *Conform to format requirements.* Some law offices double-space certain documents, single-space others. Margin requirements appear in many rules for filing documents in court, and some law offices put a Table of Contents on a contract, no matter what its length.

• *Check cover pages and captions.* Make sure you know the jurisdiction's requirements for any cover pages or captions on documents to be filed with courts. For other documents, such as letters to federal agencies, international contracts, wills in another state, try to find samples in your office or in form books so that you adjust the document to look as its audience expects.

• *Honor the local citation form.* Similarly, despite the Bluebook's widespread usage, many offices have invented citation forms to suit their purposes. Usually it is not worth fighting these, no matter what experience you have had. Even if you worked in a government agency that prefers a particular form, you may not be able to convince your new law office to conform if they have been doing otherwise for years. Calculate the best use of your adjustment time, but keep both your ultimate and your intermediate audiences in mind.

- *Honor filing requirements.* With anything that needs to be filed, make sure you have the correct information. At the start of your project, you probably counted the appropriate number of days before filing, calculated the correct number of pages, and noted particular caption or citation requirements. Adjusting at the end requires you to make sure you have accurately fulfilled these requirements or that you have changed whatever necessary in response to recently developed requirements. This is a vote against extensions of either time or space: follow the rules to keep your audience happy.

These conventions make your job at once gratifying and maddening. Once you know the conventions, you can conform your document to them quickly enough, or build them in as you go. You do not usually have to agonize too much about them because your choices are predetermined and predictable. The agony comes in mustering concentration after doing so much substantive work. The content is fine, you say to yourself, and you want to release the document. But your attention to these conventions allows you to put the finest finish on your document.

You may have found it easy to follow these conventions as you built your document, or you may have found some of them nonsensical. The danger lies in mindlessly following conventions that are outmoded or that lead to inaccuracy in your document. You may more often decide to break the mold.

BREAKING THE MOLD

Other conventions may be more difficult to honor. They may be outmoded, unnecessary, or mystifying, all of which may cost you time—or
accuracy. You already investigated any conventions that stalled you or
obstructed your document's purpose. Once you knew the reasons behind
the language—the format, the conventions—you may have been able to
invent a better way to accomplish the same thing. Now eliminate all irrelevant material. Refine the document to meet any evolving use and context.
As you proofread, be alert to what conventions you may have broken and
make sure that the document still fulfills its purposes and will be acceptable to its audiences.

Ultimately, you will probably compromise more than accept or reject
conventions out of hand. As you finish the document, you can make sure
that it conforms to those conventions your readers will be most sensitive
to, and then be creative about the rest. You can combine two sections that
say essentially the same thing; use the boilerplate language for motions for
summary judgment, but weave in your client's situation; or punctuate the
presentation of authority with points of your own.

TECHNIQUE

• *Balance time with client's needs.* It is probably only at this point that you know the document well enough to make it perfect. Can your client afford one more remake? If not, adjust the pillows, so to speak, but leave the rest alone. As much as you are tempted to translate arcane language, for example, you may find that your intermediary readers or your supervisors will ask you to leave it alone. You may want to focus instead on the most prominent parts of the document to make sure that it says what you want it to and leave untouched the parts that your readers expect.

FINISHING THE DETAILS

Finishing also involves a number of detailed tasks, most of them quite small, all of them quite important. It includes making sure that the citations are correct, that the punctuation is correct, that there are no typographical mistakes, and that there are no words left out, among other things. The following techniques can work in finishing, but you may have to invent your own. Remember that the idea is to keep the concentration high and allow enough time to do this well.

TECHNIQUES

- *Read the document backwards.* This seems to work for catching typos and citation errors. It does not work for leaving out words, like "not."
- *Read the document by using a ruler to read each line.* Your eye will not wander.
- *Use a ruler and cross each word out.* Your eye will not wander and your pen will keep you awake.
- *Read aloud.* Sometimes you can hear what you cannot see.
- *Read in non-sensical pieces*, such as page two, page seven, page five, page one, page three. Try not to read from beginning to end because there will be twice as many mistakes at the end as at the beginning. Your nonsensical reading keeps you focused on details.

REFLECTING ON YOUR REPERTOIRE

You have just built a document. You have added another design to your portfolio. You may have created something larger than you had before, something more streamlined, more compact, or more complex than any you have done before. In a way, there should be a sort of ceremony, a cutting of the ribbon, some champagne and wishes for the success of the document. In the more formal world of brief filing, there is a kind of ceremony; when a contract is signed, the parties are sometimes gathered together. But many legal documents are filed by others in the office, and you have already moved on to the next project.

Pause, if just for a moment. As you complete a project, you usually have a keen idea of what worked well in the project and what did not. That idea often breaks into at least two distinct categories: what worked well in the document itself and what design techniques served the document best. As you place the document into your portfolio, note what worked and why. What about the design was unique, appropriate, or particularly effective? It may have been a contract provision that solved an unusual conflict, an argument that synthesized two seemingly disparate points, a suggestion that saved the client a great deal of money. Give yourself credit for that

and make a note of how you did it, when the idea came, and what happened that allowed you to solve the problem.

If parts of the document did not satisfy you, note those, too. An argument may have gone on for too long, a contract may have been too boilerplate, or a letter too sarcastic. Your idea may have seemed like a good one at the time, but now you see it does not fit that well, but must be sent off to the client anyway. Alright. Do so, but rather than forgetting about it, make more than a mental note about what you would do differently next time: change the proportions, think of a good theory sooner, do less unnecessary research.

Note, too, what may have worked on one project, but will be a waste of time if you do it on another. Transfer your ideas and techniques from one project to another. What did you discover that you can use again? What was a perfect design, but unique to that landscape? Recognize when you have added a unique document to your portfolio or when you have invented something that will work in several settings. Even for those ideas that transfer, fight the temptation to create a "cookie cutter" solution to several problems, which could make your work so generic that it does not affect audiences properly. While the law may be the same in Kansas as in New York, you may want to frame the briefs differently for judges in those disparate settings.

Make similar notations about your writing techniques. You know when a project moved smoothly, when a technique focused you better, when another technique saved you hours in the library. You know when collaborating helped you break open an idea for a negotiation or particular progress on a case. Mark those successful techniques and why they worked. Keep inventing more. Admit, too, when you have taken too long on a document, when you have gotten stuck at particular points, when you have bowed to your bad propensities for over-researching, over-writing, or over-refining. Why? When? How much are you holding on to habits from pre-law school days? How much are non-law voices trying to drive your legal writing process? Free them to go elsewhere while you invent and invoke techniques appropriate to building these practical legal documents.

Your design repertoire can expand as you gain experience. As an increasingly experienced legal architect, you can become more versatile in using different techniques for different situations. Try some form of dictation, rather than holding tight to typing; try some form of quick drafting, rather than correcting every sentence as you go; try talking a design through with others, rather than getting set on one way to do it. Keep searching for easier, faster, better, more creative ways of designing documents. Then, no matter what your time frame, you will be able to build with ease and confidence.

As architects and lawyers know, you may not always like your client or the landscape or what you have been asked to build. You may not agree with your colleagues' choices or your client's taste; you may not always believe in the underlying soundness of the idea. But you can always become a better legal architect. Every situation offers a challenge to your problem-solving abilities and your writing techniques. Every building offers some kind of design question—even one unit of tract housing may be built over a water vein where another was not. And sometimes the worst situations evoke your best creativity. Enjoy that. Enjoy becoming a better, faster legal architect. Celebrate. Then move on to your next design.

APPENDIX A
SUMMARY OF WRITING PROCESS TECHNIQUES

- *Record the document's rhetorical features, as you observe them, perhaps as "rhetorical outlines." (page 81)*

- *Record your reactions as you read. (page 119)*

- *Write a descriptive outline of the document that captures its analytical progression. (page 119)*

- *Read for one thing at a time. (page 119)*

- *Read separate sections out of order. (page 120)*

- *Read as mentor. (page 120)*

- *Read for the document's most important needs. (page 120)*

- *Read actively, rather than passively. (page 120)*

- *Keep notes from project to project. (page 120)*

- *Interview the assigning attorney. (page 145)*

- *Discover the rhetorical elements. (page 146)*

- *Collect the facts. (page 156)*

- *Analyze the facts. (page 161)*

- *Compare the arguments. (page 163)*

- *Use interviewing documents or checklists. (page 164)*

- *Try to get client to identify issue. (page 164)*

- *Get partner to identify issue. (page 164)*

- *Balance buisness concerns against legal ones. (page 164)*

- *Evaluate the economics of the deal. (page 164)*

- *Research the forms. (page 165)*

- *Then get the right "flavor" for the form. (page 165)*

- *Create a library of master forms. (page 165)*

- *Choose an organizational plan. (page 165)*

- *Ask for written directions. (page 169)*

- *Write out the facts and have them checked. (page 169)*

- *Write out the theme, including any specific issues and answers, and have it checked. (page 169)*

- *Brainstorm. (page 169)*

- *Interview the audience himself. (page 170)*

- *Discuss the audience with the assigning attorney. (page 170)*

- *Interview people who have written for that audience before. (page 170)*

- *Write down the page limit you would want for this document if you were the primary reader. (page 170)*

- *Estimate the number of appropriate sources before you research. (page 171)*

- *Select, prepare, and repair forms. (page 171)*

- *Write out all preliminary question or legal issues. (page 171)*

- *Before you write, consider the level of detail that will be appropriate for the audience. (page 171)*

- *Write out all the issues, using the three-part schema. (page 180)*

- *Put the issues in a preliminary order. (page 180)*

- *Consider what will make some issues irrelevant. (page 180)*

- *Talk to others. (page 180)*

- *As you research, fill in the charts. (page 180)*

- *Take notes about both content and organization. (page 180)*

- *Percolate, rather than procrastinate. (page 180)*

- *Address practical matters. (page 180)*

- *Try out several theories; write them out. (page 183)*

- *Use your preliminary issue to cull appropriate materials. (page 205)*

- *Create a research strategy and write it out. (page 211)*

- *Write down the date. (page 221)*

- *Write down the full citation in whatever form you will use in your final document. (page 221)*

- *Create a system for taking notes. (page 221)*

- *Create files on a disk. (page 221)*

- *Use separate legal pads for separate topics . (page 221)*

- *Color code. (page 222)*

- *Use a pyramid to organize information. (page 222)*

- *Be meticulous: filter, translate, paraphrase, quote. (page 222)*

- *Record specific page and document numbers. (page 222)*

- *Record your own thoughts about the source. (page 222)*

- *Allow for development of your theme or message—and record it. (page 222)*

- *Record connections and sketch an overall design. (page 223)*

- *Keep track of sources, showing their relative importance. (page 223)*

- *Write out Purpose, Audience, Scope, Stance; prioritize . (page 223)*

- *Write memos to intermediate readers. (page 223)*

- *Create your own macros for recording and sorting information. (page 223)*

- *Connect all subparts to the whole. (page 228)*

- *Paraphrase a source so it means something to you; then translate for the reader. (page 228)*

- *Tape record a summary of the document's content. (page 228)*

- *Test the validity of the syllogism in an argument, opinion, or memo. (page 257)*

- *Make your hypothesis the conclusion; then use the primary sources to discover the major and minor premises . (page 257)*

- *Observe the similarities and differences among the syllogisms in all documents you are researching; is there a pattern? (page 257)*

- *Extract and synthesize your major premise from your resources. (page 257)*

- *Test the validity and consistency of a contract by combining all parts into a syllogism. (page 258)*

- *Sketch or outline. (page 313)*

- *Don't get it right, get it written. (page 313)*

- *Decide on your document's theme. (page 324)*

- *Check the headings to make sure that each advances the theme. (page 324)*

- *Use a descriptive, or reverse, outline to make sure you can justify each paragraph and its place in your analysis. (page 324)*

- *Fill in any holes you left or omit any repetitive parts. (page 324)*

- *Check the first sentences of each paragraph to make sure they are connected to each other. (page 325)*

- *Rearrange the text if necessary. (page 325)*

- *Avoid making small-scale changes simultaneously. (page 325)*

- *Create a rewriting checklist. (page 328)*

- *Do several designs. (page 349)*

- *Let the document sit for a while. (page 357)*

- *Write the document as your last task of the day, then rewrite it first thing in the morning. (page 357)*

- *Change the medium. (page 357)*

- *Read aloud. (page 357)*

- *Change your environment to get a new perspective. (page 357)*

- *Pretend that the document has already been turned in. (page 358)*

- *Delegate the rewrite to someone else. (page 358)*

- *Literally cut and paste. (page 358)*

- *Synthesize comments from others. (page 358)*

- *"Front" the main sentence in the document. (page 428)*

- *Reorder sentences to unify the paragraph. (page 435)*

- *Read for one thing at a time. (page 441)*

- *Use cohesive devices. (page 445)*

- *Look for patterns. (page 454)*

- *Create your own revision list. (page 457)*

- *Rewrite and revise with modern interior elements in mind. (page 462)*

- *Adjust appropriately for the document's context. (page 471)*

- *Use the appropriate level of formality. (page 475)*

- *Review expected scope. (page 475)*

- *Honor business practices. (page 475)*

- *Honor the office "stamp." (page 475)*

- *Check the use of jargon. (page 476)*

- *Check salutations and closings in letters. (page 476)*

- *Conform to format requirements. (page 476)*

- *Check cover pages and captions. (page 476)*

- *Honor the local citation form. (page 476)*

- *Honor filing requirements. (page 477)*

- *Balance time with client's needs. (page 479)*

- *Read the document backwards. (page 480)*

- *Read the document by using a ruler to read each line. (page 480)*

- *Use a ruler and cross each word out. (page 480)*

- *Read aloud. (page 480)*

- *Read in non-sensical pieces. (page 480)*

APPENDIX B
MANAGING YOUR TIME

As you finish your project, you have a keen sense of how well you have used your time. If you are working in a private law office, you may have had to account for every tenth of an hour. If you work in a public office, you may have been aware of shifting priorities as you worked on your most recent document. In either case, you may have "cheated," billing fewer hours than you actually worked or staying late and coming in early to finish this project.

The end of the project is a good moment for assessing your time management abilities. Document production is art and architecture, but with deadlines and demanding clients. Your ability to streamline your time is essential to your sense of success and satisfaction. You are not writing the proverbial Great American Novel; instead, you are producing documents that must be sturdy enough to withstand scrutiny from the most hostile users. And producing them quickly.

Before you move on to the next project, you might want to assess your habits. Look for clues in the Writing Process techniques sandwiched in the green pages of this book. In those sections, you may discover what places bog you down, what places you devote too much time to because you just enjoy those places more, and what places you simply stopped. What follows are some added suggestions for using each project as a means for improving your time management.

Intermingled with the tenths and quarters of an hour devoted to client work are countless minutes of idea development, office management, recruiting, long-range planning, travel time, financial projections, training, and coordinating. The same is true in law school: writing projects are intermingled with the reading for classes, volunteer work, student organizations, and day-to-day activities. In order to maximize each day's returns for the respective investments of time and energy, you may want to revitalize time management techniques and explore means of doing more work in less time.

Doing more work in less time involves not only creating efficient strategies for accomplishing tasks unique to your practice goals, but also balancing personal goals with professional ones. Time for family, hobbies, relaxation, physical fitness, and personal development must integrate with work time. Balancing personal with professional development means balancing the time spent on each, and balancing takes planning.

You may not feel that you have enough time to read this appendix, for example, because most legal writers have trouble finding the time to do casual reading. You may expect to have the time, but the unexpected often occurs: a frantic client calls and needs immediate attention; an associate returns a draft to you that is incomplete, unfocused and late; a hearing that should have taken only two hours takes six. Time evaporates unexpectedly and pushes projects further along on the calendar. Your days become longer, your weekends are spent at the office, and your vacation continues to be postponed.

As lawyers compete more for clients, become more sensitive to clients' demands to know how time is spent, and take on more to make ends meet, managing the working day and year has become an increasingly important issue. Many lawyers bristle at traditional time management courses whose approaches do not speak to their needs. Traditional advice such as "keep your desk clear of all paper" may be impractical for attorneys who are often out of the office while mail and phone calls continue to come in.

You can create and sustain a healthy balance, not only between personal and professional time, but also among the varied complex tasks you meet in a sophisticated practice. You can create an individualized approach that will make your time more structured when necessary, more flexible when called for, and generally more useful for you in planning your professional time. Overall, time invested early will save much more time later. Invest early to manage what you can: your office, your own desk, your research and writing, and your client contacts. And investing early allows you room for the time you cannot manage: court appearances, length of hearings, client emergencies. You can fashion your time so that you will be running your projects; the projects will not be running you. The calendar and the clock will become your allies so that you can consistently create "win-win" solutions: you will spend less time accomplishing more. As usual, take what is useful for you, share your techniques with colleagues, create joint strategies—and enjoy the balance. Take a moment now to make some notes on what works and what does not in your time management scheme.

PUTTING TIME IN PROFESSIONAL PERSPECTIVE

To create your own best approach, put your time in professional perspective. This perspective is the balance of your tasks, your limits, and your breaks. Each of us has a different list, one that depends on our practice, our experience, and our goals. But while it may be tempting to begin by defining all the work that you do and trying to fit the rest of your life around your work, try reversing the order to build your best techniques for your time management.

TECHNIQUES

• *Define when you do not want to work.* Your productivity is related to your energy level, and your energy level is usually related to how much time off you take. So define your breaks. Start with the next two years and decide how much vacation you would like to have, or are allowed to have, over that period. If you would like a two-week vacation or longer next year, put down the dates for that vacation now. Then do the same on the monthly and weekly levels. Decide when you want to spend time at home, with loved ones, pursuing a hobby, or simply relaxing. Then bring your ideal down to the daily level by setting aside time for jogging, for lunch, for reading the newspaper, or for chatting with associates. All of these matters take time -- and should. Seeing them as a part of your professional life may hone your time-managing techniques. Enjoy this picture of your breaks for the year, the week, and each day. Resolve to take those breaks.

• *Define your working limits.* Having so resolved not to work at certain times, define your limits. Decide how many billable, or working, hours you would like to put in this year, and divide that by the number of weeks you would like to work. If you are being asked to do 2200 billable hours each year, then consider how much you can do beyond those official hours. Whatever your situation, do the same time definition for the week: decide how many hours you would like to work each week. Then decide when you would like to arrive at the office and when you would like to leave. Try

Weekly Working Limits

__ *hours per year* = __ *hours per month* = __ *hours per day*

	Current Schedule	Preferred Schedule
Arrive at work:	7:30 am	8:00 am
Breaks:	12:30 pm -- 1:00 pm	11:30 am--12:15 pm
		3:30 pm -- 4:15 pm
Leave Work:	8:30 pm	6:00 pm
Night Work:	Irregularly 11:00 pm	none
Weekend:	Sunday evening	none

writing all of this down (one technique suggested below for investing time early and managing time overall). Look at your picture, enjoy it, erase and scribble until you have a comfortable and realistic sense of your preferred daily, weekly, monthly, and yearly schedules.

To enjoy your breaks, to stay within your limits, and to accomplish all of your tasks, you now must speed up your work by doing more in less time. You will need to invest your time in projects up front. You might need to eliminate non-productive professional groups or informal commitments around the law firm. And do not worry: if you feel overwhelmed now, decide how you can gradually pare down tasks over the next two years.

FACTORING IN SEVERAL AUDIENCES

Once you have put your time in professional perspective by defining your breaks, limits, and tasks, consider the audiences with whom you

One of the easiest ways to find out about your audience is to ask finish them, and what are their likes and dislikes. If you delegate, make sure you also make clear your preferences and propensities. You may be strict about deadlines, which helps in time management, and will want to let them know this well ahead of time. Being strict about deadlines requires quick turnaround on your part, as well, to reinforce the importance of timely submissions to you.

And you need to know yourself. You may be excellent on the phone with clients, but take too long to chat; you may dislike going through piles of mail, so put off sorting it and throwing it away; you may write your own drafts, but can no longer afford the time. Examine what habits you have that work, and what do not. If you are not sure, ask those who work with you. Assess all of your audiences and yourself, and consider how they can help or hurt you in staying within your time limits.

One of the modern lawyer's concerns in managing time is how to manage one's own time when others cannot manage theirs. Many projects now involve several people and incorporate several rounds of feedback before they leave the office. In a highly specialized practice, a product's quality level must be high, and the corresponding pressures build. In particular, the time it takes to move a product from good to excellent may be twice the time it takes to make it good. How to minimize this "excellence" time, then, becomes the task of all those working on the project.

Consider a project on which you are working right now. Assess the goals as you understand them. For example, the firm's goals on this project may be to keep the client informed of complex legal developments; your goals may be to write this document in less time but with more focus than you did on the last similar document.

Working Backwards

Knowing your limits and your audiences will allow you to work backwards, using a kind of reverse engineering to manage your time. You probably have a good sense of what tasks each project demands. Left unnamed and untamed, those tasks may run wild, taking as much time as they like. Identified, separated, and harnessed, they will pull you neatly to the end of the project in an appropriate amount of time. And you will be the driver.

Decide what date you want to finish the project, even if there is no official deadline. Be realistic, and sketch those major dates into your calendar. For each major project, consider at least two other deadlines in addition to the major deadline. The first is the practical deadline, which occurs a few days before the project must be completed. This will give you some breathing room should any unexpected delays occur. The second is the halfway mark between now and the final deadline. Decide that you will finish the draft, or the major portion of the project, by then. That will allow you time for feedback, discussion, completion of the research, or changes in approach.

To please a multiple audience in accomplishing all of a project's goals, you also might want to begin sensitizing the community to the time it should take to accomplish this. Sometimes the exact amount of time is

TECHNIQUE

- *Create an interim deadline schedule.* If you are so inclined, you can create a series of interim deadlines: one for research, one for sketching a picture of the project or outlining, one for drafting, one for cutting and pasting, one for making small-scale changes, and one for polishing. Or you may want to create interim deadlines with a supervisor or supervisee so that you have meeting times to check on particularly difficult steps in the process such defining the issues, outlining the shape of the document, or finalizing a theory of case. You will probably find that,by working backwards from the deadline and defining and separating each task, you will need to start sooner than you thought. Allow yourself some breathing room between these interim deadlines so that if you miss one, you do not feel hopelessly behind in the project.

impossible to project. In such cases, you might choose a reasonable deadline and work backwards.

CREATING A SYSTEM

Once you have defined the tasks your work requires and have also become sensitive to its time line, you can start creating a system unique to your tastes and good habits. A system for time management is built on individual strengths. Every lawyer has strengths that can translate into excellent time management. Having identified your limits, your tasks, your strengths, and your bad habits, create a system tailored to you.

Begin by outlining your strengths in time management. These may be closely tied to your motivations. For example, you may find you organize yourself very efficiently right before you take a vacation; or you might do things more quickly knowing you have a racquetball tournament that evening; or you find yourself more thorough and fast when you are working with someone whom you would like to impress.

Clarify these strengths, recognizing what works for you in time management. Then identify your stubborn habits. As your strengths may be tied to motivations, so your bad habits may be tied to procrastination. Most of us resist a system, or resist someone else telling us how to organize ourselves. This is partly because we are mavericks as lawyers—individual creative thinkers who often work best "under pressure"—or so we think. It is when the pressure becomes a constant cooker that we are forced to admit that we may have remained inefficient for too long. Identify those habits that are the enemy of efficiency and resolve to eliminate them—systematically.

Then compose your own theme and variations. Decide how you want to be viewed as a time manager. You may decide, for example, that you want to be seen as a strong leader who conducts short meetings, as an organized lawyer who responds quickly to client demands, as a trial lawyer whose documents are filed on time and who never asks for extensions, or some combination of all of the above. From your theme, develop techniques suited to you so that you can replace bad habits with specific techniques that invest time early and allow space for the unexpected. Choose from among the following techniques to get started.

TECHNIQUES

• *Eliminate paper.* Delegate to your secretary or a paralegal the task of organizing your files. Or delegate this to yourself, making an appointment with yourself to get this organization started. Your organization scheme may work better if you design the system in writing or approve it before it is implemented. Store on disk what you can and clear your office of paper copies. Also, read each day's mail immediately. Eliminate, or have your secretary eliminate, all unnecessary mail and envelopes and divide the mail into piles, such as client correspondence, CLE materials, bar notices, and personal correspondence. Touch each piece of paper only once. As you read the mail, immediately throw away anything you can and dictate a response or directions for the rest. For each piece of paper you decide to keep, give it a "home" by returning it to a file or telling your secretary where to file it immediately.

• *Write down directions.* If you have had any trouble with people misunderstanding what you want - including yourself—write it down. That way, if you are busy or absent, the person to whom the task has been delegated can continue to work on the task without having to interrupt you. Even though writing appears to take unwarranted time, this investment into precise directions will save hours of needless and annoying volleying between you and your supervisees, and hours of "start-up" time reminding yourself where you should be going on the project. If you are being supervised by a poor time manager, you might try writing a gentle clarifying memo. "As I understand it, you have asked me to research whether or not....Please let me know if this is incorrect. Otherwise, I will continue with the project."

• *Delegate more.* This is hard, especially when you are not sure what direction a case may be taking. Neverhtheless, try to give more responsibility to others. This will take training, which will absorb time up front. But if you make your directions specific and build in time for checkpoints, you may find that, over time, your associates learn your likes and dislikes and take pride in helping you out. Give them credit, encouragement, discipline, and frequent, constructive feedback. Let go. Save your time for matters that only you can handle, and guide others to do the less demanding, but more time-consuming, tasks.

THE THREE "C"s:

COMPARTMENTALIZE, CONCENTRATE, CONDENSE

• *Compartmentalize tasks.* Pull together similar tasks, such as sorting through mail, dictating letters, or answering phone calls. As much as you can, do these in blocks of time. Then your legal mind can gear up for a certain kind of task rather than leaping through several throughout the day. Such an approach eliminates unnecessary "switch" time, which occurs when you try to do too many things at once. Compartmentalizing will allow you, then, to devote your full attention to each type of task.

• *Concentrate deeply on each task.* Having compartmentalized tasks, devote 100% of your attention to each, in sequence. This focus will increase your efficiency because your mind will be clear of other matters. You know that you will reach that matter in another compartment later, so you can release yourself from that compartment and concentrate on the present one. You should find that your mind works more easily and more quickly when it has agreed with itself to do one thing at a time.

• *Condense the time it takes to do each task.* Once you have created compartments and increased your concentration, try to speed up your work on each task. For example, if you took twenty minutes to dictate a five-page document, try taking fifteen minutes to do the same task the next time. Try to decrease the quantity of time without jeopardizing the quality. Concentrate on condensing, and time yourself.

• *Say "no."* This is hard, whether you are speaking to clients, supervisors, or supervisees. But do it. Plan ahead, so that you are not forced to refuse, but rather can kindly refuse because you know your professional limits. You know when you are taking on too much. You can refuse gently (*I would love to, but I don't think I can do a good job. . .*), firmly (*I cannot do that for you. I'm sorry.*), or you can flat ter *(Of all the people I love to work with, you are the one I enjoy most. But I cannot do it for you at this time. Please ask again.).* If you know that your refusal will get you into trouble, try asking them to use you as a back-up *("This is very inconvenient for me right now. Can you find someone else? If not, then get back to me.)* or give a long-term no *(I will do this last project for you, but I cannot be called upon with such short notice in the future.)* Find ways that work best with your personality and that of your associates. To take on too much is to do mediocre work that will damage your reputation for quality lawyering; to say "no" when appropriate keeps the quality of your work high and may win you respect.

• *"Percolate," rather than procrastinate.* Resolve to start each project immediately. But take only one step at a time. Gather the facts and sketch some issues; then turn to another project and allow yourself to percolate on the direction you will take on the first case. Research just one issue at a time; stop; let that sink in while you read the mail. Rather than simply put a project at the bottom of the pile, make some notes, sketch some thoughts, and allow those to percolate. Percolating is not only necessary, but also often better than doing the project all at once.

• *Use the calendar and the clock.* Keep your eye on both at all times. Know the major deadlines and pace yourself. Watch the clock and be aware of how long you take to do any task. Without becoming a slave to the clock, use it as a helpful friend who reminds you when the mind is wandering unnecessarily, when a meeting is going on too long, or when you are tempted to come in on the weekend. Things do take longer than we think, so use the calendar and the clock to define exactly how long they do take.

• *Choreograph your day.* Whatever your strengths are, program the least amount of time for them. You like those tasks, they come easily, so you are likely to do them faster. Conversely, save your high energy times for the tasks you like the least. Rather than doing what you like when you feel best, try doing what you like least then. You will do it faster. And when your energy wanes, answer calls, hold meetings, schedule activities that will keep you awake.

CHECKLIST FOR CREATING YOUR OWN SYSTEM

To refine your system, select those tasks or traits from the following list that appeal to you in making your personal time management system work effectively. Having identified certain items on the list, decide in what order you would like to implement them.

Long-Range Planning

___ 1. Review personal life goals, balancing professional, personal, financial, physical, social, spiritual, intellectual, and cultural goals.

___ 2. Review the goals of the law office and the department.

___ 3. Write down, refine, and order personal and professional goals by a certain date.

___ 4. Plan long-range goals into the future as far as is comfortable.

___ 5. Refine goals by making them concrete and measurable.

___ 6. Check periodically to make sure goals are balanced.

Daily Planning

___ 7. Create a system that highlights important tasks for each day.

___ 8. Keep information in one source.

___ 9. Communicate effectively with secretary and associates in keeping an up-to-date calendar.

___ 10. Try to accomplish something each day that stretches skills, attitudes: relax into the stretch.

___ 11. Connect daily goals to long-range goals.

___ 12. Avoid the pull of bad habits by recording those ideas, attitudes, people, actions, readings, activities that drain energy or unnecessarily lengthen time spent.

___ 13. Factor in energy levels in "choreographing" the day.

___ 14. Factor in energy levels with others working on the same project.

___ 15. Allow for breathing room in the day's schedule.

___ 16. Make appointments with a project.

___ 17. Compartmentalize activities, doing "bunches" of similar tasks at the same time.

___ 18. Concentrate 100% on one task at a time.

Delegating

___ 19. Be active rather than passive in solving problems.

___ 20. Encourage others to create solutions to problems before they are discussed in a group.

___ 21. Encourage brainstorming at the creative end of a problem.

___ 22. Clarify issues as early as possible.

___ 23. Give clear, written directions.

___ 24. Set up short sessions for clarifying issues, dimensions of the project.

___ 25. Give specific feedback at crucial stages of a project to avoid undirected research or writing on tangential issues.

___ 26. Build skills from one project to the next by giving feedback that focuses on patterns, overall work habits, development of analytical, research, and writing skills.

___ 27. Ask for useful criticism.

___ 28. Allow time for effective feedback throughout the project.

___ 29. Be proactive by learning colleagues' strengths and weaknesses, not reactive.

___ 30. Set an example of efficiency, high productivity, balance.

___ 31. Give away tasks that others can do.

___ 32. Mentally let go of tasks others are doing now.

__ 33. Eliminate tasks that are unnecessary.

__ 34. Reduce the time that is imposed on you by others by thinking through all the tasks a project requires and assigning those tasks efficiently.

__ 35. Gently, but firmly, monitor a project's time line.

Working With Others

__ 36. Plan projects by creating together a generous time line.

__ 37. Ask others for their suggestions on how the project should be shaped.

__ 38. Together create specific goals for the project.

__ 39. Together create specific goals for analytical, research, writing, time-management development.

__ 40. Create feedback times that concentrate on overall development and are pressure-free, removed from any specific project.

__ 41. Look for patterns in development that promote effective work habits.

__ 42. Give specific, positive feedback when tasks are done well.

__ 43. Anticipate problems and use examples from past history to teach others to avoid making similar mistakes.

__ 44. Create a manual for your department that outlines procedures, forms, feedback guidelines, goals.

__ 45. Create a book of "good examples" of work product from your department.

__ 46. Ask others for suggestions on improving manuals, examples.

__ 47. Cut meeting times in half by preparing a careful agenda.

__ 48. Start and end on time.

__ 49. Listen carefully for contributions from others.

__ 50. Ask others to prepare portions of the meeting and call to ask if there are any questions before the meeting begins.

__ 51. Prepare solutions to items on the agenda and suggest them to the supervising attorney well before the meeting.

__ 52. Factor in the schedules of all those involved in a project, including the secretary.

__ 53. Periodically ask for suggestions on how to supervise a project more effectively.

__ 54. Say "no" when it is appropriate.

Organizing

__ 55. Analyze the best way to use technology to organize.

__ 56. Create together a system for your department.

__ 57. Decide on a system for your office.

__ 58. Decide on a system for each project.

__ 59. Handle papers only once.

__ 60. File -- or have filed-- papers immediately.

__ 61. Keep the desk clean; have on it only the project being worked on now.

__ 62. Keep the office as clean as possible; file papers when they are not in use.

__ 63. Ask secretary, associates for ideas on organizing.

__ 64. Delegate organization of files, correspondence.

__ 65. Have secretary open mail and separate into files or piles: personal, correspondence, documents, and so on.

__ 66. Dictate responses as you read when possible, including directions to secretary on where and when to file.

Avoiding Procrastination

__ 67. Do the most difficult task first.

__ 68. Set a deadline for each project.

___ 69. Set a deadline for each task.

___ 70. Use the task to improve performance and development.

___ 71. Plan tasks according to energy levels.

___ 72. Contract for no interruptions during crucial times.

___ 73. Ask secretary's help in enforcing no interruptions and no returns to bad habits.

___ 74. Recognize bad habits tampering with time: kill them.

___ 75. Work against the clock.

___ 76. Take breaks as rewards.

___ 77. Break large tasks into smaller ones.

___ 78. Use vacations, off-times as rewards.

___ 79. Don't get it right -- get it written.

___ 80. Get it right in shorter, focused, critical sessions.

___ 81. Honor a daily action list.

Creating Energy

___ 82. Concentrate deeply on tasks and balance periods of intensity with release.

___ 83. Be calmly active, actively calm.

___ 84. Be on time for meetings, appointment, deadlines.

___ 85. Release bad habits.

___ 86. Have paper and pencil handy to record thoughts.

___ 87. Dictate more, using speaking abilities to enhance reading and writing abilities.

___ 88. Read and write faster and better.

___ 89. Set up a physical fitness program.

___ 90. Balance mental activity with physical, spiritual, emotional activity.

__   91. Enjoy humor where appropriate.

__   92. Write longhand less and less.

__   93. Talk less and say more.

__   94. Assign work appropriately to others, including clients.

__   95. Handle phone calls all at once if possible.

__   96. Reduce drop-in traffic, setting up shorter appointments.

__   97. Focus attention 100% on people present.

__   98. Talk about non-law subjects occasionally at work.

__   99. Expect the unexpected.

__   100. _____.

Begin implementing your system in a small way so as not to upset either your own or your associates' balance. You might start with one major project and try a new technique, not worrying about other projects. At the end of that project, assess how the technique worked, and try again. Then try the technique on two projects at once, and so on. Fold your new techniques into your schedule gradually, giving yourself a year or three to transform yourself into a good time manager.

The system you adopt can simply become a string of good habits that crowds out the bad. Make a list on the next page of the good habits on which you want to build your own system. Tailor this to your energy level and to your practice. You might decide to delegate more tasks to your secretary, realizing that at the outset there might be some intensive training involved, but that that investment will ultimately free up more of your time. You might try bunching together similar tasks, and compartmentalizing your correspondence for the day by dictating letters. Or you might consider implementing more and more technology into your practice, learning and using increasingly sophisticated software to speed up in-house memos and proofing and cite-checking. Having made the list, number the approaches in the order in which you would like to implement them.

DOING FIRST THINGS FIRST

Having an overall approach sets up and concentrates smaller tasks. With the time line in mind for a large project, and with an approach defined that reflects your strengths, energy levels, standards, and techniques, you can make small-scale tasks easier and faster to handle.

Break the project into smaller and smaller pieces. Then parcel out time for those pieces, and handle each piece with a specific technique. For example, you might have to meet with the partners on the project, do some research, answer the client's phone calls, organize complex documents, delegate some other issues for research, and create a unique strategy for solving the client's problem. Designate time, as precisely as is practical, for each task.

Then make the most of that time. For example, if you must organize complex documents, you might choose to delegate that. But rather than just telling a clerk to do the work, you might set aside ten minutes to explain the task, outline what results you want, define the purpose, and even choose the materials you want used, such as looseleafs notebooks. Ask for questions. Set up a date for the result, and then let go of the task.

If it is a project you must do yourself, such as the research on a complex tax question, define the issue precisely. Outline a research strategy that covers three or four sources and decide the order in which you are going to read them. Decide how you are going to take notes. Use this strategy to allow you to resume work more easily after the inevitable interruption. Interrupted, you know exactly where you were in your research, and can return. Feeling tired, you can interrupt yourself with the same efficient start-up when you return.

Make appointments with the project, letting it say "no" for you when you know the task must be done in order to do it with quality. You are not saying "no" to someone, but rather your project is letting you know that it needs your time in order to be of high quality. Make sure you let others requesting your time know this: "The time you are asking me to give to this new project will diminish the quality of the one I am working on." Better yet, find ways to speed up your work without compromising quality.

Make sure these strong, but gentle messages sent to others are matched by even stronger messages to yourself. When you feel yourself starting to procrastinate, analyze the reason: energy level? nature of the task? audience? perfectionism? Then break down the procrastination into a task that incorporates the reason. For example, if you are procrastinating because it is late in the day and your are tired, make a deal with yourself to do only the first few minutes, take a break to work on another project, and then come back for a few more minutes. If perfectionism is hounding you, tell yourself that you will get it done perfectly - but step by step. Be clear with others and with yourself about the nature of the task and its importance in relation to your other work.

EXPECT THE UNEXPECTED

Despite the best efforts to organize offices, desks, teams, and selves, disasters do occur. Part of managing time in law practice involves handling all those matters that can be handled now -- now. Anticipating problems should avoid many disasters, but creating a system to handle daily affairs will avoid catastrophes.

Practice law as a good tennis player plays: on the soles of your feet. Whatever the serve, you are ready. Part of this readiness comes from practice, that is, using daily tasks to become better and faster at performing them. Another part of the readiness comes with enjoying the challenge of the unexpected.

Being organized, careful about deadlines, attentive to necessary details, concerned about others, and willing to stretch and improve-- allows time for unanticipated problems. Being proactive avoids being reactive. Managing your time helps others manage theirs, and gives you enough time to anticipate and handle their problems.

Whatever system you create, make sure that it is tailored to you, that it allows for steady development throughout your career, and that it is responsive to your personal and professional goals. Enjoy so-called disasters as a challenge to your system or as proof that your system is working. Enjoy "losing control" as a way of delegating: trusting and teaching others. Enjoy taking control of your own system and of more and more responsibility as you become a creative problem-solver.

Practicing law brings surprises and disasters. But some disasters, some "busy"-ness, are direct results of poor time management. Because you know that the unexpected will occur, take care of the expected. Clear your desk of all the mundane and petty tasks, keep your phone conversations short and business-like, and use the clock to keep production high. Then, you will be poised in emergencies, clear-headed when others are confused, and ready when a last-minute change occurs. You can expect the unexpected. Your job will be more satisfying, more productive - and more enjoyable.

PHOTO CREDITS

COVER

Monona Terrace®
Skyline of Madison,
Wisconsin

Courtesy of the City of Madison.

Monona Terrace Community and Convention Center is located on the shore of Lake Monona in Madison, Wisconsin. Designed by Frank Lloyd Wright in the 1950s, bestowed on Madison as a gift, and finally built in the 1990's, Monona Terrace is a working piece of art. It hosts a wide array of groups, including conventions, meetings, banquets and community groups. Monona Terrace also hosts free educational and cultural programming for the community and is open to the public daily for educational tours of the facility.

INTRODUCTION

Pyramide du Louvre

Architect: Ieoh Ming Pei.
Photo by the author.

CHAPTER 1

Page 1: *Pyramids at East Wing, National Gallery*

Architect: I. M. Pei.
Photo by the author.

Page 3: *Imperial Hotel*

Courtesy of the Meitsu Museum.

Page 3: *Tent at Lake*

Photo by Alexis Martin Neely.

Page 6: *Architectural Drawings*

Gallery MA Project / Copyright 1996, Neil M. Denari, Architect/ Director: Southern California Institute of Architecture.

Page 14: *Palais du Luxembourg*

Photo by the author.

Page 21: *Pentagon*

Courtesy of Pentagon Press Office. Photo by Master Sgt. Ken Hammond, United States Air Force.

Page 22:   *Independence Hall*   Photo by Kirstin Miller.

Page 23:   *Bottling Co. Building*   Library of Congress, Prints and
                                            Photographs Division, Historic
                                            American Buldings Survey or
                                            Historic American Engineering
                                            Record, Reproduction Number
                                            HABS Cal 19 - Losan 31-1.

Page 23:   *Federalist Hospital*   Library of Congress, Prints
                                            and Photographs Division,
                                            Historic American Bulding
                                            Survey or Historic American
                                            Engineering Record
                                            Reproduction Number
                                            HABS Ark 26 - Hosp 1C-5. B-5.

Page 25:   *Ancient Theater*   Photo by Kirstin Miller.

Page 25:   *Modern Theater*   Library of Congress, Prints and
                                            Photographs Division, Historic
                                            American Buldings Survey or
                                            Historic American Engineering
                                            Record, Reproduction Number
                                            HABS No. PA 2- Pitbu 28-5.

Page 27:   *Cabin*   Library of Congress, Prints and
                                            Photographs Division, Historic
                                            American Buldings Survey or
                                            Historic American Engineering
                                            Record, Reproduction Number
                                            HABS 10-8 IDC1 V. 2A-1.

Page 27:   *Smithsonian Castle*   Library of Congress, Prints and
                                            Photographs Division, Historic
                                            American Buldings Survey or
                                            Historic American Engineering
                                            Record, Reproduction Number
                                            HABS DC Wash. 520B-3.

Page 28:   *William H. Winslow House,*   The Frank Lloyd Wright
            1898, River Forest, Illinois Home and Studio Foundation.

Page 28:   *La Valencia Hotel*   Photo courtesy of the hotel.
            La Jolla, California.

Page 30:	*Hardware*	Photo by the author.
Page 31:	*Materials*	Photo by the author.
Page 31:	*Doorknobs*	Library of Congress, Prints and Photographs Division, Historic American Buldings Survey or Historic American Engineering Record, Reproduction Number HABS NY 31- NEYO. 120-32.
Page 33:	*Sagrada Familia*	Photo by Corner/Young from www.Greatbuildings.com.
Page 33:	*Sidney Opera House*	Photo by Corner/Young from www.Greatbuildings.com.
Page 33:	*Solomon R. Guggenheim Museum*	Photograph by David Heald © The Solomon R. Guggenheim Foundation. New York.
Page 35:	*Jefferson Memorial*	Library of Congress, Prints and Photographs Division, Historic American Buldings Survey or Historic American Engineering Record, Reproduction Number HABS DC Wash 453-7.
Page 36:	*Architectural drawing*	Courtesy of Howard Sharlach.
Page 37:	*Blueprint*	Library of Congress, Prints and Photographs Division, Historic American Buldings Survey or Historic American Engineering Record, Reproduction Number 762-119163.
Page 38:	*Sketches of homes*	Public domain.
Page 40:	*Tibetan Home Interior*	Photo by the author.
Page 40:	*Interior, Governor's Mansion, Madison Wisconsin*	Photo by Judy Mahr

CHAPTER 2

Page 86:   *Ghiberti Door, Florence*   Photo by the author.

Page 87:   *Rough Roof Scaffolding*   Photo by Rob Lorey.

Page 87:   *Materials*   Library of Congress, Prints
                                          and Photographs Division,
                                          Historic American Buildings
                                          Survey or Historic American
                                          Engineering Record,
                                          Reproduction Number
                                          HABS NY 31-NEYO 76-40.

Page 88:   *Cabin in New Hampshire*   Photo by Elisabeth Ritter.

Page 90:   *Rustic House*   Photo by Rob Lorey.

Page 91:   *Patio Bullrich, Buenos Aires* Photo by the author.

Page 92:   *Detail of B'hai Temple,*   Photo by the author.
           Delhi, India

Page 93:   *Largo do Boticaro,*   Photo by the author.
           Rio de Janeiro

Page 93:   *Office Building*   Photo by the author.

Page 94:   *B'hai Temple, Delhi, India*   Photo by the author.

Page 97:   *Office Building,*   Photo by the author.
           Buenos Aires

Page 99:   *Turreted House*   Library of Congress, Prints
                                          and Photographs Division,
                                          Historic American Buldings
                                          Survey or Historic American
                                          Engineering Record,
                                          Reproduction Number
                                          HABS PA 51-Phila 615-2.

Page 100: *Brick House*   Photo by the author.

Page 101: *View from the Thames*   Photo by the author.

Page 103: *Architectural Sketch*   Public domain.

Page 108: *Blueprint of Lounsbury*   Library of Congress, Prints
                                          and Photographs Division,

Historic American
Engineering Record,
Reproduction Number
710860 262-119171.

Page 109: *Interior,*
Governor's Mansion,
Madison, Wisconsin

Photo by Judy Mahr.

Page 111: *Cabin Living Room*

Library of Congress, Prints
and Photographs Division,
Historic American Buldings
Survey or Historic American
Engineering Record,
Reproduction Number
HABS CONN 5-New Ha B-4.

Page 112: *Modern Interior*

Photo by Judy Mahr.

Page 117: *Man Finishing Entrance*

Photo by the author.

Page 119: *Barn*

Courtesy of Vermont.com.
Photo by George Kalinsky.

Page 127: *Interior with Reflection*

Photo by Judy Mahr.

CHAPTER 3

Page 129: *French Country Home*

Public domain.

Page 130: *Bank of China*

Photography: Pei Cobb Freed/
John Nye.

Page 130: *Chartres Cathedral*

Photo by the author.

Page 132: *Roman Ruins*

Photo by the author.

Page 133: *Greek Ruins*

Photo by Kirstin Miller.

Page 138: *Parts of Supreme Court*

Library of Congress, Prints and
Photographs Division, Historic
American Buldings Survey or
Historic American Engineering
Record, Reproduction Number
HABS DC Wash 535-2.

Page 139: *Paris Doorway*   Photo by Judy Mahr.

Page 139: *Tibetan Doorway*   Photo by the author.

Page 140: *Paris Doorway*   Photo by Judy Mahr.

Page 140: *Hawaiian Church*   Photo by the author.

Page 142: *View from Eiffel Tower*   Photo by the author.

Page 143: *Building Foundation*   Photo by the author.

Page 144: *Ranch House*   Photo by the author.

Page 144: *Town House*   Photo by the author.

Page 145: *Construction Site*   Photo by the author.

Page 149: *Chapel*   Photo by the author.

Page 150: *Tudor House*   Photo by Dr. David P.
                                              Harris.

Page 151: *Swedish Cathedral*   Photo by Kristin and
           Kalmar, Sweden   Grant Miekle.

Page 152: *Row of Trees*   Photo by the author.

Page 159: *4 Marilyns*   © 2000 Andy Warhol
                                              Foundation for the Visual
                                              Arts/ ARS, New York.

Page 165: *Spa at Rhodes*   Photo by Kirstin Miller.

Page 171: *Lyon's Gate at Mycenae*   Photo by Kirstin Miller.

Page 172: *Classical Temple*   Photo by Kirstin Miller.

Page 179: *Isaac Bell Home and*   Illustration by Wolcott Etienne
           Carson Pirie Scott   in CLUES TO AMERICAN
           Department Store   ARCHITECTURE, Starrhill Press
                                              (an imprint of Black Belt
                                              Publishing, LLC).

Page 181: *Brazilian Embassy*   Photo by the author.

Page 185: *Doorway to Argentine*   Photo by the author.
           Cathedral.

CHAPTER 4

Page 187: *House Graphic*	Library of Congress, Prints and Photographs Division, Historic American Buldings Survey or Historic American Engineering Record, Reproduction Number 710860 262-119173.
Page 188: *Country home*	Public domain.
Page 189: *Minaret*	Photo by Kirstin Miller.
Page 190: *House in Disrepair*	Photo by the author.
Page 191: *Kalorama Home*	Photo by the author.
Page 192: *Floor Plan*	Library of Congress, Prints and Photographs Division, Historic American Buldings Survey or Historic American Engineering Record, Reproduction Number 712860 Z62-119161.
Page 193: *Eiffel Tower*	Photo by the author.
Page 194: *Doorway*	Photo by Rob Lorey.
Page 194: *Entrance*	Photo by the author.
Page 195: *Large Doorway*	Photo by the author.
Page 201: *House Front*	Library of Congress, Prints and Photographs Division, Historic American Buldings Survey or Historic American Engineering Record, Reproduction Number HABS Mass 10 Nant 72-2.
Page 201: *Notre Dame de Paris*	Photo by the author.
Page 203: *Gateway*	Photo by the author.
Page 203: *Gateway*	Photo by Rob Lorey.
Page 204: *Rotunda Entrance*	Photo by the author.

Page 207: *Hut*   Photo by Rob Lorey.

Page 208: *Panthe'on, Paris*   Photo by the author.

Page 210: *Cartoon*

Page 220: *Stairway to Nowhere*   Photo by Kirstin Miller.

Page 229-32: *Housing Sketches*   Library of Congress, Prints and
Photographs Division, Historic
American Buldings Survey or
Historic American Engineering
Record, Reproduction Number
710860 Z62-19173 as rendered
by Elisabeth Ritter.

Page 233: *Temple at Agrigento*   Photo by the author.

Page 235: *Pyramid*   Photo by the author.

Page 238: *Pyramide du Louvre*   Architect : Ieoh Ming Pei.
Photo by the author.

Page 246: *Sphinx, Giza, Egypt*   Photo by the author.

Page 247: *Parthenon*   Photo by the author.

Page 249: *Classical Entrance*   Library of Congress, Prints and
Photographs Division, Historic
American Buldings Survey or
Historic American Engineering
Record, Reproduction Number
HABS NY 60-RY 1-2.

Page 256: *Deteriorating Building*   Library of Congress, Prints and
Photographs Division, Historic
American Buldings Survey or
Historic American Engineering
Record, Reproduction Number
HABS NY 31-NE40 76-26.

Page 261: *Ruins*   Photo by Kirstin Miller.

Page 266: *House on Stilts*   Photo by Rob Lorey.

Page 274: *Apartment Buildings*   Photo by the author.

Page 276-77: *Atheneum, New*   Illustrations by Wolcott Etienne
            Harmony, Indiana;   in CLUES TO AMERICAN
            Dulles Airport;   ARCHITECTURE, Starrhill Press
            Robie House   (an imprint of Black Belt
                                         Publishing, LLC).

CHAPTER 5:

Page 279: *Supreme Court*   Library of Congress, Prints and
                                        Photographs Division, Historic
                                        American Buldings Survey or
                                        Historic American Engineering
                                        Record, Reproduction Number
                                        HABS DC Wash 535-1.

Page 280: *East Wing, National*   Architect: I.M.Pei.
          Gallery of Art   Photos by the author.

Page 281: *East Wing Interior,*   Architect: I.M.Pei.
          National Gallery   Photo by the author.

Page 282: *Architectural Rendering*   Public domain.

Page 283: *Gothic Cathedral*   Library of Congress, Prints and
                                        Photographs Division, Historic
                                        American Buldings Survey or
                                        Historic American Engineering
                                        Record, Reproduction Number
                                        HABS Conn 5-New HA 6B6.

Page 283: *Home with Tower*   Library of Congress, Prints and
                                        Photographs Division, Historic
                                        American Buldings Survey or
                                        Historic American Engineering
                                        Record, Reproduction Number
                                        HABS Cal 43-Cup 4-6.

Page 283: *Apartment Buildings*   Library of Congress, Prints and
                                        Photographs Division, Historic
                                        American Buldings Survey or
                                        Historic American Engineering
                                        Record, Reproduction Number
                                        HABS NY 31- NEYO 55-1.

Page 293: *Monona Terrace®*
Madison, Wisconsin

Courtesy of the City of Madison.
Photo by the author.

Page 294: *Skyscraper*

Library of Congress, Prints and
Photographs Division, Historic
American Buldings Survey or
Historic American Engineering
Record, Reproduction Number
HABS NY 31-NEYO-157-1.

Page 294: *House on Hill*

Library of Congress, Prints
and Photographs Division,
Historic American Buldings
Survey or Historic American
Engineering Record,
Reproduction Number
HABS Mass 10-Nant 4-1.

Page 298: *Small house*

Public domain.

Page 299: *La Madeleine*

Photo by the author.

Page 304: *United States Capitol*

Photo by the author.

Page 308: *National Archives*

Photo by author.

Page 325: *Icelandic Church*

Photo by Beau Kaplan.

Page 326: *Roman Ruins in Sicily*

Photo by author.

Page 327: *Monona Terrace®*
Madison, Wisconsin

Courtesy of the City of Madison.
Photo by author.

Page 331: *Northwestern Law School*

Photo by Elisabeth Ritter.

Page 331: *Modern Building*

Photo by author.

Page 360: *Apartment*

Photo by Howard Sharlach.

Page 362: *Detroit Airport Terminal*

Photo by Elisabeth Ritter.

Page 365: *Iolani Palace,*
Honolulu, Hawaii

© 1993 Friends of Iolani
Palace.

Page 367: *Detroit Airport*

Photo by Elisabeth Ritter.

Page 389: *Hallway*   Library of Congress, Prints and
                                       Photographs Division, Historic
                                       American Buldings Survey or
                                       Historic American Engineering
                                       Record, Reproduction Number
                                       HABS DC Wash 520B-13.

Page 393: *Shape Drawing*   JMI & Associates, Inc.

Page 395: *Hotel Interior*   Photo by the author.

Page 396: *Interior, Buzios, Brazil*   Photo by the author.

Page 397: *Interior,*   Photo by Judy Mahr.
           Governor's Mansion
           Madison, Wisconsin

Page 399: *Round Room*   Library of Congress, Prints and
                                       Photographs Division, Historic
                                       American Buldings Survey or
                                       Historic American Engineering
                                       Record, Reproduction Number
                                       HABS,ILL,ChiG 40-4.

Page 401: *Living Room*   Photo by the author.

Page 402: *Tiffany Hotel*   Photo by Todd Eberle.

Page 403: *Colorful interior drawing* JMI & Associates, Inc.

Page 404: *Detail of Rug,*   Courtesy of the City of Madison.
           Monona Terrace®   Photo by the author.
           Madison, Wisconsin

Page 404: *Café Interior*   Photo by the author.

Page 405: *Rhythm Interior drawing*   JMI & Associates, Inc.

Page 406: *Rhythmic Interior*   Photo by Eric Roth, Interior
                                       Design by C & J Katz Studio,
                                       Boston, Massachusetts.

Page 407: *Sinks*   Photo by the author.

Page 408: *Chairs and lamp*   Photo by the author.

Page 409: *Governor's Mansion, Madison, Wisconsin* Photo by Judy Mahr.

Page 410: *Lighted Hallway* Photo by Judy Mahr.

Page 411: *Interior* Library of Congress, Prints and Photographs Division, Historic American Buldings Survey or Historic American Engineering Record, Reproduction Number HABS Wis 51-RACI 5-7.

Page 411: *Round Room* Library of Congress, Prints and Photographs Division, Historic American Buldings Survey or Historic American Engineering Record, Reproduction Number HABS Ill 16-ChiG 40-4.

Page 411: *Kitchen* Library of Congress, Prints and Photographs Division, Historic American Buldings Survey or Historic American Engineering Record, Reproduction Number HABS NY 31-NEYO 118A-7.

Page 416: *Fireplace room* Library of Congress, Prints and Photographs Division, Historic American Buldings Survey or Historic American Engineering Record, Reproduction Number HABS Conn 1-Fair F 1-5.

Page 416: *Traditional Interior Naval Chapel* Photo by the author.

Page 419: *Interior of Restaurant* Photo by Judy Mahr.

Page 421: *Frank Lloyd Wright's Home and Studio, 1895, Oak Park Illinois:Interior, dining room* The Frank Lloyd Wright Home and Studio Foundation.

Page 422: *Weisman Art Museum*
at the University of
Minnesota

Architect: Frank O. Gehry.
Photo by Don F. Wong.

Page 422: *Interior,*
Pyramide du Louvre

Architect: Ieoh Ming Pei.
Photo by the author.

Page 425: *Unity Temple*
1905, Oak Park, Illinois

The Frank Lloyd Wright
Home and Studio Foundation.

Page 427: *Glass Storefront*

Photo by Judy Mahr.

Page 431: *Keyhole Room*

Photo by Tim Street Porter.

Page 433: *Stairs*

Photo by the author.

Page 434: *Interior,*
Governor's Mansion,
Madison, Wisconsin

Photo by Judy Mahr.

Page 436: *Interior,*
Governor's Mansion,
Madison, Wisconsin

Photo by Judy Mahr.

Page 437: *Chairs in Windows*

Photo by the author.

Page 438: *Comfortable Den*

Photo by Tim Street Porter.

Page 439: *Restaurant Interior*

Photo by Judy Mahr.

Page 440: *Unusual chair*

Photo by the author.

Page 442: *Living Room with Stairs*

Photo by Tom Bonner.

Page 444: *Parallel Structure*

Photo by the author.

Page 445: *Beachfront*

© Steven Brooke Studios.

Page 448: *Medieval Interior*

Photo by the author.

Page 448: *Fallingwater*

Photograph of Fallingwater
courtesy of the Western
Pennsylvania Conservancy.

Page 459: *Beach view*   © Steven Brooke Studios.

Page 460: *Cluttered Floor Plan*   JMI & Associates, Inc.

Page 460: *Uncluttered Floor Plan*   JMI & Associates, Inc.

Page 464: *Dining Room*   Photo by the author.

Page 465: *Comfortable Bedroom*   Photo by Elisabeth Ritter.

Page 465: *Boston Federal Courthouse*   Architects: Pei, Cobb Freed & Partners Architects LLP. Photo © Steve Rosenthal.

CHAPTER 7:

Page 467: *Pyramide du Louvre*   Architect : Ieoh Ming Pei. Photo by the author.

Page 468: *Pyramid Cleaning*   Photo by Nicholas Pioch.

Page 469: *Portico, Arlington National Cemetary*   Photo by the author.

Page 470: *Pyramide du Louvre*   Architect : Ieoh Ming Pei. Photo by the author.

Page 472: *Poorly apportioned house*   Library of Congress, Prints and Photographs Division, Historic American Buldings Survey or Historic American Engineering Record, Reproduction Number HABS NY 1-DUNV. 1-2.

Page 473: *Kalorama Home*   Photo by the author.

Page 474: *Steeple*   Library of Congress, Prints and Photographs Division, Historic American Buldings Survey or Historic American Engineering Record, Reproduction Number HABS GA 123 AUG. 17-1.

Page 477: *Sticks House*   Photo by the author.

Page 478: *House in Uruguay*   Photo by Howard Sharlach.

Page 479: *Bruges, Belgium*   Photo by Kirstin Miller.

Page 480: *Mosque*   Photo by Howard Sharlach.

Page 481: *Neo-Tudor House*   Photo by the author.

Page 482: *Hotel in Uruguay*   Photo by Howard Sharlach.

Page 483: *Milan Galleria*   Courtesy of Elisabeth Ritter.

Page 484: *Passageway*   Photo by the author.

BIBLIOGRAPHY

1.   LOUIS A. ARENA, LINGUISTICS AND COMPOSITION: A METHOD TO IMPROVE EXPOSITORY WRITING SKILLS (1975).

2.   ARISTOTLE, THE COMPLETE WORKS OF ARISTOTLE: THE REVISED OXFORD TRANSLATION (1984).

3.   Kathleen M. Bailey, *An Introspective Analysis of an Individual's Language Learning Experience, in* ISSUES IN SECOND LANGUAGE ACQUISITION: SELECTED PAPERS OF THE LOS ANGELES SECOND LANGUAGE RESEARCH FORUM 58 (S. Krashen & R. Scarella, eds. 1981).

4.   V.K. Bhatia, *Language of the Law*, 20 LANGUAGE TEACHING 227 (1987).

5.   Patricia Bizzell, *Cognition, Convention, and Certainty: What We Need to Know About Writing*, 3 PRE/TEXT 213-41 (1982).

6.   JAMES BRITTON ET AL., THE DEVELOPMENT OF WRITING ABILITIES 11-18 (1975).

7.   H. DOUGLAS BROWN, PRINCIPLES OF LANGUAGE LEARNING AND TEACHING 154 (2d ed. 1987).

8.   SCOTT J. BURNHAM, DRAFTING CONTRACTS 272 (1993).

9.   Patricia L. Carrell & Joan C. Eisterhold, *Schema Theory and International Reading Pedagogy, in Methodology in* TESOL: A BOOK OF READINGS 220 (Michael H. Long & Jack C. Richards eds., 1987).

10. Robert Chaim, *A Model for the Analysis of the Language of Lawyers*, 33 J. LEGAL EDUC. 120 (1993).

11. Craig Chaudron, *Language Research on Metalinguistic Judgments: A Review of Theory, Methods, Results*, 33 LANGUAGE LEARNING 343 (1983).

12.   RICHARD M. COE, TOWARD A GRAMMAR OF PASSAGES (1988).

13.   MORRIS L. COHEN ET AL., HOW TO FIND THE LAW (9th ed. 1989).

14.   THOMAS COOLEY, THE NORTON GUIDE TO WRITING (1992).

15.   EDWARD P.J. CORBETT, CLASSICAL RHETORIC FOR THE MODERN STUDENT (3D. ED. 1990).

16.   Brenda Danet, *Language in the Legal Process*, 14 L. & SOC'Y REV. 444 (1980).

17.   JOHN C. DERNBACH, RICHARD V. SINGLETON II, CATHLEEN S. WHARTON, JOAN M. RUHTENBERG, A PRACTICAL GUIDE TO LEGAL WRITING AND LEGAL METHOD (2d ed. 1994).

18.   PETER ELBOW, WRITING WITHOUT TEACHERS (1973).

19.   LINDA HOLDEMAN EDWARDS, LEGAL WRITING: PROCESS, ANALYSIS, AND ORGANIZATION (1996).

20.   Christopher Ely, *An Analysis and Writing Pedagogies*, 25 TESOL Q. 123 (1991).

21.   ENGLISH FOR SPECIFIC PURPOSES (Ronald Mackay & Aland Mountford, eds., 1978).

22.   EPISODES IN ESP (John Swales, ed., 1985)).

23.   William N. Eskridge, Jr., *Dynamic Statutory Interpretation*, 135 U. PA. L. REV. 1479 (1987).

24.   William N. Eskridge, Jr. & Philip P. Frickey, *Legislation Scholarship and Pedagogy in the Post-legal Process Era: Statutory and Constitutional Interpretation*, 48 U. PITT. L. REV. 691 (1987).

25.   William N. Eskridge, Jr. & Philip P. Frickey, *Statutory Interpretation as Practical Reasoning*, 42 STAN. L. REV. 321 (1990).

26.   LESTER FAIGLEY, NONACADEMIC WRITING: THE SOCIAL PERSPECTIVE IN WRITING IN NONACADEMIC SETTINGS 231 (Lee Odell & Dixie Goswamie eds., 1985).

27.   ELIZABETH FAJANS, MARY J. FALK, SCHOLARLY WRITING FOR LAW STUDENTS (1995).

28.   Daniel A. Farber & Suzanna Sherry, *Telling Stories Out of School: An Essay on Legal Narratives*, 45 STAN. L. REV. 807 (1993).

29.   STANLEY FISH, IS THERE A TEXT IN THIS CLASS? (1980).

30.   Felix Frankfurter, *Some Reflections on the Reading of Statutes*, 47 COLUM. L. REV. 527 (1947).

31.   Susan Gass, *From Theory to Practice, in* ON TESOL '81 (M. Hines & W. Rutherford eds., 1982).

32.   John Gibbons, *The Silent Period: An Examination*, 35 LANGUAGE LEARNING 255 (1985).

33.   Lynn M. Goldstein & Susan M. Conrad, *Student Input and Negotiation of Meaning in international Writing Conferences*, 24 TESOL Q. 443 (1990).

34.   Peter Goodrich, *The Role of Linguistics in Legal Analysis*, 47 MODERN L. REV. 523, 530-531 (1984).

35.   Angela P. Harris, *Foreward: The Jurisprudence of Reconstruction*, 82 CALIF. L. REV. 741 (1994).

36.   SHIRLEY BRICE HEATH, WAYS WITH WORDS: LANGUAGE, LIFE, AND WORK IN COMMUNITIES AND CLASSROOMS (1983).

37.   HOLLIS T. HURD, WRITING FOR LAWYERS (1982).

38.   TOM HUTCHINGSON & ALAN WATERS, ENGLISH FOR SPECIFIC PURPOSES (1987)

39.   Richard Hyland, *A Defense of Legal Writing*, 134 U. PA. L. REV. 599 (1986).

40. J. Myron Jacobstein et al., Fundamentals of Legal Research (7th ed. 1998).

41. Ann M. Johns, Coherence and Academic Writing: Some Definitions and Suggestions for Teaching, 20 TESOL Q. 247, 250 (1986).

42. Ann M. Johns, Written Argumentation for Real Audiences: Suggestions for Teacher Research & Classroom Practice, 27 TESOL Q. 75 (1993).

43. Alex M. Johnson, Jr., Defending the Use of Narrative and Giving Content to the Voice of Color: Rejecting the Imposition of Process Theory in Legal Scholarship, 79 Iowa L. Rev. 803 (1994).

44. Robert Kaplan, A Further Note on Contrastive Rhetoric, 24 Comm. Quart. 2 (1976).

45. Robert B. Kaplan, Cultural Thought Patterns in Inter-Cultural Education, 16 Language Learning 1 (1966).

46. Donald Knapp, A Focused, Efficient Method to Relate Composition Correction to Teaching Aims, in On Teaching English to Speakers of Other Languages (V.F. Allen ed., 1965).

47. Christina L. Kunz et al., The Process of Legal Research (4th ed. 1996).

48. Judith N. Levi & Anne Graffan Walker, Language in the Judicial Process 1-35 (1990).

49. JoAnne Liebman-Kleine, Toward a Contrastive New Rhetoric--A Rhetoric of Process (Mar. 1986), microformed on U.S. Dep't of Educ. OERI No. ED 271 963 (ERIC).

50. Molly Mack, Theoretical Linguistics and Applied Linguistics Research: Perspectives on Their Relationship to Language Pedagogy, 5 Ideal 65 (1990).

51. Bonnie J.F. Meyer, *Basic research on prose comprehension: A critical view, in* COMPREHENSION AND THE COMPETENT READER: INTER-SPECIALTY PERSPECTIVES (Dennis F. Fisher et al. eds., 1981).

52. Bonnie J.F. Meyer & G. Elizabeth Rice, T*he interaction of reader strategies and the organization of text*, 2 TEXT 155 (1982)).

53. Heikki Nyyssönen, *Lexis in Discourse, in Nordic Research on Text and Discourse* 73 (Ann-Charlotte Lindeberg et al. eds., 1992).

54. Teresa G. Phelps, *The New Legal Rhetoric*, 40 SW. L.J. 1089 (1986).

55. Elizabeth D. Rankin, *Revitalizing Style: Towards a New Theory and Pedagogy, in* THE WRITING TEACHER'S SOURCEBOOK 300 (Gary Tate, et al. eds., 3d ed. 1994)

56. MARY B. RAY & BARBARA J. COX, BEYOND THE BASICS (1991).

57. MARY B. RAY & JILL J. RAMSFIELD, LEGAL WRITING: GETTING IT RIGHT AND GETTING IT WRITTEN (3d. ed. 2000).

58. J. Christopher Rideout & Jill J. Ramsfield, *Legal Writing: A Revised View*, 69 WASH. L. REV. 35 (1994).

59. BETTY W. ROBINETT, TEACHING ENGLISH TO SPEAKERS OF OTHER LANGUAGES: SUBSTANCE AND TECHNIQUE 244 (1978).

60. ANTHONY J. SANFORD & SIMON C. GARROD, UNDERSTANDING WRITTEN LANGUAGE (1981).

61. DEBORAH SCHIFFRIN, DISCOURSE MARKERS (1987).

62. DONALD SCHON, THE REFLECTIVE PRACTITIONER: HOW PROFESSIONALS THINK IN ACTION (1983).

63. DAVID SKOVER & PIERRE SCHLAG, TACTICS OF LEGAL REASONING (1986).

64.   Nancy Sommers, *Responding to Student Writing*, 33 COLLEGE COMPOSITION & COMMUNICATION 148 (1982).

65.   WILLIAM STRUNK & E.B. WHITE, THE ELEMENT OF STYLE (3RD ED. 1979).

66.   GARY TATE, NANCY MYERS, EDWARD P.J. CORBETT, THE WRITING TEACHERS' SOURCEBOOK (4th ed. 2000).

67.   JOHN SWALES, GENRE ANALYSIS 6 (1990).

68.   LEV VYGOTSKY, THOUGHT AND LANGUAGE (Eugenia Hanfmann & Gertrude Vakar trans. 1962).

69.   Robin West, *Jurisprudence as Narrative: An Aesthetic Analysis of Modern Legal Theory*, 60 N.Y.U. L. REV. 145 (1985).

70.   Walter O. Weyrauch and Maureen A. Bell, *Autonomous Lawmaking: The Case of the "Gypsies,"* 103 YALE L.J. 323, 374-380 (1993).

71.   Joseph M. Williams, *On the Maturing of Legal Writers: Two Models of Growth and Development*, 1 LEGAL WRITING 1 (1991).

72.   CHRISTOPHER G WREN, JILL ROBINSON WREN, THE LEGAL RESEARCH MANUAL: A GAME PLAN FOR LEGAL RESEARCH AND ANALYSIS (2d ed. 1986).